T0320392

Before Banks

This innovative work delves into the world of ordinary early modern women and men and their relationship with credit and debt. Elise Dermineur focuses on the rural seigneuries of Delle and Florimont in the south of Alsace, where rich archival documents allow for a fine cross-analysis of credit transactions and the reconstruction of credit networks from c. 1650 to 1790. She examines the various credit instruments at ordinary people's disposal, the role of women in credit markets, and the social, legal, and economic experiences of indebtedness. The book's distinctive focus on peer-to-peer lending sheds light on how and why pre-industrial interpersonal exchanges featured flexibility; diversity; fairness; solidarity and reciprocity; and room for negotiation and renegotiation. *Before Banks* also offers insight into factors informing our present financial system and suggests that we can learn from the past to create a fairer society and economy.

Elise Dermineur is an associate professor of economic history at Stockholm University, Sweden and the author of *Gender and Politics in Eighteenth-Century Sweden* and editor of *Women and Credit in Pre-industrial Europe*.

Cambridge Studies in Economic History – Second Series

Cambridge Studies in Economic History

Cambridge Studies in Economic History comprises stimulating and accessible economic history which actively builds bridges to other disciplines. Books in the series will illuminate why the issues they address are important and interesting, place their findings in a comparative context, and relate their research to wider debates and controversies. The series will combine innovative and exciting new research by younger researchers with new approaches to major issues by senior scholars. It will publish distinguished work regardless of chronological period or geographical location.

A complete list of titles in the series can be found at:
www.cambridge.org/economichistory

Before Banks

The Making of Credit and Debt in Preindustrial France

Elise M. Dermineur

Stockholm University

CAMBRIDGE UNIVERSITY PRESS

Shaftesbury Road, Cambridge CB2 8EA, United Kingdom

One Liberty Plaza, 20th Floor, New York, NY 10006, USA

477 Williamstown Road, Port Melbourne, VIC 3207, Australia

314–321, 3rd Floor, Plot 3, Splendor Forum, Jasola District Centre, New Delhi – 110025, India

103 Penang Road, #05–06/07, Visioncrest Commercial, Singapore 238467

Cambridge University Press is part of Cambridge University Press & Assessment, a department of the University of Cambridge.

We share the University's mission to contribute to society through the pursuit of education, learning and research at the highest international levels of excellence.

www.cambridge.org

Information on this title: www.cambridge.org/9781009502641
DOI: 10.1017/9781009502634

First published 2025

A catalogue record for this publication is available from the British Library

A Cataloging-in-Publication data record for this book is available from the Library of Congress

ISBN 978-1-009-50264-1 Hardback

A la mémoire de mes grands-parents, Marguerite Mathieu (1936–2021) et Raymond Mathieu (1934–2012)

Contents

Figures

Tables

Acknowledgements

It is certainly not very original to begin by acknowledging that I have incurred many debts while writing a book precisely on debt.

First and foremost, I would like to acknowledge the generous funding of Riksbankens Jubileumsfond, the Bank of Sweden Tercentenary Foundation, via a Pro Futura Scientia Fellowship, and the Marcus & Amalia Wallenberg Foundation via grant MAW2018–0015. I also would like to thank the Swedish Institute in Paris for supporting a writing stay in their beautiful *hôtel particulier*.

I would like to thank warmly Christina Garsten and Björn Wittrock at the Swedish Collegium for Advanced Study (SCAS) in Uppsala. While in residence there in 2015–16 and again in 2017, I benefited from the expertise of the late Barbro Klein, Maria Ågren, and members of the Pro Futura committee. I am also grateful to other Pro Futura Fellows for their support and friendship over the years.

Part of the manuscript was written at the Center for Advanced Studies in the Behavioral Sciences (CASBS) at Stanford University in 2018–19. I would like to thank director Margaret Levi for welcoming me there. While in residence at CASBS, car rides offered by Ruth Milkman on rainy days led to thought-provoking conversations.

At CASBS, stimulating conversations and pleasant lunches owed much to Eva Anduiza, Federica Carugati, Andrew Elder, Jennifer Freyd, Daniel Kelly, Elizabeth Lonsdorf, Kim Williams, Linda Woodhead, and Kirsten Wysen. Special thanks to Sally Schroeder for her helpful assistance with all kind of practical matters. The CASBS volley-ball team interrupted long writing hours with the joy of sharing good laughs and fun on the court.

The last efforts on the manuscript were produced at the Robert Schuman Center for Advanced Studies at the European University Institute (EUI) in Florence. I would like to thank Ramon Marimon for inviting me there. While in Florence, Yane Svetiev shared not only his wisdom but also his mastery of Italian cuisine. Both helped the manuscript tremendously. Over the years, he has also been the perfect partner in crime. I am looking forward to our future projects together.

I am also grateful to librarians at Umeå University, Lund University, Stockholm University, SCAS, CASBS, and the EUI. I would like to thank warmly the staff at the *archives départementales du Territoire de Belfort* for their help and patience over the years. Olivier Billiot in particular has always been both helpful and generous with his time.

Many different academic audiences have read parts of this manuscript and have offered much appreciated feedback and encouragement. I would like to thank especially the participants at seminars at Umeå University, Lund University, the Stockholm School of Economics, Uppsala University, SCAS, CASBS, Stanford University, Stockholm University, the University of Vienna, and the University of Antwerp.

Over the years, I have talked about this book with many friends and colleagues whose suggestions and advice undoubtedly made the manuscript better. Among them, I would like to particularly acknowledge Christiaan van Bochove, Rodney Edvinsson, Laurence Fontaine, Oscar Gelderblom, Linn Holmberg, Åsa Karlsson Sjögren, Unathi Kolanisi, Erik Lakomaa, Margareth Lanzinger, Håkan Lindgren, Peter Lindström, Craig Muldrew, Anders Perlinge, Janine Maegraith, Svante Norrhem, Matteo Pompermaier, and Jaco Zuijderduijn. My colleagues at Stockholm University have read and commented on the manuscript on several occasions. I am grateful for their support.

Alyson has wholeheartedly supported this project from day one. Her patience and meticulousness are invaluable. I would also like to thank my parents for always supporting me. My daughter Adèle came into the world in the middle of this project and made everything more meaningful. And finally, I owe the greatest debt to Emelie. She knows why.

Currency and Surface

Currency

The livre tournois was worth 20 sous or 240 deniers.

From 1726, one Louis d'or was worth 24 livres tournois.

The livre bâloise was also in use in the south of Alsace. One livre bâloise equalled about 1 livre 6 sous and 4 deniers tournois.

I use nominal values throughout the book. After 1726, the value of the livre tournois was stabilized.

Surface

1 *journal* of arable land equals between 32.4 and 36 *ares* or 3,240 and 3,600 square metres

1 *fauchée* of meadow equals 28.8 *ares* or 2,880 square metres

Introduction

In 2008, the American housing bubble unexpectedly burst sending property values plummeting. Thousands of American families had ceased
refinancing their household loans. Their adjustable-rate mortgages far
outpaced the value of their homes, causing a wave of foreclosures across
the country. An estimated nine million households lost their homes
because the subprime loans they had subscribed to were subject to
speculation on the stock market and to predatory lending, making them
incredibly toxic.[1] In the meantime, banks and insurance companies,
which had neither anticipated the bubble nor the high number of failed
payments, faced huge difficulties. Real estate is not only the largest single
form of wealth, it is also the most important form of collateral for
borrowing.[2] Lehman Brothers Holdings in the United States, one of
the most infamous investment banks, and one of the most important,
could not avoid bankruptcy. Other banking insitutions had to be bailed
out at the expense of the American taxpayer simply to avoid a crash of the
world's financial system. Yet, the 2008 financial crisis, which led to the
eviction of millions of people, decimated stocks and hard-earned family
savings, and shut down businesses, was the result of human action. It is
perhaps one of the worst self-inflicted economic disasters. Highly complex, sophisticated, and heavily intermediated financial mechanisms,
coupled with moral hazard and deregulation in this sector, contributed
to this situation and to the ensuing worldwide financial and social crisis
in the following years.

The 2008 financial crisis is the result of at least three combined factors:
massive deregulation in the banking and finance sector since the 1970s;
heavy financial intermediation; and increased use of complex financial
engineering and mathematical models disconnected from human life

---

[1] Noelle Stout, *Dispossessed: How Predatory Bureaucracy Foreclosed on the American Middle
Class* (Oakland, CA: University of California Press, 2019), p 4.
[2] Adam Tooze, *Crashed: How a Decade of Financial Crises Changed the World* (New York:
Viking, 2018), p 43.

experience. Financialization is the designated culprit. It embodies not only the de-personification and disembeddedness of exchanges but also an ever-growing institutional distrust.[3] As a result, the 2008 crisis bruised workers and their families badly. How did we find ourselves in this situation? What happened? This book proposes to rewind the course of time and invites the reader to explore the world of financial exchange *before* banks. Then, in early modern Europe, well before the advent of financialization and technologization of finance, peer-to-peer lending prevailed.[4]

Today, the main function of western commercial banks is – supposedly – to facilitate the allocation and deployment of financial resources between savers and users of capital in a manner that efficiently assesses and transfers risk.[5] Most credit transactions occur via banking institutions. Private individuals turn to their banks when they want to purchase a house, a car, finance their studies, or start a business. Borrowing from another channel has become negligible. Bank loan contracts are, for the most part, highly standardized. Terms and conditions vary only slightly from one commercial bank to another. For most of us, interest rates on a bank loan are only marginally negotiable. After careful screening of personal information such as zip codes and credit scores, the bank may or may not agree to a loan. A borrower's character, morals, grit, or sense of ethics are criteria not taken into account. Working as a nurse and contributing to saving lives every day, for example, is considered irrelevant to the final decision. But the person's risk of dying while performing the job (the higher the risk of dying at work the less likelihood of good terms) does matter. The trust relationship between the bank and its clients is no longer personal but has turned mathematical.[6] If the bank gives the green light, the borrower is bound to the terms of the agreement and must respect them. Renegotiations of those provisions, *ex post*, are putatively rigid and difficult to justify for the modifications to be granted. Any breach of the contract is subject to strict legal rules.

---

[3] Mariana Mazzucato, *The Value of Everything: Making and Taking in the Global Economy*. Illustrated ed. (New York: Public Affairs, 2018).

[4] By peer-to-peer, I mean exchanges between two private individuals or households. It did not entail both parties entering the contractual arrangement on an equal footing.

[5] Robert Patalano and Caroline Roulet, "Structural Developments in Global Financial Intermediation: The Rise of Debt and Non-Bank Credit Intermediation," OECD Working Papers on Finance, Insurance and Private Pensions, No. 44, OECD Publishing, Paris, 2020.

[6] Cathy O'Neil, *Weapons of Math Destruction: How Big Data Increases Inequality and Threatens Democracy*. 1st ed. (New York: Crown, 2016); Josh Lauer, *Creditworthy: A History of Consumer Surveillance and Financial Identity in America* (New York: Columbia University Press, 2017).

Enforcement of the terms come at a high cost, especially for the borrower.

In early modern Europe, in contrast, and in France in particular where this present study is located, the allocation and deployment of financial funds was mainly assured by private lenders.[7] There was no bank, no credit score, and no algorithm to determine who was eligible for a loan.[8] Credit then, in the sense of moneylending, was defined as a negotiated arrangement between two parties pertaining to the transfer of capital. The contract appeared as a reciprocal, conventional inducement.[9] Terms and conditions, including the exchange of promises and modalities regarding repayment and compensation, were included in the initial agreement.[10] Renegotiation and mitigation of the initial agreement might occur *ex post* if both parties agreed. Enforcement of the agreement provisions might occur either via institutional channels such as a court of justice or informally. Women and men borrowed from and lent to each other, often at the local level, in tight-knit networks. Households financed investments in real estate, land, livestock, shops, or even venal offices via the allocation of capital from their peers. They also made ends meet, paid their taxes, and fed their families via deferred payments and small loans from family members, friends, and neighbours. The degree of risk transfer, the availability of capital and the terms of the agreement were often tailored according to the needs, capabilities, and expectations of all the parties involved. These features varied depending on the source of credit and the type of contractual agreement the parties chose. In the absence of banks, a wide range of credit channels did exist. The majority of households were not constrained to seek capital from a unique source.[11] The existing constellation of credit providers offered parties, to some extent, flexibility and choice.

Throughout France, pre-industrial credit markets were therefore characterized by their diversity. Credit transactions ran the gamut from daily

---

[7] The first commercial and savings banks emerged in the nineteenth century in most European countries. Before that, private individuals in search of funds turned to their relatives, extended family, friends, acquaintances, business partners, and even strangers.

[8] The term 'banks' used here refers to commercial banks.

[9] Oliver Wendell Holmes, *The Common Law*. Revised ed., first published 1881 (New York: Dover Publications, 1991).

[10] See Bruce G. Carruthers, *The Economy of Promises: Trust, Power, and Credit in America* (Princeton, NJ: Princeton University Press, 2022).

[11] See the recent work of Matteo Pompermaier, *"Le vin et l'argent": osterie, bastioni et marché du crédit à Venise au XVIIIe siècle*, (Rome: Publications de l'École Française de Rome, 2019). See also Marcella Lorenzini, Cinzia Lorandini, and D'Maris Coffman, *Financing in Europe: Evolution, Coexistence and Complementarity of Lending Practices from the Middle Ages to Modern Times* (Cham, Springer, 2018).

exchanges to shop foodstuffs at the local market, notarial contracts to purchase land, to promissory notes for domestic servants' wages. A wide range of credit contracts existed; either official contracts sanctioned by an official seal or non-official – written or verbal – agreements. Contrary to our modern experience with banking loans, the credit experience of early modern French people was marked by both lender's and borrower's high input and expectations. Until the mid eighteenth century, most written contracts were not standardized. Parties' preferences were reflected in the guarantees offered and the conditions of repayment. In general, fairness and flexibility prevailed not only in contract design but also in *ex post* renegotiations.[12]

Credit was also highly personalized and entailed a social dimension. Contracting parties often knew each other, worked alongside each other, frequented the same social places, and so on. Homophily and geographical propinquity prevailed in pre-industrial credit networks. This social proximity in tight-knit networks featured strong social norms, which governed credit exchanges. Solidarity, reciprocity, cooperation, and fairness, the main social features of local communities, were at the heart of most exchanges.[13] Economic transactions were strongly embedded in the social fabric of local communities, prompting the preservation and reproduction of these social ties.[14] In a context of repeated interactions, there was little space for individualistic behaviour.

Yet, we should not be fooled by the so-called romantic and chivalrous flavour of these social ties. Credit relations were never unproblematic. The mutual help system of small communities featuring self-enforcing norms was not necessarily the most economically efficient system, nor one deprived of social conflicts. Communalism and embeddedness did not preclude clashes. They were in fact common.[15] Personalized credit thus entailed power struggles and frictions precisely because of the deep embeddedness of the economic in the social. These conflicts were often exposed at courts only after renegotiations and parleys had failed. Small

---

[12] See Elise Dermineur and Yane Svetiev, "The Fairness of Contractual Exchange in a Private Law Society: A Case Study of Early Modern Credit Markets," *The European Review of Contract Law* 11, no. 3 (2015): 229–51.

[13] Marshall Sahlins, *Stone Age Economics* (New York: Routledge, 2020); David Graeber, *Debt: The First 5,000 Years* (Brooklyn, NY: Melville House, 2011).

[14] Mark Granovetter, "Economic Action and Social Structure: The Problem of Embeddedness," *American Journal of Sociology* 91, no. 3 (1985): 481–510.

[15] Claire Lemercier and Claire Zalc, "Pour une nouvelle approche de la relation de crédit en histoire" *Annales. Histoire, Sciences Sociales* 67, no. 4 (2012): 979–1009. Craig Muldrew, "Credit and the Courts: Debt Litigation in a Seventeenth-Century Urban Community," *The Economic History Review*, 46, no. 1 (1993): 23–38.

communities could also embody narrow-mindedness and localism, slow-ness, and even prevent changes.[16]

This book is about the world of ordinary women and men and their relationship with credit/debt and its practises. It examines in detail the various credit instruments at their disposal, the credit and debt experiences, the role of women in credit markets, the social, legal, and economic experiences of indebtedness and the development of these practises over time. The study concentrates on a rural area, the seigneurie of Delle and the seigneurie of Florimont, located in the extreme south of Alsace (an area located today in the Territoire de Belfort). There, the numerous documents left in the archives allow for a fine cross-analysis of credit transactions between ordinary people and the reconstruction of credit networks between roughly 1650 and 1790.[17] The emphasis is strictly on peer-to-peer lending. The book does not dig into the world of international merchants, nor public debt. It analyses how and why pre-industrial interpersonal exchanges featured flexibility, diversity, fairness, solidarity, and reciprocity, allowing more room for negotiation and renegotiation. To a lesser extent, the book sheds light on factors that contribute to an understanding of our present situation. This monograph proposes a reflection: to rethink our current system with special reference to its flaws. I am not enough of a utopian to suggest a complete revolution in banking and finance. But, as the book shows, adjustments and alternative choices based on past experiences can be (re) implemented for a fairer society and economy.[18] Early financial markets offered human-oriented features, as the book highlights, features we have lost.

The Ubiquity of Credit

Credit, and its twin debt, were ubiquitous in the early modern economy. Borrowing and lending were common features of economic *and* social life. A simple look at probate inventories suffices to fully understand credit's economic significance. Most people left liabilities behind on their death, evidence of the prevalence of credit and debt. In Paris, at the

---

[16] Abhijit V. Banerjee and Esther Duflo, *Good Economics for Hard Times: Better Answers to Our Biggest Problems* (London: Penguin, 2020). See also Michael Taylor, *Community, Anarchy and Liberty* (Cambridge: Cambridge University Press, 1982).

[17] Registers and archival documents kept at the Archives Départementales du Territoire de Belfort (ADTB hereafter).

[18] Yane Svetiev, Elise M.Dermineur, and Unathi Kolanisi, "Financialization and Sustainable Credit: Lessons from Non-intermediated Transactions?" *Journal of Consumer Policy* 45, no. 4 (2022): 673–98.

beginning of the eighteenth century, 65% of day labourers died with debt. Towards the end of the Old Regime, 80% did so.[19] In Alsace, 80% of the deceased bequeathed debts to their heirs,[20] and only a third of households left a positive balance on their deaths.[21] In fact, before the ascent of modern banks, the stock of mortgage debt to GDP was 10% in 1807, a percentage highlighting the vitality of early financial markets.[22] To put things in perspective, the stock of mortgage debt relative to GDP was comparable to the level in the United States after the shock of the Great Depression and World War II.[23] This figure, however, is only the tip of the iceberg, largely because the calculation is based solely on transactions extracted from notarial records and does not include unregistered and/or verbal loan agreements. If one adds up these undocumented transactions, then the significance and ubiquity of credit in the early modern economy is stunning.[24] And its importance even increased throughout the early modern period. Several interconnected reasons explain the general development and rise of early capital markets.

First, the scarcity of cash prompted the resort to credit. In early modern Europe in general, and in France in particular, small coins did in fact circulate. But demand far exceeded supply.[25] Coins made up barely 20% of the money supply in eighteenth-century France.[26] The monetary stock was estimated at two billion livres tournois on the eve of the Revolution. This represents 100 livres per inhabitant.[27] To alleviate

---

[19] Rebecca L. Spang, *Stuff and Money in the Time of the French Revolution* (Cambridge, MA: Harvard University Press, 2015), p 45.

[20] Jean-Michel Boehler, *Une société rurale en milieu rhénan: la paysannerie de la plaine d'Alsace (1648–1789)* (Strasbourg: Presses universitaires de Strasbourg, 1995), p 1180.

[21] Elise M. Dermineur, "Peer-to-Peer Lending in Pre-industrial France," *Financial History Review* 26, no. 3 (2019): 359–88, p 365.

[22] Philip T. Hoffman, Gilles Postel-Vinay, and Jean-Laurent Rosenthal, *Dark Matter Credit: The Development of Peer-to-Peer Lending and Banking in France* (Princeton, NJ: Princeton University Press, 2019), p 3.

[23] Philip T. Hoffman, Gilles Postel-Vinay, and Jean-Laurent Rosenthal, "Entry, Information, and Financial Development: A Century of Competition between French Banks and Notaries," *Explorations in Economic History* 55 (2012): 39–57.

[24] Dermineur, "Peer-to-Peer Lending in Pre-industrial France."

[25] Philip T. Hoffman, *Growth in a Traditional Society: The French Countryside, 1450–1815.* New ed. (Princeton, NJ: Princeton University Press, 2000), p 71. Gérard Béaur, "Credit and Land in Eighteenth-Century France." In Thijs Lambrecht and Phillipp R. Schofield, eds. *Credit and the Rural Economy in North-Western Europe, c. 1200–c. 1850,* (Turnhout: Brepols Publishers, 2009), 153–67, p 153.

[26] Spang, *Stuff and Money in the Time of the French Revolution,* p 13.

[27] Fernand Braudel, *Civilisation matérielle, économie et capitalisme, XVe–XVIIIe siècle. 1 – Les Structures du quotidien,* (Paris: Le Livre de Poche, 1993), p 411. To give a more precise idea to the reader, 100 livres represented about a third to half of the annual income of a peasant.

this lack of cash, households exchanged fungible promissory notes, used reciprocal credit, lent in kind, and expected repayment in cash when it became available again, and used a mix of ready cash and barter in lieu of payment. This system was sustained by mutual trust and was often possible because of the embeddedness of credit markets in the social life of local communities.

Second, the period also witnessed significant economic development. Characterized by substantial growth resulting from improvements in a period of proto-industrialization and boosts in agricultural output, the local economy required more capital and financial exchange for further investment.[28] Purchasing land, for example, often required substantial financial means and had to be financed through credit as only a very few could afford to pay outright. Intensification of production and the development of trade and commerce meant new manufactured items flooded the market, prompting a rise in consumption.[29] Such items were often purchased on credit.

Apart from these macroeconomic trends, households needed credit for various reasons. The poorest turned to borrowing to make ends meet until the next harvest or the next wage. Irregular income and uncertain revenue due to factors beyond their control (a bad harvest, an increase in taxation, unexpected physical disabilities, death, etc.) hindered visibility and budget planning. Minor loans repayable on demand served mainly to ensure continuity in the access to consumption for those households with an irregular income.[30] Additionally, individuals borrowed to invest in their business, shop, or farm. Land was almost always bought on credit with repayments rolling over several years, if not generations. Venal offices were also purchased thanks to credit. Life events such as baptisms, weddings, and funerals were often financed via loans. In other words, credit was not only the lifeblood of the economy but also of people's social life.

Finally, a growing population of non-manual workers; civil servants; service-oriented professionals such as lawyers, doctors, and early

---

[28] Ulrich Pfister, "Rural Land and Credit Markets, the Permanent Income Hypothesis and Proto-Industry: Evidence from Early Modern Zurich," *Continuity and Change* 22, no. 3 (2007): 489–518. See also Gilles Postel-Vinay, *La terre et l'argent: l'agriculture et le crédit en France du XVIIIe au début du XXe siècle* (Paris: Albin Michel, 1997); Gérard Béaur, "Foncier et crédit dans les sociétés préindustrielles: des liens solides ou des chaînes fragiles?," *Annales. Histoire, Sciences Sociales* 49, no. 6 (1994): 1411–28; Hoffman, *Growth in a Traditional Society*.

[29] Jan de Vries, *The Industrious Revolution: Consumer Behavior and the Household Economy, 1650 to the Present* (Cambridge: Cambridge University Press, 2008).

[30] Laurence Fontaine, *L'économie morale: pauvreté, crédit et confiance dans l'Europe préindustrielle* (Paris: Editions Gallimard, 2008).

industrialists; and merchants derived economic sustenance primarily from service, trade, and manufacture. They were thriving economically, especially in the second half of the eighteenth century. This emerging bourgeoisie is often labelled 'middling class' in British historiography.[31] They often reinjected their savings into the local economy. The nobility and the urban non-aristocrat elite had traditionally invested their capital in the land market. Purchasing land to rent out to farmers generated a regular income in the form of rents. But increasingly in the late eighteenth century, service-oriented professionals preferred to turn to the financial markets where they could collect regular revenue to ensure their assets were productive. Lesser civil servants often preferred the accessible local credit markets rather than the world of high finance where they could not compete with the elite. And they preferred local financial markets over land markets because they did not pay taxes on the extension of money, contrary to the ownership of land for non-noble individuals. The term *rentier* now also applied to this category of savers investing in the credit markets to generate a profit.[32] In turn, they contributed to boosting local credit markets.

Credit, Debt, and the Economy

It is often assumed that early modern households were ensnared in insurmountable webs of debt. Desperate farmers, Marxist historians have argued, experiencing bad harvests and fiscal pressure turned to credit markets to make ends meet.[33] Often unable to meet their engagements, they were forced to cede their land to their rapacious creditors, who in turn always stood ready to deprive peasants of their plots. Recent studies have now dramatically altered this representation of credit relations.[34]

---

[31] Margaret R. Hunt, *The Middling Sort: Commerce, Gender, and the Family in England, 1680–1780* (Berkeley, CA: University of California Press, 1996).

[32] For the concept of *rentier* see especially Brett Christophers, *Rentier Capitalism: Who Owns the Economy, and Who Pays for It?* (London: Verso Books, 2020); Thomas Piketty, Gilles Postel-Vinay, and Jean-Laurent Rosenthal, "Inherited vs Self-Made Wealth: Theory & Evidence from a Rentier Society (Paris 1872–1927)," *Explorations in Economic History* 51 (2014): 21–40.

[33] Pierre Goubert, *Beauvais et le Beauvaisis de 1600 à 1730: contribution à l'histoire sociale de la France du XVIIe siècle* (Paris: Publications de la Sorbonne, 2013). See also Craig Muldrew's criticism of Marx's failure to appreciate credit: Craig Muldrew, "'Hard Food for Midas': Cash and Its Social Value in Early Modern England," *Past & Present* 170 no. 1 (2001): 78–120.

[34] See for example Thijs Lambrecht and Phillipp R. Schofield, eds., *Credit and the Rural Economy in North-Western Europe, c. 1200–c. 1850*, (Turnhout: Brepols Publishers, 2009); Chris Briggs, *Credit and Village: Society in Fourteenth-Century England.* (New York: Oxford University Press, 2009).

Indebtedness did exist and was undoubtedly endemic, but debt did not necessarily imply the manifestation of distress and systemic plunder.[35] It could also represent 'a positive strategy to serve productive purposes'.[36]

Debt hovered over the vast majority of French households. The level of indebtedness varied in intensity and significance across time and space. The early modern period can be divided into two rough chunks of time. First, the seventeenth century, which was hardly propitious to economic development. A series of armed conflicts and poor harvests due to cold weather hindered growth.[37] Famines, wars, and epidemics were recurrent throughout the century. The long pan-European Thirty Years' War (1618–48), in particular, deeply disturbed the economy. In the south of Alsace, where this present study is situated, this particular conflict put a heavy strain on inhabitants. The incessant passing of troops, the devastation of harvests and burning of villages, especially in the second half of the war, left behind only desperation. Several villages were totally erased from the map, their inhabitants having died or fled. The reconstruction that followed took a long time.[38] Once credit was primed again, the severe winter of 1694 killed many and left the survivors starving. Borrowers who could present security turned to credit in great numbers as a survival strategy, to finance consumption and reconstruction. This being said, if the conjuncture was dreadful in general, some people managed to play their cards right. After the famine caused by the winter of 1694, much land was left without an owner. Opportunistic farmers purchased land on credit for a trifle.

The eighteenth century, on the other hand, was more propitious to economic development. In the south of Alsace, the second half of the century witnessed, in general terms, fewer armed conflicts, famines, and

---

[35] Thomas Brennan, "Peasants and Debt in Eighteenth-Century Champagne," *Journal of Interdisciplinary History* 37, no. 2 (2011): 175–200, p 178. See also Jean-Laurent Rosenthal, "Rural Credit Markets and Aggregate Shocks: The Experience of Nuits St. Georges, 1756–1776," *The Journal of Economic History* 54, no. 2 (1994): 288–306.

[36] Sheilagh Ogilvie, Markus Küpker, and Janine Maegraith, "Household Debt in Early Modern Germany: Evidence from Personal Inventories," *The Journal of Economic History* 72, no. 1 (2012): 134–67, p 136. It is also the view of Jan de Vries, "Peasant Demand Patterns and Economic Development: Frieland 1550–1750." In William N. Parker and Eric L. Jones, eds. *European Peasants and Their Markets. Essays in Agrarian Economic History* (Princeton, NJ: Princeton University Press, 1976), 81–124.

[37] Hoffman, *Growth in a Traditional Society.*

[38] Jean-Michel Boehler, "Quelle reconstruction dans la campagne alsacienne au lendemain des guerres du XVIIe siècle?" *Revue d'Alsace*, 142 (2016): 11–25; François Jacques Himly, *Les conséquences de la guerre de Trente Ans dans les campagnes alsaciennes*, (Strasbourg: F. X. Leroux, 1948).

deadly epidemics. Yet, if no major armed conflicts took place in the region considered in this study, the fiscal impact of France's warmongering foreign policy was certainly not negligible.[39] And increases in wheat prices, especially after 1760, meant that many households encountered increasing difficulty in making ends meet.[40] Yet, boosted by the general expansion of trade and commerce, early financial markets began to grow and exchange intensified throughout the period. This is true for major cities like Paris, for example, but also for smaller rural areas like Alsace.[41] Between 1740 and 1780, the volume of credit exchanged more than doubled.[42] Inflation or demographic growth cannot justify this development as both prices and population increased by 0.3% annually in eighteenth-century France.[43] In parallel, we witness the perfection of credit instruments in the course of the eighteenth century. Significant progress in the literacy rate contributed to the spread of written credit instruments (contracts and account books in particular). These innovations benefitted and served directly the increasingly commercialized economies. Commercial and loan contracts became more sophisticated and standardized. As a consequence, these written instruments 'marked the intrusion of impersonal market relations into lives that until then had been governed more commonly'.[44]

The Circuits of Credit

Today, in the western world, most people looking for a loan likely turn to their banks. There is almost no other option available to finance either consumption-related goods or to make an investment when one does not have the necessary capital. But it was not until the nineteenth century that banks as we know them today entered the picture. From then on, banks have crushed the competition and have remained the main provider for household lending.

---

[39] Troops crossed Alsace in the 1740s on the occasion of the Austrian War of Succession. Battles took place in the north of Alsace, near Saverne.

[40] René Grevet, "Les intendants des généralités septentrionales et le commerce des grains à la fin du règne de Louis XV," *Revue du Nord* 400–1, no. 2–3 (2013): 335–49.

[41] Philip T. Hoffman, Gilles Postel-Vinay, and Jean-Laurent Rosenthal "Information and Economic History: How the Credit Market in Old Regime Paris Forces Us to Rethink the Transition to Capitalism," *American Historical Review* 104, no. 1 (1999): 69, p 76.

[42] Hoffman, Postel-Vinay, and Rosenthal, *Dark Matter Credit*, p 66.

[43] Postel-Vinay, *La terre et l'argent: l'agriculture et le crédit en France du XVIIIe au début du XXe siècle*, p 134.

[44] Bruce H. Mann, *Republic of Debtors: Bankruptcy in the Age of American Independence* (Cambridge, MA: Harvard University Press, 2009), p 4.

In pre-industrial France, however, in the absence of commercial banks, a variety of credit channels coexisted allowing households to borrow but also lend money.[45] Credit exchange most often took place in local credit markets between individuals of prior acquaintance largely through concentric social circles as individuals sought credit first from their relatives, friends, neighbours, and other economic partners before turning to more distant potential lenders.[46]

Borrowers favoured certain channels for borrowing money based on at least two considerations. First, their degree of social inclusion within their community granted them access to important information regarding funds availability. They knew whom to turn to. Their social network often offered various options to choose from. Second, borrowers were evidently limited in their choice by their own financial means, social credit, and reputation. The poor and the landless, for instance, had drastically less opportunity to obtain credit lines than the better-off of the community. They often had to pay a higher if not usurious price for their loans, a situation that still persists today as loan sharks target the poor to offer their pricey services.[47]

Obtaining credit from a lender often meant that the borrower had to *have* credit; credit referring thus to both moral and economic capital. In Antoine Furetière's dictionary, the first definition given of credit refers to this aspect: 'belief, esteem one acquires in the public thanks to one's virtue, probity, good faith and merit'.[48] In the absence of credit scores or other thorough screening methods, little information was de facto available regarding both the borrower's honesty, solvency, probity, and proclivity to repay the debt. Individuals compensated for this asymmetry of information by basing their judgement on personal reputation, in other words, credit. A good reputation consisted of not only past dealings but also integrated a more holistic judgement of a person's way of life and moral bearing. *In fine*, a person's credit worked and circulated as a currency. Craig Muldrew rightly points out that credit 'was a public means of communication', which 'circulated judgement about the value

---

[45] Laurence Fontaine, Gilles Postel-Vinay, Jean-Laurent Rosenthal, and Paul Servais, *Des personnes aux institutions: réseaux et culture du crédit du XVIe au XXe siècle en Europe. Actes du colloque international «Centenaire des FUCAM» (Mons, 14–16 Novembre 1996)* (Louvains-la-Neuve: Bruylant-Academia, 1997).

[46] Fontaine, *L'économie morale*.

[47] Charles A. Bruch, "Taking the Pay Out of Payday Loans: Putting an End to the Usurious and Unconscionable Interest Rates Charged by Payday Lenders Comment," *University of Cincinnati Law Review* 69, no. 4 (2000–1): 1257–88; Creola Johnson, "Payday Loans: Shrewd Business or Predatory Lending," *Minnesota Law Review* 87, no. 1 (2003 2002): 1–152.

[48] Antoine Furetière, *Dictionnaire universel* (Paris: Arnout et Reinier Leers, 1690).

of other members of the community'.[49] Evidently this system of reputation could only function because of the hermeticity and *hyperlocality* of most credit markets.

Similarly, if credit worthiness was paramount for the borrower to obtain a loan, a good reputation was equally important for the creditor. Demonstrating moderation, fairness, empathy, and comprehension remained correspondingly vital in a world where tables could suddenly be turned. A lender often was or could later become a borrower. In such a world of repeated interactions, fairness and cooperation necessarily had to prevail. Reciprocal loans over time were nothing but common. A significant degree of mutual insurance can be found mostly because of the existence of lasting relationships between self-interested members.[50] Credit networks were therefore often mutually advantageous relationships.[51]

Borrowers in need of funds generally solicited their family and extended family first. That is the first circle.[52] Written records, however, show a low rate of inter-familial credit transfer in general. This can be explained by the fact that no agreement needed to be written down for a loan between family members, presumably because trust and solidarity between kin was automatically implied and deemed sufficient.[53] Families also had the opportunity to resort to other transfer strategies – especially intergenerational ones – such as dowries or donations to help out a family member, especially an heir. Similarly, loans between family members needed to be well balanced to avoid jeopardizing familial financial strategies, especially between generations and between heirs.

Beyond the financial aspect, borrowing from kin entailed a certain emotional and psychological dependency that could be uncomfortable at times, especially in the case of repayment difficulties. Family members acting as lenders might have proven savvy in how they responded to loan requests. A lender's response needed to take into consideration the

[49] Craig Muldrew, *The Economy of Obligation: The Culture of Credit and Social Relations in Early Modern England* (Basingstoke, Palgrave Macmillan, 1998), p 2.
[50] Marcel Fafchamps, "Solidarity Networks in Preindustrial Societies: Rational Peasants with a Moral Economy," *Economic Development and Cultural Change* 41, no. 1 (1992): 147–74.
[51] Robert Sugden, *The Community of Advantage: A Behavioural Economist's Defence of the Market* (Oxford: Oxford University Press, 2018).
[52] Laurence Fontaine also describes these circles in Fontaine, *L'économie morale*.
[53] Laurence Fontaine, "Introduction." In Maurice Berthe, ed. *Endettement paysan et crédit rural: dans l'Europe médiévale et moderne* (Toulouse: Presses universitaires du Midi, 2020), p 13.

emotional complexity of kinship ties via a well-balanced dramaturgy.[54] Oftentimes, such requests could not be turned down, precisely because of the nature of such ties. It is what sociologists describe as 'negative social capital', 'the pressure on an individual to incur costs by virtue of membership in social networks or other social structures'.[55] A self-defeating financial behaviour such as depleting savings, for example, in order to lend money to a family member came within the scope of the mutual advantage framework.

A second circle, slightly more distant, consisted of co-villagers, friends, acquaintances, and neighbours. Loans between dwellers in the same village were extremely frequent. This can be explained by several factors. First, co-villagers had fairly good information on each other. Geographical and social proximity enabled access to information on neighbours' assets, harvest yield, business financial health, capabilities, and so on. Information on reputation and good morals circulated within the community as a parochial currency.

At the local level, community members often socialized with people similar to themselves, especially with the same socio-economic background. Rural dwellers, for instance, were often related to each other. High endogamy favoured ties between various households. Most people also engaged in the same activities. In rural communities, agriculture represented the primary source of income for most, emphasizing the relative homogeneity of the group. Evidently economic inequality did exist in these small communities, but its spread was often lower than in urban areas. There was no big gap in wealth or bargaining power. Overall, these features helped foster trust and prompted cooperation between individuals. Co-villagers often worked on each other's plots of land during the harvest or performed other cooperative acts. The necessities of agricultural life induced social and economic interdependency. No one could succeed alone.[56] Even today, in the small familial farms of rural France, family members and neighbours often give a hand during the harvests. This interaction ultimately created strong bonds of solidarity and cooperation between the inhabitants. One can also add that size did matter. Cooperation is generally more difficult in a larger

[54] On this, see especially Frederick F. Wherry, Kristin S. Seefeldt, and Anthony S. Alvarez, "To Lend or Not to Lend to Friends and Kin: Awkwardness, Obfuscation, and Negative Reciprocity," *Social Forces* 98, no. 2 (2019): 753–93.

[55] Rourke L. O'Brien, "Depleting Capital? Race, Wealth and Informal Financial Assistance," *Social Forces* 91, no. 2 (2012): 375–96.

[56] Catharine Anne Wilson, *Being Neighbours: Cooperative Work and Rural Culture, 1830–1960*, (Montreal: McGill Queen's University Press, 2022).

group. Small communities had a fair advantage in this respect.[57] In the same vein, individuals frequented the same social spaces. Repeated interactions took place at church, at the local market, at the village inn, and so forth. This favoured not only sociability but also the diffusion of information. Information regarding capital availability, social credit, and capabilities circulated more easily in communities with shared social affiliations.

But, lastly, one should add a pinch of salt to all of this. In such an environment, lenders and borrowers enacted what Bourdieu called 'a collective self-deception'.[58] In such a framework, lenders could be somewhat hampered in their choices. The more socially legitimate a loan request, the greater the moral obligation to comply with it.[59] Nor could the economic consequences for lenders of the loan be ignored. In the eyes of the community the lenders were charitable benefactors, doing their Christian and family duty. The emotional requirements of the relationship could be onerous for the borrowers, placing them in a state of dependency in which gratitude was strongly expected.

The furthest credit ties, the third circle, consisted of extended networks, brokered relationships, and decentralized circuits. In search of money, individuals turned to lenders of last resort whom they did not know well or at all. The number of these available lenders remained limited. In order to reach them, borrowers often relied on intermediaries or known third parties who could vouch for them. Institutionalized brokers like the notary or simply informal intermediaries, put in contact potential borrowers and lenders.[60] Evidently, the lack of strong and close personal ties rendered the bargain unequal. Borrowers often had to sign a notarized contract with clear binding conditions. Initial security was offered by these third parties who enabled proxy of trust by reputational mechanisms.[61] Guarantees and pledges were often added to the deal to reassure lenders. And the price paid could be higher than in the closest circles.

The last circle, the fourth, consisted of professional moneylenders competing with private creditors and institutions. Private individuals could lend their excess surplus to strangers. But this profit-oriented

---

[57] The average size of successful villages is around 176 individuals. Marco Casari and Claudio Tagliapietra, "Group Size in Social-Ecological Systems," *Proceedings of the National Academy of Sciences* 115, no. 11 (2018): 2728–33.

[58] Pierre Bourdieu, *Pascalian Meditations* (Cambridge: Polity Press, 2000), p 192.

[59] Wherry, Seefeldt, and Alvarez, "To Lend or Not to Lend to Friends and Kin," p 758.

[60] Philip T. Hoffman, Gilles Postel-Vinay, and Jean-Laurent Rosenthal, *Priceless Markets: The Political Economy of Credit in Paris, 1660–1870.* (Chicago, IL: University of Chicago Press, 2001).

[61] Karen Schweers Cook. "Networks, Norms, and Trust: The Social Psychology of Social Capital-2004 Cooley Mead Award Address." *Social Psychology Quarterly* 68, no. 1 (2005): 4–14, p 8.

behaviour required a large amount of available capital, which most ordinary people did not have. These figures belonged to the local bourgeoisie, often urban. Most rural dwellers did not often engage in financial dealings with perfect strangers.

Religious minorities, often Jewish and Anabaptist livestock farmers in Alsace, frequently specialized in credit activities because their rights to own land were limited. They sold cows, horses, and meat, often on credit.[62] But their primary occupation also enabled them to handle cash, which they could redistribute via credit instruments. They tended to lend primarily to people living in the communities with whom they had repeated contact. In that sense, they were not complete strangers. But resorting to their services often meant that all the other options had been exhausted. Jewish moneylenders, often depicted as usurers, were in fact not as usurious as other groups.[63] This depiction worked as part of a borrower's strategy to avoid repayment.[64]

One should add that non-personalized lenders existed alongside private ones. Hospitals, orphanages, monasteries, nunneries, local parish vestries, and monts-de-piété (pawnshops) often financed their charitable activities via moneylending. Revenues for land and rents were converted to cash which, if not used, was subsequently reinjected into the local economy via loans. These organizations granted credit to strangers after a careful screening process. In the case of non-repayment, such organizations showed little empathy towards their debtors. The hospital of Delle did not hesitate to plunder its borrowers' houses to retrieve due payments, for example.[65]

In theory, borrowers were not limited in their options. They could turn to different lenders. They could find a channel tailored to their needs and expectations. They could defer repayments with their neighbours, borrow from the local hospital to purchase a piece of land and borrow money from an acquaintance with a promissory note. Circuits of credit were not mutually exclusive. They coexisted. Evidently, the more security and social credit one could bring to the table, the broader the options. There was a strong correlation between the wealth and social credit of debtors and their access to certain types of contract, opening or closing certain doors. A wealthy landowner, for example, could pledge a piece of

[62] Debra Kaplan, "Transactions financières entre Juifs et chrétiens dans l'Alsace du XVIe siècle," *Archives Juives* 47, no. 2 (2014): 29–46, p 19.

[63] L. Gehler, "Les Juifs de Marmoutier," *Bulletin de La Société d'histoire et d'archéologie de Saverne*, no. 3–4 (1954): 25–28, p. 28.

[64] Kaplan, "Transactions financières."

[65] Jules Joachim, *La fondation des pauvres ou vieil hôpital de Delle 1600–1820*. (Belfort: Bulletin de la Société Belfortaine d'Emulation, 1936), p 169.

land in exchange for capital. But a poor widow might have no other alternative than to pawn some of her valuables. Often, borrowers did not limit themselves to one channel. They regularly funded their investments and smaller expenses using different channels depending on their needs. However, the supply of funds could have been low in certain circles at certain times restricting borrowers' choices in practise.

Information and Motivations

This simplified model as described often proved more complex in practise. It needs to be supplemented with two additional layers. The question of trust and information between parties and the intrinsic motivation of lenders to lend their savings tell us about the complexity of the making of credit.

In small communities, trust was sustained by strong social norms built on personal ties and networks but also by available social and economic information regarding the parties.[66] The question of information asymmetry is much discussed in credit and banking studies.[67] For traditional communities, however, informational problems are, in theory, almost non-existent.[68] Agents could come by the information they needed because of the close-knit character of the community. Tied social networks encompassed more or less everyone in the community. Information access was thus made easy. For example, people knew about their neighbours' land holdings, harvests, livestock, personal difficulties, and so on. Yet, some information remained difficult to come by.

In among the vital information lenders needed, security encumbrance certainly appeared as the most critical.[69] It was nearly impossible for a

---

[66] Douglass C. North, *Institutions, Institutional Change and Economic Performance* (Cambridge: Cambridge University Press, 1990), p 55. Elise M. Dermineur, "Trust, Norms of Cooperation, and the Rural Credit Market in Eighteenth-Century France," *Journal of Interdisciplinary History* XLV, no. 4 (2015): 485–506.

[67] See for example Hoffman, Postel-Vinay, and Rosenthal, "Information and Economic History"; Philip T. Hoffman, Giles Postel-Vinay, and Jean-Laurent Rosenthal, "The Role of Trust in the Long-Run Development of French Financial Markets." In Karen Cook, Russell Hardin, and Margaret Levi, eds. *Whom Can We Trust? How Groups, Networks, and Institutions Make Trust Possible* (New York: Russell Sage Foundation, 2009), 249–85; Timothy W. Guinnane, "Trust: A Concept Too Many," Working Paper (Economic Growth Center, Yale University, 2005).

[68] Jean-Philippe Platteau, "Solidarity Norms and Institutions in Village Societies: Static and Dynamic Considerations." In Serge-Christophe Kolm and Jean Mercier Ythier, eds. *Handbook of the Economics of Giving, Altruism and Reciprocity* (Amsterdam: Elsevier, 2006), 819–86, p 855.

[69] Chris Briggs and Jaco Zuijderduijn, *Land and Credit: Mortgages in the Medieval and Early Modern European Countryside* (Cham, Palgrave Macmillan, 2018).

lender to find out if the borrower's proposed security, in most cases a plot of land, was already mortgaged or not. Where the said plot of land was already pledged to another creditor, the risk of losing the capital lent was very high. In case of foreclosure of the borrower's assets, the land pledged could be auctioned and the profits distributed in order of seniority to the creditors. In cases of over-collateralization of a piece of land, thus, the lender ran the risk of recovering little or nothing.

In the Middle Ages, a public announcement, the *cri public*, warned people against bad borrowers.[70] But it was often too late. Deceived lenders could only warn others. In the early modern period, to remedy this problem, the French crown published an edict creating the *bureau des hypothèques* in 1771.[71] Its main goal was the creation of a register to precisely identify over-collateralization. The register, however, recorded only land sales listing plots' encumbrances. The ledger was not enforced in all regions; it was never implemented in Alsace, for example. The register also presented the disadvantage of charging a fee for the procedure. For small transactions, the cost was so heavy that most people exempted themselves from registration. The fee for a sale of 50 livres amounted to 8.7%. For larger transactions, over 500 livres, the registration fees oscillated between 1% and 2%.[72] Overall, despite this attempt by the authorities to protect lenders' capital, the problem of information asymmetry remained.

Ex ante, personal reputation and social credit often filled the gap and were a proxy for reliable information. But while people could have access to a lot of information about each other, the problem of over-collateralization of securities often remained. People relied thus on intermediaries' information. Scholars have argued that notaries' primary role was to bridge the gap of information and alleviate asymmetry.[73] The notary, in theory, provided their clients with information on the borrower's assets.[74] Notaries who also drafted familial contracts such as wills, land sales, donations, and marriage contracts disposed of an enormous

---

[70] Julie Claustre, "Vivre à crédit dans une ville sans banque (Paris, XIVe – XVe siècle)," *Le Moyen Age* CXIX, no. 3 (2013): 567–96, p 586.

[71] Land might be subjected to a *hypothèque*, i.e., pledged as security in a loan contract.

[72] Postel-Vinay, *La terre et l'argent: l'agriculture et le crédit en France du XVIIIe au début du XXe siècle*, pp 119–21.

[73] Hoffman, Postel-Vinay, and Rosenthal, *Dark Matter Credit*; Hoffman and Postel-Vinay, "Information and Economic History"; Hoffman, Postel-Vinay, and Rosenthal. "The Role of Trust in the Long-Run Development of French Financial Markets"; Philip T. Hoffman, Gilles Postel-Vinay, and Jean-Laurent Rosenthal, *Des marchés sans prix: une économie politique du crédit à Paris, 1660–1870* (Paris: Editions de l'Ecole des Hautes Etudes en Sciences Sociales, 2001).

[74] Hoffman, Postel-Vinay, and Rosenthal, *Dark Matter Credit*.

pile of data on households' wealth. That might be true for urban notaries because they competed with each other to attract clients. Most of the rural notaries filled other functions as we shall see.

A second question needs to be raised. Why would lenders prefer to invest their savings in the credit market as opposed to the land market, livestock market, or any other productive items? I think the answer can be divided into two parts. On the one hand, households' financial strategies need to be taken into account, and on the other, households' intrinsic motivations to lend money needs to be explained further.

First, it is extremely difficult to track household budgets closely. One ignores the part of household savings invested in land, livestock, or in the credit market. In traditional communities, most savings came from surpluses in harvest yield and inheritance. And investing in the land market was a logical development of the activity. In the eighteenth century, harvest yield and wheat prices increased steadily in France and in particular in the south of Alsace;[75] and so did the price of land.[76] As the population increased, land was more and more fragmented among the legitimate heirs under partible inheritance. Competition for land pushed prices up, although it did not prevent some farmers from continuing to buy. Land remained a long-term investment and a familial strategy. Yet, an additional plot of land to work on could be an additional burden for some households, especially those with ageing members. Similarly, livestock farming was common in the south of Alsace. Surpluses could therefore be directed to extending the existing cattle. An extra animal on the farm also meant more work. It needed to be fed, thus risking exhausting the limited resources available.

Non-manual workers, whose main income was not tied to agricultural revenue, had good reason to invest in the credit market. For the non-nobility, land ownership was subject to the payment of taxes. Land, therefore, was not an attractive investment. In the eighteenth century, this fiscal burden encouraged the new emerging bourgeoisie to place their savings in the local credit markets.

Yet, these preferences do not suffice to explain why most households would be tempted to invest their savings in the credit market. The credit market gave the opportunity – in theory – to retrieve the liquidity invested if needed. Moral hazard and risks existed but so did it exist in the land and livestock markets. A borrower could disappear with one's savings.

---

[75] Elise Dermineur, *Women in Rural Society: Peasants, Patriarchy and the Local Economy in Northeast France, 1650–1789* (West Lafayette, IN: Purdue University, 2011), p 112.
[76] Ibid., p 152.

Similarly, a cow or a horse could die unexpectedly. And bad harvests were not infrequent. But an annual return of 5% was obtained almost effortlessly with credit. It did not require hard physical work or additional resources to be drawn to see it fructify. This type of investment was deemed unproductive by contemporary thinkers like Adam Smith.[77] It partly explains why the credit market was greatly favoured by the ageing households as a strategy to cope with old age. Towards the end of life, working was often not an option anymore. Many old people, especially widows, invested in the credit market to secure a regular annual income. Similarly, domestics, especially female maids, were also inclined to turn to the credit market to invest their income. Unmarried maids saw an opportunity there to fructify their savings before marriage. Ultimately, some better-off households turned to the credit market seeking a good return for their money.

What about the social motivations and considerations for lending? First, solidarity, cooperation, and reciprocity, features of mutual help arrangements in traditional communities, were often at work. These norms represented strong incentives to extend money to familiar faces with whom actors had repeated interactions. Because of these repeated interactions (social and economic) and force of habit, taking place over the long run – including over generations – a significant degree of mutual insurance prevailed.[78] It manifested itself in kinship, neighbourhood, and friendship ties but also in unequal and unbalanced ties such as patron–client relationships. Credit created quasi-kinship.[79] This system of mutual help worked well in small, close-knit communities of prior acquaintance with repeated interactions. But once members of the community sought opportunities outside, mutual arrangements became vulnerable and subject to collapse. Second, the pressure of these ties often constrained the lender to extend credit to their kin or fellow villagers in the name of these bonds and relations.[80] The transaction, then, instead of being the result of a voluntary cooperation, turned into a forced act in which the lender's self-interest was silenced. Credit became an obligation

[77] Adam Smith and Alan B. Krueger, *The Wealth of Nations*. Annotated ed. (New York: Bantam Classics, 2003), book 2, chapter 3.

[78] See for instance Fafchamps, "Solidarity Networks in Preindustrial Societies."

[79] Jeanne Semin, "L'argent, la famille, les amies: ethnographie contemporaine des tontines africaines en contexte migratoire," *Civilisations. Revue internationale d'anthropologie et de sciences humaines*, no. 56 (2007): 183–99.

[80] See also Wherry, Seefeldt, and Alvarez, "To Lend or Not to Lend to Friends and Kin"; Jean-Marie Baland, Catherine Guirkinger, and Charlotte Mali, "Pretending to Be Poor: Borrowing to Escape Forced Solidarity in Cameroon," *Economic Development and Cultural Change* 60, no. 1 (2011): 1–16.

(not mutually exclusive from the notion of quasi-kinship), an obligated form of solidarity.[81]

Overall, financial channels varied across different French regions. Credit markets varied in size, in frames, in outcomes, and presented many variations in local conventions and practises. The most important and valid conclusion lies in the variety of credit channels offering both lenders and borrowers choice, flexibility, and possibilities for input and preferences. Households' access to these markets, regardless of which circuits they favoured, remained conditional on the availability of credit, good social standing, and existing guarantees. But both negotiations and the existence of community norms such as cooperation, reciprocity, and fairness could grant access to capital. In this sense, flexibility is the keyword.

Formal and Non-intermediated Credit

A multitude of documents attest to the ubiquity of lending. Before the seventeenth century, the documentation available in the south of Alsace is rather limited. For the eighteenth century, on the other hand, documents have been well preserved. Notarial loan records, probate inventories, annuity registers, and judicial litigations are among those which have reached us. They allow the study of credit markets over long and continuous periods of time. *Livres de raison* or shopkeepers' account books can also be found, but this seldom happens. Probate inventories, for example, often name the various account books of private individuals, but these have not survived or have never been archived. A lot of evidence for credit transactions will continue to elude us.

Borrowers could turn to different circuits and actors in order to find the funds they needed. In turn, these circuits featured different types of contracts. Individuals had the choice between formalized (often notarized) contracts and private agreements (non-intermediated), between regulated access to credit or semi-informal exchanges. I shall specify that for most people, this line between formalized and unformalized credit appeared in fact blurry, if not non-existent. Credit was not conceived nor perceived in those terms. But for us to grasp the essence of early financial exchanges, their nature and specificities, I have de facto divided credit exchanges into two groups along these lines. In a traditional assumption, regulated credit markets are standardized and regulated by law. They offer protection against risks precisely because of the rule of law.

---

[81] Muldrew, *The Economy of Obligation.*

Notarial credit has received plenty of attention.[82] Philip T. Hoffman, Gilles Postel-Vinay, and Jean-Laurent Rosenthal are pioneers in examining in great detail the mechanisms of notarized credit markets. They show, in particular, the significance of intermediated capital markets with the colossal size of notarized lending across the entire kingdom before the advent of banks.[83] More specifically, they have paid special attention to the role of the notaries. Their privileged positions as brokers gave them the capacity to reduce asymmetric information allowing complete strangers to safely contract, thus precluding the role of banks until later in the nineteenth century. Notaries not only prevented asymmetry of information but also matched parties efficiently. Notaries as creators of trust appear as the centerpiece of the credit edifice.[84]

Regulated or notarized exchanges are often contrasted with 'informal' exchanges, transactions outside the legal framework and the scope of the authorities and its institutions, unregulated by law, often illegal, and not subsidized. Some historians have often labelled non-notarial transactions 'informal'. These loans were informal in the sense that they were negotiated and concluded outside the scope of the authorities, without formal intermediation, and were not subjected to tight regulation.[85] Private lenders and borrowers agreed privately on a loan, at their discretion, either on an actual transfer of resources or a deferred payment for an item or a service. In practise, implicit rules and shared legal norms inspired by regulated credit practises were often used. Many of these transactions, however, retained an ungoverned essence, allowing parties flexibility and freedom.

But in the early modern period, these private peer-to-peer transactions were in fact more hybrid than informal. Parties could choose – as a last resort – to settle disputes pertaining to this type of agreement before the local court of justice.[86] This dispute resolution mechanism was de facto not informal. These transactions retained a degree of informality and

---

[82] See for example Lambrecht and Schofield, *Credit and the Rural Economy in North-Western Europe, c. 1200–c. 1850*; Maurice Berthe, ed., *Endettement paysan et crédit rural: dans l'Europe médiévale et moderne.* (Toulouse: Presses universitaires du Midi, 2020); Collectif et al., *Notaires et crédit dans l'Occident méditerranéen médiéval* (Rome: Ecole Française de Rome, 2004).

[83] See especially Hoffman, Postel-Vinay, and Rosenthal, *Priceless Markets*; Hoffman, Postel-Vinay, and Rosenthal, *Dark Matter Credit*, p 3.

[84] See for example Juliette Levy, *The Making of a Market: Credit, Henequen, and Notaries in Yucatan, 1850–1900* (University Park, PA: Pennsylvania State University Press, 2012).

[85] Some regulation such as usury laws did exist. But authorities did not have institutional enforcement mechanisms.

[86] See for example James E. Shaw, "The Informal Economy of Credit in Early Modern Venice," *The Historical Journal*, 61, no. 3, (2018): 623–42.

privacy in the negotiation and contract design. But their informal character vanished when the agreement terms had to undergo arbitration by a judge, the legal representative of the local or central authorities. I refrain from employing the term 'informal' for early modern credit transactions. The concept of the informal economy, coined in the 1970s, as opposed to the formal and regulated economy, would be anachronistic in our period.[87] Indeed, it was framed in opposition to the existence of strong institutions of regulation. In comparison, these institutions were embryonic in early modern France. Instead, I prefer the term non-intermediated.

Credit was in fact far from always being notarized. Not much has been written on the characteristics and features of private transactions.[88] Documentation often provides us with fragments of evidence rather than long time series. The study of probate inventories, however, highlights the existence and even the ubiquity of non-intermediated credit.[89] Deferred payments were certainly the most common types of credit transactions.[90] People used non-intermediated transactions often and for a wide range of reasons, as we shall see.

Both categories, intermediated (notarized) and non-intermediated, coexisted. Individuals navigated from one to the other or used both at the same time. In the probate inventory of Henri Babey from 1763, one finds traces of this intermingling of credit circuits.[91] Loans from the local parish vestries and notarized obligations coexisted with informal loans from Jewish moneylenders, women, and neighbours. Most of the households and individuals featured in this book present the same portfolio as Babey. Credit was not only ubiquitous, it presented polymorphous characteristics.

The Regulation and Price of Credit

As rural and urban households alike financed their investments or made ends meet thanks to credit, the authorities – the Church and later the State – concerned themselves with the regulation of credit. One aspect of

[87] Keith Hart, "Informal Income Opportunities and Urban Employment in Ghana," *The Journal of Modern African Studies* 11, no. 1 (1973): 61–89.

[88] Ogilvie, Küpker, and Maegraith, "Household Debt in Early Modern Germany."

[89] Jean-Michel Boehler, *La terre, le ciel et les hommes à l'époque moderne: des réalités de la plaine d'Alsace aux horizons européens: 35 années de recherches d'histoire rurale, 1968–2003* (Strasbourg: Société savante d'Alsace, 2004).

[90] Peter Spufford and Dominique Taffin, "Les liens du crédit au village: dans l'Angleterre du XVIIe siècle," *Annales. Histoire, Sciences Sociales* 49, no. 6 (1994): 1359–73, p 1363. Chris Briggs, *Credit and Village: Society in Fourteenth-Century England* (Oxford: Oxford University Press, 2009), p 41.

[91] ADTB 2E4/436.

credit in particular drew their attention: its price. Both the secular and religious authorities had incentives to regulate interest rates.

The interest rate is not a modern invention of our profit-oriented economies. We do not know precisely when interest-bearing loans originated. They seemed to have predated writing.[92] Well before the advent of financialization, individuals applied a price to credit exchange. Interest on loans already existed in ancient Rome and Athens. And regulation of interest rate is not a modern phenomenon either. Around 1800 BCE, King Hammurabi of ancient Babylonia had already enacted the first formal code of laws. The maximum rate of interest was set on loans in kind and silver.[93] Throughout the world, secular and religious authorities have always had a say regarding the charging of interest, not only as a matter of economic stability but also as an ethical and moral issue.

In the pre-Reformation Catholic world, charging for interest was often – wrongly – associated with usurious practises. Aristotle had already long denounced the unproductive use of interest. 'Money begetting money' was something he considered unnatural.[94] The Scriptures also expressed clearly the idea that a loan was an act of Christian charity and could not be rewarded with interest.[95] The Vulgate featured the famous motto 'mutuum date, nihil inde sperantes', lend hoping nothing thereby.

In the eleventh and twelfth centuries, as trade and commerce expanded, theologians vigorously reasserted the Church's doctrine on usury. The Scriptures forbad the charging of interest; lending shall entail solely a charitable dimension and remain interest-free. Aquinas was the most vocal opponent to interest as he, just like Aristotle, considered money 'sterile'. Unlike animals, 'money does not beget money (...) to take usury from any man is simply evil'.[96] In 1139, the second Lateran council prohibited usury and declared that usurers shall be excommunicated. This regulation mostly targeted urban pawnbrokers, Christians and Jews alike, albeit the Jewish pawnbrokers remained unaffected by excommunication. Then, usury tended to equal the lending of money with any interest.

---

[92] Graeber, *Debt*, p 64.

[93] Sidney Homer, *A History of Interest Rates* (New Brunswick: Rutgers University Press, 1963), p 3.

[94] *Complete Works of Aristotle, Volume 2*, 1984, https://press.princeton.edu/books/hardcover/9780691016511/complete-works-of-aristotle-volume-2, p 1258b.

[95] In the Old Testament, interest was considered a problem of social justice. See for example Exodus 22:25, Leviticus 25:35–38 (no interest-bearing loans for poor people), and Deuteronomy 29:19–21 (no interest to be charged to your countrymen, only to foreigners). In the New Testament, see Matthew 5:42, Luke 6:34 and 19:23.

[96] John Thomas Noonan, *The Scholastic Analysis of Usury*, 1st ed. (Cambridge, MA: Harvard University Press, 1957).

Yet, the reality of commerce and trade in the Middle Ages clashed with Church doctrine.[97] Credit fuelled exchange between merchants and individuals. It facilitated the production and circulation of goods. One can also add that, paradoxically perhaps, the Catholic Church was quite fond of financial instruments itself. From the top of the Church institution down to monasteries and convents and the local priests, interest-bearing loans helped to fructify the member of the clergy's personal savings, generating enormous wealth in return. In the fifteenth century, in order to circumvent the usury problem, the Church favoured a specific loan contract, the annuity contract, *la rente perpétuelle*.[98] Real estate, land in general, had to back the contract, interest could not exceed 10% of the capital and more importantly the debtor had the option to repurchase the property.[99] This particular financial instrument also had the particularity of omitting a repayment deadline. The combination of both a deadline and interest constituted the crime of usury as time could not be monetized; it belonged only to God.[100] The Church's compromise emphasized the apparent fairness of such contracts as the debtor could repurchase the annuity.

Fast forward to the sixteenth century; the Reformation also took up the question of interest. Martin Luther, who had initially preached on usury, gradually modified his approach. The local prince, Luther argued, had to regulate interest-bearing loans. The political power could enact interest rates as long as they remained fair. John Calvin also insisted that interest had to entail fairness. Both reformers tacitly recognized the need for a price on loans. The Catholic Church, thus pressured both by the Reformers and the changes pertaining to the development of commerce and trade, progressively accepted the charging of interest at a fair price, which would only compensate the lender for any loss. Usury came to mean the charging of *excessive* interest rates. Charging more than the fair price was still considered usurious.

In the seventeenth century, the State progressively encroached on the Church authority over the question of credit and interest rate. French secular authorities were interested in the regulation of the interest rate for

---

[97] This is true even if credit was not well perceived in the fifteenth century in certain commercial areas. See Hans-Jörg Gilomen, "La prise de décision en matière d'emprunts dans les villes suisses au 15e siècle." In Marc Bookne, Karel Davids, and Paul Janssens, eds. *Urban Public Debts, Urban Government and the Market for Annuities in Western Europe (14th–18th Centuries)*, (Turnhout: Brepols Publishers, 2003): 127–48.

[98] Martin V published in 1425 the papal bull "Regimini universalis."

[99] Bernard Schnapper, *Les rentes au 16e siècle. Histoire d'un instrument de crédit* (Paris: Editions de l'Ecole des Hautes Etudes en Sciences Sociales, 1995).

[100] Homer, *A History of Interest Rates*, pp 67–79.

at least two reasons: the prevention of usury and the control of the capital market. First, in order to maintain public peace, avoid excesses, and keep a relative economic equilibrium, the fight against usurious practises naturally fell upon the State, especially in the context of the State-building process. This being said, the lack of sufficient surveillance and coercive organization easily allowed the circumventing of rules. Second, and perhaps more importantly, the French State guzzled a lot of money for its war effort. Credit became a means to finance the Crown's belligerence and territorial ambitions. As early as the thirteenth century, one finds traces of public bonds.[101] In order to make sure capital would remain available for the State, the French Crown protected itself against harsh competition. In 1665, the French Crown opted for an arbitrary 5% maximum rate applicable to its entire territory for peer-to-peer lending, which did not correspond to any market equilibrium.[102] This rate remained more or less unchanged until the French Revolution.[103] As a result, the French State could then offer a superior return on its public bonds, hoping investors would place their capital with the Crown.[104] The State's strategy made de facto competition with private individuals unfair, diverting savings and capital from private markets to the royal treasury. Most households, however, did not have enough resources to invest in such bonds. In any case, the rate ceiling did not result in a deficit of available resources for private individuals as credit markets were quite segmented.

In theory, imposing a price of one's choice on a credit transaction was illegal if it exceeded 5% of the capital lent. In practise, however, nothing hindered individuals from doing just that. No system of control existed to ensure the terms agreed upon between private individuals respected the rate ceiling. Notaries were obligated to stipulate an interest equal or inferior to 5%. In effect, they always wrote down 5%; early modern French credit markets were de facto 'priceless'.[105] This, therefore, offered legal courts a benchmark for assessing compensations. But what about the private negotiations undertaken by the parties at their discretion? In practise, interest could be disguised in the terms of the agreement and the loan overpriced, highlighting a critical level of user input.[106]

---

[101] Schnapper, *Les rentes au 16e siècle. Histoire d'un instrument de credit*, p 45.

[102] Postel-Vinay, *La terre et l'argent: l'agriculture et le crédit en France du XVIIIe au début du XXe siècle*, pp 86–87.

[103] Between 1766 and 1770, the legal interest rate ceiling was 4%.

[104] Postel-Vinay, *La terre et l'argent: l'agriculture et le crédit en France du XVIIIe au début du XXe siècle*, pp 37–38.

[105] Hoffman, Postel-Vinay, and Rosenthal, *Des marchés sans prix*.

[106] James E. Shaw, "Market Ethics and Credit Practices in Sixteenth-Century Tuscany," *Renaissance Studies* 27, no. 2 (2013): 236–52, p 243.

Private arrangements on the side did take place. Payments in kind were not rare as an additional compensation, as we shall see.

Overall, the efforts of both secular and religious authorities to regulate credit took some time before turning into a general legal rule collectively followed and assimilated. Enacted in 1665, the legal interest rate of 5% was not necessarily followed with rigour until the beginning of the eighteenth century.[107] In the newly conquered provinces on the margins of the kingdom where praxis varied, the transition was also slow. The progressive institutionalization of credit and the efforts to regulate interest rates did not prevent individuals' input and latitude of action.

Social Norms, Power, and Embeddedness

This book insists on the embeddedness of economic activity in social relations.[108] I have already mentioned that economic exchanges were deeply embedded in the social fabric of local communities. Building upon the work of Karl Polyani and Mark Granovetter, I consider that economic activity, and in particular credit exchanges, were not disembedded from society.[109] All economic behaviour in market societies is rooted in socialized networks.[110] Building upon Granovetter's idea of embeddedness, Brian Uzzi has theorized further how social relations may facilitate and/or derail economic exchanges.[111] For him, several preconditions, or social structural antecedents, are needed to create the conditions of embeddedness. For our purpose, face-to-face interaction (information), reciprocity, and an absence of option (joint problem-solving arrangements) are the most relevant. The seigneuries of Delle and Florimont exhibited those features as we shall see throughout the book.

---

[107] Postel-Vinay, *La terre et l'argent: l'agriculture et le crédit en France du XVIIIe au début du XXe siècle*, p 91.

[108] See in particular Ronan Le Velly, "La notion d'encastrement: une sociologie des échanges marchands," *Sociologie du travail* 44, no. 1 (2002): 37–53. Ronan Le Velly, "Le problème du désencastrement," *Revue du MAUSS* 29, no. 1 (2007): 241–56. Marcel Mauss, *The Gift: Forms and Functions of Exchange in Archaic Societies*, trans. Ian Cunnison (Jefferson, NC: Martino Fine Books, 2011).

[109] Karl Polyani, *The Great Transformation: The Political and Economic Origins of Our Time* (Boston, MA: Beacon Press, 2001); Granovetter, "Economic Action and Social Structure."

[110] Also see the argument of Laurence Fontaine. *Le marché: Histoire et usages d'une conquête sociale* (Paris: Gallimard, 2014).

[111] Brian Uzzi, "The Sources and Consequences of Embeddedness for the Economic Performance of Organizations: The Network Effect," *American Sociological Review* 61, no. 4 (1996): 674–98.

Traditional historiography contends that credit relations in pre-capitalist societies often come under the umbrella of shared norms.[112] Members of the local community shared the same living conditions, socio-professional background, and the same 'mental state', fertile ground for cooperation.[113] Trust between parties was sustained thanks to strong norms of social proximity and a sense of community belonging. Cooperation, reciprocity, and solidarity being natural answers to communities facing the same hurdles, a significant degree of mutual insurance thus existed. Social norms and shared moral codes attenuated market failures.[114]

Current historiography on the subject of early financial markets refers to these norms. Mauss in his seminal work underlines that debt upsets the balance of power between the lender and the debtor. But, more importantly for our purpose, he argues that these power struggles and hierarchies of domination are key to effective cooperation and buiding group cooperation.[115]

More recently, Laurence Fontaine insists on social motivation and consideration as the engine behind the lending mechanisms in early modern Europe.[116] For her, solidarity, cooperation, and reciprocity, features of mutual help systems, were often at work in peer-to-peer lending. These norms represented strong incentives to extend money to familiar faces with whom actors had repeated interactions. To another extent, a 'lending moral', in other words, lending fairly and to the poorest, was a moral obligation and found echo in the Middle Ages.[117] Christian charity emphasized the necessity to lend to those with meagre means. But Fontaine clearly demonstrates the limits of this model by taking into consideration the complexities of social interaction in such communities. Trust did not appear magically simply because people belonged to a certain community.[118] Information that was both social (social credit and reputation) and economic (assets, capabilities, and past

---

[112] E. P. Thompson, "The Moral Economy of the English Crowd in the Eighteenth Century," *Past & Present*, 50 no. 1 (1971): 76–136 ; James C. Scott, *The Moral Economy of the Peasant: Rebellion and Subsistence in Southeast Asia*, (New Haven: Yale University Press, 1977). Ferdinand Tönnies, *Community and Society* (Mineola, NY: Dover Publications, 2003).

[113] Joseph Heath, "The Benefits of Cooperation," *Philosophy & Public Affairs* 34, no. 4 (2006): 313–51.

[114] Samuel Bowles, *The Moral Economy: Why Good Incentives Are No Substitute for Good Citizens* (New Haven: Yale University Press, 2016).

[115] Mauss, *The Gift*.   [116] Fontaine, *L'économie morale*.

[117] Claustre, "Vivre à crédit dans une ville sans banque (Paris, XIVe – XVe siècle)," p 577.

[118] See for instance Dermineur, "Trust, Norms of Cooperation, and the Rural Credit Market in Eighteenth-Century France"; Guinnane, "Trust."

repayments), in fact also prevailed in the exchanges. This set of information, easily available in small networks and local communities, determined the conditions and the terms of the exchanges between parties. Trust did depend on both social interdependency and on the collection of information.[119] Access to credit markets was therefore subordinate to both. In addition, the complexity of interaction in a small community adds another layer. Communities were not homogeneous, their social dynamics could and did differ. There was a necessary power struggle between creditors and debtors. In the Alpine valleys she studied, Laurence Fontaine shows that creditors often controlled the manpower of their debtors. As debts went on not being repaid, lenders had access to their borrowers' harvests, often allowing the creditor-merchant to supply their urban shops. Alain Corbin points to a similar appropriation and display of power in Limousin. There, lenders often paid impromptu visits to their debtors and families during mealtimes, sitting down and consuming their provisions.[120]

This imbalance in the relationship between a creditor and a borrower has also been examined by Craig Muldrew in England. Also considering the embeddedness of credit activities in social settings, he refers to an economy of obligation.[121] For him, an economy of obligation consisted of a set of social norms often establishing a relationship of power between lenders and borrowers.[122] Credit relations between acquaintances became a social *and* economic obligation. Lenders with financial capacity or shopkeepers who could offer lines of credit felt obliged to comply with the demand and pressure of the borrowers around them. Credit, then, instead of being the result of voluntary cooperation, turned into a forced act in which the lender's self-interest was de facto constrained. Credit became an obligatory form of solidarity or forced solidarity.[123] Along the same lines of thought, Pierre Bourdieu talks about 'the exercise of gentle violence' when referring to credit.[124] For him, it is 'an attack on the

---

[119] See the argument of Gilles Laferté, "Théoriser le crédit de face-à-face: un système d'information dans une économie de l'obligation," *Entreprises et histoire*, 2 no. 59 (2010): 57–67.

[120] Alain Corbin, *Archaïsme et modernité en Limousin au XIXe siècle, 1845–1880: la rigidité des structures économiques, sociales et mentales* (Limoges: Presses Universitaires de Limoges, 1999), p 167.

[121] Muldrew, *The Economy of Obligation*.

[122] Marcel Mauss's gift theory also emphasized the fact that financial exchanges bind individuals together in a social relationship. Marcel Mauss, *The Gift: Forms and Functions of Exchange in Archaic Societies*.

[123] See also Baland, Guirkinger, and Mali, "Pretending to Be Poor."

[124] Pierre Bourdieu, "Outline of a Theory of Practice". Translated by Richard Nice. Cambridge: Cambridge University Press, 1977, p 193.

freedom of one who receives it (...) it creates obligations, it is a way to possess, by creating people obliged to reciprocate'.[125]

The pre-industrial period, and more specifically the eighteenth century, represents a crossroads in which the embeddedness of economic exchange in social relations slid towards a growing disembeddedness. Several scholars have sought to explain this phenomenon. Karl Marx and Friedrich Engels contend that the rise of industrialism in the West has dissolved the traditional social bonds and obligations that glued communities together. Industrial capitalism with all its novel attributes (property rights, wage labor, etc.) destroyed the sociality of the peasantry with 'power-laden transactional relations'.[126] Ferdinand Tönnies was the first to propose a distinction between *gemeinschaft* (community) and *gesellschaft* (society) to emphasize the decline of neighbourliness and the rise of individualism. He described the transition from medieval rural communities, in which ties were principally with kin and neighbours, to modern urbanized, industrialized, and bureaucratized societies, where structural and social arrangements had superseded communal obligation.[127] David Graeber argued that a transition from 'everyday communism' – before the advent of capitalism – to 'impersonal arithmetic', oriented towards profit-making and the depersonification of exchange, took place at some point in time, ending the reign of traditional exchange and replacing it with our modern practise.[128] Douglass North also referred to this shift from personal exchanges to impersonal exchanges.[129] While Graeber pointed to capitalism in general as being responsible, North argued that the progressive institutionalization of exchanges was responsible for this shift.

This phenomenon is especially observable in credit relations. Indeed, as institutions sustaining and supporting credit markets – such as the notaries and judicial courts of justice – started to gain more and more importance in the fifteenth and sixteenth centuries, practises and arrangements were then determined on a case-by-case basis, often retaining the values and norms pertaining to the old system, in other words, customary systems. In the seventeenth and eighteenth centuries, however, these institutions increasingly started to be represented by standardization, as rules and routines were developed and codified. The process of institutionalization in the second half of the eighteenth

---

[125] Pierre Bourdieu, *Practical Reason: On the Theory of Action*, trans. Randall Johnson, 1st ed. (Stanford, CA: Stanford University Press, 1998), p 94.
[126] Stout, *Dispossessed*, p 20.   [127] Tönnies, *Community and Society*.
[128] Graeber, *Debt*.
[129] North, *Institutions, Institutional Change and Economic Performance*.

century, on the other hand, meant these institutions became largely invulnerable to contestation, especially in conjunction with a higher demand for their services.[130] At this point, disembeddedness began to spread to all strata of society.

Today, markets rely on efficient institutions to ensure their functioning, but they have drifted apart and extracted themselves from collective social norms and obligations. Institutions that facilitate and regulate transactions – making interpersonal relations and their values supposedly superfluous – engender a de-personification of exchange as David Graeber puts it, or disembeddedness.[131] This is one of the issues identified in the 2008 financial crisis. And this is the subject of the final chapter.

The Legal Framework of Debt

Since the financial crisis of 2008, the idea that a debt does not necessarily have to be repaid has (re)emerged.[132] A distinction between so-called bad and good debt is currently fuelling many heated ideological debates about the essentialism of debt and the legitimacy of reimbursement.[133] In pre-industrial Europe, however, this discussion did not take place on the same terms. A debt was considered a contract between two parties that ultimately needed to be repaid in one way or another. It was both a legal agreement, with clear rules of the game as defined and regulated by law, and a moral obligation towards one's community. More importantly, debt also entailed a Christian's obligation. Several verses of the Bible made clear that borrowers had a Christian duty to fulfil their agreements.[134] Defaulting on one's debt equated to failing to

---

[130] John W. Meyer and Brian Rowan. "Institutionalized Organizations: Formal Structure as Myth and Ceremony." *American Journal of Sociology* 83, no. 2 (1977): 340–63.

[131] Graeber. *Debt*. See also Michael Taylor, *Community, Anarchy and Liberty* (Cambridge: Cambridge University Press, 1982). In a previous work, I have shown how trust migrated from peer-to-peer exchanges to institutions, from informal to formal institutions, highlighting the phenomena of disembeddedness. Dermineur, "Trust, Norms of Cooperation, and the Rural Credit Market in Eighteenth-Century France."

[132] See for instance Graeber, *Debt*; Michael Hudson, …. *And Forgive Them Their Debts: Lending, Foreclosure and Redemption from Bronze Age Finance to the Jubilee Year* (Dresden, ISLET-Verlag, 2018).

[133] See Piketty's opinion on this: www.lemonde.fr/idees/article/2019/01/12/thomas-piketty-1789-le-retour-de-la-dette_5408120_3232.html?fbclid=IwAR00CICQrSP6_WbbrR8 NqevchhWGyo7mQPIfl31NdDhwvnEPykDVNjjW5JE. Gustav Peebles, "The Anthropology of Credit and Debt," *Annual Review of Anthropology* 39, no. 1 (2010): 225–40.

[134] See for example: Romans 13:7: 'Pay to all what is owed to them: taxes to whom taxes are owed, revenue to whom revenue is owed, respect to whom respect is owed, honor to

act charitably toward another Christian, a sin in 'communal Christianity'.[135]

One of the medieval amercements available to society for debtors defaulting on their debt was excommunication, the exclusion from the sacraments and services of the Church. An excommunicated man or woman became an outcast, living on the margins of the community. Between roughly 1300 and 1600, creditors had the possibility of bringing a defaulting debtor before an ecclesiastical court. Citing a borrower to appear before a Church tribunal constituted a great tool of coercion and worked as an enforcement mechanism. If a summoned debtor failed to appear before the Church court, he was automatically excommunicated for disobeying the Church's command.[136] The procedure was fairly accessible at a reasonable price. Most of the excommunication for debt lawsuits took place in urban centres. Lenders could thus have a means to enforce the terms of an agreement, which was often a verbal one. These litigations frequently stopped short and did not go through the whole judicial process. It was enough to resort to a summons in order to discredit a debtor in the eyes of the community and force him to take action. It is unclear however if and how the summons prompted imme-diate repayment. Informal renegotiation might have prevailed afterwards. Medieval debt was thus entangled not only in economic and social relations but also in religious morality.

Jealous of their prerogatives, kings progressively and successfully diminished the power of the Church. Justice became one of the areas in which early modern kings strongly affirmed their authority over any other competing institutions. The Edict of Villers-Cotterêts in 1539 is a notable illustration of this royal awakening. This edict de facto pro-scribed the use of Church tribunals. Lay people had to resort to lay justice, a royal prerogative, outsourced to many local seigneurs.[137] After 1600, cases of excommunication for debt decreased significantly as debt became a matter for lay courts.[138] The changes in economic and religious norms also played a role in the disappearance of excommuni-cation as a punishment for debt.

---

whom honor is owed.' Romans 13:8: 'let no debt outstanding'. Ecclesiastes 5:5: 'It is better that you should not vow than that you should vow and not pay.'

[135] John Bossy, *Christianity in the West 1400–1700* (New York: Oxford University Press, 1985).

[136] On this question, see Tyler Lange, *Excommunication for Debt in Late Medieval France: The Business of Salvation* (Cambridge: Cambridge University Press) 2016, p 4.

[137] The late medieval and early modern justice system was complex and multi-layered. See Elise M. Dermineur, "The Civil Judicial System in Early Modern France." *Frühneuzeit-Info* 22 (2011): 44–53.

[138] Lange, *Excommunication for Debt in Late Medieval France*, p 28.

In the meantime, the proportion of verbal agreements began to decrease as well. Church courts very seldom based their rulings on notarized contracts: the ecclesiastical judges ruled on all sort of agreements and especially verbal ones. If verbal and private agreements could be enforced through the Church court, it was unnecessary to add an additional transaction cost with a notary's fee. Contracting verbally could suffice. But when the Church court system lost its attraction and its legitimacy to the lay courts, the number of verbal agreements began to decrease.

Church courts did not possess the monopoly over debt collection lawsuits. Civil courts, in the case of simple default, and criminal courts, in the case of *mala fide* bankruptcy, ruled on most debt matters, often with blurry limits over each other's jurisdiction. Fraudulent debtors risked capital punishment imposed by criminal courts. In 1619, in a famous example, accused and convicted of the crime of bankruptcy, a merchant of Lyon was condemned to capital punishment by a court. But first, Antoine Trouillet had to reveal to the authorities where he had hidden his assets from his creditors. Torture was used to obtain his confession. He was then forced to march to the scaffold holding a sign reading 'fraudulent bankruptcy'. After he was hanged, Antoine Trouillet's body remained on the main square for twenty-four hours, to be seen by all.[139] Justice considered deceitful debtors to be criminals. Trouillet's case is an extreme example. In pre-industrial Europe, deceiving creditors deliberately could lead to capital punishment. We can count only a handful of debtors who suffered such a fate. There is no current estimate available for early modern France. But in England, for example, only four fraudulent bankrupts died on the scaffold between 1706 and 1820.[140]

Insolvent debtors who did not have the capacity to repay their dues must be distinguished from deceiving debtors. Simple failure and incapacity to repay one's debt was a common phenomenon. Yet, defaulting on one's debt was taken seriously. Failing to repay one's creditor could lead to prison and to excommunication. But increasingly, these types of amercement tended to disappear and remained rare in eighteenth century France.

In the case of default for simple insolvency, lay courts could jail a defaulting debtor. Yet, since the reign of Louis IX, prison for reason of

---

[139] Quoted by Julie Hardwick, "Banqueroute: la faillite, le crime et la transition vers le capitalisme dans la France moderne." *Histoire, économie & société* 30e année, no. 2 (2011): 79–93, p 80.

[140] Emily Kadens, "The Last Bankrupt Hanged: Balancing Incentives in the Development of Bankruptcy Law," *Duke Law Journal* 59 (2010): 1229–319, p 1231.

private debt had been prohibited. The great *Ordonnance* of 1254 reserved this punishment uniquely for money owed to the crown. In the 1380s, however, obligation contracts began to feature a new clause. In addition to pledging one's assets to guarantee a loan, it became possible to pledge one's body as well. This new *proviso* might reflect the difficulty encountered by borrowers to locate available funds in a period when creditors might have been apprehensive. To bridge the trust deficit between the parties, pledging one's body might have been perceived as a strong guarantee. This new input from debtors and creditors led to the development of imprisonment for reason of debt.

In late medieval Paris, the Châtelet prison housed the defaulting debtors until full repayment to their creditors was made. Julie Claustre estimates that in 1488–89 one fifth of prisoners had been jailed for insolvency. Half of the Châtelet prisoners for debt spent less than 48 hours in prison and 75% were released after a week. In most cases, debtors and creditors renegotiated the terms of their agreement within the walls of the prison through an intermediary, either a notary or a clerk.[141] Yet, despite the *Ordonnance de Moulins* in 1566, which recognized the validity of pledging one's body in a loan contract, prison for debt gradually lost its attraction. In the eighteenth century, French judges very seldom sent debtors to prison. By contrast, approximately 10,000 English men were imprisoned each year for debt in the eighteenth century. This practise continued well into the nineteenth century.[142] Other regions, such as the American states, also sent defaulting debtors to prison and continue to do so up to this day.[143] In France, imprisoning a debtor gradually turned out not to be the most efficient strategy to get one's capital back, but it did remain a possibility for the creditor. But suing the guarantor became an increasingly common practise instead, revealing itself to be more effective. In the meantime, a royal decree enacted in 1670 and again in 1680 required the creditor to pay for the

---

[141] Julie Claustre, "De l'obligation des corps à la prison pour dette: l'endettement privé au Châtelet de Paris au Xve siècle" in Julie Claustre (ed) *La dette et le juge. Juridiction gracieuse et juridiction contentieuse du XIIIe au XVe siècle (France, Italie, Espagne, Angleterre, Empire). Actes de la Table ronde, 15–16 mai 2003 au Collège de France*, (Paris: Publications de la Sorbonne, 2005), pp 121–34. See also Julie Claustre, *Dans les geôles du roi. L'emprisonnement pour dette à Paris à la fin du Moyen Âge* (Paris: Publications de la Sorbonne) 2007.

[142] Prison for debt was abolished in 1867 in France. See also Daniel Lord Smail, *Legal Plunder: Households and Debt Collection in Late Medieval Europe* (Cambridge, MA: Harvard University Press, 2016) p 157; and Gustav Peebles, "Washing Away the Sins of Debt: The Nineteenth-Century Eradication of the Debtors' Prison," *Comparative Studies in Society and History* 55, no. 3 (2013): 701–24.

[143] Mann, *Republic of Debtors*.

debtor's subsistence in prison, which possibly discouraged creditors from pursuing this sort of punishment.[144] In the seventeenth and eighteenth century, the registers of hearings in the seigneuries of Delle and Florimont mentioned prison as an amercement but never for defaulting debtors.

Throughout the Old Regime, the central authority legislated on debt collection. The most notable changes were introduced by the civil *Ordonnance* of 1667. It made claiming a verbally agreed upon debt at court more difficult, reinforced the validity of written evidence, and facilitated the pursuit of guarantors. But despite this legal set, lenders and borrowers adapted their debt collection practises to the conditions of the market and above all to their community structure. They rarely seized land, for instance, preferring renegotiating the terms of their initial agreement, as we shall see in Chapter 5.

Before the implementation of the Napoleonic Code, it was clear that premodern civil courts offered an *à la carte* service to creditors. Lenders could indeed choose the amercement *they* wished to be applied to their defaulting debtor. It was they who required imprisonment or foreclosure, not the judge. The magistrate embodied the figure of justice only to avoid private vendettas. Despite the multiple-choice strategies available to creditors, they seldom sought the harshest sentences. Norms of cooperation and fairness prevailed in tight-knit communities.

Overall, the legal framework seemed highly advantageous to creditors. Debt collection, however, required some participation on the part of the debtor, especially in disclosing and turning over assets. In an age in which the coercive reach of the authorities was limited, the delay between the first hearing and the auction of assets could sometimes spread over several months, if not years. Cooperation and negotiation between parties was therefore necessary.

Both parties often met halfway by renegotiating, with or without mediators.[145] Facing the justice apparatus, it is clear that a debtor's best strategy lay in informal renegotiation. At court, they were exposed to the possibility of foreclosure, less often to imprisonment for debt. They were rarely granted a sufficient delay to repay their dues. But debtors did use one tool to save some of their assets from being taken. Married couples often sought separation of property as a strategy to avoid the complete

---

[144] De Boug, François Henri, *Recueil des édits, déclarations, lettres patentes, arrêts du Conseil d'État et du Conseil Souverain d'Alsace, ordonnances et règlemens concernant cette province avec des observations* (Colmar: Jean-Henri Decker) 1775, vol 1, p 80.

[145] Anne Bonzon, *La paix au village – clergé paroissial et règlement des conflits dans la France d'Ancien Régime* (Paris: Champ Vallon Editions, 2022).

disappearance of their estate in foreclosure. Such a legal step supposedly allowed a woman to counter her husband's financial mismanagement. Married women granted the separation could withdraw their assets and property, often in the form of lineage property and dowry. Most of these separations took place before foreclosure.[146]

Overall, the theory and practise of credit and debt varied tremendously. There were legal rules. Authorities interefered to some degree in the conclusion of contracts and their execution. But households often ignored, disregarded, or reintepreted those rules. They preferred to revert to social norms and their local culture to conclude agreements or deal with repayment issues.

Space, Time, and Structure of the Book

In order to reconstruct the world of early modern credit and debt and uncover its complexities, this book focuses on two adjacent rural seigneuries located in the extreme south of Alsace on the border with the Swiss cantons: the seigneurie of Delle and the seigneurie of Florimont. There, between roughly 1650 and 1790, from the end of the Thirty Year's War to the eve of the Revolution, households and individuals lent and borrowed on a daily basis.

The empirical research presented in this book is based on large datasets of mainly notarial and judicial records pertaining to the south of Alsace.[147] For the period c. 1650 to 1790, I gathered and cross-analysed about 12,000 documents: probate inventories, notarial loan records, and local judicial court records. This area is of interest for at least two reasons. First, these two seigneuries represented well a typical French rural area of the time and therefore made an appropriate point of departure. Second, the abundance of source material made the region promising for an empirical study. By focusing on a small area, I was able to trace and cross-analyse the experiences of debtors and creditors. While the book examines a specific area, I nonetheless believe its results will be extendable and applicable to other European regions.

The book explores a broad array of topics, such as the development of credit markets and instruments, the role of formal and informal institutions, and enforcement mechanisms among others. The main guiding thread of the book is that social norms prevailed in peer-to-peer lending within tight-knit societies before the advent of commercial banks. Loans

---

[146] Julie Hardwick. "Seeking Separations: Gender, Marriages, and Household Economies in Early Modern France." *French Historical Studies* 21, no. 1 (1998): 157–80.

[147] Registers and archival documents kept at the ADTB.

were flexible and could be renegotiated. Norms of cooperation, solidarity, reciprocity, and fairness prevailed. Predatory lending remained rare.

Chapter 1 presents a detailed overview of the area under consideration. It focuses on the seigneurie of Delle and the seigneurie of Florimont between c. 1650 and 1790 with special attention given to the social and economic life of these communities. This chapter presents *the milieu* in which dwellers in the south of Alsace lived and experienced credit. The aim is to equip the reader with the necessary background to comprehend the making of credit.

Chapter 2 focuses on the non-intermediated market and its actors from c. 1650 to 1790. These credit markets functioned as peer-to-peer or interpersonal lending, exchanges that featured either a private written agreement or a verbal promise. Considered merely as simple daily transactions made to alleviate a lack of cash in circulation and to smooth consumption, they are often eclipsed by notarial credit. In this chapter, the probate inventories of seigneuries in the south of Alsace highlight the various features of these peer-to-peer exchanges and give particular attention to the profiles of lenders and borrowers, the purpose of the loans, and the networks of exchange at work. This chapter shows that these exchanges were in fact of significance. The volume of exchange competed well with notarized loan contracts, which prompts questioning the nature and function of non-intermediated credit.

This intermediated credit is the subject of Chapter 3. It focuses on notarial credit. Because notaries drafted various kinds of contracts related to individual, family, and household wealth, scholars have emphasized the exceptional access they had to a vast array of information. With such information, especially regarding creditworthiness, notaries could overcome asymmetric information, lower transaction costs, and match lenders and borrowers effectively, precluding the role of banks until the nineteenth century. Recent historiography highlights their role as intermediaries between investors and borrowers.[148] In rural areas, where most individuals knew each other or were related to each other and conducted business on a daily basis with each other, this brokerage role bore another meaning. This chapter looks closely at the various types of notarial contract and their characteristics. Despite the official character of such loans, they did retain a high degree of flexibility and input.

Chapter 4 moves away from the different forms of credit. It focuses on the role and activities of women in credit transactions. That women made economic contributions to their households in the management,

---

[148] See Hoffman, Postel-Vinay, and Rosenthal, *Priceless Markets*; Hoffman, Postel-Vinay, and Rosenthal, *Dark Matter Credit*.

care, and sale of livestock and farm products, and in the production of various marketable items, is incontrovertible. Yet, the significance and extent of their larger economic role has been neglected, especially when it comes to financial exchange and credit. For the most part, much remains to be written about the extent of women's capacity to lend *and* borrow, of gendered practises related to credit, of the impact of female involvement in credit networks traditionally dominated by men, and of the effects of female participation in the economic life of their household and community.[149] This chapter sheds light on their roles and motivations as particular actors. But it also aims to show their significance in credit networks at large.

Chapter 5 focuses on the enforcement of credit contractual agreements and questions the meaning of trust in credit networks. Despite the norms of solidarity, cooperation, and fairness that characterized pre-industrial society, breach of agreement did occur. When lenders and debtors had exhausted all the possibilities available to settle their disagreement, taking the matter to court was often the last resort. The aim was to recover the money owed, but often the emotional and social implications of a lawsuit went beyond the simple economic dimension. Throughout the period, the burden of debt increased rapidly, as did the number of discontented creditors. The apparent dichotomy is intriguing: on the one hand, financial arrangements were flexible and renegotiable, but on the other, contract enforcement at court was sought after. These lawsuits are rich sources of information for the historian. They highlight the shortcomings and failures of debtors, and the (im)patience of creditors. But above all, they display the dynamics of complex and multiple layers of social and economic relationships. Overall, this chapter reconstructs both transactional and dispute resolution practises in non-intermediated and intermediated credit relationships via judicial records.

Finally, Chapter 6 focuses specifically on the last two decades of the Ancien Régime. As argued in the book, the traditional local credit market featured norms of solidarity, fairness, and cooperation and allowed its agents considerable input regarding the terms of their agreement before contracting and/or afterwards. But structural changes in the 1770s, such as an increase in credit activities, drawing on the power and profitability of such exchanges, and especially the appearance of new investors, affected the social and legal norms and nature of these markets. The gradual and massive resort to external parties – such as the notary and the local court – to handle and manage financial transactions remodelled these institutions into specialized and incontrovertible experts.

---

[149] Elise Dermineur, ed., *Women and Credit in Pre-Industrial Europe* (Turnhout, Brepols Publishers, 2018).

Embedded in society, the local court system traditionally responded to the demands of its users and their input shaped the form of the institution. It can be argued that when a new category of investors emerged, their requests, in turn, tended to shape the judicial institution, serving their interests first, above those of other users, allowing the evolution of the judicial institution into a more specialized one. These institutions became more efficient in debt conflict resolution, which left aside other litigation, such as assault and battery for example. Not only did the judge's expertise gradually appear indisputable, but he also helped to standardize contracts and legal norms.

1 The Setting: Mutual Arrangements in Small Communities in the South of Alsace 1650–1790

Introduction

Before the institutionalization of credit in the nineteenth century, credit exchanges were both a personal and a local affair. As highlighted in the Introduction, credit transactions were embedded in social relations. The negotiation and conclusion of contracts and their enforcement were subjected to both economic and social dynamics.

Yet, credit relations were also deeply rooted in a geographical and temporal milieu. Locality mattered.[1] Some local environmental features influenced individual and collective practises of credit. This chapter presents some of these features to equip the reader with the necessary background to comprehend the making of credit.

In the south of Alsace, just like in many French villages, people abided by certain norms, part of a local culture.[2] This set of norms was made of legal, social, and moral norms supported by local structures and conventions. The specificities of village structures, organizations, and institutions; the nature of land tenure; the form of inheritance practised; and the place of women in the local society, and so on governed individual and collective behaviour. These local specificities can be labelled local culture. In turn, it influenced the formation, characteristics, and sustainability of mutual arrangements.

This chapter draws thus the contours of the geographical, demographical, economical, and political milieu. First, it describes the living conditions of the rural dwellers in the south of Alsace with particular reference to the population and its access to resources. Then, this chapter turns to the various socio-professional categories of people living in Delle and Florimont. Finally, it examines how people were governed.

---

[1] James C. Scott, *Seeing Like a State: How Certain Schemes to Improve the Human Condition Have Failed* (New Haven, CT: Yale University Press, 1998). Emmanuel Le Roy Ladurie, *Montaillou, village occitan de 1294 à 1324.* Édition revue et corrigée. (Paris: Folio, 2008).

[2] These norms could have been different just a few kilometres away.

Living in the South of Alsace in the Seventeenth and Eighteenth Centuries

Topography

The villages studied in this book are located in the extreme south of Alsace, in the narrow corridor between the Vosges and the Jura mountains, cramped between Swiss cantons and the Protestant duchy of Montbéliard. About twenty-five kilometres north of these seigneuries lies the town of Belfort, the nearest commercial centre with 4,000 inhabitants towards the end of the Ancien Régime. Further away are the cities of Mulhouse, Colmar, Basel, and Besançon (see Figure 1.1 and Figure 1.2). Strasbourg, the regional royal administrative centre, the *intendance*, is located about 150 kilometres north.

This hilly area of two dozen villages is veined with small streams and rivers and thick with lush forests. Oak trees, hornbeams, chestnuts, and pine trees stand at the edge of the villages. Yellow fields of wheat, barley, and oats cut across green pastures where red-pied dairy cows and flocks of sheep graze. To the east lie lowlands, dotted with a multitude of

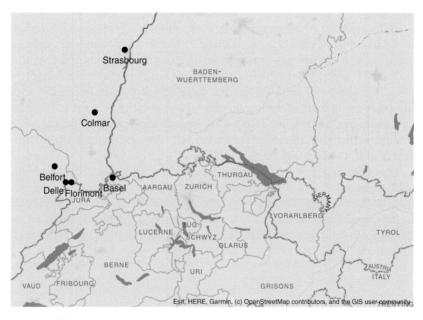

Figure 1.1 Map of the area.
(*Source*: Compiled by the author)

Figure 1.2 Map of the area by Robert de Vaugondy, 1754.
(*Source*: ATDB 1Fi326)

ponds. To the south is the first plateau of the Jura mountains. On a cloudless day, it is possible to catch sight of the snowy tips of the Alps. Summers are warm and thunderstorms frequent, while ice and snow are common in the winter. It is one of the regions of France where it rains the most. Many villages are subject to frequent floods.

Settlment in this area is ancient. Most of the villages date back to at least Roman times if not earlier. Clusterings of rural dwellings were usually aggregated and dense as represented in Figure 1.3, Figure 1.4, and Figure 1.5. One direct implication of this was that the spheres of private and social life were not neatly separated.[3] Each village, even the smallest, featured social areas where people met on a daily basis: a washing house, an inn, a chapel, or a church. Other social spaces included the seigneurial mill and oven. Some of those villages even had

---

[3] Platteau, "Solidarity Norms and Institutions in Village Societies," p 823.

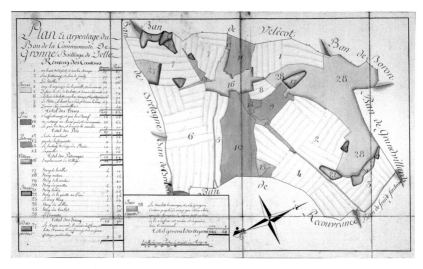

Figure 1.3 Map of the village of Grosne, 1766.
(*Source*: ADTB, 1C92)

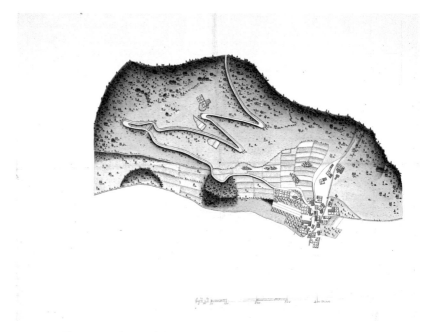

Figure 1.4 Map of the village of Bourogne in 1770.
(*Source*: ADTB 1C165)

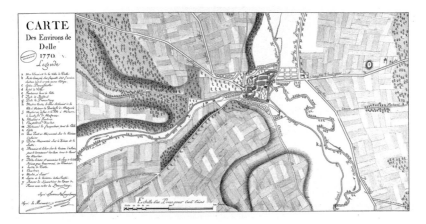

Figure 1.5 Map of the town of Delle in 1770.
(*Source*: ADTB 1Fi323)

a school in the eighteenth century. Weekly markets and annual fairs were organized in the little square at the centre of the village.

The Local Population

The seigneuries of Delle and Florimont counted together a total of twenty-four villages throughout the period. In the mid-seventeenth century, at the conclusion of the Thirty Years' War (1618–48), the region was in a poor state and its population decimated.[4] The raging conflict had displaced inhabitants and had wiped several villages from the map. From 1632 to 1640, Swedish and French forces clashed regularly in the region. Swedish soldiers distinguished themselves by their extreme violence, plundering several towns and villages, terrorizing and molesting the local population. In 1633, the peasants of the south of Alsace, outraged by these abuses, took up arms and defied the occupying forces.[5] In response to this uprising, the Swedish troops massacred the local population.[6] A local chronicler mentioned 3,000 dead among the

---

[4] Rodolphe Reuss, *L'Alsace au dix-septième siècle au point de vue géographique, historique, administratif, économiqe, social, intellectuel et religieux* (Paris: É. Bouillon, 1897), p 71.
[5] Henri Bardy, "Les Suédois dans le Sundgau (1632–1648)," *Revue d'Alsace*, vol. 7 (Fédération des sociétés d'histoire et d'archéologie d'Alsace, 1856), 241–56.
[6] Philippe Dattler, *La métallurgie dans le Comté de Belfort: 1659–1790.* (Belfort: Société Belfortaine d'Emulation, 1980), p 5.

peasants.[7] In the village of Florimont, for example, the castle was burnt and the walls torn down in retaliation.[8]

The region had barely started to heal its wounds when another raging conflict took place. The Franco-Dutch war (1672–78) added another wave of population movements and desolation, especially after 1674. Twenty years later, the cold winter of 1693–94 provoked a catastrophic famine starving many families in the area. Thus, it is not until the beginning of the eighteenth century that the region began to regain its vigour.

In the eighteenth century, in the absence of major conflicts and epidemics, the population grew continuously. In 1720, in both seigneuries, 483 households were listed on the official censuses, representing an estimated total of 2,173 inhabitants. In 1777, the population had increased to 1,011 households, totalling 4,559 inhabitants.[9] More specifically, for the seigneurie of Delle, for which we have good and long series estimates, the number of inhabitants increased by a total of 195%, from 1667 to 1751, which is equivalent to an increase of 1.29% per year. From 1751 to 1803 this growth slowed down, increasing to a total of 52%, which is equivalent to an increase of 0.81% per year.[10]

The main town of Delle was small and counted about 288 inhabitants within its walls in 1720. In 1777, there were about 450 people living there. In the seigneurie of Florimont, the eponymous town counted 103 inhabitants in 1720, and 211 in 1777. In 1793, their number had jumped to 467. On average, each village counted about 40 hearths (households), or about 180 inhabitants each at the end of the eighteenth century.[11]

It is worth mentioning the presence of several Jewish and Anabaptist families in this area. Anabaptists were expelled from the Swiss cantons in the late sixteenth century and migrated to Protestant lands, especially in Alsace and in the county of Montbéliard.[12] They settled in the south of

[7] Hugues Bois de Chêne, *Recueil mémorable de Hugues Bois-de-Chesne, chronique inédite du XVIIe siècle* (Montbéliard: Charles Deckherr, 1856), p 83.

[8] Anne Lerch-Boyer, *Esquisse d'une seigneurie de Haute Alsace au XVIIIe siècle: la seigneurie de Florimont*, Mémoire de maîtrise, (Strasbourg: Université de Strasbourg, 1973), p 10.

[9] I follow Yvette Baradel's estimate of 4.5 individuals per household for this region. Yvette Baradel, *Belfort: de l'Ancien Régime au siège de 1870–1871: fonction régionale, impact national, 1780–1870* (Belfort: Société belfortaine d'émulation, 1993).

[10] Michel Colney, *Delle au XVIIIe siècle* (Colmar: Coprur, 1989), pp 91–92. ADTB 1C31, 21J1.

[11] See Baradel, *Belfort*.

[12] Odile Birgy, "Une occupation originale de l'espace rural. La communauté Anabaptiste de Normanvillars dans le Sundgau au XVIIIe siècle," *Histoire & Sociétés Rurales* 41, no. 1 (2014): 17–54.

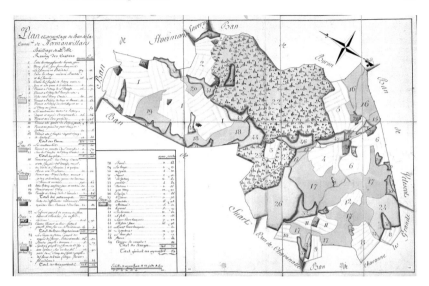

Figure 1.6 Map of the village of Normanvillars.
(*Source*: ADTB 1C111)

Alsace later, in the eighteenth century, despite Louis XIV's expulsion Act of 1712. In 1747, the seigneurie of Florimont welcomed several Anabaptist families to settle in what was left of the village of Normanvillars, an abandoned settlement in the middle of a thick forest dotted with several ponds (see Figure 1.6). The Barbaud family, who owned the seigneurie, was eager to take advantage of these territories to increase their revenues.[13] There, the Anabaptists became sharecroppers of the seigneur, taking over the existing scattered farms and creating new ones.[14] Besides farming, they made a living mostly by raising and selling cattle.[15] Some of these families also specialized in weaving.[16] In 1780, there were twelve families living in the forest of Normanvillars, ninety-nine inhabitants in total.[17] In 1791, one counts twenty-three Anabaptist families out of ninety-seven living on the territory of the village of Florimont.[18] Anabaptists were successful farmers. In the eighteenth century, one finds traces of their credit activities as lenders attesting to

---

[13] The Barbaud family were also Protestant.   [14] ADTB 2E4/352.
[15] Odile Birgy, *Histoire & Sociétés Rurales* 41, no. 1 (2014): 17–54.
[16] ADHR (Archives départementales du Haut-Rhin) C1284.
[17] Archives départementales du Bas-Rhin (ADBR hereafter), C 338.
[18] Birgy, "Une occupation originale de l'espace rural."

their capacity to create surpluses. Contrary to the Jewish population, the Anabaptists were well integrated and were on friendly terms with their Christian neighbours.[19]

The area also counted several Jewish families. About fifteen families lived in the seigneurie of Delle, principally in the village of Seppois-le-Haut.[20] An important Jewish community was also established in the neighbouring village of Foussemagne, across the seigneurie limits. Just like Anabaptists, Jewish families were not allowed to own property. They specialized instead in raising livestock, especially horses and cows, and in meat production.[21] We find traces of their numerous interactions with Christian dwellers via their credit activities. They acted principally as lenders. But contrary to the Anabaptist creditors who often extended cash, Jewish lenders sold their cattle on credit. Only a few seemed to have specialized in moneylending per se.

Living Conditions

In the south of Alsace, most dwellers lived on modest farms. Houses were often made of wattle and daub; stone was more unusual (see Figure 1.7 and Figure 1.8). Bundles of straw usually covered roofs. In the second half of the eighteenth century, people began to coat them with tiles, more resistant and less prone to fire. The living quarters were often small. Most houses had only a few rooms. It was not rare that the main living room (called *stùb* in Alsatian or *poêle* in French dialect) served as a kitchen, dining room, and main bedroom. After all, it was the warmest room in the house, usually equipped with a ceramic wood-burning stove (*kachelofe*) in better-off farms. The parents often slept there in a bed with thick feather cushions and a quilt covered with a *kelsch*, a checked plaid made of hemp. It is also in this room that families spun and wove in the long winter evenings. In most houses, a door directly connected this space with the stable where cows, pigs, horses, and other farm animals were confined.

It is in the stable that animals spent the night and the winter and where cows were milked. This space led directly to the barn, where stocks of hay and straw were placed, as well as the ploughing equipment and carts.

[19] Ibid. Charles Hoffman, *L'Alsace au XVIIIe siècle au point de vue historique, juridique, administratif, économique, intellectuel* (Colmar: A.M.P. Ingold, 1899), vol 1, p 192.

[20] Dominique Varry, "Les campagnes de la subdélégation de Belfort au milieu du XVIIIe siècle." In Michel Balard, Jean-Claude Hervé, and Nicole Lemaitre, eds. *Paris et ses campagnes sous l'Ancien Régime* (Paris: Éditions de la Sorbonne, 2021), 15–26, p 19.

[21] Freddy Raphaël, "Les Juifs de la campagne alsacienne: les marchands de bestiaux," *Revue des sciences sociales de la France de l'Est*, 9, 1980, pp 220–45.

Figure 1.7 A house made in wattle and daub from the eighteenth century, from the village of Recouvrance now visible at the Musée des Maisons comtoises de Nancray.
(Photo: Wikipedro, CC BY-SA 4.0, https://creativecommons.org/licenses/by-sa/4.0/)

Figure 1.8 An old farm in stone in Croix in 1981, probably dating from the eighteenth century.
(*Source*: photo by Raymond Mathieu, personal collection)

On top of the barn, granaries stored bags full of grains from the harvests. In the middle of the courtyard, a water pit was common. A small cellar was usually built underground, under the house or somewhere near the house, under a heap of soil, to store fruits, vegetables, wine, and home-made spirits. Some farms also had a smokehouse where meat, bacon, sausages, and freshwater fish were smoked to ensure long preservation.

Most of the farms had their own garden and orchard where families grew vegetables and fruits. The orchards were particularly rich in pears, apples, plums, and walnuts. All of these were often transformed illegally into strong liquor.[22] Most of the households also owned a pig and poultry for their personal consumption. Overall, nearly all of what families consumed was produced locally and most households were self-sufficent.

Agriculture and Livestock Farming

The overwhelming majority of the dwellers in this region relied on agriculture to make a living. Many contemporary commentators observed that the province of Alsace was very fertile thanks to its rich soil. Jacques de Lagrange, the new *intendant* of Alsace at the beginning of the eighteenth century, observed that 'all Alsace is a very fertile land in all sorts of grains, wine, forage, gardens, and other vegetables'.[23] However, the part located at its extreme south – notably the regions of Delle and Florimont – did not receive the same generous praise. The royal engineer Taverne de Longchamps wrote in 1774 that the region 'is located in the most unproductive part of the province of Alsace, the land is generally speaking only good for the less precious kind of commodities such as oat, rye, barley, *metiel* [mix of rye and wheat], potatoes, black wheat or buckwheat, etc.'[24]

In this area, as Taverne de Longchamps rightly noted, peasants mainly practised mixed farming. They cultivated different kinds of grains, usually the cheapest. Spelt wheat and rye were planted in September and harvested over the summer, while the spring cereals such as oat, barley, and hemp, and vegetables such as potatoes, peas, and lentils were planted in the spring to germinate immediately and were harvested

---

[22] ADTB 1C22.

[23] 'Toute l'Alsace est un pays très fertile en toutes sortes de grains, vins, fourrages, jardinages et autres légumes', Jacques de Lagrange, *L'Alsace en 1700: Mémoire sur la Province d'Alsace de l'Intendant Jacques de La Grange* (Colmar: Ed. Alsatia, 1975), p 44.

[24] 'La ville de Belfort est située dans la partie la plus ingrate de la province d'Alsace, les terres de son voisinage sont généralement parlant seulement propres aux espèces de denrées les moins précieuses, tel que l'avoine, le seigle, l'orge, le metiel, les pommes de terre, le blé noir ou sarrazin, etc...'. Taverne de Longchamps, "Mémoires" in Bulletin de la Société belfortaine d'émulation, 1886, no 8, p 79.

within a few months.[25] Climatic conditions with a lot of rain and frequent freezing temperatures called for polyculture to spread risks.

Overall, 50% of the surface area was dedicated to the cultivation of grains. About 17% was reserved for livestock grazing and hay production. Forests occupied more than a quarter of the surface. Wine cultivation, popular on the slopes of the Vosges mountains, was almost non-existent in the south of Alsace. The area, colder and frequently frozen, was not particularly well-suited for viniculture.

Stock raising, on the other hand, was a very important activity for many households. Most farmers reared dairy cows, horses, chickens, pigs, and other farm animals. Several livestock fairs were organized throughout the two seigneuries as sales contracts show. Arthur Young, the celebrated British agronomist, even noted the good quality of cows in this region.[26] In the south, in the villages of Villars-le-Sec, Saint-Dizier, and Croix, villagers also raised sheep and goats.[27] In the seigneurie of Florimont, peasants engaged in pisciculture and raised carp in the numerous ponds scattered throughout the seigneurie.[28]

In 1667, the new intendant for Alsace asserted that 'most of the peasants owned their land'.[29] In the absence of proper tax registers for this region (such as *compoix* or *taille tarifée*), it is difficult to assess the exact nature of land tenure. *Terriers*, registers listing who owned what at a given time, give only a truncated picture.[30] Overall, the south of Alsace was a region of small proprietors. Land-holding patterns and occupational structures are of utmost importance in this book, not only because land tenure was often a proxy for wealth but also because land was frequently used as collateral in financial transactions.

Jean-Michel Boehler estimates that about 60% of Alsatian land was indeed owned by peasants.[31] Among the other proprietors, the local lords, nobles, religious institutions, and, to a lesser extent, urban elites, shared about 40% of the land. Religious and charitable institutions might

---

[25] Varry, "Les campagnes de la subdélégation de Belfort au milieu du XVIIIe siècle," pp 15–26.

[26] Arthur Young, *Voyages en France en 1787, 1788 et 1789* (Paris: Armand Colin, 1976), p 1121.

[27] ADTB 21 J 1 *'Il y a plusieurs terrains en friches et c'est sur des hauteurs ou la pâture est bonne pour les moutons, aussy ces habitants en tiennent beaucoup et c'est un de leur commerce.'*

[28] Georges Bischoff, "Les blancs de la carpe. Pisciculture et pouvoir: l'exemple de l'Alsace autrichienne (14e–17e siècle)." In Jean-François Chauvard et Isabelle Laboulais, eds. *Les fruits de la récolte, études offertes à Jean-Michel Boehler* (Strasbourg: Presses Universitaires de Strasbourg, 2007), 179–95.

[29] Cited in Hoffman, *L'Alsace au XVIIIe siècle au point de vue historique, juridique, administratif, économique*, p 181.

[30] Boehler, *Une société rurale en milieu rhénan*, p 504.   [31] Ibid., p 45.

have owned up to 25% while the urban bourgeoisie might have owned between 5% and 10%. The rest was owned by the seigneurs.[32]

The reality of this property, however, was very different from our modern standards and understanding.[33] Peasants could sell, inherit, exchange, and transmit the land they owned even though originally the land belonged to the seigneur.[34] These transactions were subject to a fee and had to be registered at the notary's office (*droit de mutation*).[35] The weight of taxes on land marred the very meaning of property. The *cens foncier*, for example, was a tax on the plot itself due to the seigneur, a reminder of his ultimate right to the land (*propriété éminente*). One should also add that some lands were rented *longissimi temporis*. Emphyteutic leases were long-term agreements that were inheritable.[36]

In the seigneuries of Delle and Florimont, a peasant and his family owned about five hectares of arable land on average (see Table 1.1). This number tended to decrease throughout the eighteenth century. These figures are consistent with other Alsatian villages. In the Kochersberg, close to Strasbourg, 77% of the peasants owned less than two hectares.[37] On the other side of the Rhine, 70% of the landholders had less than four hectares in 1780.[38]

Throughout the eighteenth century, peasants owned less and less land (Table 1.1). This was mainly due to two factors: partible inheritance associated with demographic pressure and an increase in prices.[39] First, in this region, peasants practised egalitarian inheritance. All legitimate heirs regardless of sex inherited equally from their parents. As living conditions improved, the proportion of surviving children increased. The population rose throughout the period. More heirs meant de facto a smaller portion of land inherited. Second, land prices surged in the eighteenth century. In the seigneurie of Delle, for example, land prices grew by 1.57% annually between the beginning of the eighteenth century and the 1780s. In the period 1700–1705, the mean for one *journal* of land

[32] Boehler, *La terre, le ciel et les hommes à l'époque moderne*, p 131.

[33] Jean-Michel Boehler, "L'art d'être propriétaire sans l'être tout en l'étant," *Revue d'Alsace*, no. 140 (2014): 79–96.

[34] In Alsace, 'collonge' and 'maix' were the terms in use for these plots of land.

[35] Some of these peasants 'owned' land via an emphyteutic lease, a contract signed for ninety-nine years and tacitly renewable.

[36] Hoffman, *L'Alsace au XVIIIe siècle au point de vue historique, juridique, administratif, économique, intellectuel*, pp 208–9.

[37] Jean-Michel Boehler, "Communauté villageoise et contrastes sociaux: laboureurs et manouvriers dans la campagne strasbourgeoise de la fin du XVIIe au début du XIXe siècle," *Études rurales* 63, no. 1 (1976): 93–116, p 100.

[38] Boehler, *Une société rurale en milieu rhénan*, p 515.

[39] Boehler, *Une société rurale en milieu rhénan*, p 504.

Table 1.1 *Surface area for arable land in hectares in the seigneuries of Delle and Florimont according to probate inventories (1670–1790)*

Period	Mean surface area ownership per deceased (hectare)	Number of probate inventories[a]
1670–89	4.85	46
1690–1709	7.008	99
1710–29	6.072	42
1730–49	5.080	66
1750–69	4.029	125
1770–90	3.072	262

[a] Probate inventories dataset (hereafter): ADTB 12B165, 2E4/10, 53, 54, 55, 56, 85, 86, 87, 114, 203, 210, 228, 252, 260, 261, 262, 287, 288, 296, 299, 309, 315, 317, 348, 349, 350, 351, 397, 399, 401, 402, 403, 404, 405, 407, 411, 435, 436, 437, 438, 439, 440, 441, 442.

(about a third of one hectare of land) equalled 46 livres. In the period 1780–85, it increased to 160.[40]

Overall, the south of Alsace was a region of small proprietors. Yet, it is important to stress that small land tenure did not preclude solidarity. On the contrary, the nature of agricultural work required a certain amount of reciprocal neighbourliness. Collective labour was required for the harvests, for sowing, but also for other particular tasks.[41] And heirs had an interest in participating in the collective work effort. Interestingly, this pattern of cooperative work continued long into the twentieth century when farms were heavily mechanized and subsidized.

Craftsmanship and Early Industries

Besides agriculture and livestock farming, dwellers engaged in subsidiary economic activities additional to their main occupations such as manufacturing, crafting, and/or service-oriented activities. There was a plethora of peasants-turned-artisans who toiled in the villages and towns across the area. Exactly how many peasants engaged in such activities is difficult to say. By-employments were often part-time, temporary, and/or seasonal activities. They were meant to generate additional revenues on the side. Apart from some master artisans living in Delle, these rural

---

[40] Nominal prices. For both periods, the mean of one journal might have been undervalued. Some land was sold for a trifle to repay a debt, dragging down the mean price in our series.

[41] Wilson, *Being Neighbours*.

craftsmen were usually not members of any guild and thus were not subject to many rules and constraints.

Peasants engaged in a wide range of by-employments. In the south of Alsace, the early textile industry was a sector generating additional revenues for many families. Probate inventories frequently list various tools and instruments such as looms and spinning wheels. Peasants cultivated flax and hemp. Some in the south raised sheep for their wool. Often in the winter, men and women spun flax fibres and wove linen. They also carded or combed raw wool and spun it into yarn (usually a female task). Peasants sold their production to the local market but also to merchants, often from the neighbouring region of Mulhouse, an area where the early textile industry was booming.[42] In 1762, a hosiery manufacture opened in the town of Belfort.[43]

Since livestock farming was an important activity, a small group of artisans specialized in the processing of leather. Delle had its own tannery. Some households made garments and shoes. Seamstresses, tailors, and shoemakers were well represented. Those craftsmen, often landless or with too little land available, however, often featured among the poorest members of their community.

Construction craftsmen such as carpenters, builders, stone carvers, and tilers could frequently be found scattered in various villages. But it is perhaps those who toiled over food and beverages who were the most numerous. Innkeepers, who were often also farmers, were present in almost all the villages. Some villages even had several inns. Butchers and bakers, on the other hand, tended to open their shops only in the most populated areas.

The early metallurgy sector also generated some extra income for a few families. Iron ore was extracted in the north of the region, at the foot of the Vosges mountains. The village of Florimont had a small blast furnace. Small foundries and establishments using trip-hammers employed a few workers in both seigneuries.[44] Blacksmiths could be found in nearly every village.

The eighteenth century saw the rise of retail shopkeeping. This was particularly noticeable in Delle. There, several grocers sold a wide range of products including spices, tobacco, coffee, and other luxury products to a growing bourgeoisie. This new clientele also visited the wigmaker,

---

[42] Jean-Marie Schmitt and David Jenkins, "The Origins of the Textile Industry in Alsace: The Beginnings of the Manufacture of Printed Cloth at Wesserling (1762–1802)," *Textile History* 13, no. 1 (1982): 99–109.
[43] ADTB 1C34.   [44] Dattler, *La métallurgie dans le comté de Belfort.*

barber, arquebusier (a craftsman who makes and sells harquebuses and other portable firearms), and haberdashery shop, among others.

The Population and Its Wealth

Estimating Wealth

In the absence of proper tax registers, it is difficult to assess the wealth of Alsatian households with any precision.[45] In a common assumption, the rural population of Alsace was wealthier than other parts of the French kingdom thanks to fertile soil and reputable wine production.[46] Probate inventories help us to distinguish several broad categories.[47]

Yet, probate inventories are not flawless. They were in general drawn for at least two reasons. First, a probate was often necessary to divide the estate among legitimate heirs. Second, the settlement of debts required an official list of liabilities. Only estates with something left to be divided and debts to be paid (or claims to be received) underwent such a process. As a result, not all households had an inventory made.[48]

The comprehensive nature of probate can be problematic. The appraisers, for the most part, listed carefully all items that were considered of some worth. Yet, the heirs and surviving spouse could have diverted some items for themselves. Micheline Baulant estimates that 10% of the value of the estate was in fact diverted.[49] Second, the estimation of goods and assets was not systematically applied in monetary value. If the succession was not problematic, the family divided the land and estate between themselves without estimating their value, which would have engendered additional costs. Third, probate inventories were aimed at households with something to leave behind. Many rural dwellers died penniless. And therefore the surviving probates give a skewed picture of households' wealth. One should add that probates did not assess an individual's wealth but household wealth, often considering the assets of both spouses together. Finally, most probated estates were ageing households whose accumulated wealth might have

---

[45] There were no proper individualized tax records such as *compoix* or *taille*. The *taille* was a tax on household wealth but these taxrolls do not exist for the region.

[46] Young, *Voyages en France En 1787, 1788 et 1789*.

[47] Gérard Béaur, "Les catégories sociales à la campagne: repenser un instrument d'analyse," *Annales de Bretagne et des pays de l'Ouest* 106, no. 1 (1999): 159–76.

[48] In addition, the preservation of such documents for the seventeenth century is rather low compared to the post-1750 period.

[49] Micheline Baulant, "Niveaux de vie paysans autour de Meaux en 1700 et 1750," *Annales. Histoire, Sciences Sociales* 30, no. 2–3 (1975): 505–18.

been higher than younger households.[50] Considering all these biases, wealth estimates need to be taken with a pinch of salt.

The criteria for establishing social differentiation need to encompass several variables.[51] Since assessments often lacked monetary value, arable land ownership is a decent proxy for wealth, as well as access to local responsibilities.[52] Dwellers in the south of Alsace can thus be divided into several general categories. First, the poor and the landless stand at the bottom. Then, the small-landed proprietors form the vast majority of households. And finally, the better-off, either big landowners or non-manual workers make up the rising new bourgeoisie.

The Poor and Landless

In pre-industrial Europe, between 25% and 50% of the population lived in poverty.[53] For the late eighteenth century, about 10% of the French population was deemed poor.[54] In Alsace, in 1791, a report estimates that 36.6% of households in the town of Wissembourg needed assistance and 2.1% were begging. In Truchtersheim, a village close to Strasbourg, about 22% of the households needed assistance and a stunning proportion of 20% of the households were begging.[55] Poverty was ubiquitous.

Every household could potentially find itself in an uncomfortable, if not dramatic, situation in a world full of risks and uncertainties.[56] Poor households, in general, were sensitive to price changes and economic slowdown. In rural areas, crop failures causing shortages of various degrees, ranging from insufficient stocks to subsistence crisis and famine, were the main reasons households struggled. In the eighteenth century, wheat prices experienced periods of boom and bust, as Figure 1.9 shows. In the second half of the eighteenth century, in particular, wheat prices

[50] See for example Håkan Lindgren, "The Modernization of Swedish Credit Markets, 1840–1905: Evidence from Probate Records," *The Journal of Economic History* 62, no. 3 (2002): 810–32; Dermineur, "Peer-to-Peer Lending in Pre-Industrial France"; Sebastian A. J. Keibek, "Correcting the Probate Inventory Record for Wealth Bias," Working Paper No. 28, Cambridge Group for the History of Population and Social Structure & Queens' College (March 2017).

[51] Béaur, "Les catégories sociales à la campagne."

[52] Yann Lagadec, "Elites villageoises et pouvoir local," *Enquêtes rurales*, no. 11 (2007): 45–61.

[53] Catharina Lis, and Hugo Soly, *Poverty and Capitalism in Pre-Industrial Europe* (Atlantic Highlands, NJ: Humanities Press, 1979).

[54] Stuart Woolf, *The Poor in Western Europe in the Eighteenth and Nineteenth Centuries* (London: Routledge, 2016).

[55] Boehler, *Une société rurale en milieu rhénan*, p 1447.

[56] Laurence Fontaine, *Vivre pauvre. Quelques enseignements tirés de l'Europe des Lumières* (Paris: Editions Gallimard, 2022).

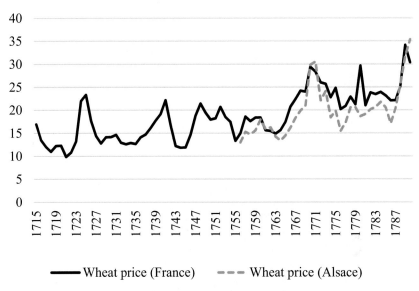

———— Wheat price (France)   – – – Wheat price (Alsace)

Figure 1.9 Wheat price in France and in Alsace in livre tournois according to Labrousse.[57]

rose significantly in Alsace. For those struggling to make ends meet, increases in prices could have dramatic consequences.

Most of the poor were landless. Right before the Revolution, Condorcet pointed to the link between property and wealth; for him a poor person was 'the one who does not own anything, neither assets nor furniture and who is meant to fall into misery upon the slightest incident'.[58] In the south of Alsace, probate inventories indicate that 10.2% of the deceased did not own any land at all and 35% owned less than one hectare (see Figure 1.10).[59] Most households (93%) owned less than ten hectares, a threshold Pierre Goubert has deemed indispensable to reach food security.[60]

A few alternatives were therefore available to the landless. They could sell their manpower to others, often for temporary or periodic work tasks.

[57] Ernest Labrousse, *Esquisse du mouvement des prix et des revenus en France au XVIIIe siecle* (Paris: Editions des archives contemporaines, 1984).

[58] Quoted in Fontaine, *Vivre pauvre. Quelques enseignements tirés de l'Europe des Lumières*, p 15. My translation.

[59] Some households, especially the ageing ones, could have donated their land to their heirs before their deaths.

[60] Goubert, *Beauvais et le Beauvaisis de 1600 à 1730*, p 182. The average holding of arable land decreased throughout the eighteenth century mostly because of demographic pressure and fragmentation of land under partible inheritance. Hoffman estimates that food security could be reached with five hectares. Hoffman, *Growth in a Traditional Society*, p 36.

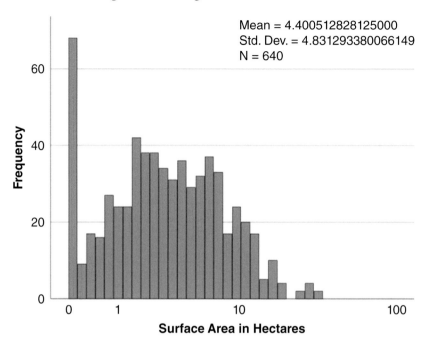

Mean = 4.400512828125000
Std. Dev. = 4.831293380066149
N = 640

Figure 1.10 Land ownership per household in hectares (logarithmic scale) based on 640 probate inventories, 1670–1790. (*Source*: probate dataset)[61]

They could rent out plots from others – provided they owned the necessary tools. They could also use the commons to feed their livestock. This option was necessarily subsidiary. And/or they could make ends meet thanks to what Olwen Hufton calls the makeshift economy, a diversification of activities to ensure a livelihood.[62] In the south of Alsace, the production and the sale of small textile items was an activity many undertook during winter. Some craftmanship activities, such as carpentry or shoemaking, required small tools. But manufacturing activities requiring more sophisticated tools and raw products were not necessarily accessible to all. Finally, to make ends meet and palliate the lack of cash/income, the landless could turn to the credit market. Without much guarantee to offer, they were often barred access to substantive loans. The generosity of others often granted them delays and cash to survive.

---

[61] The graph does not include seven probates from the period before 1670.
[62] Olwen H. Hufton, *The Poor of Eighteenth-Century France 1750–1789* (Oxford: Clarendon Press, 1974).

Those without land often struggled. Jacques Cottet was a shoemaker living in the village of Bourogne. He and his wife owned a piece of garden and an orchard next to their house where they could grow some vegetables and fruits, probably for their own consumption and for the sale of the surplus in the form of liquor. They also owned a piece of meadow, but no animal was listed in their probate inventory. When Cottet died in 1773, the tanner Jean-Baptiste Touvet recalled 242 livres he had lent the shoemaker, likely linked to the purchase of leather so he could perform his craft. Cottet's household was also indebted to the priest of the community for 53 livres, for seeds and the rent of a piece of land. Craftmanship and agriculture often complemented each other in rural areas to make ends meet.[63]

Young people without land or awaiting inheritance to establish their own household often sold their manpower to others.[64] In the eighteenth century, service-oriented labour was fast developing. While this kind of occupation was supposed to be temporary, some of these landless domestics remained in service throughout their lives. In February 1781, the appraisers of the village of Suarce drafted the probate inventory of the community's herdsman in charge of the cows. Henri Barbier owned very little. He did not own a house and likely rented one or was hosted by the community. He did not own land either. He had a few pieces of furniture, three livres in cash, two pigs, two goats, and various poultry. He did not have any debts, but nine livres were owed to him by the community and a few households for his services as the village's herdsman.[65]

Migrants were often among the poor. They had migrated in search of better opportunities and sold their services wherever they could. Catherine, whose last name was not known either by the probate appraisers or by her lodger, came from a Swiss village. She was employed as a domestic. No property or items were listed in her probate when she died in 1787. Two individuals owed her money. Catherine Bourquardez owed her twenty-one livres, perhaps as the remainder of her salary. And Georges Bandelier owed her three livres, also for an unknown reason.[66] Those two claims were her only wealth.

The very destitute could find some respite at the local hospital in Delle. *L'hôpital des pauvres* was established in the late seventeenth

---

[63] ADTB 2E4/260.
[64] Cissie Fairchilds, *Domestic Enemies: Servants and Their Masters in Old Regime France* (Baltimore, MD: John Hopkins University Press, 2019).
[65] ADTB 2E4/442.   [66] ADTB 2E4/288.

century to house the poor and the sick.[67] Incidentally, this institution would finance its charitable activities mainly via moneylending.

Landed Peasants and Rural Artisans

The vast majority of the dwellers in this region were smallholders and worked their land (see Figure 1.10). In the probate sample examined, the average holding of arable land per household was about five hectares for the period. In a traditional assumption, with five hectares a family could reach self-sufficiency and pay taxes provided the soil was fertile and commons available.[68]

Those with too little land took on by-employment. Jean-Pierre Monnier died in 1778 in the village of Chavanatte. The clerk writing down his inventory mentioned that Monnier was a shoemaker. With a little over two hectares of arable land, Monnier likely needed to add to his revenue.[69] It was also certainly the case for the cooper Jean-Jacques Hosenat from the village of Réchesy who also owned about two hectares of arable land and the blacksmith Jean Claude Gainey from Suarce who also had just over two hectares.[70] Some of these rural artisans accumulated reasonable wealth but nonetheless continued their agricultural activities. Jean-Pierre Chappuis from the village of Croix was not only a farmer but also a blacksmith. He seemed to have also sold tobacco. At some point before his death, he was a tax collector for the *dixme* tax of his village, a move highlighting his wealth.[71]

Yet most of the smallholders struggled. Several poor harvests in a row or poor economic conditions could push some of these households below the poverty line. Some of them could bounce back with time but others never recovered. These households are not easy to track. We can take a glimpse at their struggle by looking at land sale registers. In the period 1780–85, the mean for one *journal* of land equalled 160 livres. Yet, several transactions were agreed upon well under market price. About 33% of transactions for arable land were under market price by at least half, and 13% of the sales stipulated a price below or equal to forty livres, only a quarter of the mean price. Those transactions seemed, in fact, to have been transactions to repay a debt or a creditor, a desperate move.[72]

---

[67] Joachim, *La fondation des pauvres ou vieil hôpital de Delle 1600–1820*.
[68] Hoffman, *Growth in a Traditional Society*, p 36. Goubert, in contrast, mentions ten hectares for a family to be self-sufficient. Pierre Goubert, *Beauvais et le Beauvaisis de 1600 à 1730: Contribution à l'histoire sociale de la France du XVIIe siècle* (Paris: Publications de la Sorbonne, 2013).
[69] ADTB 2E4/435.   [70] ADTB 2E4/440.   [71] ADTB 2E4/287.
[72] This pattern might correspond to what Ulrich Pfister called the permanent income hypothesis, Pfister, "Rural Land and Credit Markets, the Permanent Income Hypothesis and Proto-Industry." Households balanced capital assets with labour supply.

Overall, the majority of peasants were small proprietors. As a result, these communities were often more egalitarian with little disparity in wealth or in bargaining power. Pierre Barral qualifies these societies as 'rural democracy'.[73] This terminology is certainly too romantic. Yet, the wealth gap between the vast majority of the households seems to have been quite narrow, which might have prompted greater cooperation.

The Rural Elite and the Bourgeoisie

If the majority of the peasants were struggling small proprietors juggling various activities to make ends meet, some accumulated quite substantial wealth. The biggest landowner recorded, Jean Michelat from the village of Saint-Dizier, owned 34.9 hectares.[74] He was, incidentally, the mayor of his village. Nicolas Jeantine from Suarce had two houses, twenty-eight hectares, six ponds, a large amount of livestock, and 5,000 livres in claims at his death. Jean-Claude Dadey, mayor of Chavanatte, also had two houses covered in tiles, twenty-seven hectares of arable land, a large flock of sheep, and a herd of cows. In 1675, the mayor of Courtelevant, Jean-Pierre Prudon, owned more than thirty hectares of arable land.[75] Overall, 1% of the biggest landowners owned more than 26.7 hectares. Wealth accumulation often went hand in hand with access to local responsibilities. Mayors and churchwardens were likely to be among the better-off. French historians often labelled these better-off peasants *coqs de village* (village roosters), the ones with money and power.

At a higher level, the rural bourgeoisie also counted non-manual workers such as judges, notaries, lawyers, and bailiffs in its numbers. While there were only a few of them in the seventeenth century, the venal offices multiplied their numbers in the eighteenth century. These families often intermarried and thus created powerful networks of influence. The better-off often participated in the local credit market, lending but also borrowing money.

Governance and Administration

Early modern Alsatian communities were governed by two different sets of rules. First, there were law and legal ordinances enacted by the French crown since the conquest of Alsace after the Thirty Years' War; alongside the traditional customs proper to each local community. While the legal sets enacted by the central authorities kept growing throughout the

[73] Pierre Barral, "Note historique sur l'emploi du terme 'paysan,'" *Études Rurales*, no. 21 (1966): 72–80.
[74] ADTB 2E4/56.   [75] ADTB 2E4/436.

period, the traditional customs nonetheless persisted. The second set of rules governing small communities consisted of informal rules, referred to as social norms.

The Royal Power

This study begins in 1648. That year marked the end of the long and deadly Thirty Years' War (1618–48). The Treaty of Westphalia, sealing the European peace, recognized France as one of the war's winners. Louis XIV was granted new territories on the northeast side of his kingdom. The region called 'Haute Alsace', once under the domination of the Austrian Habsburgs, was now integrated into the French jurisdiction and administration.[76] Among these new territories figured the villages of this study.

Before 1648, the dwellers of Haute Alsace were part of the Holy Roman Empire. As a borderland region, they used the rights, rules, and justice of the Empire. They paid taxes to the Austrian authorities. Vienna was nevertheless a distant master. 'Every time the house of Austria wanted some assistance from Alsace', writes the intendant Jacques de la Grange, 'the provincial estates had to be summoned in Ensisheim'.[77] No decision regarding taxes or conscription could be taken without the express consent of these estates.

After the war, to ensure a smooth transition and the implementation of a new administration, the French authorities decided to leave much of the traditional uses of Alsace in place. 'Il ne faut point toucher aux usages de l'Alsace' (one must not touch the habits and practises of Alsace) affirmed the Controller-General of Finances in 1701.[78] There were several reasons for this. First, Alsatian territory was a mosaic of small territories belonging either directly to the king or the local nobility, in other words an administrative conundrum featuring the superposition of various jurisdictions, rights, and prerogatives.[79] A quick glance at a map suffices to understand the complexity of such territory. Second, Cardinal Mazarin, the faithful minister of Louis XIV, did not want to engage in an

---

[76] The rest of Alsace minus a few cities was added to the French kingdom in 1697 by the treaty of Nimègue. 'Haute Alsace' is often called Sundgau in Alsatian.

[77] Cited by Georges Bischoff, *Gouvernés et gouvernants en haute Alsace à l'époque Autrichienne*, Société savante d'Alsace et des régions de l'est (Strasbourg: Librairie Istra, 1982), p 5.

[78] Georges Livet, *L'intendance d'Alsace sous Louis XIV, 1648–1715* (Paris: Société d'Edition Les Belles Lettres, 1956), p 642.

[79] Reuss, *L'Alsace au dix-septième siècle au point de vue géographique, historique, administratif, économiqe, social, intellectuel et religieux*, p 271.

unnecessary struggle in Alsace, 'une querelle d'allemand' as he coined it.[80] France already had a long list of hostile neighbours and internal issues. Third, the cultural aspect certainly played a role in this decision. Alsatians, the majority of whom did not speak French but instead spoke Alsatian or German, were de facto culturally closer to the Habsburgs than the Bourbons. In the fifteenth and sixteenth centuries, several incidents in the region pushed the Alsatian historian Georges Bischoff to conclude that Alsatians were not particularly fond of their French neighbours. The Alsatian identity was strong.[81] In 1648, when the treaty of Münster – part of the treaty of Westphalia – gave the city of Colmar to Louis XIV, its inhabitants rose in discontent. Their resistance led to the destruction of their walls in retaliation. Finally, Alsatians, observed the new intendant La Grange, 'are reluctant to abandon their traditional customs'. To the contrary, 'novelty troubles them as they are fond of their traditional habits, whether good or bad'.[82]

One should add that the French language was only spoken in the south and in small pockets on the flanks of the Vosges. Most Alsatians continued to draft their contracts in Gothic characters. They carried on measuring their plots in *acker* or *journal*, not in *arpent de roi*. In most of Alsace, inhabitants used several different currencies well into the eighteenth century.[83]

In any case, any major change would have been difficult to implement. The region had experienced violent battles and plunder for several years. Villages had been erased from the map. Populations had been displaced. Crops had been lost. The reconstruction would surely take a long time. As a result, Alsace was granted a particular status.

A few months after the peace of Westphalia, the French annexation became a tangible reality. The status quo was respected. The former administrative entities were preserved. But the French administration came on top of the former structures with, notably, the powerful *intendants de justice, de polices et des finances*.[84] From his seat in Strasbourg, the intendant took his orders directly from the capital and represented the royal power and authority in the region. He could count on faithful

---

[80] Ibid.

[81] Bischoff, *Gouvernés et gouvernants en haute Alsace à l'époque Autrichienne*, p 214.

[82] Cited by Boehler, *Une société rurale en milieu rhénan*, p 8.

[83] Jean-Michel Boehler, "Étrangers et étranges: terre et paysans d'Alsace vus par les ressortissants d'outre-Rhin et d'outre-Vosges aux XVIIe et XVIIIe siècles." In Dominique Dinet and Jean-Noël Grandhomme, eds. *Les formes du voyage: approches interdisciplinaires*, Sciences de l'histoire (Strasbourg: Presses universitaires de Strasbourg, 2019), 11–23, p 14.

[84] The *intendances* were created by Louis XIII in 1635 to better manage and control local provinces.

officers scattered throughout Alsace in the newly created *subdélégations* to execute his orders locally. The seigneuries of Delle and Florimont were part of the Belfort *subdélégation*. Below the *subdélégation*, the administrative *baillage*, matching more or less seigneurial limits, headed by a bailiff, fulfilled principally fiscal and justice functions at the local level. Perhaps the most careful change was the creation of the Conseil Souverain d'Alsace in 1657 in Ensisheim.[85] The monarchy did not call it a parliament like in other regions, yet its role was very similar. It served notably as a court of appeal.

What was the weight and reach of the royal authority on the seigneuries of Delle and Florimont? The royal fiscal administration imposed the payment of fixed taxes such as the subvention (resembling the *taille*), the *capitation* since 1695, the *dixième* (replaced by the *vingtième* in 1749) and various periodic taxes aiming at specific objectives.[86] These latter became common in the eighteenth century. All in all, Dominique Varry estimates that each household in the area contributed, on average, five livres each year to the royal coffers.[87] It was perhaps the fiscal burden that was the most salient aspect of the royal domination for the inhabitants of Delle and Florimont.

The Seigneurial Authority

After the Thirty Years' War, therefore, most of southern Alsace was in the hands of the French king. In 1659, Louis XIV rewarded his faithful minister, Cardinal Mazarin, for his services with the territories newly gained from the Habsburgs. This is known as the *donation Mazarin*. The small seigneurie of Delle was included in this gift, along with most of the south of Alsace. The Mazarin family resided in Paris or Versailles. They

---

[85] It was transferred in Colmar upon the treaty of Nimègue in 1679.

[86] Charles Hoffman, *L'Alsace au XVIIIe siècle au point de vue historique, juridique, administratif, économique, intellectuel*. The taille was a tax paid by the non-elite households. Both the nobility and the clergy were exempt. It was a distributive tax. The king set an overall sum to be collected for the entire kingdom. This sum was then divided between the various administrative regions who in turn divided it between the various parishes. Collectors were appointed in each parish and drew up a list of taxable households, assessing the ressources of each household. The capitation tax was introduced by Louis XIV in 1695 to help finance his wars. It was design to be a universal tax, paid by all. The taxpayers were divided into classes based on their status and ranks, not their wealth. The dixième was a temporary tax on the revenue of each individual, at the rate of one tenth of annual revenue. The vingtième tax was introduced in 1749 to replace the dixième. It was one-twentieth or 5% of the annual income collected by the government for all people regardless of their rank or status, although it was abrogated during the French Revolution.

[87] Varry, "Les campagnes de la subdélégation de Belfort au milieu du XVIIIe siècle," p 25.

almost never visited their eastern estates, delegating the management of their possessions to seigneurial agents.

While the seigneurie of Delle was the property of the Mazarin family, the seigneurie of Florimont belonged to a new ennobled local family, the Barbaud. Originally from the Protestant duchy of Montbéliard, the Barbaud made their fortune in metallurgy.[88] In 1672, Gaspard Barbaud bought the seigneurie of Florimont for 80,000 livres tournois. And in 1675, Louis XIV ennobled the family.

While there was no direct presence of the royal authorities in rural areas, the rights and privileges of the local seigneur were more tangible in the villages. First, the fiscal burden was important. The most important taxes were the *taille* and the *cens foncier* on the land, both direct contributions. Indirect taxes not only on the sale of grains, wine (*angal* or *umgeld*), and salt, but also on land transfers could generate substantial profits for the seigneur. Second, the local judge, notary, prosecutor, tax collector, and forest warden were the visible figures of the seigneurial authority. They assured the smooth daily operation in the seigneurie.

For our purpose, two officers played roles of utmost importance, the notary and the judge. A semi-public figure, the notary's duties consisted of the drafting, certifying, and archiving of legal records. Land sales, wills, donations, leases, marriage contracts, and in particular loan contracts, figured among the most common deeds a notary drafted.[89] Throughout the period, the role evolved; in 1597 the office became venal. From then on notaries could not only purchase their office but also transmit it to their heirs, thus creating local oligarchies.[90] The local judge, on the other hand, handled petty conflicts between villages. He notably helped to enforce debt contracts.

---

[88] Dattler, *La métallurgie dans le Comté de Belfort: 1659–1790*, p 34.

[89] See for instance Philip T. Hoffman, Gilles Postel-Vinay, and Jean-Laurent Rosenthal, "What Do Notaries Do? Overcoming Asymmetric Information in Financial Markets: The Case of Paris, 1751," UCLA Economics Working Paper (UCLA Department of Economics, 1994); Jean L. Laffont, *Le notaire, le paysan, et la terre dans la France méridionale à l'époque moderne* (Toulouse: Presses Universitaires du Midi, 1999); Claire Dolan, *Le Notaire, la famille et la ville: Aix-en-Provence à la fin du XVIe siècle* (Toulouse: Presses Universitaires du Midi, 1998); Levy, *The Making of a Market*; Kathryn Burns, "Notaries, Truth, and Consequences," *The American Historical Review* 110, no. 2 (2005): 350–79; Francois Menant and Odile Redon, eds., *Notaires et crédit dans l'Occident méditerranéen médiéval* (Rome: Ecole Française de Rome, 2004); Jean-Yves Sarazin, "L'historien et le notaire: acquis et perspectives de l'étude des actes privés de la France moderne," *Bibliothèque de l'école des Chartes* 160, no. 1 (2002): 229–70.

[90] Albeit after the payment of a tax. A short pause in this hereditary system took place between 1722 and 1743. But after 1743, the hereditary nature of their office was uncontested. In Delle, venality of offices began in 1700.

The role of the seigneurial institutions changed throughout the period. In the seventeenth century, the seigneur aimed to coerce the peasants into respect for rules and, above all, respect for his authority. The local court of justice, for example, often prosecuted misdemeanours connected to infringements on the seigneur's rights and prerogatives, the disruption of public peace, or even infringements on Christian morals. In September 1682, the prosecutor of Delle brought Noël Challemey to court because he had not used the services of the notary to write his will. In June 1682, the prosecutor brought Simon Gainon to court for blasphemy. In January 1681, the prosecutor accused Melchior Hennemend of having worked on a Sunday.[91] Yet, in the eighteenth century, these cases progressively disappeared from the docks and were replaced by the dwellers' own concerns. The defence of property rights and the repayment of debt then became major concerns.

The seigneurial authority, closer to the peasants, is traditionally depicted as constraining, an inheritance of the medieval feudal system.[92] Yet, in the south of Alsace, peasants were no longer serfs. The seigneurs did own the *haute justice* and various rights and privileges, but peasants met in general assembly, wrote down the tax rolls to distribute the fiscal burden among themselves, often collected the taxes themselves, managed the finances of their parish, and did not even consult their seigneur before using the justice system. Their degree of autonomy was real, so was their latitude of action.[93]

Village Institutions

The early modern village was not simply a group of households living in close proximity to each other. It was also a social and political institution, an economic environment, and a legal entity. As a result, several formal and informal institutions provided the necessary structures to ensure the continuity and smoothness of cooperation.[94]

The community – *la communauté* – as a legal and economic institution, was administrated by its inhabitants under the (often distant) supervision of the seigneur. Villagers elected their representatives to administer their

---

[91] ADTB 8B19.

[92] See for instance Philippe Goujard, "L'abolition de la féodalité dans le Pays de Bray (1789–1793)," *Annales Historiques de La Révolution Française* 224, no. 1 (1976): 287–94.

[93] René Le Cerf, "Le général d'une paroisse bretonne," *Revue de Bretagne et de Vendée. Etudes d'Histoire Local*, (July 1888:, 54–65.

[94] Heath, "The Benefits of Cooperation."

affairs, especially complex fiscal and financial questions.[95] These officers took on various tasks. Some chores aimed at securing a form of cooperative benefit for all (administering the commons for instance) and some other tasks had rather an extractive purpose (establishing the tax roll for example).[96] The key official was the mayor. Elected by his peers – the *bourgeois,* heads of their households – the mayor was often a wealthy individual. It was not rare to encounter dynasties of mayors succeeding each other from father to son.

Alongside the mayor, one finds the churchwardens (*marguilliers* or *fabriciens*). These officials were lay people administering and managing the local church via an institution called the *fabrique*.[97] It was common that the churchwardens also participated in decisions regarding the community at large.[98] In France, a parish vestry's main purpose was to deal with the maintenance of the religious buildings and cemetery. The budget was based on two types of revenue. First, the revenue from the collections during services, funerals, bench rental, sale of fruits or grass from the cemetery, for instance. Second, the vestry also collected revenue by renting bequeathed land, the payment of mass foundations, and from the annual payment of annuity contracts extended to hundreds of individuals in the community.

Money was spent on keeping the parish church in good shape. Purchase of candles, religious ornaments, payment of the priest for the service of the mass, and payment to the administrators of the parish vestries constituted the most essential of the expenses. With excess money, the administrators were able to lend cash to individuals.

Overall, peasants self-governed their communities. Michael Taylor labelled these communities as 'quasi-anarchic'.[99] Yet, one should not get an impression of egalitarian democracy. The community had real prerogatives and room for action. But those steering its affairs were a handful of better-off men enjoying a status of prestige and power among their peers. Wealth mattered. After all, *'qui paie, decide'* – 'the one who pays, decides'.[100] All the mayors were among the wealthiest – if not the wealthiest – of their village. Patriarchal structures prevailed. Women,

---

[95] Antoine Follain, "L'administration des villages par les paysans au XVIIe siècle," *Dix-septième siècle* 234, no. 1 (2007): 135–56, p 143.

[96] Heath, "The Benefits of Cooperation."

[97] Antoine Follain refers to the 'officiers de village'. Antoine Follain, "L'exercice du pouvoir à travers les fonctions communautaires dans les campagnes françaises modernes." In Jean-Pierre Jessenne and François Menant, eds. *Les élites rurales: dans l'Europe médiévale et moderne,* (Toulouse: Presses universitaires du Midi, 2020), 149–62, p 150.

[98] Antoine Follain, *Le village sous l'Ancien Régime* (Paris: Fayard, 2008).

[99] Taylor, *Community, Anarchy and Liberty,* p 35.

[100] Follain, *Le village sous l'Ancien Régime,* p 270.

dependants, and many men were excluded from the decision-making process. In theory, widows had a say in the village assembly as head of their household, but one can question their real influence.

Traditional Customs

In the north of France, and in Alsace in particular, local traditional customs prevailed. They were a set of accepted, ancient, legal norms based loosely on Germanic and Roman law as well as on the Justinian Code. Customary law played a critical role in civil matters as it covered a wide range of familial issues. 'Royal' law applied where customary law remained silent.[101] The French kings did not repeal these customary laws because 'self-governance in certain provincial matters was largely in the interest of the crown.'[102]

In the south of Alsace, inhabitants followed the local custom of Ferrette.[103] Its origins are not well known but legal scholars contend that it has heavy Germanic and Celtic influences. Its transmission was oral until the sixteenth century when the custom was written down.

Among the various articles featured in this custom, the ones related to inheritance are of importance. The custom of Ferrette specified two rules for succession. First, children, regardless of their sex, inherited equally from their parents. This was called partible inheritance. De facto, it means that women were entitled to some property upon the death of both parents. Access to property and assets gave them economic agency.[104]

Land and houses were divided accordingly, not without incongruities. It was common, for example, to inherit one sixth of a house, or less. One of the heirs had to buy their siblings out to keep the parental house, an operation almost always done via credit arrangements.[105] If no one had

---

[101] Elise M. Dermineur "The Civil Judicial System in Early Modern France." *Frühneuzeit-Info* 22 (2011): 44–53.

[102] Zoë A. Schneider, *The King's Bench: Bailiwick Magistrates and Local Governance in Normandy, 1670–1740* (Rochester, NY: University of Rochester Press, 2008), p 18.

[103] Édouard Bonvalot, *Coutumes de la Haute-Alsace dites de Ferrette* (Colmar: Barth et Held-Baltzinger, 1870); Marie-Lyse Storti, "Coutume de Ferrette et/ou coutume du comté de Belfort," *Revue d'Alsace*, no. 132 (2006): 205–44. Other local customs existed but were less important than the custom of Ferrette. See also Bonvalot, Édouard. *Les coutumes du val de Rosemont.* (Paris: Durand, 1866); *Les coutumes de l'Assise et les terriers de 1573 et de 1742.* (Paris: Durand, 1866).

[104] Dermineur, "Women in Rural Society"; Elise Dermineur, "Widows' Political Strategies in Traditional Communities: Negotiating Marital Status and Authority in 18th c France." In Daybell and Norrhem, eds. *Gender and Political Culture, 1500–1800* (Farnham: Routledge, 2016), 123–39.

[105] Janine Maegraith, "Financing Transfers: Buying, Exchanging and Inheriting Properties in Early Modern Southern Tyrol." *The History of the Family* 27 (1), (2021): 11–36.

the means to buy the whole house, the heirs proceeded to its sale and divided the benefits equally. Under partible inheritance, debt also had to be shared equally.

Second, spouses inherited from each other following the one-third – two-thirds custom rule. The surviving male spouse was entailed to two thirds of the community property and the heirs – legitimate children – one third. The surviving female spouse, on the other hand, only took one third, leaving the heirs with two thirds of the family property. Gradually, this legal rule was amended in practise. In the second half of the eighteenth century, men and women *chose* to inherit from each other equally.[106]

Social Norms in Traditional Communities: A Blueprint for Social and Economic Behaviour

The local context influenced the practises of credit. The history and environment of a particular area weighed heavily on local practises and customs. Yet, this is not the full picture. Social norms need to be added to this complex equation. 'People want to act as they have to act' writes Erich Fromm, but 'at the same time find gratification in acting according to the requirements of the culture'.[107] Social norms had powerful oversight of all forms of exchange in small communities.

Social norms are the informal sets of rules that govern individual and group behaviours and actions. They have been referred to as the 'grammar of society' or the 'collective consciousness'.[108] They are 'the language a society speaks'.[109] They are not legal norms, but they can offer similar expectations. Social norms are public, shared, transmissible, and understood by all. They prescribe or proscribe behaviour. They govern what is acceptable and what is not in a society or a group.[110] They reflect

---

[106] Dermineur, "Women in Rural Society." On movables and immovables as a concept see especially Margareth Lanzinger, "Movable Goods and Immovable Property: Interrelated Perspectives." In Annette Cremer ed., *Gender, Law and Material Culture* (London: Routledge, 2020).

[107] Cited by Jean-Philippe Platteau, *Institutions, Social Norms, and Economic Development* (London: Routledge, 2000), p 17.

[108] Cristina Bicchieri, *The Grammar of Society: The Nature and Dynamics of Social Norms* (Cambridge: Cambridge University Press, 2006). Jon Elster, *Explaining Social Behavior: More Nuts and Bolts for the Social Sciences*, 1st ed. (Cambridge: Cambridge University Press, 2007), p 347.

[109] Bicchieri, *The Grammar of Society*, p ix.

[110] Cristina Bicchieri, Ryan Muldoon, and Alessandro Sontuoso, "Social Norms." In Edward N. Zalta, ed. *The Stanford Encyclopedia of Philosophy*, Winter 2018 (Stanford, CA: Stanford University, 2018), https://plato.stanford.edu/archives/win2018/entries/social-norms/.

people's expectations. Infringement of the norms is sanctioned by punishment.

In traditional communities like those in the south of Alsace, social norms are essential for the cohesion, stability, and perpetuation of the community.[111] In such communities, inhabitants usually abide by strong social norms.[112] Expression of and adherence to these norms offer a blueprint for people's social and economic behaviour. Local variations obviously existed. But one finds strong similarities and common traits in these small and traditional communities.

Among the social norms of interest are collaborative norms. Collaborative norms were especially prominent in small traditional communities because of the frequency of repeated interactions and the adversities households could face.[113] The size of these communities, but also the limitations they experienced in terms of technology, communication, and transportation, led people to interact and cooperate predominantly with their fellow villagers for all sorts of matters. In fact, most people's daily interactions took place at the village or seigneurie level. As a result, with repeated exchanges comes 'familiarity and social interaction'.[114] In the early modern world, households faced risks and uncertainties on a nearly daily basis. In the absence of the welfare state and insurance schemes, it is the solidarity of others that softened adversities. The mutualization of risks and efforts was of tremendous importance. Yet, solidarity arrangements in those communities were largely motivated by self-interest. By helping others, one expected to receive back. The solidarity arrangement works as an insurance against risk. Collaborative norms and other regarding norms did not mean people completely sacrificed their own interests. 'Individuals' writes Joseph Stiglitz 'are concerned that in their dealings they are treated fairly'.[115] It is fairness that greased social interactions and activated commitments.

These social norms were at the core of credit transactions. They were collectively understood, transmitted, and experienced within local

[111] Taylor, *Community, Anarchy and Liberty*, 1982, p 26.

[112] Michele J. Gelfand et al., "Differences Between Tight and Loose Cultures: A 33-Nation Study," *Science* 332, no. 6033 (2011): 1100–4.

[113] Russell Hardin, *Collective Action* (Baltimore, MD: Johns Hopkins University Press, 1982).

[114] Marcel Fafchamps, "Formal and Informal Market Institutions: Embeddedness Revisited." In Jean-Marie Baland, Thierry Verdier, and Jean-Philippe Platteau, eds. *The Handbook of Economic Development and Institutions* (Princeton, NJ: Princeton University Press, 2020), 375–413.

[115] Joseph Stiglitz, "Rational Peasants, Efficient Institutions, and The Theory of Rural Organization: Methodological Remarks for Development Economics," Working Paper (Princeton, NJ, Woodrow Wilson School, 1988).

communities, often communities of fate.[116] In such a setting, the decision-making process regarding transactions often defied the law of rationality and economic profitability, making way for credit exchanges featuring a certain degree of fairness and mutual gain within a community of advantage.[117] Economic behaviour was closely embedded in networks of interpersonal relations.[118]

Concluding Remarks

The villages of the seigneuries of Delle and Florimont were unoriginal and dull in many ways. Peasants carried out the same tasks as in many other villages. Yet, the local context matters. It gives us keys to understanding why some features of credit transactions looked the way they did.

---

[116] I borrow the expression community of fate from John S. Ahlquist and Margaret Levi, *In the Interest of Others: Organizations and Social Activism* (Princeton, NJ: Princeton University Press, 2013).
[117] Robert Sugden, *The Community of Advantage.*
[118] Granovetter, "Economic Action and Social Structure," p 504.

2   Peer-to-Peer Lending in Non-intermediated Credit Markets

Introduction

Marie Catherine Acreman and her husband, Jean Pierre Paumier, lived on a farm in the village of Suarce. The couple was one of the village's well-to-do households. This was reflected in their large house filled with many pieces of furniture and linen, and in their barn, which housed one of the largest herds of cows in the community. The couple owned several hectares of arable land. The running of their farm required the help of no less than four domestics. Paumier died in 1765.[1] From then until her death in 1782, Marie Catherine Acreman headed the farm alone. Her probate inventory, and in particular the list of claims, is a thorough portrayal of the couple's wealth. In total, together with Paumier at first, and then Acreman on her own, they had extended twenty loans to various households for a total of 3,130 livres, a small fortune. All of these loans had been arranged privately, without either the intercession of the notary or his seal. The parties had negotiated the terms of their agreements, including the interest rate and the deadline for repayment. They wrote down the contracts themselves – or with the help of someone who could write – all of them as promissory notes.[2]

Similarly, when the priest of Suarce died in 1768, his probate inventory also showed the ubiquity of these private agreements. Ursanne Buessard owed money to forty-two different individuals. He had borrowed money here and there, always via a promissory note, outside any formal and official channels. In addition, he owed money for various services and products to artisans and shopkeepers who had recorded the dues in their ledgers. Upon the priest's death, they presented themselves to the appraisers who recorded their claims.[3] None of these debts bore the seal of the notary.

In these two examples, lenders and borrowers arranged their transactions, either an actual transfer of capital in cash or the deferred payment

---

[1] ADTB 095 E-dépôt GG 1-5.   [2] ADTB 2E4/442.   [3] ADTB 12B65.

of a due, privately, without intercession and without certification. No notary was needed to record their arrangements. Negotiations and provisions were left to the discretion of the parties. And enforcement of these contracts often remained informal and private. Thus far, these non-notarized credit networks and markets have been unduly neglected.[4] In a common assumption, small-scale credit interested primarily poor households.[5] These families could neither borrow substantial amounts, present sufficient guarantees, nor pay the fees for certification. As a result, the documentation is often scarce. In medieval England, historians estimate that most small-scale credit agreements were 'conducted orally and without evident security'. The same goes for the early modern Flemish countryside.[6] Most of their transactions remained therefore 'informal' or non-intermediated. Yet, small-scale credit did not concern only the poor. In early modern Venice, many transactions of all sorts were non-intermediated.[7]

We know little about loans contracted outside notaries' offices in pre-industrial France. The historiography of credit, indeed, has long focused on the rich and continuous notarial records to the detriment of these non-notarized transactions.[8] It is true that notarial records have helped historians to draw a sophisticated picture of early financial French markets. Philip Hoffman, Gilles Postel-Vinay, and Jean-Laurent Rosenthal estimate that notarial loan contracts represented 16% of the GDP in 1740 and 23% in 1780.[9] Given these impressive figures, scholars often – wrongly – assume that people lent and borrowed money primarily via these notarial intermediaries. While notarial obligations and annuities

---

[4] Stephan Nicolussi-Köhler, ed. *Change and Transformation of Premodern Credit Markets: The Importance of Small-Scale Credits* (Heidelberg: heiBOOKS, 2021); Paul Johnson, "Small Debts and Economic Distress in England and Wales, 1857–1913," *Economic History Review* 46, no. 1 (1993): 65-87, p 65; Margot C. Finn, *The Character of Credit* (Cambridge: Cambridge University Press, 2003); James E. Shaw, "The Informal Economy of Credit"; Håkan Lindgren, "Parish Banking in Informal Credit Markets: The Business of Private Lending in Early Nineteenth-Century Sweden" 24, no. 1 (2017): 83–102; Christiaan van Bochove, "Seafarers and Shopkeepers: Credit in Eighteenth-Century Amsterdam," *Eighteenth-Century Studies* 48, no. 1 (2014): pp 67–88; Beverly Lemire, "Petty Pawns and Informal Lending: Gender and the Transformation of Small-Scale Credit in England, circa 1600–1800," Kristine Bruland and Patrick O'Brien, eds. *From Family Firms to Corporate Capitalism: Essays in Business and Industrial History in Honour of Peter Mathias* (Oxford: Clarendon Press, 1998) pp 112–38.

[5] See Laurence Fontaine and Jürgen Schlumbohm, *Household Strategies for Survival, 1600–2000: Fission, Faction and Cooperation*, (Cambridge: Cambridge University Press, 2000).

[6] Lambrecht and Schofield, *Credit and the Rural Economy in North-Western Europe*, p 4.

[7] Shaw, "The Informal Economy of Credit."

[8] See in particular Hoffman, Postel-Vinay, and Rosenthal, *Priceless Markets*; Hoffman, Postel-Vinay, and Rosenthal, *Dark Matter Credit*.

[9] Hoffman, Postel-Vinay, and Rosenthal, *Dark Matter Credit*, p 3.

played a critical role in the allocation of credit, in the circulation of capital, and the backing of investments, non-notarized – and often undocumented – transactions have also come to be seen as significant.[10]

This chapter explores these non-intermediated loans, in the form of either credit sales or actual transfer of capital. Overall, those transactions certainly represented most of the financial exchanges taking place in early modern France.[11] These non-intermediated credit markets featured either a written or a verbal promise, developing outside of the scope of the authorities. Private lenders and borrowers agreed privately on a loan, at their discretion, either on an actual transfer of resources or on a deferred payment for an item or a service. In theory, the conclusion of the contract was not subject to regulation and did not have to follow a pre-established template. But in practise, implicit rules and shared legal norms inspired by notarial credit practises could be used to draft and enforce the contract. However, many of these transactions retained an unofficial character, allowing parties flexibility and input. The transactions were not regulated and supervised until a breach of contract occurred; judicial courts could then enforce the terms of the agreement only if they were in writing, certified by witnesses, and respected the legal ceiling for interest rates. While a written agreement could be executed at court, it was often enforced via private means, in other words, informally.

This chapter examines in detail the small petty debts, the daily financial transactions between households and individuals that were contracted privately either in written or in verbal form. Most of these transactions are difficult to track and often come into view through the local judicial records in the case of a repayment dispute.[12] But lawsuits often remain silent regarding the exact terms of the contracts or their purposes. Historians, nevertheless, can get a glimpse of these transactions thanks to probate inventories, which allow the partial reconstruction of these small credit markets and networks. These inventories, collected from the 1650s to the 1790s in the seigneurie of Delle and Florimont, are analysed in detail here.

---

[10] See for example Sheilagh Ogilvie, Markus Küpker, and Janine Maegraith, "Household Debt in Early Modern Germany: Evidence from Personal Inventories," *The Journal of Economic History* 72, no. 1 (2012): 134–67; Elise M. Dermineur, "Peer-to-Peer Lending in Pre-Industrial France." So Nakaya, "Credit Networks between City and Countryside in Late Medieval Lucca." In Stephan Nicolussi-Köhler, ed. *Change and Transformation of Premodern Credit Markets: The Importance of Small-Scale Credits* (Heidelberg: heiBOOKS, 2021), 133–56.

[11] Laurence Fontaine, "Pouvoir, relations sociales et crédit sous l'Ancien Régime," *Revue Française de Socio-Économie* 9, no. 1 (2012): 101–16, 104.

[12] Something Craig Muldrew studied; Craig Muldrew, *The Economy of Obligation*.

Tracking Non-intermediated Transactions: Probate Inventories

It is through the prism of probate inventories we can gain an overview of interpersonal financial transactions and recreate credit networks. Upon the death of an individual, local officers drafted a probate inventory to assess the extent and worth of the deceased's estate (see Figure 2.1 and Figure 2.2). Besides the real estate, various types of land, livestock, and movables, officers drew up a list of claims and liabilities. The probate served as a basis to divide the estate fairly among all legitimate heirs. It was also used to settle any existing claims or liabilities. It is this list that is of particular interest to us (*dettes actives* and *dettes passives*); it usually included (but not always) the names of lenders and borrowers, their place of residency, the sum owed, and sometimes its purpose.[13]

While probate inventories are a great source for the study of small daily transactions between people, they are not without their flaws.[14] We have seen in Chapter 1 their limitations to estimate population wealth. Probate inventories featured deceased people who were generally older than the rest of the living population, which in turn could skew their indebtedness level and their saving capacity. Deceased people who had a probate drawn up after death had something to leave behind and might have been wealthier on average.

Probates exhibit several limits when it comes to reconstructing credit and debt networks. The list of claims and liabilities gives a truncated and residual picture of credit transactions within the community at time *t*. The transactions recorded were not exhaustive. Moreover, out of the 647 probated estates examined, 80 (12.36%) did not record any claim or liability. We cannot be sure that no debt at all existed for those households. Some debts were not written down for various reasons. Between the time of a person's death and the drafting of their inventory, some debts might have already been settled and thus were not

---

[13] Probate inventories have been used elsewhere to examine non-intermediated financial transactions, see especially Lindgren, "The Modernization of Swedish Credit Markets"; Lindgren, "Parish Banking in Informal Credit Markets"; Elise M. Dermineur, "The Evolution of Credit Networks in Pre-Industrial Finland," *Scandinavian Economic History Review* 70, no. 1 (2022): 57–86.

[14] There has been a lot of discussion regarding the flaws in probate inventories. See in particular Jan Kuuse, "The Probate Inventory as a Source for Economic and Social History," *Scandinavian Economic History Review* 22, no. 1 (1974): 22–31; Håkan Lindgren, "The Modernization of Swedish Credit Markets," Carole Shammas, "Constructing a Wealth Distribution from Probate Records," *The Journal of Interdisciplinary History* 9, no. 2 (1978): 297–307. See also Keibek, "Correcting the Probate Inventory Record for Wealth Bias."

Figure 2.1 First page of the probate inventory of Thienette
Paulmier, 1693.
(*Source*: ADTB 2E4/56, photo by the author)

listed.[15] Marie-Catherine Arnoux, the widow of the innkeeper
César Taburon, declared to the appraisers that she did not know if
they owed money to anyone because she did not have the account

[15] Also observed by Muldrew, *The Economy of Obligation*, p 104.

Figure 2.2 First page of the probate inventory of Jean Chaboudé and Claudine Schick, 1691.
(*Source*: ADTB 2E4/56, photo by the author)

book.[16] Some inventories seem therefore to have been incomplete and were sometimes updated at a later stage; albeit the archived copy might

[16] ADTB 2E4/228.

not have been updated at all.[17] In addition, many probate inventories were not drawn up immediately after the death of a person. A certain sloppiness could engender a gap of several months, even years, between the death and the actual listing.

In the south of Alsace, probate inventories were not individualized. In most cases, assessors evaluated the worth of a household's estate, merging both the wife's and the husband's assets after the death of one of them. The probate comprised their lineage property and community property. If the widow survived her husband, the clerk in charge of writing the inventory distinguished – sometimes but not systematically – the wife's assets, especially her dowry, from the rest. A debt could be personal, but most of the debts were in fact household debts, a burden shared by the head of the household, the spouse, their dependents, and their heirs. I should add that probate inventories undermine our understanding of women's financial activities. Officers preferred to list the names of the household's male head rather than the individual at the origin of the transactions. All activities were understood to take place in the name of the household. Women who appeared under their own name in the probate inventories' transactions were often widows and never-married women rather than married women.[18]

Yet, given all those challenges, we can nonetheless recreate a comprehensive picture of early financial networks by concentrating on the list of claims and liabilities. In our sample of 647 probate inventories from the seigneuries of Delle and Florimont, 565 featured claims or liabilities or both. Together, this represents a grand total of 6,389 transactions. I have deliberately excluded funeral costs from the sample because these specific debts were incurred only following death. After correction, the number of interpersonal transactions in both seigneuries reached 6,154, including 268 without a specified amount, for a total of 537,909 livres tournois (see Table 2.1).[19] The mean for each liability equalled 77.4 livres tournois while it reached 123.4 livres tournois for a claim.[20] Overall, the number of liabilities owned by each household reached an average of 8.

---

[17] The dataset is constituted of probate inventories kept by the notary.

[18] More on this in Elise M. Dermineur, ed., *Women and Credit in Pre-Industrial Europe*.

[19] ADTB 12B165, 2E4/10, 53, 54, 55, 56, 85, 86, 87, 114, 203, 210, 228, 252, 260, 261, 262, 287, 288, 296, 299, 309, 315, 317, 348, 350, 351, 397, 399, 401, 402, 403, 404, 405, 407, 411, 435, 436, 437, 438, 439, 440, 441. In the case of two probate inventories written up per household (one per spouse), I have eliminated potential double entries. The total amount excludes funeral costs.

[20] The currency is the livre tournois. One livre equals 20 sols, and each sol was divided into 12 deniers. I have converted the sol and denier in livre, which explains the decimal point.

Table 2.1 *Overview of claims and liabilities in the seigneuries of Delle and Florimont, 1650–1790 in livres tournois (based on the probate dataset, nominal prices, funeral costs excluded)*

	Seigneurie of Delle	Seigneurie of Florimont	Total
Number of probates	318	247	565
Number of transactions	3,762	2,392	6,154
Claims	1,107 (v = 118,385.2)	560 (v = 74,973.1)	1,667
Liabilities	2,655 (v = 236,311.7)	1,832 (v = 108,239.3)	4,487
Sum	354,696.96	183,212.31	537,909.4 (excl. funeral costs)
Mean/claim[a]	110.5	136.31	123.4
Mean/liability[b]	93.9	60.91	77.4

[a] Several claims did not feature a specific amount.
[b] Several liabilities did not feature a specific amount.

Categorizing the nature of the transactions recorded in probate inventories is not without difficulty. Scribes were often sloppy and vague in their descriptions. Some transactions did not record any purpose or nature (24% of our sample), simply the name of the debtor/lender and the amount due. Sometimes first names and/or amount went missing. Françoise Michelat from the village of Saint-Dizier died in 1782; her household left behind a trail of unspecified debts. She owed the miller of her village 100 livres, two smiths, respectively, 27 livres and 29 livres, the innkeeper of Delle 10 livres, another miller in Delle 18 livres, and so on.[21] None of these entries mentioned any purpose or nature of the contract binding the parties. The occupation status of her creditors tends to suggest plausible connections with their trade/what she owed them, but we cannot be entirely certain. About a quarter of the transactions fall into this category of unspecified loans (see Figure 2.3).

In this chapter, the focus is exclusively on non-intermediated transactions. These transactions are mainly in two categories. First, deferred payments, also referred to as sale credits, constitute 30% of our sample (all transactions). Second, peer-to-peer credit exchanges contracted privately, without intermediaries such as the notary, represent about 15% of

[21] ADTB 2E4/299.

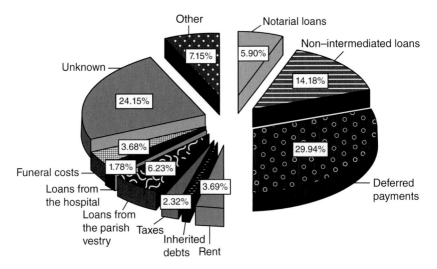

Figure 2.3 Overview of the different claims and liabilities found in the probate inventories of the seigneuries of Delle and Florimont, 1650–1790.
(*Source*: probate inventory dataset)

all the transactions recorded (minus funeral costs). If we add to these 15% the 25% of unspecified interpersonal transactions, the proportion reaches 40%. Overall, non-intermediated exchanges (credit sales and promissory notes) represent about 70% of the total transactions in the sample (see Figure 2.3 and Figure 2.4). Notarial loans (5.9% in number and 15.6% in volume), loans from institutions such as the parish vestry (6.2% in number and 6.8% in volume) and non-personalized entities such as the hospital (1.8% in number and 2.2% in volume) made up the rest.

Did debt become more personal with time? On the one hand, only 8% of the debts recorded were related to institutions (the local hospital and the parish vestries).[22] And this tendency did not recede. The proportion of both deferred payments and non-intermediated transactions increased throughout the period considered and especially in the second half of the eighteenth century, while the proportion of notarial loans did decline in probate inventories (Figure 2.4). But on the other hand, as stated before, probate inventories often present a truncated picture of reality. It is possible that deceased people preferred to repay notarial obligations as

---

[22] In Wildberg, in contrast, this proportion reached 19%. Ogilvie, Küpker, and Maegraith, "Household Debt in Early Modern Germany," 134–67, p 147.

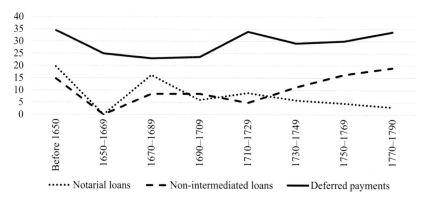

Figure 2.4 Proportion (%) of financial transactions by category in the probate inventories of the seigneuries of Delle and Florimont, 1650–1790.
(*Source*: probate inventory dataset)

a priority over any other debts in the second half of the eighteenth century (more on this aspect in Chapter 6). And it is also possible that ageing households did not want to contract formal obligations towards the end of their lives, as we shall see in Chapter 3.

In any case, many debts were thus not formally documented. The same pattern can be found elsewhere in rural areas. On the other side of the Rhine, in Wildberg, for example, only 4.7% of inventoried debts by value were formalized in the seventeenth century.[23] In a common assumption, peasants who lived in tight-knit communities exonerated themselves from certification. The intimate character of personal exchanges often made formalization superfluous, and unnecessarily costly. In more urban and more developed economies, on the other hand, formalization was in general higher. In early modern Kent, 25% of debts in probate inventories were formalized.[24] In seventeenth-century Canterbury, about 30% of debts found in probates were formalized.[25] Yet, this rural/urban divide is not entirely satisfactory and should be nuanced. Contracting practises varied a lot from one area to another, but also within the same region. Local practises and conventions often

[23] Ibid.
[24] Peter Spufford, "Long-term Rural Credit in Sixteenth- and Seventeenth-Century England: The Evidence of Probate Accounts." In Christopher Marsg, Tom Arkell, Nesta Evans, and Nigel Goose, eds. *When Death Do Us Part: Understanding and Interpreting the Probate Records of Early Modern England* (Oxford: Leopard's Head Press, 2000): 213–28, pp 216–17.
[25] Spufford and Taffin, "Les liens du crédit au village," p 1364.

prevailed. In rural Flanders, for example, three-quarters of inventoried debts were bonds or annuities.[26]

The Deferred Economy

Joseph Couleaux was an industrious man. He traded firearms at his shop in Delle. Clients came all the way from towns in southern Alsace and Franche-Comté and even from the Swiss cantons for his handcrafted weapons. His rifles, pistols, and powder sold well. His wife also had her own shop next door. She ran a haberdashery boutique with equal success. When Couleaux died in 1777, fifteen clients owed him a total of 2,297 livres for his products. The account book of the haberdashery shop also listed pending payments for a total of 607 livres.[27] Couleaux and his wife were wealthy shopkeepers but nearly 3,000 livres of pending payments represented a huge amount of money. Most of the couple's clients could not pay outright, either they did not have enough ready cash or enough resources at the time of the purchase.

Their neighbour, Jean-Jacques Girardin, also ran a shop in Delle. He sold various items such as haberdashery goods but also exotic imported products such as coffee, tea, olive oil, ginger, and tobacco. In his account diary, left after his death in 1759, 88 clients from Delle and nearby villages owed him a total of 2,179 livres, almost 25 livres on average per customer.[28] Credit sales were a common practise to ensure the continuity of commerce and trade.[29]

A substitute for credit, often featuring a small amount of money, deferred payments allow us to measure the pulse of local economic life.[30] Just like the use of credit cards today, deferred payments were a form of

---

[26] Thijs Lambrecht, "Rural Credit and the Market for Annuities in Eighteenth-Century Flanders." In *Credit and the Rural Economy in North-Western Europe, c. 1200–c. 1850* (Turnhout: Brepols Publishers, 2009), 75–97, p 78; and pp 91–93.

[27] ADTB 2E4/288.   [28] ADTB 2E4/203.

[29] Natacha Coquery, "Tenir boutique à Paris au XVIIIe siècle: luxe et demi-luxe" (Paris, Éd. du Comité des travaux historiques et scientifiques, 2011). See also the 'dette à la main' described by Ulrich Pfister in Switzerland, Ulrich Pfister, "Le petit crédit rural en Suisse aux XVIe-XVIIIe siècles," *Annales. Histoire, Sciences Sociales*, 49, no. 6 (1994): 1339–57, p 1342.

[30] Yet, deferred payments and credit sales have perhaps not thus far received the attention they fully deserve. Consumer credit has been well covered for the nineteenth and twentieth centuries. See for instance Lendol Calder, *Financing the American Dream: A Cultural History of Consumer Credit* (Princeton, NJ: Princeton University Press, 2009); Anaïs Albert, "Le crédit à la consommation des classes populaires à la Belle Époque: Invention, innovation ou reconfiguration?," *Annales. Histoire, Sciences Sociales* 67, no. 4 (2012): 1049–82; Steven Finlay, "The History of Credit." In Steven Finlay, ed. *Consumer Credit Fundamentals*, (London: Palgrave Macmillan, 2009), 33–53.

loan. Credit sales for a handcrafted item, for foodstuff or livestock, or even for services, overall mostly for household consumption, were ubiquitous throughout early modern Europe. They were perhaps the most common form of payment. Because of irregular incomes, the hazardous nature of harvests, the various domestic accidents and contingencies, and the general lack of coins in circulation, cash was often scarce. Like Girardin and Couleaux, many small shopkeepers, artisans, and service providers accommodated customers with a line of credit facilities. This practise of delaying payment had become the norm long before the period examined here. And it persisted long into the twentieth century in many rural regions. It was common for customers asking the baker to put the daily bread on their 'tab', or the tobacconist to do the same for cigarettes and magazines, up until at least the 1990s.[31] People would simply pay at the end of the month or whenever cash became available.

Deferring payments went beyond shopkeeping practises. Anyone who had something to sell – land, livestock, handcrafted items, etc. – allowed delayed payments. When Marcel Cuenin, a tailor living in the town of Delle, died in 1783, his probate inventory mentioned several deferred liabilities. He owed, for example, five livres for grain to a certain Beuné, forty-nine livres for flour to the local miller, twelve livres for wine purchased from a certain Erard, one livre to the innkeeper of Lebetain, nine livres to the butcher of Delle, and the list goes on.[32] Most of what Cuenin consumed was purchased on credit. This strategy was very common for most households and was especially significant for the most disadvantaged. For the shopkeepers, artisans, or sellers, it was largely a matter of having the patience to await payment for everything one had sold.[33]

The practise of deferred payment was widespread and commonly accepted within the community. As a result, it was not only people in dire straits who resorted to it, but also better-off households. Some individuals might have had the means to pay the shopkeepers outright, but it seems the practise of delaying payment turned into an accepted norm. The notary Jean-Baptiste Emporte owed a couple of merchants from Belfort money for their products, as well as a certain Dauvin from Delle for the purchase of liquor.[34] The former military officer Urs Courvoisier had incurred several debts to merchants and innkeepers. For instance, he owed 237 livres to a couple of innkeepers in Delle,

---

[31] See also Gilles Laferté et al., "Le crédit direct des commerçants aux consommateurs: persistance et dépassement dans le textile à Lens (1920–1970)," *Genèses* no. 79, no. 2 (2010): 26–47.

[32] ADTB 2E4/288.   [33] Claustre, "Vivre à crédit dans une ville sans banque," p 580.

[34] ADTB 2E4/203.

probably for food and wine consumed there.[35] His line of credit might have been extended as it was understood he was wealthy enough to repay at some point. Villagers might have preferred to reserve cash for some other debt to be repaid, perhaps more urgent ones, older ones, or ones with less flexible deadlines, such as taxes.

Deferred payments also cancelled each other out in reciprocal exchanges; ungoverned reciprocity prevailed. In 1785, the widow Marie-Catherine Reyne declared that she owed money to the blacksmith Pierre Hans for a job he had done. But Hans owed her money for wood sold to him and some ploughing work done on her land. They therefore needed to settle their accounts.[36] Their example was quite common among villagers.[37]

Sellers and shopkeepers practising credit sales had no guarantee the required payment would be completed at all. In the majority of cases, no security backed such agreements, especially if the good or item bought was edible. In 1707, Jean Henri Fériez, the innkeeper and butcher of Boron declared upon the death of his wife that 'several people owe him money (…) including several who are insolvent for expenses made at his inn'.[38] Similarly, Deyle Bourquard ran a bakery in the town of Delle together with his wife Claudine Rassinier. She died prematurely at the age of 39 in 1790.[39] Upon her death, officials found among the baker's wife's papers a *livre journal* listing clients who owed the couple money for their bread. Claudine Rassinier had listed 25 clients liable for 175 livres tournois, almost a year's income for a skilled worker. The bakers, like other shopkeepers and artisans, offered lines of credit to their clients. Claudine Rassinier had specified that some of these debts might very well never be repaid at all. The inventory does not mention at what point the bakers' forbearance broke down and when they stopped delivering the bread to those insolvent customers. One of Rassinier's indebted clients, who might not have had ready cash available, did '*un travail a la maison pour cette somme*' (a job at our house for this amount) showing clearly that barter existed alongside monetized transactions. Debt was sometimes transformed into labour power. When the necessary means could not be found, flexibility often prevailed.

In fact, because cash was scarce, rural dwellers often accepted the possibility to receive repayment in kind. In 1741, the innkeeper Jacques

---

[35] ADTB 2E4/261.   [36] ADTB 2E4/296.
[37] Also noted by Craig Muldrew, "Interpreting the Market: The Ethics of Credit and Community Relations in Early Modern England," *Social History* 18, no. 2 (1993): 163–83.
[38] ADTB 2E4/55.   [39] ADTB 2E4/288.

Roueche accused a customer of not having paid him despite his promise that he 'would repay either in cash or in kind'. The innkeeper Erard also proposed repayment in kind from an indebted customer.[40]

Over time, several of these deferred payments remained unpaid.[41] Probate inventories are full of small, deferred transactions labelled '*douteuses*' (uncertain) whose origin dated to well over a few years earlier. Craig Muldrew sees this as an act of voluntary charity on the part of sellers in granting a line of credit to customers who could not or would not pay their debt. He argues that the amount of small unpaid debts was in fact many times larger than charitable bequests, and probably amounted to about 5% of the total yearly expenditure of most of the middling sort.[42] Debt forgiveness might very well have existed. We may also wonder, for example, if the bakers were bound to some ethical norms and a Christian duty not to leave a neighbouring household to starve. After all, feeding the poor was part of the Christian ethic.

The motivation for some of these deferred payments might often have been an act of charity. Madeleine Kolbin died a year after her husband.[43] Her status as newly widowed might have encouraged the sympathy of her neighbours. Her probate inventory listed several small debts owed to various individuals for foodstuff and services. She owed the miller Voissard 33 livres for grain. She was indebted to the innkeeper Thomas 37 livres for wine and bacon he delivered to her. The innkeeper Taburon had also sold her some bread for 12 livres. She also owed money to a shoemaker, a mason, a seamstress, and a carpenter for small jobs they did for her. And several individuals had lent her money in cash. She and her husband might have incurred some of these debts together. But some of these were directly connected to her new status of widow. In total, she owed 690 livres of debt for various items and services she did not or could not pay outright.

Yet, the incentive for repayment was strong in tight-knit communities with repeated interactions. And that is precisely what replaced securities in credit sales: social networks, long lasting relationships, the prospect of repeated future interactions, and mutual trust. A defaulting buyer/debtor would witness his line of credit become extinct and his reputation tarnished. Households with meagre means would be cut off from subsistence consumption. Not only would a bad payer lose opportunities for future deals with the seller he defaulted on, but also with other potential

---

[40] ADTB 8B90.
[41] Something Laurence Fontaine also notes in Laurence Fontaine, "Antonio and Shylock: Credit and Trust in France, c. 1680–c. 1780," *The Economic History Review*, 54, no. 1 (2001): 39–57, p 43.
[42] Muldrew, *The Economy of Obligation.*   [43] ADTB 2E4/288.

Figure 2.5 Livre journal of the notary Jacques Etienne Lajanne, 1696–1704.
(*Source*: ADTB 12B183, photo by the author)

sellers as well. Reputation travelled fast. Defaulting and abusing trust would inevitably lead to a form of social and economic ostracism. Finally, it should be noted that repaying a debt was also a charitable act towards a fellow Christian.[44] In late medieval Europe, the promise to repay was made both to the lender and to God. A broken promise was as much towards the other party as before God.[45]

To track payments appropriately, sellers and shopkeepers wrote down their transactions in account books (see Figure 2.5).[46] Oftentimes, the two accounts columns were non-existent or not filled in properly.[47]

---

[44] John Bossy, *Christianity in the West*.

[45] Tyler Lange, *Excommunication for Debt in Late Medieval France*, p 4.

[46] A practise that did not necessarily require the skills of writing and reading as shown by Duccio Balestracci, Betsy Merideth, and Paolo Squatriti, *The Renaissance in the Fields: Family Memoirs of a Fifteenth-Century Tuscan Peasant* (University Park, PA: Pennsylvania State University Press, 1999). See also Daniel Lord Smail, *Legal Plunder*, p 93; and Francesca Trivellato, *The Promise and Peril of Credit: What a Forgotten Legend about Jews and Finance Tells Us about the Making of European Commercial Society* (Princeton, NJ: Princeton University Press, 2019), p 93.

[47] Very few of these account books have been preserved in the archives for the south of Alsace.

In fact, these books often featured erratic, cryptic, and scribbled entries.[48] And people tended to record only what was due to them, not what they owed to others.[49] Upon the death of Marguerite Page in 1707, her husband Jean Henri Feriez, an innkeeper in the village of Boron, lost track of the couple's budget. He could not recall exactly how much was due to them from pending payments, knowing only that some of these debts would be lost because of insolvent customers.[50] Jean Baptiste Bichet, the innkeeper of Puis was less sloppy. He kept a *livre journal* to keep track of his clients' running tabs.[51] He made them sign every time they consumed food and drink in his house. Jean-Francois Sandrin, a dyer in Delle, had 'A *livre de remarque* written in "German" in which the deceased wrote down all what could be owed to him by various persons'.[52] He also had 'two other account books, both very old', underlining the habit of registering dues and payments but also showing the importance of archiving and preserving past transactions.[53] A blacksmith in Delle had an account book specially devoted to tracking sums due to him.[54] And the barber of Delle also had one for the 'clients he used to shave'.[55] In 1741, Francois Erard, a *cabaretier* (innkeeper) in Delle, pursued before the judge the repayment of a debt contracted by Jean Ignace Maître from Villars-le-Sec. He showed his account book. On page 43, dated 11 August, we can read that Maître had consumed to a total of 16 livres 8 sols at his tavern.[56] In 1741, Jacques Roueche, the innkeeper of Brebotte came before the judge to ask redress. He accused Jacques Scheneberg of not paying him his dues for wine Scheneberg consumed at his place. Scheneberg responded that the '*compte est imaginaire*' (account is imaginary). Roueche replied that he did not think it was necessary to have Scheneberg sign the livre journal because he was his brother-in-law.[57]

Not only professionals but also households kept their own account books. Pierre Malraget, the weaver of Delle, owed 3.5 livres to the

---

[48] Julie Hardwick, "Banqueroute", p 90. See also Pierre Gervais, "Why Profit and Loss Didn't Matter: The Historicized Rationality of Early Modern Commerce," in Pierre Gervais, Yannick Lemarchand, and Dominique Margairaz, eds., *Merchants and Profit in the Age of Commerce, 1680–1830* (London: Pickering & Chatto, 2014). Daniel Vickers, "Errors Expected: The Culture of Credit in Rural New England, 1750–1800," *Economic History Review* 63, no. 4 (2010): 1032–57.

[49] Claustre, "Vivre à crédit dans une ville sans banque," p 584.   [50] ADTB 2E4/55.

[51] ADTB 2E4/439.

[52] The probate states 'German' but I believe it was rather a form of German, Alsatian.

[53] ADTB 2E4/288.   [54] ADTB 2E4/288.   [55] ADTB 2E4/288.

[56] ADTB 8B90; it should be noted that the bill concerned several individuals who had consumed at the inn. The bill was to be footed by Maître.

[57] ADTB 8B90.

household of Pierre Desronces as specified in his 'livre de raison' (book of reason).[58] And Marie Barbe Tourtelier, a widow from Delle, had 'a notebook used as a livre de raison (…) in which there are several articles amounting to 50 livres and 13 sols'.[59] Interestingly, women seemed to be able to maintain the books as well. Such account books could also be presented before the judge as evidence in the case of default of payment.

While the use of account books might have been common, many of these debts were never recorded. How many deferred payments remained verbal agreements? Some artisans never used account books. Françoise Michelat from the village of Saint-Dizier in our example above left behind such unspecified debts. She owed money to several artisans (smiths, innkeepers, millers, etc.) without the mention of any form of record.[60] Some of these might very well have been verbal agreements, sanctioned only by a handshake.[61]

Artisans, retailers, and other sellers needed to trust that their customers would pay them at some point. As Daniel Smail mentions, 'the state of obligation was ordinary and temporary rather than pathological'.[62] A screening process allowing certain clients to run expenses on their tabs might have taken place. Presumably bad payers or those with a reputation for failing to pay in the past might not be allowed to defer payment at all or to run their tab above a certain ceiling at the discretion of the seller. Of this, we can know very little. But in the absence of a credit ledger and credit score, memory and the account book of a shopkeeper, his own forbearance, and screening of his customers based on their characters and reputations played a role in the allocation of deferred payments.

The negotiation and agreement for credit sales remained private and discreet until a breach occurred or the patience of the creditor broke down. After failed parleys, parties could turn to the local judge for mediation; the account book served as evidence against an indebted borrower. Deferred payments then stopped being a private matter when they were brought into the public eye. The maintenance of account books indicates a willingness to keep track of transactions in a world in which deferred payments were the norm. But it also underlines a preoccupation with remembering, and to a lesser extent with the limits of trust.

Today, throughout the developed world, big retailers and large department stores offer buy now, pay later schemes for customers who do not want to wait to accumulate enough savings or to consume via their credit

---

[58] ADTB 2E4/85.   [59] ADTB 2E4/114.   [60] ADTB 2E4/299.
[61] See Ulrich Pfister, "Le petit crédit rural en Suisse," p 1342.
[62] Daniel Lord Smail, *Legal Plunder*, p 109.

cards.[63] These stores charge exorbitant interest rates, even superior to regular bank credit cards. Did deferred payments in the past also feature interest rates? This thorny issue has failed to win unanimous support among historians. Craig Muldrew argues that these transactions were not subject to any interest rate in early modern England.[64] Recently, however, James Shaw contends that interest rates were often hidden in any sort of transaction, either notarized or non-intermediated.[65] He argues convincingly that shopkeepers and artisans could account for the deferred payment in the price. Natacha Coquery estimates that interest for deferred payments could vary between 10% and 14% a year, based on her examination of a jeweller's account books.[66] And Laurence Fontaine has shown that after a private agreement deadline for repayment expired, the borrower had to pay the legal interest rate, *l'intérêt composé*.[67] It is reasonable to assume that retailers' forbearance came at a price. An immobilization of capital required a form of compensation, either as disguised interest included in the price, in the form of moral interest (e.g., service, moral debt), or as a form of compensation in kind given on the side. A shopkeeper had leverage to indemnify himself for the delay in payment. Similarly, movements in the price level, especially for goods such as grain, surely needed to be accounted for. And finally, it must be that shopkeepers and other artisans knew that some of their clients would never pay them. Did they insert a premium in the price of their products as security? Or did they just consider unpaid dues an act of charity? The sources are not prolific on this. We can only hypothesize that the price might have accounted for both the delay in repayment and eventual defaults to keep the shopkeeper afloat.

In the seigneuries of Delle and Florimont, deferred payments and credit sales represent 30% of all transactions recorded in the probate inventories dataset (21% in terms of volume). Between 1650 and 1789, the number of deferred payments remained more or less constant (see Table 2.2).[68]

---

[63] A practise that started in the nineteenth century, see for instance Lauer, *Creditworthy*. See also Gunnar Trumbull, *Consumer Lending in France and America: Credit and Welfare* (Cambridge: Cambridge University Press, 2014).

[64] Craig Muldrew, *The Economy of Obligation*.

[65] James E. Shaw, "The informal economy of credit in early modern Venice." *The Historical Journal* 61, no. 3 (2018): 623–42.

[66] Natacha Coquery, "Vente, troc, crédit: les livres de comptabilité d'un joailler-bijoutier parisien à la fin du XVIIIe siècle," in *Actes des sixièmes journées d'histoire de la comptabilité et du management, faculté Jean Monnet, 23–24 mars 2000, p. 133–44.

[67] Fontaine, *L'économie morale*.

[68] In fact, credit sales seemed to have been popular at least until World War I. See Gérard Jacquemet, "Belleville ouvrier à la Belle Epoque," *Le Mouvement Social*, no. 118 (1982): 61–77. Between 1869 and 1910, the number of civil litigations concerning unpaid credit sales jumped from 17% to 23% of all litigations in the working-class neighbourhood of Belleville.

Table 2.2 *Deferred payments and credit sales in the probate inventories in the seigneuries of Delle and Florimont, 1650–1790. The table excludes 120 transactions which do not feature any amount*

	N	% N compared to other transactions recorded	Volume	% V compared to other transactions recorded	Mean	Median	Stand Dev
Before 1650	21	34.4	108.96	8.2	6.81	4.10	8.46
1650–69	1	25	1.91	3.8	1.91	1.91	
1670–89	149	23	2,580.54	12.7	19.85	7.62	34.23
1690–1709	221	23.6	4,234.2	14.5	22.64	5.08	85.36
1710–29	126	33.9	3,630.14	26.2	31.29	15.00	42.44
1730–49	199	29.1	13,085.29	22.8	68.51	18.55	152.32
1750–69	381	30	28,815.79	16.7	84.26	12.75	471.26
1770–90	815	33.7	60,421.78	24.7	76.19	15.00	230.16
Total	1,913		112,878.61		38.93	10	146.3

Source: probate inventory dataset

In the period 1770–1790, 33% of all the transactions recorded were in fact deferred payments for more than 24% of the volume exchanged. The range for these transactions was low, under 100 livres (Figure 2.6 and Table 2.2).

Evidently, the category of deferred payment uncovers a complex reality in a world where revenues were too irregular and coins too scarce for people to pay cash. Besides the pending payments expected by artisans, retailers, innkeepers, and other service providers, credit sales also concerned grain, foodstuffs, wine, livestock, and all kinds of goods and items. Grains such as wheat, oats, rye, and spelt were often sold to peasants who did not have enough left for the impending sowing season (12% of the credit sales). Millers were often solicited for such transactions. For some peasants, deferred payments enabled them to bounce back. Because of a bad harvest or grain shortage, some households found themselves forced to buy grain, either to survive or to sow. Pierre Monnier and Marguerite Hans, a couple of peasants from Suarce, had to purchase grain for several years in a row. In 1731, hail had destroyed their crops. In 1732, the harvest was insufficient. The same happened all the years afterwards up until 1740. For those nine years, the couple incurred a debt of 1,118 livres tournois just for grain, a significant amount of money, which they had difficulty in repaying.[69] They might

---

[69] ADTB 2E4/350.

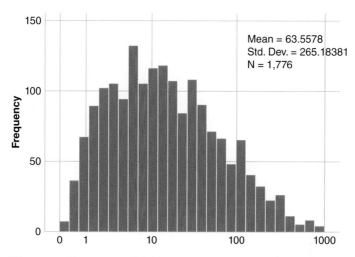

Figure 2.6 Frequency of deferred payments in livres tournois in the seigneuries of Delle and Florimont per value, 1650–1790 (N = 1,776 as 137 transactions did not specify any amount, logarithmic).
(*Source*: probate inventory dataset)

very well have agreed on the purchase of overpriced grain or to a credit sale with hidden interest. But nonetheless, they could continue their activity thanks to the deferred payment for grain and they somehow kept afloat.

Apart from grain, households often deferred payment for foodstuffs they did not or could not produce. Bread, wine, salt, and meat were the most common food supplies purchased on credit (foodstuffs represent 6.7% of the deferred transactions). However, vegetables, fruit, dairy products, and eggs were rarely purchased on credit as most households, even the poorest ones, could produce these items or exclude them from their diet at times. Towards the end of the eighteenth century, households purchased exotic products such as coffee and tobacco, also on credit. However, these transactions still remained rare for rural dwellers.

Households also delayed the payment of livestock they purchased (7.3% of all credit sale transactions). Horses, cows, oxen, and pigs could not usually be paid outright. Small repayments were made later when cash became available again. Jewish and Anabaptist livestock farmers were quite active in this market segment. We might ask whether their customers took longer to repay them on the basis of their religious confession. Based on court records, Jewish livestock farmers seem to have had to encounter some hurdles in this respect (see Chapter 5).

It is interesting to note that if 7.3% of these transactions for livestock were not officially documented, many households chose to certify this type of transaction with an obligation contract (12% of all obligations), as we shall see in Chapter 3.

Finally, a rather large proportion of deferred payments involved land sales (8.9% of all credit sales in number and 24% in terms of volume). These appear in the probate inventories without mention of any sort of formalized contract. In a common assumption, land transactions were secured by notarized loans because of the amount of money at stake. But it seems that some households chose either not to contract at all for land transfers or chose to delay contracting at the notary's office. As we shall see in the next section, land sales were also executed via *promesses sous seing privé* (private promises).

Overall, everything was monetized and had monetary value. People did not hesitate to charge for small services, making deferred payments ubiquitous.

It does not come as too much of a surprise, and as stated previously, that artisans, shopkeepers, and innkeepers (in this order) appear therefore among the socio-professional categories allowing lines of credit to their customers.[70] Most of these artisans and retailers extended credit for at least two reasons. First, households did not necessarily have ready cash to purchase goods and services. To remain in business, extending lines of credit was of ultimate necessity. Second, some of these professionals hoped to bind customers to them.[71] Steve Kaplan argues that deferred payments helped in fact to stabilize ties between sellers and buyers.[72]

Among these professionals, innkeepers are an interesting case. They could be found in nearly every village, even the most remote and poorly populated. While their main activity and income remained anchored in agricultural labour, together with their spouses, they opened one room in their house or their barn to host customers. They provided rudimentary furniture such as wooden chairs, benches, and tables. They sold mainly wine. People came there to socialize, gossip, and play cards, often in the late afternoon and over the long winter days and nights. Customers also sat down to negotiate or seal a deal, often with a glass of wine. This practise was also used to settle conflicts.[73] Some of these *cabaretiers*

---

[70] On this see also Bernadette Angleraud, "Les boulangers lyonnais aux XIXe-XXe siècles (1836–1914): une étude sur la petite bourgeoisie boutiquière" (Doctoral thesis, Université Lyon 2, 1993). Steven Laurence Kaplan, *The Bakers of Paris and the Bread Question, 1700–1775*, (Durham, NC: Duke University Press Books, 1996). Coquery, "Tenir boutique à Paris au XVIIIe siècle."

[71] Kaplan, *The Bakers of Paris*, p 378.   [72] Kaplan, *The Bakers of Paris*.

[73] Anne Bonzon, *La Paix au village: clergé paroissial et règlement des conflits dans la France d'ancien Régime* (Paris: Éditions Champ Vallon , 2022).

became successful and offered not only wine but also food to their customers. Antoine Grimont and his wife Anne-Marie Monnier ran such an establishment in the village of Suarce.[74] When Grimont died in 1727, his inventory featured, among other things, eight wooden tables, four brand new chairs, and several casks of wine. Twenty-seven clients owed him a total of 463.9 livres, a substantial amount (17.2 livres per client).

Similarly, when the *cabaretier* Jean-Thibaud Louis died in 1762, 102 livres in cash were found in his house.[75] Because the *cabaretier* handled cash, he was often able to redistribute part of it to others via loans.[76] Jean-Baptiste Bichet, the innkeeper of Puis, also presented such a profile. He was able to lend (and borrow) money. His customers and others surely knew they could find ready cash available to borrow at his place. Innkeepers could also certainly provide information to potential lenders and borrowers thanks to information gathered daily.[77] Craig Muldrew argues that some innkeepers brokered credit relations between distant parties who would not otherwise have known each other.[78] I have not found evidence of this in the south of Alsace. There, these rural innkeepers differed from the city types who were professional brokers.

Cabaretiers were not the only informal credit intermediaries. Other retailers and shopkeepers offered their clients the possibility to borrow money. Tripet Dumond, a grocer in Florimont, allowed the deferred payment for 'some coffee and other merchandise' to Jeanne Baptiste Franquin. He also lent her money as 'a loan of 3 livres to purchase some iron' from another merchant.

Service providers such as domestics and medical healers also participated in this economy of redistribution. The wages of many domestics lagged behind by several months and even years, and they did charge interest for the delay (24% of all deferred payments). It is therefore common to find them claiming their dues upon the death of their masters. Jean-Pierre Jobin recalled twenty-four livres for his past year's annual wage upon the death of Marie Catherine Acreman. Marie Catherine Frery claimed 'a half year wage' from Jean Baptiste Bichet, the innkeeper of Puis, upon his death in 1773.[79] These domestics did lend part of their salary either to their acquaintances or back to their

---

[74] ADTB 2E4/351.   [75] ADTB 2E4/440.

[76] See for example Pompermaier, *Le vin et l'argent*; Oscar Gelderblom, *Cities of Commerce: The Institutional Foundations of International Trade in the Low Countries, 1250–1650* (Princeton, NJ: Princeton University Press, 2015), pp 43–62; and James M. Murray, *Bruges, Cradle of Capitalism, 1280–1390* (Cambridge: Cambridge University Press, 2005).

[77] Regarding the role of innkeepers in credit exchanges see in particular Pompermaier, *Le vin et l'argent*.

[78] Muldrew, *The Economy of Obligation*, p 40.   [79] ADTB 2E4/439.

employers. François Patingre, a farm domestic employed by Jeanne-Marie Dermineur claimed 109 livres upon her death in 1783, not only for his wages but also for money he had lent to her.[80] Payments often came in late for medical healers and medical practitioners. Morally and ethically pressed to perform their duties, many of them waited weeks if not months to be paid.

Sellers tended to allow deferred payments to households not only in their villages but also from other villages nearby. This was obviously a practise out of necessity, for the sustainability of their business. André Arnoux was a farrier in Delle.[81] Upon his death in 1783, his *livre journal* indicated that 16 clients from Delle, but also from five neighbouring villages, owed him a total of 445.5 livres for his labour and for items sold to them. A farrier might often visit farms to perform his craft (to shoe horses for example). In early modern England, rural shopkeepers rarely offered lines of credit to customers living further than 10 miles from their shops. The same practise is observed in the seigneuries of Delle and Florimont.[82]

Jean Jacquart remarks that 'facing a due date of whatever nature, the natural reaction was to delay its repayment'.[83] Credit sales were ubiquitous; almost all buying and selling involved a form of credit.[84] This mode of consumption remained important throughout the period. Deferred payments certainly sustained and encouraged the rise of a consumer society.[85] In rural areas, income from harvests was often irregular and cash was often in poor circulation. Credit sales allowed households to balance their budgets. This system allowed for flexibility as well as the continuity of consumption. Alongside these deferred payments, we find another category of non-formalized loans: interpersonal loans.

Peer-to-Peer Lending: Interpersonal Loans Without Intermediation

Loans between households, individuals, or groups of individuals certified by a private written or verbal agreement, without the imprimatur of the notary, entered into the category of private non-intermediated

---

[80] ADTB 2E4/439.   [81] ADTB 2E4/288.

[82] Carole Shammas, *The Pre-Industrial Consumer in England and America* (Oxford: Clarendon Press, 1990), p 247.

[83] Jean Jacquart, "L'endettement paysan et le crédit dans les campagnes de la France modern." In Maurice Berthe, ed. *Endettement paysan et crédit rural dans l'Europe médiévale et moderne*, (Toulouse: Presses universitaires du Midi, 2020), 283–97, p 285.

[84] As also argued by Muldrew, *The Economy of Obligation*, p 95.

[85] Margot C. Finn, *The Character of Credit*; Craig Muldrew, *The Economy of Obligation*; Jan De Vries, *The Industrious Revolution*.

transactions. Lender and borrower negotiated and agreed privately, at their discretion, on the transfer of capital. This transfer could be a monetary loan or a deferred payment for something sold. The written promissory notes, IOUs, were called alternatively *cédules*, *billets*, or *promesses sous seing privé*. It is unclear, however, how often people resorted to the verbal agreements.[86] Other peer-to-peer loans without mention of either their nature or any specific contract can be found in probate inventories. These were possibly promissory notes or verbal agreements.[87]

All of these non-formalized financial transactions presented the same characteristics of non-intermediation.[88] This is the main difference with notarial loans. Promissory notes were negotiated privately by individuals, at their discretion, without supervision and intermediation. Non-intermediated loans usually entailed the transfer of capital from one party to the other. But deferred payments had found their way into this type of transaction as well. The boundary between credit sales and cash loans was often blurry and porous, and almost impossible to distinguish for the historian. It seems, however, that deferred payments for small amounts did not necessarily require a promissory note; people used their private account books instead or preferred verbal agreements. The mean value for deferred payments seems to confirm this hypothesis. The mean for deferred payments equalled 63 livres, while it was 161 livres for interpersonal loans (see Table 2.3).

---

[86] Probate inventories only mention a few of these transactions. But probates did not usually specify the minutiae of the type of agreement made. See Ulrich Pfister, "Le petit crédit rural en Suisse," p 1342.

[87] Note that in some parts of France, the term obligation sometimes referred to a private contract. In the seigneuries of Delle and Florimont, 'obligation' designated a notarial contract. We will see in the next chapter that *obligation* and *rente* were often synonymous. Jean Jacquart, "L'endettement paysan et le crédit dans les campagnes de la France moderne."

[88] I shall briefly mention that bills of exchange also entered this category. Their main function was the transfer of funds between distant locations. They were thus widely used by merchants, in particular international dealers. A merchant could order one of his agents in another town to pay a specified amount, in a set currency and at a set date, to a third party. Bills of exchange distinguished themselves from other contracts by the absence of collateral to secure the transaction. The reputation, probity, solvency, and social credit of its signatories worked *in lieu* of security. In essence, merchants used a bill of exchange to lend money, defer payments for merchandise, and to speculate thanks to currency conversion. Because the purpose of this type of contract was to move money from one distant place to another, only the mercantile elite used them. Peasants did not use them as a financial instrument. In my investigation, bills of exchange are almost non-existent in all the credit transactions recorded. I found only one. They will, therefore, not feature in this chapter. On this, see Francesca Trivellato, *The Promise and Peril of Credit*, p 2.

Table 2.3 *Intermediated and non-intermediated interpersonal agreements in the seigneuries of Delle and Florimont between 1650 and 1789*

Main categories	N	N with value	V	Mean	Median	Max	StdDev
Non-intermediated agreements	906 (14.2%)	897	121,788.46 (22.6%)	135.77	56	10,000	425.41
Deferred payments	1,913 (29.9%)	1,176	112,878.61 (20.9%)	63.56	12.63	6,857	425.41
Parish vestry loans	398 (6.2%)	397	35,438.81 (6.6%)	89.27	89.27	2,400	143.66
Notarial loans	377 (5.9%)	376	76,481.34 (14.2%)	203.41	80.48	5,000	477.36
Unknown	1,543 (24.2%)	1,505	115,242.57 (21.24%)	76.57	17.78	24,000	641.48

(*Source*: probate inventory dataset)

In the following example, Jean Pierre Chatelot bought two horses from a livestock farmer. The parties signed a promissory note. They agreed that the repayment would take place in a year and that interest would be paid in grain. A witness even certified the precision of the deal (in this case, the witness also wrote down the contract):

Je soussigné Jean Pierre Chatelot bourgeois de Perouse connais et confesse de devoir justement à Meyer Piquard juif à Foussemagne la somme de quatre vingt une livres tournois provenant ladite somme pour deux chevaux que ledit Piquard juif lui a vendu à son gré et contentement avec quatre quartes de gru mesure de Belfort dont je promets lui payer la ditte somme d'aujourd'hui en un an à peine de tous frais depens dommage interest faute de payement aud. terme. Fait à Perouse ce neuvième août mil sept cent cinquante huit en presence de François Lamblé recteur d'école à Perouse témoin.

(I, Jean Pierre Chatelot, inhabitant of Perouse, hereby confess to rightly owe Meyer Piquart, Jew from Foussemagne, the amount of eighty-one livres tournois for the purchase of two horses that the said Jew Piquart has sold to my will and satisfaction with four bags of grain, in the measure of Belfort, for which I promise to repay the said amount within one year from today. Judicial fees, damages, and interest due for lack of payment within the repayment deadline are mine. Established in Perouse on the 9th of August 1758 with François Lamblé, schoolmaster in Perouse, witness.)

Most promissory notes were initially verbal agreements.[89] It is impossible to determine how many were converted to written agreements. But considering the large number of promissory notes in probate inventories, we can hypothesize that a large proportion of verbal agreements were indeed converted into promissory notes. People usually wrote down their names, the amount due, the length of the loan, the interest rate, the guarantees offered (if any), and the name of a pledge (if any). A witness could also be included to testify to the authenticity of the document. It seems that the witness might also be the person writing down the contract in a world where literacy was not always a guarantee, just as in the example above. Interestingly, even though parties could neither read nor write, they were deeply attached to written contracts as evidence of their dealings. This did not necessarily reflect a distrust of the other party. But it did perhaps emphasize a strong will to keep track of multiple dealings. Very few of these contracts have survived physically in the archives, making it difficult to grasp all their nuances and details. Sometimes they are to be found attached to a probate inventory or a court register to serve as evidence (see Figure 2.10). Typically, people kept these promissory notes safely at home, usually in locked wooden boxes.

[89] See Laurence Fontaine, "Antonio and Shylock," p 51.

Non-intermediated, these loans offered leeway and flexibility to the parties. Lender and borrower could negotiate the terms of their agreement privately, at their discretion, with their own rules and expectations. Conditions of repayment, security on the loan, interest rate, and other potential compensation could be discussed and (re)negotiated (see Figure 2.10 for example).

The only norm to be strictly observed in these contracts was a limit of 5% on the interest rate.[90] Above this ceiling of 5%, such loans were considered usurious, therefore illegal, and could not be enforced at court. The parties had the choice to decide on a price right away upon agreement. Or they could delay the payment of interest after the deadline for repayment had passed.[91] However, there is no evidence that lenders charged more for a loan than the official and legal ceiling of 5%. There is no evidence either that they charged less than 5%.[92] And nothing prevented a lender asking for monetary or non-monetary compensation on the side.[93]

Compensation in goods (grains, vegetables, meat, etc.), just like in our example above, was common. Jean-Christophe Hoigné from the village of Grosne borrowed six livres and fifteen sols bâlois (almost nine livres tournois) from Antoine Merat, living in the neighbouring village of Brebotte. The agreement between the two men stipulated that the lender would farm a piece of land belonging to the borrower until full repayment had been made, a compensation understood as 'a security' for the loan.[94] Livestock was often used as security. Called 'retenue', this was a form of pledge.[95] Claude Riche lent thirty-three livres tournois to Jean Perreney and kept one of his cows as security for the deal.[96] The milk produced was his, but he had to take good care of the animal. In the same vein, it seems that a promissory note could include securities in the form of mortgaged land, just like a notarial loan. Some plots of land could be used as temporary or usufruct property. The lender could harvest or pasture on the land pledged. Jean-Bourquin Perreney left a plot of land for growing flax to Jean Tallon for his exclusive use until full repayment

---

[90] The legal cap for notarized loans was 5%, with the exception of the years 1766–1770 when it was 4%. It seems that the practise of applying interest rates on promissory notes varies between regions. In Alsace, promissory notes stipulated an interest rate. In some other regions, the interest rate was payable after the IOU period finished.

[91] Pierre Gervais, "Early Modern Merchant Strategies and the Historicization of Market Practices", *Economic Sociology*, Cologne: Max Planck Institute for the Study of Societies (MPIfG: 2014), 15, 3, 19–29. p 25.

[92] There is evidence that private promissory notes were also subject to the legal rate enforceable.

[93] James E. Shaw, "The Informal Economy of Credit."   [94] ADTB 2E4/55.

[95] On pledges see especially Daniel Lord Smail, *Legal Plunder*, chapter 2.

[96] ADTB 2E4/56.

of the twenty-five livres bâloises lent.[97] This practise often replaced the payment of interest. In theory, the land pledged could be seized in case of default.

A promissory note sometimes included pawned objects as securities. When the sixty-year-old widower Joseph Berlincourt died in March 1780, his inventory contained several pieces of jewellery for women and objects made of gold. These had been deposited by Samuel Levy and his wife, a couple of Jewish livestock farmers living in a nearby village, as securities for a private loan.[98]

Similarly, a promissory note could include a pledge. In 1780, Jean-Baptiste Dermineur borrowed 260 livres from Louis Fleury. The pair wrote a promissory note. Perhaps because Dermineur did not have a good reputation, or because the amount at stake was quite important, the contract included a third party, a guarantor.[99] Sureties were often friends or relatives of the debtor whose debt they guaranteed, creating a vast web of local obligations.[100] In case of default, pledges were liable for the debt. The next chapter will delve into this question further.

In theory, a promissory note was informally assignable and could circulate among members of the community as a currency. How frequent was the assignability of such a debt? It is difficult to estimate. The examination of probate inventories and marriage contracts shows that the practise existed. The probate inventory of a blacksmith in 1783 featured two promissory notes initially written between a Jewish creditor and two different parties. The two individuals who had initially contracted with the Jewish lender now owed the capital and the interest to the blacksmith.[101] In another example, George Herbelin owed 200 livres to the Jewish livestock merchant Samuel Levy. But Levy had given the contract to his relative Cerf Levy and the debt was now due to him.[102] We cannot exclude that the exchange of promissory notes featured some speculation, especially if the contract has passed the initial repayment deadline. If the interest had not been paid, the new bearer could make a substantial profit.[103]

People, however, preferred to exchange notarial obligations, a more secure currency. The practise seems to have been that daughters and sons were endowed with notarial obligations rather than promissory notes upon their marriage.[104] Assignability of promissory notes might have remained

---

[97] ADTB 2E4/56.   [98] ADTB 2E4/436.   [99] ADTB 2E4/296.
[100] Mann, *Republic of Debtors*, p 15.   [101] ADTB 2E4/288.   [102] ADTB 2E4/436.
[103] Thierry Nootens and Nathalie Ricard, "Petites gens, petites dettes: monétarisation de la vie sociale et rapports de domination dans le district judiciaire d'Arthabaska (Québec), 1880–1930," *Histoire Sociale/Social History*, vol 53, no 109 (2019): 491–518, p 499.
[104] Elise Dermineur, "Widows' Political Strategies in Traditional Communities."

limited to the close circle, a very tight social network. Assignability equated flexibility but also introduced an impersonal dimension, which might explain people's reluctance to endow their children with promissory notes. Contests of authenticity and legitimacy could drag out repayment or even hinder it. In the case of difficulties, parties would have to turn to the local court to arbitrate their disagreement.

Regarding default, indeed, the lender could sue the borrower at the local court, showing the private contract as written evidence. About 35% of summons to court for default concerned non-intermediated loans, outnumbering notarial loans (see Chapter 5). But because of the private and intimate character of non-intermediated loans, resolution of conflicts mainly occurred in the private sphere via personal interaction and negotiation. Cases finding their way to court might very well have worn out the lender's forbearance.

The authorities grew concerned over the lack of supervision of non-intermediated transactions. The loss of tax income, especially, might have prompted the State to act. In 1666, the State ruled that loans superior to 100 livres had to be registered before the notary against a fee or had to be written down between private parties.[105] This legal disposition underlines the effort of the authorities to rule out verbal agreements, control the flux of exchanges, and arbitrate disputes. However, it does not appear that people took up the habit of registering their loans with the notary on a regular basis before the beginning of the eighteenth century.[106] In 1693, the State subjected the notaries to the registration of all their acts via a new institution, the *contrôle des actes*. Against a fee, the *contrôle des actes* enabled the certification and authentication of notarial deeds and later private promissory notes.[107] Did people dutifully register their promissory notes against a fee? Private promissory notes had to be registered with the *contrôle* before being accepted as evidence at court. It is unclear if people chose to record private loans only when difficulties arose or not. The *contrôle des actes*, however, was

---

[105] Isambert, François-André, *Recueil général des anciennes lois françaises, depuis l'an 420 jusqu'à la révolution de 1789: contenant la notice des principaux monumens des Mérovingiens, des Carlovingiens et des Capétiens, et le texte des ordonnances, édits, déclarations, lettres-patentes, réglemens, arrêts du Conseil, etc., de la troisième race, qui ne sont pas abrogés, ou qui peuvent servir, soit à l'interprétation, soit à l'histoire du droit public et privé, avec notes de concordance, table chronologique et table générale ...* 18. Paris: Belin-Le-Prieur, 1824, p. 137.

[106] More on this in Dermineur, Elise M. "Rethinking Debt: The Evolution of Private Credit Markets in Preindustrial France." *Social Science History* 42, no. 2 (2018): 317–42.

[107] This step might have blurred the difference a bit more between notarial loans and promissory notes.

never established in Alsace.[108] Alsatians did not have to pay the fees and did not have to register their private contracts to use them as evidence at court. For this reason, it might be that Alsatians used non-intermediated loans more often than their fellow countrymen.[109]

Historians have argued that promissory notes and other non-formalized arrangements were frequent for small, reciprocal, and usually short-term loans. Creditor and borrower often knew each other and were bound either by family ties or by geographical proximity. These intimate ties often exempted them from the burden of registering their transaction with the notary. The small amounts exchanged supposedly did not necessarily require official certification for the promise to be respected. One can imagine that some debtors might have been offended to be offered a loan certified by an external party.[110] In their eyes, this step could imply distrust, and could be interpreted as a provocation. Since promissory notes could be enforced at court, we might ask why some lenders and borrowers preferred to pay the service of a notary. This question will be tackled in Chapter 3.

Probate inventories give very little information on the purpose of promissory notes and other non-formalized interpersonal loans. Why did people borrow from one another using these arrangements? The meagre evidence at hand suggests a wide range of purposes, often involving complex ties. Monetary loans often served to pay a third party or pay for something bought that could not wait any longer for repayment. Sometimes, sellers and/or shopkeepers requested immediate payment. In 1756, Jean Grimont borrowed 200 livres from Claude-Antoine Monnier to build his house.[111] Louis Monnier borrowed 39 livres from one of his relatives to pay his taxes. The widow of Francois Ducloux borrowed 100 livres in cash 'to employ the money for her and her children's subsistence and pay the most pressing debts in order to avoid judicial lawsuits'.[112] And Pierre Jolié *le vieux* borrowed 240 livres from one of his neighbours to 'repay a Jew from Durmenach'.[113] In 1706, Simon Gainon borrowed 76 livres from Joseph Py to buy a couple of

[108] Françoise Hildesheimer, "Insinuation, contrôle des actes et absolutisme," *Bibliothèque de l'école des Chartes* 143, no. 1 (1985): 160–70.
[109] The *conseil souverain d'Alsace* (CSA) the equivalent of the local parliament for the province, however, ruled in 1778 that Jewish lenders and Jewish borrowers had to register their promissory notes with the local authorities against a fee. Reacting to and surfing on the rise of antisemitism in the province, the authorities sought to limit and control the activities of Jewish moneylenders in Alsace.
[110] Fontaine, "Introduction." In Maurice Berthe, ed. *Endettement paysan et crédit rural*, p 13.
[111] 2E4/407.   [112] ADTB 2E4/402.   [113] ADTB 2E4/442.

oxen from someone else.[114] In this case, it could be that Gainon bought the oxen from a seller he was perhaps not familiar with. The seller might have denied him credit. Livestock were often bought at a livestock fair and merchants from distant villages sometimes required full or partial payments in cash. And promissory notes also served to acknowledge a debt for something bought which would be paid for later in time. It is impossible to distinguish with certitude the proportion of effective loan and deferred payments in promissory note contracts. Overall, most of what was for sale was purchased on credit.

Yet, the average for a promissory note was more than double the amount of a deferred payment. The mean in the seigneuries of Delle and Florimont reached 135.8 livres (see Table 2.3 and Figure 2.7). People did lend to each other significant amounts of money via a promissory note. On the other hand, notarial loans did feature larger amounts.

A dramatic increase took place in the second half of the eighteenth century (see Table 2.4 and Figure 2.5). Not only did the number of non-intermediated interpersonal loans increase but their volume and mean rose as well. The same trend can be observed in the notarial credit market (see Figure 2.8). How can we interpret this growth? As the fragmentation of land continued in the eighteenth century, capital was needed to purchase new land, build new houses, and improve agricultural techniques in order to increase productivity.[115] A general climate of growth prevailed, favourable to credit activities of all kinds.[116]

Promissory notes were supposedly short-term loans whose full repayment was expected within a few weeks or a few months. Yet, in the seigneuries of Delle and Florimont, the promissory notes for which we have information of their length (34.7%) had, on average, a level of more than five and a half years. It seems that promissory notes could be rolled over and informally renewed, at least as long as the interest payments continued.[117] We cannot exclude the fact that some of these debts appearing in probate inventories had become insolvent with time. Often, the best option lenders had besides a lawsuit was to wait until the borrower's death to then line up and claim the sum due to the heirs. In fact, it was not rare that promissory notes were transformed into a

---

[114] ADTB 2E4/56.   [115] Ulrich Pfister, "Le petit crédit rural en Suisse," p 1340.
[116] Hoffman, *Growth in a Traditional Society.*
[117] It is also a practise one finds in the Netherlands. See Christiaan van Bochove and Heleen Kole, "Uncovering Private Credit Markets: Amsterdam, 1660–1809," *Tijdschrift Voor Sociale En Economische Geschiedenis* 11, no. 3 (2014): 39–72, p 54. See also Laurence Fontaine, "Antonio and Shylock," p 45. Jean Louis de Rodolp's portfolio presented several promissory notes paid well after the deadline.

Table 2.4 *Overview of non-intermediated credit between households in the seigneuries of Delle and Florimont between 1650 and 1790, for cases with a specified amount (total number of cases = 906)*

Period	Number	Volume	Mean	Median	Std. Deviation
Before 1650	7 (4.3%)	73.93	10.56	8.57	7.410
1670–89	54 (8.47%)	2,432.17	45.04	24.70	58.46
1690–1709	79 (8.65%)	3,490.21	44.18	21	79.41
1710–29	18 (4.93%)	788.41	43.80	25.37	46.19
1730–49	77 (11.88%)	8,459.34	109.86	70	128.91
1750–69	206 (17.44%)	34,831.8	169.09	60	337.74
1770–90	456 (19.44%)	71,712.59	157.26	69.65	544.57
Total	897	121,788.46	135.77	56	425.41

(*Source*: probate inventory dataset)

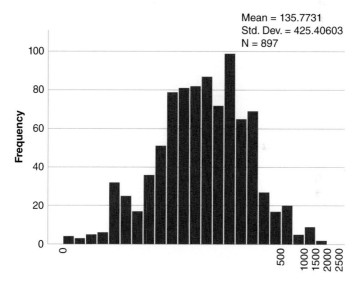

Mean = 135.7731
Std. Dev. = 425.40603
N = 897

Figure 2.7 Frequency of peer-to-peer loans in livres tournois in the seigneuries of Delle and Florimont, 1650–1790.
(*Source*: probate inventory dataset, logarithmic scale)[118]

notarial obligation upon a death. Brothers Jean-Pierre and Antoine Grimont owed 192 livres to Germain Voelin. When this latter passed away, the promissory note was converted into a notarial obligation. The widow Marie Gaijean also owed 542 livres to Germain Voelin. Her

[118] The total number is 906. Nine transactions have no specified amount.

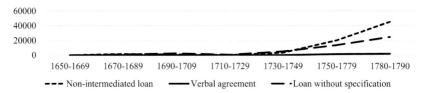

Figure 2.8 Evolution of peer-to-peer lending volume in livres tournois over time in the seigneuries of Delle and Florimont, 1650–1790. (*Source*: probate inventory dataset)

private agreement was also transformed into a notarial obligation upon her lender's death. This process can be explained because it was probably easier to renew the loan for the heirs via the notary, especially if there were several of them. And a lack of trust vis-à-vis the new debtors – the heirs – could also be responsible for this conversion.

Yet, when a promissory note was being repaid, lenders acknowledged the partial or total repayment of a promissory note via another private written instrument, a receipt (*quittance*, see Figure 2.9). Just like any other type of written document, people were careful to preserve these in wooden boxes at home for long periods of time, even well after everything was reimbursed. Just like a promissory note, a receipt was strictly a private document drafted by the parties. A few of them have survived in the archives, often attached as proof to a probate inventory.[119]

Who was engaged in lending via non-intermediated loans? Credit allocation remained a local phenomenon, highly concentrated among villagers (see Table 2.5 and Figure 2.11). Most lenders and borrowers were farmers. There was no parish banker.[120] There was no group of distinctive financiers. We do find individuals handling cash, such as innkeepers, shopkeepers, and, to a lesser extent, artisans. These professionals might have used promissory notes to charge for their products or services, or they might have simply redistributed the cash they could accumulate. There is a certain social, economic, and geographical homogeneity among creditors and debtors using non-intermediated loans. Overall, promissory notes were used in an environment in which agents did not display huge bargaining discrepancies.

---

[119] It seems that parties could register a *quittance* at the notary for their notarial contracts. However, none have been found for the south of Alsace.

[120] A term used in pre-industrial Sweden by Anders Perlinge, "Sockenbankirerna: kreditrelationer och tidig bankverksamhet: Vånga socken i Skåne 1840–1900" (Stockholm: Nordiska museets förlag, 2005).

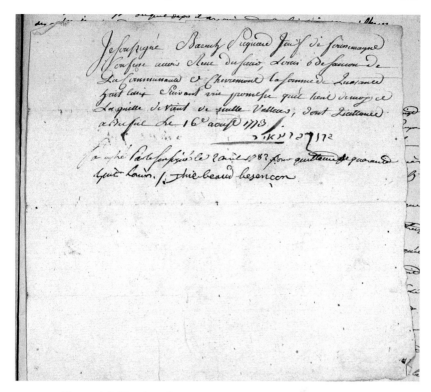

Figure 2.9 Receipt of repayment, 1773.
(*Source*: ADTB 4B249, photo by the author)[121]

As such, non-intermediated loans exhibit thus the features of a small world. A third of these transactions took place between neighbours living in the same village (35.5%, Table 2.5,[122] while about 14% of these loans were contracted between relatives.[123] Similar figures could also be found in eighteenth-century Württemberg where between 13% and 16% of

---

[121] 'Je soussigné Baruch Piquard juif de Foussemagne confesse avoir recu du sieur Louis Besancon de la communauté de Chèvremont la somme de quarante huit louis suivant une promesse qu'il tient de moi et devient de nulle valeur, dont quittance. A Belfort, le 16 août 1773.' 'I, the undersigned Baruch Piquard, a Jew from Foussemagne, confess to having received from Sieur Louis Besancon of the community of Chèvremont the sum of forty-eight louis in accordance with a promise he made to me and which is now worthless, for which receipt is given. Belfort, 16 August 1773.'

[122] Based on the information we have (173/906) we do not know their place of residence.

[123] Although this number could be higher since kinship was not always stipulated and because a third of the transactions took place among people living in the same village where high levels of endogamy prevailed.

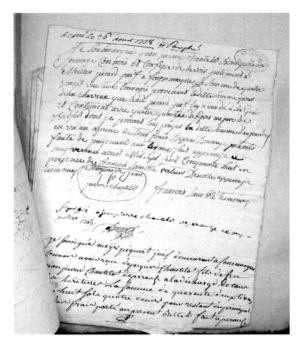

Figure 2.10 Promissory note from 1778 between Meyer Piquard and Jean-Pierre Chantelot, 1758. Receipt of payment is acknowledged at the bottom. (*Source*: ADTB 4B249, photo by the author)[124]

inventoried borrowing took place among kin.[125] In neighbouring Wildberg, in the second half of the seventeenth century, a similar

---

[124] 'Je soussigné Jean Pierre Chatelot bourgeois de Perouse connais et confesse de devoir justement à Meyer Piquard juif à Foussemagne la somme de quatre vingt une livres tournois provenant ladite somme pour deux chevaux que ledit Piquard juif lui a vendu à son gré et contentement avec quatre quartes de gru mesure de Belfort dont je promets lui payer la ditte somme d'aujourd'hui en un an à peine de tous frais depens dommage interest faute de payement aud. Terme. Fait à Perouse ce neuvième août mil sept cent cinquante huit en presence de François Lamblé recteur d'école à Perouse témoin.' 'I, the undersigned Jean Pierre Chatelot, bourgeois of Perouse, know and confess that I owe Meyer Piquard, a Jew of Foussemagne, the sum of eighty-one livres tournois, coming from the said sum for two horses that the said Jewish Piquard sold to me at my will and content with four quarters of wheat, measure of Belfort, of which I promise to pay him the said sum from today within one year, under penalty of all costs, expenses, damages, interest, in the absence of payment at the said term. Done at Perouse this ninth of August, one thousand seven hundred and fifty-eight in the presence of François Lamblé, school rector at Perouse and witness.'

[125] Cited in Ogilvie, Küpker, and Maegraith, "Household Debt in Early Modern Germany," p 149.

Table 2.5 *Financial networks in the seigneuries of Delle and Florimont, 1650–1790*

	Deferred payments (probate dataset)	Private non-intermediated loans (probate dataset)	Notarial loans (probate dataset)	Notarial loans (notarial dataset)
Same village	(572/1,913) 30%	(321/906) 35.5%	(91/377) 24.1%	38.3%
Among relatives	(160/1,913) 8.36%	(125/906) 13.79%	(27/377) 7.2%	13.5%

proportion can be found as well.[126] These numbers are higher than for deferred payments and notarial loans (see Table 2.5. Despite the intimacy existing between lenders and borrowers, writing down contracts and keeping track of them was of significance. Debt between kin and friends, the first circle, usually took place with little formalization, as we have seen. Parties recorded the debt with a promissory note or in their ledgers rather than contracting at the notary.[127] The existence of a promissory note for a transaction between family members might highlight the need to keep track of the various entangled dealings of an individual.[128]

As an example of an interpersonal lending network, let us consider the period 1770–90. Figure 2.11 represents the network of non-intermediated loans in both seigneuries at that time. One notes the presence of a large cluster in the middle. Not only does this cluster feature and connect the most active lenders but it also shows long chains of credit. Such high clustering suggests cooperative and prosocial behaviours as these relations were embedded, making lending easier.[129] But high clustering also emphasizes the interdependency of the actors in terms of the allocation of funds. If default occurred, other failures to repay could spread like fire within the cluster. The network features several important lenders but no real 'financier'. Joseph Berlincourt, for example, a retired military officer, had extended many loans but mostly to people outside his community. Such cases

---

[126] Ogilvie, Küpker, and Maegraith, "Household Debt in Early Modern Germany," p 149.

[127] Laurence Fontaine, "Introduction." In Maurice Berthe, ed. *Endettement paysan et crédit rural dans l'Europe médiévale et moderne.* "Lla dette entre parents et amis s'inscrivant normalement sur un billet privé ou dans un livre."

[128] Vickers, "Errors Expected."

[129] Matthew O. Jackson, "Networks in the Understanding of Economic Behaviors," *Journal of Economic Perspectives* 28, no. 4 (2014): 3–22, p 17. See also Matthew O. Jackson, *Social and Economic Networks.* (Princeton, NJ: Princeton University Press, 2010).

Figure 2.11 Network of non-intermediated loans in the seigneuries of Delle and Florimont, 1770–90. The nodes are coloured according to the place of residence of the agents (Blue for the seigneurie of Florimont, orange for the seigneurie of Delle, and green for outside the seigneuries).
(*Source*: probate inventory dataset)

remained rare. Jean-Baptiste Bichet was an innkeeper. As such, he often had access to cash and information, making possible the allocation of funds to people in his community. Overall, many households were connected to one another and were dependent on each other. Interpersonal lending remained extremely local with only a few outsiders.

To illustrate this point further, Figure 2.12 reconstructs the non-intermediated credit networks in the seigneurie of Florimont between 1770 and 1790. It features both deferred payments and non-intermediated private transactions.

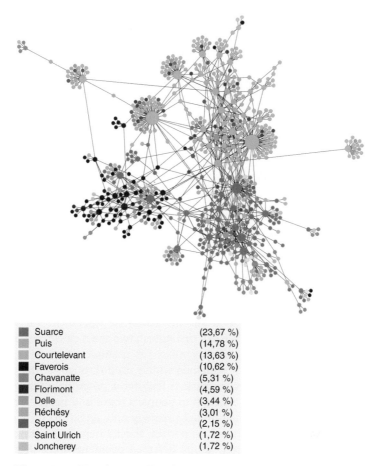

Suarce	(23,67 %)
Puis	(14,78 %)
Courtelevant	(13,63 %)
Faverois	(10,62 %)
Chavanatte	(5,31 %)
Florimont	(4,59 %)
Delle	(3,44 %)
Réchésy	(3,01 %)
Seppois	(2,15 %)
Saint Ulrich	(1,72 %)
Joncherey	(1,72 %)

Figure 2.12 Non-intermediated credit networks featuring deferred payments and private transactions in the seigneurie of Florimont 1770–90 (main cluster, nodes are coloured after villages and are weighted according to their degrees).
(*Source*: probate inventory dataset)

This graph underlines at least two aspects of non-intermediated credit relations. Households preferred to deal with familiar faces. Deferred payments and promissory notes connected people geographically close to each other. Most of the transactions were hyperlocal, between neighbours.[130] And most debtors and creditors were similar in

---

[130] In the seigneurie of Florimont, the majority of the non-intermediated transactions were between households from the same village.

status, in other words, they did not present important discrepancies in terms of wealth or bargaining power. There were households with higher out-degrees than others. But their professional occupation justified the number of transactions they made (one of this node is the local innkeeper for example with many deferred payments for the goods he sold). Added to this, most households within the community (about 70%) were connected to one another. The main cluster on the graph shows the existence of highly personalized relationships within the community.

Overall, almost all households in the community were involved in this giant web of credit. Promissory notes were common. Peasants used them extensively, which suggests that literacy was not a problem or a hurdle.[131]

Concluding Remarks

In pre-industrial Europe, peer-to-peer lending transactions realized without intermediation and without formal certification show that the credit market was not solely organized by notaries. In fact, they were ubiquitous. Yet, these transactions remain very little known. Overall, there was a wide range of arrangements with various terms of agreement in this non-intermediated category. We can distinguish two main categories: interpersonal loans (such as promissory notes for example), and deferred payments (credit sales). Both remained widely used throughout the period.

Non-intermediated credit markets featured a potpourri of transactions precisely because they pertained to people's input and needs. The terms of the agreement were negotiated privately and agreed to on a case-by-case basis at the discretion of the parties. Parties negotiated and adjusted the agreement's provisions. While deferred payments were inscribed in ledgers or were simply agreed upon verbally, promissory notes were written agreements. Lenders and borrowers were deeply attached to written proof, not necessarily because of a lack of trust but because they needed to keep track of the giant web of tangled transactions they were part of.

So, if non-intermediated transactions could be sealed in the private sphere, without intermediation and without an additional fee, why did people turn to notaries? The next chapter brings elements of an answer.

---

[131] Contrary to what Le Gendre has found in sixteenth century Poitou. Romain Le Gendre, *Confiance, épargne et notaires: le marché du crédit à Saint-Maixent et dans sa région au XVIe siècle* (Paris: Ecole des Chartes, 2020).

3   Intermediated Credit: Notarial Contracts

Introduction

In the non-intermediated credit market, households often deferred the payment of items and services and borrowed money without official certification. The reciprocity and repetition of such dealings presumably made certification superfluous. Yet, notarial contracts could also seal credit exchanges. In fact, both non-intermediated and notarial credit coexisted. In what circumstances did households prefer a notarial contract over a private deed? What elements persuaded them to turn to the notary?

This chapter focuses on the notarial credit market and notarial loan contracts.[1] It aims, particularly, to shed light on the motivations of lenders and borrowers from turning to the notary to draft and register their financial deeds. It compares notarial credit transactions with non-intermediated ones thanks to the examination of notarial loan registers in the seigneuries of Delle and Florimont from the 1730s to 1790. It first presents the various contracts available at the notary's office, then turns to the main contract provisions, emphasizing their flexible character. Attention to creditors and borrowers is paid in a third part. Finally, this chapter explores the various reasons why lenders and borrowers turned to the notary to register their financial deeds.

A Variety of Notarial Credit Contracts

In Delle and Florimont, one notary resided in each seigneurie. Their prime role was the certification of contracts thanks to their official seal

---

[1] It has been a renewal of interest lately for notarial records. See among others: Gabriel Audisio, *L'historien et l'activité notariale: Provence, Vénétie, Egypte, XVe–XVIIIe siècles* (Toulouse: Presses Universitaires du Midi, 2005); Olivier Poncet, "Nommer et décrire les actes des notaires de l'époque moderne, entre théorie, pratique et histoire," *Bibliothèque de l'école des Chartes* 172, no. 1/2 (2014): 449–53; Laurence Fontaine, "L'activité notariale (Note Critique)," *Annales. Histoire, Sciences Sociales* 48, no. 2 (1993): 475–83; and Mathieu Arnoux, and Olivier Guyotjeannin. *Tabellions et tabellionages de la France médiévale et moderne.* Mémoires et documents de l'École des chartes. (Paris: École des Chartes, 2011).

and the keeping of legal records. In case of dispute, their imprimatur suffered no contestation. These officers could also offer sound legal advice to their clients for their family and for business affairs.[2] To some extent, notaries contributed to the safeguard of property rights.

In the south of Alsace, notaries registered a certain number of contracts every year: loans, land sales, donations, wills, and other documents related to family affairs.[3] Loan registers from the period 1733–89 for Delle and 1740–89 for Florimont are continuous. The *minutes,* copy of the contracts consigned in the notary ledgers were archived.[4] Lenders and borrowers could ask for a copy of the contract, an *expedition,* at an additional cost.[5]

In general, the notary offered access to different financial instruments to his clients. Depending on the needs, capabilities, and expectations of the parties, there were four major types of notarial loan contracts to choose from: annuities in the form of *rentes perpétuelles, rente constituées, rente viagères,* and obligations. None of these credit instruments were particular to the French kingdom, they could be found throughout early modern Europe with more or less the same type of provisions.

Annuities

A *rente viagère* (life annuity) featured a lender who lent to a borrower a certain amount of capital, usually a significant amount. A fixed sum featuring both reimbursement for the capital and interest would be repaid annually until the creditor(s)'s death. Following the death of the creditor(s), the payment stopped, and his heirs could no longer claim anything from the borrower. But if the debtor died before the creditor, then their heirs had to continue the annual payments. Both lenders and

---

[2] Hoffman, Postel-Vinay, and Rosenthal, "What Do Notaries Do?" See also Oscar Gelderblom, Mark Hup, and Joost Jonker. "Public Functions, Private Markets: Credit Registration by Aldermen and Notaries in the Low Countries, 1500–1800." In Marcella Lorenzini, Cinzia Lorandini, and D'Maris Coffman, eds. *Financing in Europe: Evolution, Coexistence and Complementarity of Lending Practices from the Middle Ages to Modern Times,* 163–94 (Cham: Springer, 2018).

[3] The archiving of notarial documents is erratic and does not allow for estimating exactly how many contracts notaries drafted for each seigneurie.

[4] In Delle, these registers are preserved starting from 1733 until 1790. In Florimont, the registers are continuous from 1740 to 1790. No significant lacuna has been observed over these periods. It is possible that loans were registered on loose sheets of paper and were not included in the notary's dedicated registers, but the probability is quite low. Therefore, the notarial loan registers studied here are quite comprehensive. However, one must note that loans were often part of land sale contracts and were included in the sale deed; often not registered separately.

[5] Le Gendre, *Confiance,* pp 167–69.

borrowers bet on the life expectancy of the person for whom the *rente* was drafted; usually, the annual payments were fixed in correlation with the age of that person. This financial tool often served as a retirement pension for ageing people.[6] Oftentimes, the return was superior from the initial investment. It is still in use today in France for the purchase of real estate property. In early modern Delle and Florimont, the *rente viagère* was the least common of the three annuity contracts.[7] None could be found in the notarial ledgers.

The *rente perpétuelle* (perpetual annuity) worked differently. It started as an annual rent paid to a seller of land by a buyer who could not pay the entire price outright.[8] In the sixteenth century, however, an annuity became a payment made annually for a grant of capital, including interest, until the principal was totally repaid. Usually the amount paid every year was fixed, giving the lender the assurance of a fixed annual income. The lender could not ask for the repayment of the capital. The borrower, however, had the possibility to repay the principal of his *rente* at once. The contract was backed with specific pieces of land. An annuity did not bear a repayment deadline to comply with the Church rule on usury.[9] The annuity was transmissible to heirs in case of the lender's death and if the capital had not been repaid by then. Public institutions often turned to this credit instrument to finance their activities.[10] Scholars have argued that the indefinite duration of the *rente perpétuelle* had a negative effect on commerce and growth.[11] In rural areas, this indefinite duration often engendered indebtedness over several generations.

The *rente constituée* (annuity) resembled the *rente perpétuelle*. It was attached to a specific piece of land or an 'immeuble' such as a house. With a *rente constituée*, a lender extended money to a borrower until the latter decided to repay the capital in full. In the meantime, fixed interest – supposedly the revenues of the land – were paid every year (6.25% at the beginning of the seventeenth century and then 5% until the end of the

---

[6] Jaco Zuijderduijn, "The Ages of Women and Men: Life Cycles, Family, and Investment in the Fifteenth-Century Low Countries." In Elise M. Dermineur, ed. *Women and Credit in Pre-Industrial Europe*, (Turnhout: Brepols Publishers, 2018), 95–120.

[7] Elsewhere, they also remained marginal. Hoffman, Postel-Vinay, and Rosenthal, *Dark Matter Credit*, p 28.

[8] Schnapper, *Les rentes au 16e siècle*.

[9] Robert-Joseph Pothier, *Traité du contrat de constitution de rente*, (Paris: Béchet aîné, 1763), p 5.

[10] Katia Béguin, "La circulation des rentes constituées dans la France du XVIIe siècle: une approche de l'incertitude économique," *Annales. Histoire, Sciences Sociales* 60, no. 6 (2005): 1229–44.

[11] George V. Taylor, "Noncapitalist Wealth and the Origins of the French Revolution," *The American Historical Review* 72, no. 2 (1967): 469–96, p 480.

Ancien Régime).[12] Furetière argues that this *rente constitutée* resembled a 'sale with the option to re-purchase' the land.[13] In the seventeenth and eighteenth centuries, the seller could continue to work the land. As this type of annuity was attached to a specific piece of land, any new owner had to continue the service of the *rente*.[14] Annuities could also circulate as a means of currency. Scholars often refer to a 'second-hand market' for annuities, where they could be exchanged and traded.[15] *Rente constituée* functioned therefore somewhat as medieval British mortgages and was often assimilated and became confused with perpetual annuities with time.[16] Just like a perpetual annuity, a *rente constituée* did not specify any repayment deadline to circumvent the rules of usury.

In the seigneuries of Delle and Florimont, notaries rarely offered annuities to their clients. Only a handful of such contracts have been found. Most of them dated back to the beginning of the eighteenth century. They seem to have been relics of even older contracts being renewed.

But, by contrast, annuity contracts were the favourite financial tool of the non-private lenders such as the hospital of Delle and the local parish vestries. Little is known regarding the annuities offered by the parish vestries in the literature. In early modern France, each parish had, in theory, a parish vestry to manage the affairs of the local church.[17] In the Middle Ages, parishioners could 'buy' mass services for the repose of their souls after death, paid to the parish vestry – the *fabrique*.[18] They bequeathed goods to this end.[19] In the early modern

---

[12] With the exception of a short period of time between 1760 and 1764.

[13] Antoine Furetière, *Dictionnaire universel contenant généralement tous les mots françois tant vieux que modernes & les termes des sciences et des arts,* (La Haye: A. & R: Leers, 1701), entry: rente constituée, pp 483–84.

[14] Serge Dormard, "Le marché du crédit à Douai aux XVIIe et XVIIIe siècles," *Revue du Nord* 362, no. 4 (2005): 803–33, p 806.

[15] Paul Servais, "De la rente au crédit hypothécaire en période de transition industrielle: stratégies familiales en Région Liégeoise au XVIIIe siècle," *Annales. Histoire, Sciences Sociales* 49, no. 6 (1994): 1393–409, p 1396.

[16] On *rente constituée* see especially Paul Servais, "De la rente au crédit hypothécaire en période de transition industrielle. On British mortgages see especially Briggs, *Credit and Village;* Briggs and Zuijderduijn, *Land and Credit.*

[17] See , Marcel Pacaut et al., *L'Hostie et le denier: les finances ecclésiastiques du haut Moyen Age à l'époque moderne: actes du colloque de la commission internationale d'histoire ecclésiastique comparée, Genève, août 1989* (Genève: Labor et Fides, 1991); and Serge Brunet, "Fondation de messes, crédit rural et marché de la terre dans les Pyrénées centrales (XV–XVIIIe siècles), les communautés de prêtres du Val d'Aran." In Maurice Berthe, ed. Endettement paysan et crédit rural, dans l'Europe médiévale et moderne, (Toulouse: Presses universitaires du Midi, 1998).

[18] Brunet, "Fondations de messes."

[19] Catherine Vincent, "La vitalité de la communauté paroissiale au XVe siècle à travers quelques exemples de fondations rouennaises," *Revue du Nord* 356–57, no. 3–4 (2004): 741–56.

period, new loans were made thanks to the *fabrique*'s revenues, which sometimes included the lucrative *dîmes*. The administrators were able to lend money to a few households. In order to respect the Church rule on usury, only annuity contracts were drafted.[20] Peasants pledged a piece of land to the *fabrique* in exchange for capital received; every year they paid a *rente*. These loans were usually long-term agreements, spread over several generations. Parish vestries enjoyed modest profits. In 1682, the parish vestry of Delle received about 400 livres in revenues from the interest rates. In 1788, this increased to about 600 livres.[21] Interestingly, the *fabrique*'s debtors who could get the *fabrique's* loans were often well to do landed farmers in need of liquidities. In Delle and Florimont, many households were indebted to their local parish vestry, either on their own initiative or because they inherited land burdened with such annuities. Overall, parish vestry loan contracts accounted for 6.6% of the debt of the seigneuries' deceased in terms of volume. In terms of number, they even surpassed notarial loans in probate inventories.

Local practises, private property structures, and notarial preferences played a role in the geography of annuities.[22] Notaries, especially rural ones, might have had a preference, expertise, or habits for one type of contract only.[23] In Burgundy, for example, only 7% of the notarized loan contracts were annuities, but these accounted for 21% of the volume exchanged.[24] In the north of France, annuities were the most privileged notarial instrument of credit.[25] In the south of Alsace, another contract was popular: the obligation.

Obligations

In the eighteenth century, annuities gradually lost their attractiveness.[26] The edict of 1771 on *hypothèques* (mortgages) increased considerably the fees for the creditor, leading to a decrease in the number of annuities

---

[20] As noted in the introduction, specifying both an interest rate and a deadline for repayment was consider an usurious practise. It implied the monetization of time. Yet, the Church considered time only belonging to God.

[21] ADTB GG15/1 and GG16/37.

[22] Postel-Vinay, *La terre et l'argent: l'agriculture et le crédit en France*, p 39.

[23] This is also the conclusion of Claire Lemercier and Francesca Trivellato, "1751 and Thereabout: A Quantitative and Comparative Approach to Notarial Records," *Social Science History* 46, no. 3 (2022): 555–83.

[24] Jean-Laurent Rosenthal, "Credit Markets and Economic Change in Southeastern France 1630–1788," *Explorations in Economic History* 30, no. 2 (1993): 129–57.

[25] Dormard, "Le marché du crédit à Douai," p 803.

[26] Schnapper, *Les rentes au 16e siècle*.

drafted.[27] By the mid-eighteenth-century, another financial instrument, the obligation, gained popularity and supplanted annuities in terms of numbers. Obligations 'grew larger and more common, and by the nineteenth century, they came to dominate the credit market'.[28]

In the seigneurie of Delle, 1,468 obligations were signed for the period 1733–90. In Florimont, 624 obligations were registered for the period 1740–90. I thus estimate that in this area on average about 7% of households signed a notarial loan every year.

An obligation was not a new instrument per se. Obligations were notarized promissory notes, an agreement to repay a certain amount in a delimited and predefined time. Obligations were widely favoured by artisans and peasants because they were usually used for small amounts repayable in the short-term.

Obligations were fungible. One could pass on, inherit, and exchange obligations. When Marie Elisabeth Jeantine got married, for example, her parents endowed her with an obligation amounting to 1,000 livres.[29] Marie Ursule Vautrin was also endowed by her mother with 12,000 livres worth of obligations.[30]

The success of obligations could be further explained by their flexible character. In theory, obligations could not legally bear an interest rate since they stipulated a deadline for repayment.[31] Stipulating both would be usurious. In practise, however, the interest could be hidden in the capital or arranged on the side.[32] In the seigneuries of Delle and Florimont, obligations, however, just like annuities, specified an interest rate usually equal to the 5% legal rate.[33] We shall come back to this point shortly.

[27] Jean Jacquart, "L'endettement paysan et le crédit dans les campagnes de la France modern." In Maurice Berthe, ed. *Endettement paysan et crédit rural: dans l'Europe médiévale et moderne*, 283–97. (Toulouse: Presses universitaires du Midi, 2020), p 289.

[28] Philip T. Hoffman, Gilles Postel-Vinay, and Jean-Laurent Rosenthal. *Priceless Markets*, p 15. Obligations already dominated in the sixteenth century in Saint Maixent, Romain Le Gendre, *Confiance*.

[29] ADTB 2E4/392, 1777, marriage contract of Jean Pierre Marion and Marie Elisabeth Jeantine.

[30] ADTB 2E4/276, 1778, marriage contract of Antoine Drillot and Marie Ursule Vautrin.

[31] Hoffman, Postel-Vinay, Rosenthal. *Des marchés sans prix*, p 15. See also Claude de Ferrière, *La science parfaite des notaires, ou le parfait notaire: contenant les ordonnances, arrests & réglemens rendus touchant la fonction des notaires, tant royaux qu'apostoliques* 1, 1752, p 174.

[32] Jean-Laurent Rosenthal. "Credit Markets and Economic Change," p 132. And Hoffman, Postel-Vinay, and Rosenthal, *Des marchés sans prix*, p 31.

[33] One can explain the fact that obligations did bear an interest rate in this particular region because it was integrated into the French kingdom after the Thirty Years' War. The crown, then, decided not to touch the *us et coutumes* (habits and customs) of Alsace. This could possibly have applied to interest rates, See chapter 1.

Most obligation contracts mentioned collateral, often in the form of land, sometimes in the form of livestock.[34] In August 1783, Francois Dandelan and his wife Marguerite Tirebert purchased several plots of land. As they could not pay for the land outright, they borrowed 400 livres tournois 'in real money' from Antoine Cornuez, a shopkeeper living in the same village. The loan served to 'pay for a piece of land they bought from Sr Stoum (...) living in Belfort', a third party. To back the transaction, the land purchased served as security. In addition, the borrowers also pledged all their goods. The couple had to repay the capital the next year with a 5% interest fee.[35] As this deed bore specific interest, it does not fit the definition of an obligation. But as its duration was specified, it did not fit into the annuity category either. This hybrid format could be found in most of the obligations in our sample where both an interest rate of 5% and a repayment deadline were systematically specified.

Yet, contracts featuring an 'upon request' repayment clause resembled an annuity contract. In theory, it meant that borrowers were expected to complete the repayment at the lender's will and convenience at some point in the future. But in practise, the interest could be rolled over for a long time. In the seigneuries of Delle and Florimont, 13.2% of the notarial loan contracts were due upon request.

Obligations had thus a polymorphous and complex definition. In Alsace, obligations and annuities could be easily confused with each other. This hybrid format could be found elsewhere in the French kingdom.[36] In seventeenth-century Anjou, Maine, Touraine, and Berry obligations stipulated an interest rate.[37] The provinces of Bresse, Bugey, and Pays de Gex also exhibited this practise. But upon the annexation to the French kingdom in 1601, the monarchy forbad the mention of an interest rate in obligation contracts.[38] When Alsace was attached to the French kingdom after the Thirty Years' War, it was decided to leave the *us et coutumes* unchanged to make the integration of Alsatians as smooth as possible. As a result, Alsatians could keep specifying an interest rate and a deadline for repayment.

In the seigneuries of Delle and Florimont, notarial loan records are continuously available from the 1730s to the 1790s.[39] In total, the

---

[34] See also Le Gendre, *Confiance*, pp 159–62.   [35] ADTB 2E4/280.

[36] '[E]ven within the notarial system, the links between obligations and *rentes* remain unclear' Jean-Laurent Rosenthal, "Rural Credit Markets and Aggregate Shocks," p 291.

[37] The monarchy forced these provinces to transform these contracts into annuity contracts. See Le Gendre, *Confiance*, p 179.

[38] Ibid.

[39] From 1744 only for Florimont. Dataset consists of: for the seigneurie of Delle: ADTB2E4/155, 156, 157, 158, 159, 194, 222, 223, 257, 258, 279, 280, 281, 285; for the seigneurie of Florimont: ADTB2E4/408, 409, 410, 443, 444, 445, 446.

Table 3.1 *Overview of the notarial loans in the seigneuries of Delle and Florimont, 1733–90*

	N	V	Mean	Median	StDev	Min	Max
Delle	1,468	446,129.63	303.9	200	446.3	10	6,000
Florimont	624	307,003	491.9	200	1166	18	12,000

Table 3.2 *Overview of the notarial loans in the seigneuries of Delle and Florimont by periods, 1733–90*

	N	V	Mean	Median	StDev	Min	Max
1730–39	131	23,441.6	178.9	126	165.4	15	1,000
1740–49	233	59,796.3	256.6	150	389.5	18	3,000
1750–59	255	74,865.35	293.6	127.5	682.4	22	6,400
1760–69	278	75,723.5	272.4	150	409.9	24	3,000
1770–79	480	195,202.6	406.7	202.5	802.9	18	10,764
1780–89	715	324,103.2	453.3	252	935.6	10	12,000

notarial registers contain 2,092 loan contracts (see Table 3.1). All of these contracts were labelled 'obligations' without exception.

In total, the dataset consists of 2,092 loans for a period of about seventy years, about 29 contracts every year, for a total volume of 753,132 livres tournois (Table 3.2). In contrast, in Paris, on average, 138 million livres were exchanged annually. Parisian households borrowed on average 13,000 livres tournois. While Paris might be exceptional in every respect, the notarial credit market remained unpretentious elsewhere in the kingdom, especially in rural areas and small towns. In 1780, the mean obligation in Delle and Florimont oscillated between 300 and 490 livres. In rural Sainte-Croix-en-Plaine, in northern Alsace, it was about 259 livres for the same period.[40] In the southern town of Albi, it was just 120 livres. In Château-Thierry, a town between Paris and Reims, the mean was 278 livres per obligation contract. In Normandy, it reached 2,144 livres in the city Rouen.[41] Important variations occurred throughout the kingdom. Overall, the mean per obligation was often lower in rural areas than in urban areas.

[40] Boehler, *Une société rurale en milieu rhénan*, p 1184.
[41] Postel-Vinay, *La terre et l'argent: l'agriculture et le crédit en France*, p 84.

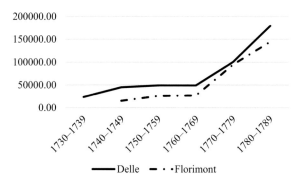

Figure 3.1 Volume of exchange in the seigneuries of Delle and
Florimont, 1733–90.

The amount per contract varied a lot in Delle and Florimont (see
Table 3.2 and Figure 3.2). Loans under 100 livres tournois remained
an exception.[42] Most people preferred not to register their loans with the
notary for small amounts. Households might have felt that the fees and
transaction costs associated with this effort were not worth it. They
preferred the costless oral transactions or promissory notes for petty
loans, as we saw in Chapter 2. Yet, loans over 500 remained rare.
Seldom were important amounts exchanged. This is not too surprising
in a local credit market where most households did not present considerable disparities in terms of wealth and bargaining power. Most of the
loans remained between 100 and 300 livres, enough to purchase livestock, plots of land, or a small house, as we shall see below (see
Figure 3.2). This is similar to what has been observed in northern
Alsace. In rural Kochersberg, 45% of the operations were between
200 and 500 livres.[43]

Throughout the eighteenth century, both the volume and the number
of loans increased (Table 3.2 and Figure 3.1). After the 1760s, the
increase became even more pronounced and notarial activity became
more dynamic. In effect, accounting for demographic changes, it means
that more households exchanged goods and capital. And they borrowed
to finance a wide range of projects: purchase of land, livestock, house,
etc. The same trend can also be observed in Paris for the same period.[44]

---

[42] In 1666, the State ruled that loans superior to 100 livres had to be registered before the
notary against a fee or had to be written down between private parties. Isambert,
François-André. *Recueil général des anciennes lois françaises*, p 137.
[43] Boehler, *Une société rurale en milieu rhénan*, p 1203.
[44] Hoffman, Postel-Vinay, and Rosenthal, *Priceless Markets*, p 101.

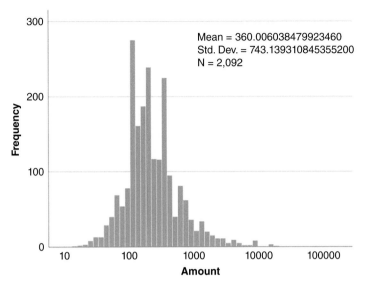

Figure 3.2 Histogram of the notarial loans in the seigneurie of Delle and Florimont, 1733–90.
(*Source*: logarithmic)

Purpose of the Loans

Notarial obligations remained vague on the purpose of loans. In theory, an obligation had to stipulate a purpose, otherwise the contract was deemed null and void.[45] Yet, many contracts featured an elusive purpose. For example, in April 1751, the widow Catherine Jeanmaire borrowed 190 livres from her sister Marie Patissier. The notary wrote that the loan was for her 'needs and necessities'. In fact, about half of the loans in our sample did not mention any specific reason for the deal (see Table 3.3).[46] The formula *juste et légal prêt d'argent* – fair and legal money loan – was often used, which was enough to validate the contract. This formula was used either because it became a standard provision for the notary or because households increasingly did not wish to provide much detail over their personal finances. As Thomas Brennan notes 'it is rarely clear how borrowers used their loans'.[47] For half of these loans, we do

---

[45] Claude de Ferrière, *La science parfaite des notaires*, p 177.
[46] In the seigneurie of Delle, 53,8% of the cases did not specify a clear purpose while the proportion reached 47% in Florimont.
[47] Thomas Brennan, "Peasants and Debt," p 177.

Table 3.3 *Overview of the loans' purposes in the seigneuries of Delle and Florimont, 1730–90*

	N	N %	Sum	Sum %
Loan without specification	1,041	49.8	328,154.72	43.6
Land	107	5.1	53,608.4	7.1
Livestock	250	12	41,836.5	5.6
House & Building	106	5.1	55,190	7.3
Debt payment and certification	260	12.4	152,782.3	20.3
Loan and sale/mix	134	6.4	49,158.9	6.5
Other	194	9.3	72,401.75	9.6

not know what the money was used for.[48] One can only speculate that cash was exchanged between the parties.

For the rest of the contracts, there were two main categories: deferred payments for the purchase of items and products and certification of old debts.

Credit sale for the purchase of livestock constituted one of the most important categories of notarized loans (12% in number). We have already seen the importance of these transactions for the non-intermediated credit market. Livestock farming was popular in this region. Several specialized fairs and markets were organized across the region not only for selling cows but also pigs, sheep, and horses. In May 1753, Jean Jacques Monnier bought two oxen at the local fair in Grandvillars. As he could not pay outright, Monnier and the seller contracted at the notary's office. Joseph Cueny and his wife Marie Anne Beuguelet bought a cow at the fair organized in Florimont. They also went to the notary to formalize their debt. Purchase of livestock at a fair often meant contracting with someone less familiar with whom an official contract might help seal the deal. Additionally, livestock sales between neighbours and people of prior acquaintance were also sometimes sealed with a notarial loan. Parties might have preferred a notarial loan after the drafting of a promissory note presumably because of a deficit of trust after a few missed payments.[49] In 1775, George Fleury and his wife Ursule Bourquenez recognized, via an obligation, that they still owed fifty-one livres to Jacques Patingre for a cow sold to them five years earlier.[50] De facto, those obligations were not proper cash transfers but

---

[48] Same proportion in Saint-Maixent. See Le Gendre, *Confiance*, p 156.
[49] Fontaine, "Antonio and Shylock."   [50] ADTB 2E4/444.

credit sales. The animal bought usually served as a guarantee. In case of non-repayment, the seller could easily seize the animals.

Besides livestock, households also purchased grains, foodstuffs, merchandise for their shops, and other items via an obligation. As we have already seen, most of these items did not require a notarial contract. A promissory note usually sufficed. Only 0.7% of the notarial contracts concerned the deferred payment of grains for example. Additionally, 6.4% of the transactions in terms of number regarded the deferred payment of an item combined with a loan in cash. For these exchanges, the borrowers might have found themselves in an uncomfortable financial situation. These cases also highlight the complexities of credit exchanges where more than one transaction between parties occurred. The cases suggest the forbearance of the lender might have broken down after they extended both time and cash for repayment on several occasions to the debtor.

Investment in land remained surprisingly limited in both seigneuries (6.5% and 7% in terms of number in the seigneuries of Delle and Florimont, respectively). In fact, seller and buyer often negotiated the payment – and instalment – of a piece of land directly in the land sale deed, also a notarial contract. They usually did not write and pay for a separate loan contract. In a land sale contract, parties specified the conditions of payment for the transfer, often a loan as a few households could not pay outright. A land sale was thus also a credit sale. More than a third of the land sales in Delle and 40% in Florimont for the period 1780–85 featured a loan provision.[51] In 1782, Henry Vienez from the village of Croix sold to Joseph Gainon a piece of land for sixty livres. The buyer promised to reimburse the sum in three years, in two terms, with interest.[52] As a land transfer was sealed by a notarial contract, the seller could easily enforce payment or seize the land sold in case of non-repayment.

I can add here that land transfers were often a means to repay a debt. Examining closely the notarial land sale records for the period 1780–85, one notes that several transactions were agreed upon well under market prize. The mean price for 1 journal of arable land equated to 160 livres. Yet, 33% of transactions for arable land were under market price by at least half the price. And 13% of the sales stipulated a price below or equal to 40 livres, only a quarter of the mean price.

Just like today, buying a house in early modern France was expensive. Most people had to borrow to this end. In the seigneuries, 7.3% of the

[51] ADTB 2E4/268, 269, 270, 428, 429, 430.   [52] ADTB 2E4/268.

total volume was dedicated to this for 5.1% of the contracts. Building, buying, or renovating a house was often done via a cash loan. In 1782, Toussaint Dauphin borrowed money from the local judge, Reiset, for a house he bought from a third party, Jean Pierre Duprez.[53] In this case, it is likely that Duprez needed cash and could not wait for the payment of his house. Some of these transactions were also credit sales. In March 1745, Jean Pierre Chavanne acknowledged he owed 300 livres to Pierre Cattey for a house that the latter sold to the borrower.[54]

Finally, the repayment of old dues and the certification of debt represented a large proportion of the notarial loans, about 12.4% of the loans representing 20.3% of the total volume fall into this category.[55] This practise consisted of the borrowing of money to repay an old debt, to service an existing debt, or to certify an existing contract (i.e., to transform a private deed into a notarial contract). In fact, various situations required parties to renew their loan contracts with the notary.

Many households chose to certify a debt because the initial trust between the parties was no longer the same or no longer existed. After a few missed payments or delays, households turned to a notarial obligation to certify their promissory note.[56] A new deal with new provisions sanctified by the notary's imprimatur might have been necessary to reassure the lender. Similarly, it was an indication to the borrower that they had exhausted their lender's forbearance. Jean Pierre Frery and his wife Madelaine Dermineur had borrowed money on several occasions from Pierre Bettevy, to a total of 420 livres. Several promissory notes from 1768 and 1770 were still standing several years later. In 1777, the parties signed a notarial obligation bundling all the previous debts to form a new one with new provisions.[57] On 12 May 1743, George Monnier from Croix signed a new obligation to Henri Daucourt for 150 livres. The three previous obligations signed in the past were now void and invalid. This new contract probably contained new and revised provisions to satisfy the parties.[58] The renewal of a loan agreement often featured no effective transfer of money.

Note that the certification of loans did not necessarily involve a change in the seniority of the debt. In 1755, Marc Fleury and his wife Anne Michelat and Nicolas Tendon signed an obligation to replace a

---

[53] ADTB 2E4/280.   [54] ADTB 2E4/157.

[55] In eighteenth century Verona, this practise was common as 45% of the new loans were used to repay a debt. Marcella Lorenzini, "The Credit Market and Notaries in Verona in the Second Half of the Seventeenth Century," *The Journal of European Economic History*, 44, 1, (2015): 123–48, p 138.

[56] Fontaine, "Antonio and Shylock," p 51.   [57] ADTB 2E4/444.

[58] ADTB 2E4/157.

promissory note written in 1753. They specified that the promissory note 'is null and void except the seniority of the date'.[59]

Upon an individual's death, their heirs often had to divide and settle an accumulation of outstanding debts. It was common to renew, renegotiate, and extend the existing loan with the original creditor. There were at least two reasons for the parties to do so at the notary. The creditor and heirs might not have known each other well and suffered from a deficit of trust. The lender might then have incentive to turn a promissory note into a notarial obligation. In 1739, the widow Jeanne Francoise Carillon and her son acknowledged together the loan granted their husband and father in 1699 by the local judge, Taiclet.[60] They renewed the loan and promised the reimbursement of ninety-two livres within three years. But, most importantly, in the presence of several heirs owing each a proportion of the loan thanks to the partible inheritance system, the lender was eager to secure his initial transaction further. Not only did the fragmentation of the debt have the potential to increase difficulties for the creditor to retrieve his entire capital, but more importantly, the security used to guarantee the initial loan was now being held by different heirs. Securities, often in the form of land, were legally binding with the notary's imprimatur. There was thus an incentive to register a loan with the local notary to secure the transfer of capital with collateral. Finally, when a borrower died, his creditors lined up in order of seniority. Death and the subsequent writing of a probate inventory listing all claims and liabilities often constituted a good assessment of the situation for creditors, who might not have known about each other's existence until then. A lender with a promissory note might feel their capital could be jeopardized by too many liabilities and too much indebtedness. The lender could choose to write a notarial obligation in order to increase the likelihood of reimbursement and ask for a guarantee from the heirs. Similarly, in the presence of minors among the heirs, tutors often chose to turn to the notary for a debt renewal (5% of the total obligations were made by a tutor representing the interests of its ward). Tutors feared being held accountable and liable if debts were not repaid.

And finally, loan renewals could be bundled up by a single lender in an effort to officialise deferred payments and promissory notes. Jacques Patingre, for instance, was a livestock dealer living in the village of Puis. He raised and sold cows, oxen, and horses. He was one of the biggest breeders – if not the biggest – in the area. Between the 1760s and 1786, he signed 139 notarial contracts, mostly to formalize the deferred

---

[59] ADTB 2E4/194.   [60] ADTB 2E4/156.

payments of his livestock. Sometimes he certified several transactions all at once. On 18 and 19 May 1775, for example, he signed 18 deeds that were in effect deferred payments. One can hypothesize that he used the notary to keep track of his different dealings. As a lot of his clients could not pay outright for the animals they bought from him, he had the incentive to certify their debt at the notary's office to avoid too many payments being dragged on for several years.

Overall, households used notarial obligations for a wide range of purposes. Deferred payments, transfer of capital, and repayment and certification of old debts were the most common reasons to sign a notarial obligation. Like non-intermediated credit, notarial credit featured both crisis credit and premeditated credit.[61]

The Art of the Deal: Contract Terms

Notarial contracts featured several enforceable terms and provisions. Interest rate, securities and pledges, and length of time for reimbursement were among the most important. In theory, each of these contractual obligations had to be respected. Any breach could give rise to judicial litigation and subsequent damages. But in practise, and despite the official and formal character of notarial loans, those terms remained flexible and negotiable.

Interest Rates Provisions

In early modern France, credit markets were supposedly 'priceless', with a price fixed by the authorities.[62] The interest rate was capped at 5% in the entire kingdom; it was the maximum lenders could officially request.[63] Anything above was usurious. In the south of Alsace, this rate was applied to most of the notarial loan contracts. Either people contracted at the maximum rate, or they – less often – opted for an interest-free agreement. Anything in between remained rare.

This price uniformity might appear surprising. De facto, it meant that there was no competition between providers of capital. Promissory notes, parish vestry loans, loans from the hospitals, all featured a 5% interest rate when mentioned. It also meant that debtors presenting better

---

[61] Paul Johnson, "Small Debts and Economic Distress in England and Wales, 1857–1913," *Economic History Review* 46, no. 1 (1993): 65–87.
[62] Hoffman, Postel-Vinay, and Rosenthal, *Priceless Markets.*
[63] Between 1760 and 1766, the interest rate was officially lowered to 4%.

guarantees, larger assets available as collateral, higher savings, or even better morals did not receive lower interest rates.

People paid a fixed price for what was considered a service. Only a few notarial loans were interest free, about 5.5% of all notarial obligations in total. Most of the deeds specifying that no interest would be paid concerned the credit sales of livestock. Yet, some of these loans were free only in appearance. In 1735, Hannelot Levy from Silisheim did not ask for interest in money but in grain when he sold livestock to André Glare.[64] In 1733, the priest Demangeon of Brebotte lent 168 livres to the miller of Recouvrance and his wife.[65] The loan was free of interest for a year. But after a year, if the capital was not reimbursed, the contract stipulated that the borrowers would have to pay the regular 5% interest fee (*l'intérêt composé*).[66]

The 5% cap on the price was the theory. In practise, things were often more complex. Households looked for flexibility. Before the middle of the eighteenth century, there was a great diversity in the guarantees offered, often the result of preliminary negotiations between the parties outside the notary's office. It reflected the needs and strategies of both creditors and debtors. This diversity of arrangements regarding the interest rate often meant greater flexibility *post ante*. For example, in June 1733, the widow Marie Barbe Tourtelier borrowed from the local medical doctor, Lacour, the sum of 300 livres in 'real' money.[67] The widow promised to reimburse her creditor in a year and pledged a selection of her meadows and arable lands as guarantees. The parties also agreed that the lender would receive hay and new growth from the mortgaged meadows and additionally 20 carp as interest.[68] In this case, the mortgaged lands served to pay interest to the creditor. In effect, this compensation in kind might have exceeded the 5% interest rate.

In March 1734, Jean Pierre Chaumé acknowledged that he owed Marc Vareschat 81 livres. Chaumé had bought two young mares from Vareschat. He promised to pay him within two years with an interest of 5%.[69] He backed this deferred payment by pledging all his goods as well as a plot of meadow '*à titre précaire*', a temporary usufruct of the land. This practise, inherited from Roman law, consisted of letting the lender use the land until the contract was fully executed.[70] Here, it

---

[64] ADTB 2E4/155.   [65] ADTB 2E4/155.

[66] Laurence Fontaine, *L'économie morale*. See also Laurence Fontaine, "Espaces, usages et dynamiques de la dette: dans les Hautes Vallées Dauphinoises (XVIIe-XVIIIe siècles)," *Annales. Histoire, Sciences Sociales* 49, no. 6 (1994): 1375–91, p 1385.

[67] ADTB 2E4/155.

[68] In this case, the contract between the parties resembled more an annuity.

[69] ADTB 2E4/155.

[70] René Fedou, *Lexique historique du Moyen Age* (Paris: Armand Colin, 1980).

is interesting to note that in addition to the legal interest, a piece of land also served to pay interest. Either the revenue of the land was considered to be the 5% interest specified or, and this seems plausible, the piece of land was given in addition to the 5% interest. That way, the lender and borrower circumvented the legal ceiling. In 1781, Marguerite Dermineur, a widow living in the village of Suarce lent 400 livres to Jean Pierre Fleury. He promised to reimburse the widow within two years at a 5% interest rate. But the contract also stipulated that he would grant her the usufruct of the land he pledged as collateral as a form of interest. This benefit also seemed to have been added to the 5% rate.

As these examples show, the 5% ceiling could be circumvented. Lenders, borrowers, and notaries could bypass the rules if needed thanks to the vagueness of provisions. Was this flexibility in contracts to the advantage of both parties? The debtor who had pledged a specific piece of land could reimburse the interest in kind. In a world of cash scarcity, this might be advantageous. Yet, the creditor charged more than the legal rate by taking both a payment in kind and in cash. This usurious practise might have been used as a premium to protect himself against moral hazard or to account for important price variations.

Guarantees and Personal Securities

Guarantees were one of the most important features of notarial deeds, as expected given the delayed nature of exchange in credit contracts and the risk of loss of capital. In general, a good reputation as an honest person – having *credit* – was perhaps the most important form of security for the lender.[71] A good reputation for trustworthiness mattered a great deal and enabled the debtor not only to find credit more easily but also, supposedly, to put fewer guarantees on the deed.[72] Reputation allowed the creditor to measure the willingness and commitment of the debtor to repay his debts and secured the transaction.[73] In small rural communities, key information about a person's reputation was relatively easy to come by, thanks to a high degree of social proximity. Despite such prior acquaintance, some information regarding a borrower's assets, capacities, reputation, and prior engagements (such as mortgaged assets with other creditors) could be missing. Moreover, repayment could also be

---

[71] Fontaine, *L'économie morale.*

[72] On reputation and the different meanings of *credit* see especially Clare Haru Crowston. "Credit and the Metanarrative of Modernity." *French Historical Studies* 34, no. 1 (2011): 7–19.

[73] Daniel Lord Smail, *The Consumption of Justice: Emotions, Publicity, and Legal Culture in Marseille, 1264–1423*, (Ithaca: Cornell University Press, 2003).

hindered, delayed, or become impossible because of moral hazard, unexpected conditions, and other factors. The degree of risk for the lender was often high.

Guarantees thus filled various functions. For the creditor, the bond served in the first place to overcome a lack of trust. In case of default, the security could be seized and auctioned to compensate the lender. In a common assumption, 'compensating the truster is often more important than reducing the probability of abuse by the trustee'.[74] For the creditor, the fundamental point was to minimize any error in the prediction.[75] For the debtor, offering sureties sent a positive signal and demonstrated willingness and commitment.

In many instances the value of the lien did not match the amount of the loan.[76] Many transactions featured securities with values that were much higher than the capital sought. One explanation for this phenomenon could be that borrowers aimed to outcompete other potential borrowers by offering larger pledges to the lender. But I would also argue that guarantees were not thought of as an object in jeopardy that could compensate a creditor in case of default. Foreclosures remained rare. I believe, instead, that parties conceived guarantees more as an item that could be exploited and used to repay interest in kind. The intrinsic value of the plot mattered very little in this respect.

Notarial loan contracts often included either a specific security in the form of land, livestock, real estate property such as houses, or simply a general lien of all the borrower's goods ('*tous ses biens meubles et immeubles*'). This latter often included all cumulative and future possessions of the debtor. Land was by far the main form of wealth. A personal guarantee from a third party – a co-signer – might also be added to the deed. In effect, it also meant that households without enough guarantees, with only their reputation to offer, were excluded from such a market. The notarial credit market was reserved for landed and well-connected households.

In the south of Alsace, collateral in the form of *specific* plots of land dominated the guarantees offered until the middle of the eighteenth century. One can posit that the specific plots added to the deed as collateral had been negotiated and chosen by the parties beforehand

---

[74] Karen S. Cook, et al. *Cooperation Without Trust?*, The Russell Sage Foundation Series on Trust, (New York: Russell Sage Foundation, 2005), p 38.
[75] Thomas Parr, Giovanni Pezzulo, and Karl J. Friston, *Active Inference: The Free Energy Principle in Mind, Brain, and Behavior* (Cambridge, MA: The MIT Press, 2022).
[76] Also observed by Fontaine, "Espaces, usages et dynamiques de la dette."

and likely without the intermediation of the notary.[77] This choice could matter to the parties if interest were to be paid in kind.

Before the middle of the eighteenth century, there was great diversity in the guarantees offered, reflecting not only the input of both parties but also the great elasticity of arrangements. Specific plots of land, harvests in kind, livestock, were among the collateral offered. As a result, in traditional communities, collateral provisions remained flexible and negotiable.

From the 1760s onwards, households began to systematically offer a general claim on their assets to their lenders. Male borrowers also increasingly associated their wives with the deed, as we will see in the next chapter. A personal guarantee was also more and more frequent. From the 1760s onwards, more guarantees thus were added. These changes and the deficit of trust are explained further in Chapter 6.

In case of non-repayment and subsequent foreclosure, a judge could seize and auction the specific plot of land mortgaged in priority (see Chapter 5). He was also able to seize and auction more property might this not be enough.

In case of immediate difficulty, some borrowers offered to pay the annual interest in kind via the specific plots mortgaged, especially if they were short on cash. In June 1733, Marie Barbe Tourtelier, a widow, borrowed 300 livres in cash from George Lacour, the medical practitioner of the seigneurie. She offered to pay the interest in kind and specified in the contract which plots would serve this purpose. The designated plots were also offered as security on the loan. As cash was often scarce, paying interest in kind could have been a valid option for the rural population.

In addition to specific plots of land pledged, creditors might require extra security on their loan. In October 1773, George Frossard and Madelaine Mougin, a couple of peasants living in Florimont borrowed 156 livres from Henri Stouff, the village innkeeper. In order to secure the transaction, they pledged all their goods and property. And to reassure their creditor further, their son-in-law agreed to guarantee the loan and acted as security.[78] In April 1778, Joseph Riat and Marie Anne Thevenin, a couple of tailors, borrowed 400 livres from Pierre Bettevy. They also pledged all their goods and property. Was it enough of a

---

[77] Pledging a particular plot to the deed might have been a form of emotional commitment by the borrower. Historians have argued that in partible inheritance regions, peasants were not attached to specific plots but rather to the notion of possession. While this argument sounds reasonable, engaging a particular plot of land, perhaps inherited, perhaps bought, in a risky and uncertain credit transaction could have had emotional significance.

[78] ADTB 2E4/444.

Table 3.4 *Underwriters in the seigneuries of Delle and Florimont, 1730–90*

	Underwriter in Delle	Proportion	Underwriter in Florimont	Proportion
	N	%	N	%
1730–39	21	16	#N/A	#N/A
1740–49	42	23.46	4	7.3
1750–59	55	28.2	10	16.6
1760–69	86	41.54	7	9.86
1770–79	112	39.8	31	15.66
1780–89	250	52.5	65	27.2

guarantee for the 400 livres of capital they borrowed? Probably not because they had to provide not one but two personal securities. In 1748, Jean Jacques Girardot from Joncherey also seemed to suffer from a deficit of trust capital. In order to secure the purchase on credit of a horse from someone living outside the seigneurie, not only did he pledge all his goods, but he also presented 5 underwriters.[79]

Pledges reassured hesitant creditors (see Table 3.4).[80] In the seigneurie of Delle, 38.5% of the contracts featured a guarantor (mean = 320 livres), while the proportion was 18.75% in Florimont (mean = 784 livres). Just like the debtor, they offered their goods and property to secure the transaction.[81]

In case of default, the lender could turn to the underwriters for the payment and even seize their goods if the debtor's property proved to be insufficient. The creditworthiness of the underwriter mattered as much as that of the debtor. Perhaps more importantly I think, a guarantor could also act as a leveller in contract enforcement. This type of security was a means to put social pressure on the debtor and represented therefore an extra incentive to respect the terms of the contract. Today, collective security is used as a strategy by microcredit institutions to force people to repay their loans.[82]

---

[79] ADTB 2E4/159.

[80] Amaury de Vicq and Christiaan van Bochove, "Historical Diversity in Credit Intermediation: Cosignatory Lending Institutions in Europe and North America, 1700s–1960s," *Social Science History* 47, no. 1 (2023): 95–119.

[81] In contrast, in thirteenth-century Barcelona for example, 80.35% of the contracts featured a guarantor presumably because they did not have much land to offer as collateral, Jordi Fernández Cuadrench, "Crédit juif et solidarité villageoise dans les campagnes barcelonaises au XIIIe siècle." In *Endettement paysan et crédit rural dans l'Europe médiévale et moderne*, 1998, 169–82, p 174.

[82] Aminul Faraizi, Taskinur Rahman, and Jim McAllister, *Microcredit and Women's Empowerment: A Case Study of Bangladesh* (London: Routledge, 2013).

Acting as a security on someone's loan, besides being an act of neighbourliness, was not only a great responsibility but also a risky one.[83] In case of default, pledges could turn to the debtor and demand to be compensated. Some obligations were in fact loans between a failing debtor and his pledge as this latter had to repay the borrower's previous debt.[84]

In the later period, the proportion of underwriters appearing on loan deeds jumped to 52.3% in the seigneurie of Delle. It increased in Florimont but not on the same scale. The seigneurie of Florimont was smaller and perhaps villagers did not require this extra provision on their contracts.

A debtor and a pledger held, thus, collective responsibility for a loan. Because of this responsibility and burden, underwriters were often blood-related to the debtor.[85] Not only might it have been easier to convince a relative to act as security, it might also reassure the lender that family pressure would be a leveller in contract enforcement. In addition, inheritance patterns might have played a role. A brother or a sister acting as security on a loan could offer part of their familial estate share in case of default. In March 1750, Joseph Bideaux borrowed 266 livres tournois to wipe out a debt. He asked his brother-in-law to act as underwriter on his notarial loan. A couple of weeks later, Bideaux returned the favour to his relative and became an underwriter on Joseph Duprez's loan. In the seigneurie of Delle, at least 33% of the securities were blood related to the debtor, and 38.5% in Florimont.

Acting as a guarantor seems to have implied a favour to return. Pierre Daucourt and Jean Pierre Chappuis lived in the same village of Croix. In March 1751, they both borrowed cash from Marguerite Vauclair, a widow living in Delle. They acted as each other's guarantor. In April 1760, Pierre Chellet and Jean Pierre Parat borrowed money from the same creditor and also acted as each other's security. These examples of shared security seem to have been common; this system reinforced bonds between households within the community. It also expanded further the network of social obligation and social indebtedness, perhaps being perceived as a mutual obligation or forced mutual help.[86] It is unclear, however, if this system constituted an effective incentive for repayment.

Some individuals acted as pledges for several borrowers. Their social and economic capital might have been such that they could bear witness

[83] Muldrew, *The Economy of Obligation*. See p 160.
[84] Also a practise observed in Saint-Maixent. Le Gendre, *Confiance*.
[85] Also noted by Laurence Fontaine, Introduction, in Berthe, p 15.
[86] Raymond Firth, *Elements of Social Organisation* (London: Routledge, 2013).

for several debtors. Among them, mayors often vouched for their co-villagers. Jean Pierre Bideaux, mayor of Villars le Sec, appeared on three different occasions as a guarantor for debtors not directly related to him.

Several women in our sample also acted as pledgers. In theory, women were legally barred from endorsing such a role, but never-married women and widows did fill this role every now and then. Spinster Elisabeth Girardin vouched for her sister and her husband on a 200 livres tournois loan. Claudine Perrinet, another unwedded woman, guaranteed the 100 livres tournois loan for Jacques Mougin. These women, albeit not numerous, did seem to carry enough social capital and respect – and possibly enough resources – to endorse such functions. Sometimes they were relatives of the debtors; through them, the familial estate secured the transaction further.

Negotiations between debtors and their security took place in the private sphere, outside the notary's office. Little is known about the consensus reached and the motivations of pledgers. How did borrowers approach guarantors and convince them? How much did they reveal about their own finances and projects? One also does not know if guarantors acted as intermediaries in contract brokering. Sources remain silent about these issues.

Length of Time for Repayment

In February 1740, Joseph Schick, a peasant from Fêche-l'Église borrowed 150 livres tournois from Jeanne Françoise Fouchard, a widow living in Delle. Schick intended to repay another – perhaps impatient – creditor with this new loan. Alongside all his goods, he pledged several pieces of land and presented a guarantor to secure the transaction. At a 5% interest rate, Schick promised to reimburse the loan in three years, but it took him nearly twelve years to do so. There is no evidence of a formal judicial complaint on the part of the widow. It is likely that both parties found themselves satisfied with the terms of their agreement. As long as the interest was paid and as long as the creditor did not need to retrieve her capital, the loan was simply 'rolled over', just like an annuity loan. One cannot exclude the possibility that they privately renegotiated the terms of their agreement and added extra compensation, both for the delay and to smooth any eventual irritation on the part of the creditor. Schick could have offered Fouchard some incentives not to pursue her dues at court, offering either money or service. In this specific example, it is possible the widow invested her savings in order to receive a yearly payment assuring her of a regular income. She might have found herself satisfied as long as she received a frequent interest payment. In total, she received at least 90 livres in interest for an initial investment of 150 livres.

In a similar example, in November 1763, Louis Bidaine, a peasant from Courcelles, borrowed 120 livres tournois in cash for an unknown purpose from Pierre Bettevy, the better-off mayor of Florimont. Bidaine promised to reimburse the loan within a year and pledged all his goods. But it took him 23 years to reimburse a capital of 120 livres, which cost him at least 138 livres in interest. Again, there was no evidence the case was ever brought to court.

Examples like these are multiple. In their ledgers, notaries often, but not systematically, wrote the repayment date on the margin of the contract. It appears that writing down the repayment date applied only to contracts that had not been copied for the parties. Parties who did not request a copy had to return to the notary to let him know the debt had been repaid.[87] How many lenders and borrowers informed the notary of this, we do not know. Private receipts acknowledging full repayment could have been exchanged as well.

In Delle, 211 loans (14.4%) specified a settled repayment. For those, on average, it took debtors 56 months (4.6 years) to repay the capital borrowed. In Florimont, 106 contracts out of 624 (16.9%) specified that the debt had been repaid, averaging 88 months (7.3 years). In comparison, promissory notes found in probate inventories had on average a similar time of 5.5 years.

In both seigneuries, most notarial loans specified a short-term deadline, usually ranging between one and three years (see Table 3.5).[88] A few contracts specified a deadline superior to five years. Note that a few loans were to be repaid *ad primam requisitionem* or 'on request'. Overall, the delay for repayment specified in the contract did not seem to have any relationship to the amount borrowed.

In most cases, as it took much longer for borrowers to reimburse, the initial length specified in the contract mattered very little. Some loans were renewed either informally or formally.[89] The parties had the possibility to extend the deadline for repayment before the notary against a fee, via a *prorogation*.[90] How many did resort to this legal device is unclear as these extensions were not included in obligation registers. Lenders and borrowers could also renegotiate the loan informally. Very little documentation about this has reached us. But since the lender did not

---

[87] Le Gendre, *Confiance*, pp 172–75.   [88] This remained stable across time.
[89] The rise in debt litigations in the eighteenth century indicates the difficulty borrowers had in repaying their debt on time.
[90] Le Gendre, *Confiance*, p 186.

Table 3.5 *Duration of the notarial loans in the seigneuries of Delle and Florimont specified in contracts, 1730–90*

	Delle		Florimont	
	N	%	N	%
Less than a year	36	2.4	10	1.6
Between 1 and 3 years	1,282	87.3	281	45
Between 4 and 5 years	56	3.8	31	4.96
Over 5 years	57	3.9	34	5.4
On request	31	2.1	246	39.4
Not specified	5	0.3	11	1.76
Other	1	0.1	11	1.76

seem to have to pursue their rights at court, the rolling over of loans might have satisfied them, as long as the interest continued to be paid.

Repayment delays were not limited to the south of Alsace and were ubiquitous in early modern France.[91] Jean Jacquart characterized this tendency to defer payment for all sorts of loans as a 'natural reaction' on the part of the peasants.[92] In fact, all the strata of society were concerned. In Saint-Maixent, in the sixteenth century, between 23% and 40% of the notarial obligations did not mention a *quittance*, in other words, an acknowledgement that the debt had been repaid.[93] In Strasbourg, out of 259 notarial contracts signed in 1751, 29.2% were repaid within 5 years, 23.4% within 10 years, 29.2% within 10 to 20 years and 18.2% within 20 to 30 years. For a further 105 debts, more than 40% of the total, there were no receipts; were these ever repaid?[94] Every type of transaction was subjected to this delay, almost as a ritualized norm.[95] A repayment deadline was therefore understood as something elastic.[96]

In fact, many loans benefited from 'rolling over', a tacit consensual agreement of both parties.[97] The borrower continued paying annual

---

[91] Ibid., p 190.

[92] Jacquart, "L'endettement paysan et le crédit dans les campagnes de la France moderne," p 285.

[93] Le Gendre, *Confiance*, p 188.   [94] Cited by Fontaine, "Antonio and Shylock," p 51.

[95] Delle and Florimont are not exceptional in this respect. Throughout Europe, individuals struggled to repay their debts on time. See Muldrew, *The Economy of Obligation*, p 174.

[96] Edward Palmer Thompson, "Time, Work-Discipline, and Industrial Capitalism," *Past & Present*, no. 38 (1967): 56–97. The notion of punctuality in repayment might, in fact, be a modern one. E. P. Thompson argued that the industrial revolution modified our perception of time.

[97] This phenomenon has also been observed elsewhere. See Jaco C. Zuijderduijn, "Foreclosures Foregone: Default, Prosecution, and Leniency in a Village in Holland

interest, the principal would remain outstanding, occasional rescheduling of the debt could take place, and the deal was consequently renewed as long as both parties agreed.[98] Agreements were not often renewed before the notary as they would be subject to additional transaction costs with an engrossment fee.[99] Such practises suggest that if the agreed upon exchange term became harsh for one party, parties jointly adjusted by continuing their agreement past the deadline, avoiding an open conflict leading to judicial enforcement. Some of these loans might roll over for several generations, resulting in much indebtedness. In fact, a loan that was renewed continued the binding relation between two households over time.

Evidently, this lasting and binding relationship was not without social consequences. Consider the following example. In 1747, Bernard Liron borrowed 100 livres in cash from the local lord, Gaspard Barbaud. Liron promised to reimburse the sum within a year and backed the deal with a new house in addition to all his assets. A year later, there is an indication in the margin of the contract that the interest had been paid but not the capital. Liron died the same year. The heirs continued to service the debt, and repayments of the capital are made here and there. In 1779, Liron's daughter Marie Liron managed to repay the debt in its entirety. As the domestic of the Barbaud household, it is unclear if she saved enough money or if she had to work without pay to repay the loan. In total, it took 32 years for the family to reimburse the loan and cost at least 160 livres in interest.[100]

As we shall see in Chapter 5, creditors did not actively pursue insolvent debtors in court. Creditors were able to bring their debtors before a judge at a low cost; in theory, filing a complaint before a court was free.[101] But most creditors preferred rolling over the notarial loans. In small communities where the economic and social contexts were highly embedded, most people chose to renegotiate the terms of their agreement rather than pursue dues in court, risking damaging personal ties. Because of the

---

(Sixteenth Century)," Paper for the workshop 'Mortgages in the European countryside, 1200–1700', Cambridge 13 July 2015; Fontaine, "Antonio and Shylock," p 51.

[98] See especially David P. Waddilove, "Mortgages in the Early-Modern Court of Chancery." Chapter 2 "Aspects of Mortgages in Society." Cambridge: Cambridge University, 2014.

[99] We know about the tacit practise of 'rolling over' contracts because the notary wrote in the margin the date of capital repayment, often well after what had been agreed upon. David P. Waddilove, "Mortgages in the Early-Modern Court of Chancery."

[100] ADTB 2E4/444.

[101] Lawyers, however, could be hired for a fee but were not mandatory. More importantly, the loser of a case had to pay the *depens*, a fee to the court. In case of debt insolvency, the creditor won in 99% of the cases.

silence of sources, historians do not know the terms and implications of these out-of-court renegotiations. I suspect that 'rolling over' loans came with a new set of social, personal, and economic obligations binding the parties further. Creditors' forbearance was not confined to the south of Alsace. Here and there across Europe, where justice was also fairly reasonably priced, lenders were willing to wait for their repayment rather than taking their debtors to court.[102]

The rolling over aspect was certainly the most crucial component of the credit relationship. It means that parties implicitly agreed to continue their relationship and to preserve the bond that tied them. Both parties were satisfied with this tacit arrangement (as long as the interest continued to be paid). De facto, the length specified in contracts mattered very little. It meant that people wished to continue their relationship with each other. For the lender, it was the insurance of a regular *rente* but also a form of power over another household. For the borrower, it meant a form of subjection and dependence towards the lender and their family. But it also meant fidelity, in the sense that the borrower hoped tacitly to continue having access to the lender's capital not only in fiduciary terms but also in terms of social capital. A debtor's allegiance to a lender could possibly grant him indirect benefits such as information, networks, and other possible benefits from their cooperation and relationship.

The seigneuries of Delle and Florimont were tight-knit communities with high homophily and endogamy. It is possible that this rolling over mechanism originated in the very nature of the parties' relationships. High sociability might have granted more room for accommodation and flexibility.

Actors on the Notarial Credit Market

After studying loan contracts and their provisions in detail, we move on to creditors and debtors. Who were the households who lent and borrowed money? And how were these households connected to each other? What were the patterns of loan distribution?

Borrowers

Who were the borrowers? Notarial deeds revealed the names, place of residence of the parties, sometimes their professions, and existing kinship relations. The majority of the contracts mentioned the name of the male

---

[102] Muldrew, *The Economy of Obligation*, p 200.

head of the household, but the capital borrowed might very well have benefitted members of his household in one way or another, such as his wife and children, or his domestics and relatives living under the same roof. In traditional communities, a debt was rarely for individualistic purposes.

In both seigneuries, men alone – presumably on behalf of their households – represented an important proportion of the debtors; 50% in Delle and 42% in Florimont. But married couples featuring both spouses also represented a large group of debtors, 39% in Delle and 47% in Florimont. Husband and wife offered not only more guarantees to the creditor but also a joint responsibility. Couples borrowing together were both liable and engaged their common property as well as their lineage property. This means that a woman's dowry and inherited property was at stake in case of difficulties and default. The proportion of married couples as debtors did increase after the 1760s, as we shall see in more detail in the next chapter.

Not surprisingly, the overwhelming majority of borrowers were farmers, mostly landowners; 72% in Delle and 80% in Florimont. These households often needed to borrow in order to purchase land and livestock. Not many were able to make purchases outright. Newly wedded couples often had to borrow money for the acquisition of land and tools upon their marriage. Entering marriage often meant entering indebtedness.

In the seigneurie of Delle, artisans, retailers, service-oriented professions, and the upper strata of the population (i.e., lawyers, judges, administrators, and civil servants as well as the local nobility) represented a non-negligible proportion of borrowers (28%). These individuals often borrowed to make a productive investment or to buy real estate. Jean Claude Girardin, Delle's *'secrétaire de ville'*, for example, owed Anne Arnoux and Christophe Belet 500 livres for a house the couple sold to him in 1743.

Creditors

In both seigneuries, the overwhelming majority of creditors was also male. But like borrowers, men alone tended to act on behalf of their households. Husbands and wives appearing together represented only a handful of creditors. Adding the wife to the deed might indicate that she either intermediated the transaction – often with a family member or a female debtor – or that part of her capital, if not all, was being lent. The son of Florimont's notary, Claude Léonard Joseph Lajanne was 25 years old when he married Justine Paillard in 1783. The bride, on the other hand, was 41 years old. It seems that the marriage was arranged between these two wealthy and locally powerful families. The bride's father was a magistrate sitting on Delle's city council. As a result, the bride brought a significant dowry to the young groom. Within a few months of their marriage, they both appeared as creditors on five different occasions between June 1784 and March 1787. In total, they lent 1,300 livres. In this case, it is possible that the couple invested the bride's dowry in the local credit market. After all, marriage 'was not the product of an obedience to an ideal rule, but the completion of a strategy'.[103] The bride had prior experience of the notarial credit market as she appeared on three occasions as a creditor on her own, a few years before her marriage.

In the seigneurie of Delle, female lenders, regardless of their marital status, signed 19% of the total contracts for a volume of 18.8% of the total exchanged, while in the seigneurie of Florimont female investors appeared on 22% of the deeds for a volume of 26.6%. If we compare these data with those currently available elsewhere, women in the seigneurie of Delle and Florimont lent a little bit more in proportion than did women in Paris around the same period. In early modern Paris, despite women being described as 'rare as lenders', 23% of lenders were female. They provided 20% of the credit.[104] Interestingly, 16% of creditors in Delle and 17% in Florimont were unmarried women, either never married or widows. Overall, if we compare with the figures available for non-intermediated transactions, women lenders chose the notarial credit market as their first choice for their investments. This can be explained by the security such contracts offered. We will explore women's activities in the credit market more deeply in the next chapter.

Alongside sex and marital status, the socio-economic status of the lenders is of significance. Most of the creditors in the seigneuries of Delle and Florimont were farmers. In Delle, 36.3% of creditors had their primary activity linked to agriculture, while they were 54.3% in Florimont. Interestingly, the proportion of farmers decreased over time, especially in Delle. The upper strata, made up of non-manual workers (civil servants, administrators, etc.), increasingly extended more and more credit, mostly to farmers. They invested their savings in the rural market to reap the benefit. They secured their transactions via a notarial contract, mostly because of the difference in status and the trust gap between themselves and their borrowers, the overwhelming majority of the latter being farmers. Yet, this strategy was not the prevalent one until

---

[103] Bourdieu, Pierre. "Les stratégies matrimoniales dans le système de reproduction." *Annales. Économies, Sociétés, Civilisations* 27/4 (1972), 1105–27, p 1107.
[104] See also Dermineur, *Women and Credit in Pre-Industrial Europe*.

the end of the Ancien Régime. We will explore this issue further in the final chapter.

Jewish and Anabaptist lenders, outsiders in the traditional communities of Alsace, also sought extra protection with a notarial loan contract (7% of creditors). Jewish households were especially careful to make their dealings with Christian households official. As we shall see in Chapter 5, Jewish creditors often had to bring their debtors to court in order to extract repayment. Religious minorities using the notary's office were gradually more numerous through the eighteenth century.[105]

Religious institutions such as abbeys, convents, and other monasteries sometimes used the services of the notary for their lending activities.[106] Yet it is possible that they had their own scribes at their disposal, perhaps wanting to keep the financial dealings of their community away from the public eye. The parish vestry did not seem to resort to the notary either, with the exception of a few cases in the seigneurie of Florimont. Some of the parish vestry loans found their way to the notary's ledger. This might be because the notary was often required to write down the parish vestry contracts as well, confusion could have arisen then.

Finally, I must add that very few outsiders were involved in this credit market. The markets were not outward looking and were quite hermetic, no very large loans were made, there simply was no need.

Networks of Exchange

On 12 June 1785, the local judge of Delle, Francois Antoine Xavier Reiset consented to lend 3,000 livres to the court bailiff Francois Xavier Bornot and his wife Marie Josèphe Verney. The couple had just bought a house from the carpenter Ambroise Terrier for the same amount.[107] The two parties signed an obligation at the notary's office, sealing the transfer. The borrowers promised to repay within a year and offered the said house as a guarantee. On the same day, Ambroise Terrier, who had just sold the couple the house, lent 300 livres to Sébastien Cattay and his wife Geneviève Fleury. It is likely that Terrier reinvested part of the down payment he received from his buyers, choosing to secure the transaction with a notarial obligation. Cattay and Fleury promised to repay within 3 years at 5% interest. They pledged all their assets and belongings and, to reassure Terrier further, Cattay's brother

---

[105] Contrary to the village of Holtzheim in northern Alsace, see Boehler, *Une société rurale en milieu rhénan*, pp 1198, 1206.
[106] Something also noted in Boehler, *Une société rurale en milieu rhénan*, p 1199.
[107] ADTB 2E4/280.

Table 3.6 *Homophily in the credit market of the seigneuries of Delle and Florimont, 1730–90*

	Same village (%)		Among kin (%)	
	Delle	Florimont	Delle	Florimont
1730–39	35.1	n/a	7.6	n/a
1740–49	39.8	56.3	11.2	9.7
1750–59	28.7	51.6	7.7	29
1760–69	29.9	50.7	10.1	2.7
1770–79	30.6	37.7	10.7	12
1780–89	27.7	33.5	19.11	28.75

Source: Notarial dataset

acted as a pledge.[108] Terrier went on to sign a second obligation two days later. He lent 700 livres to Joseph Faivre, an innkeeper in Delle.[109]

In another example from 1745, Jean Pierre Cattay and his wife Marie Berger went to the notary to acknowledge a debt of 262 livres to Marie Beuné, their neighbour from Delle. The money owed represented, in fact, several debts incurred over time: an unpaid obligation owed to Beuné's father from 1717, an outstanding promissory note from 1721, some blacksmith's work done presumably by her father, and another loan made by Beuné herself.[110] The next year, in 1746, Jean Baptiste Graff presented himself at the notary's office and acknowledged he discharged Cattay and Berger from their debt to Beuné for 100 livres as he owed money to them.[111] Now instead he owed money to her. The multi-layered debt mirrored the on-going relationships between the two families, but also the incredible complexities of debt ties.

These examples highlight how credit and capital circulated within the local community. Notarial transactions, just like any other sort of transaction, show a great deal of enmeshment suggesting complexities of ties between households. This enmeshment was in fact the result of a small world effect.

Similarity breeds connections in the notarial credit market of southern Alsace. In Delle, more than one third of the transactions took place between people living in the same village. Geographic propinquity was even higher in Florimont where between 40% and 50% of the exchanges occurred between neighbours living in the same village (see Table 3.6). On the graph representing notarial transactions between 1760 and 1790, the majority of orange nodes (seigneurie of Delle) are on one side, while the majority of blue nodes (seigneurie of Florimont) are on the other (see

[108] ADTB 2E4/280.   [109] ADTB 2E4/280.   [110] ADTB 2E4/157.
[111] ADTB 2E4/157.

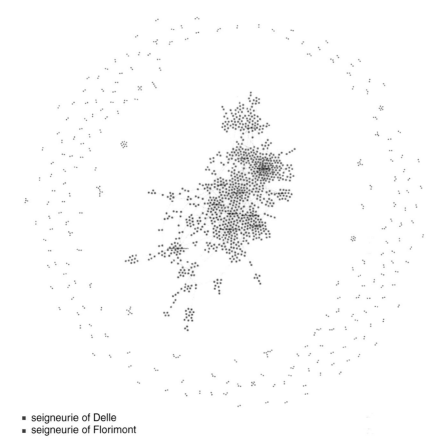

▪ seigneurie of Delle
▪ seigneurie of Florimont

Figure 3.3 Network of notarial loan transactions in the seigneuries of Delle and Florimont, 1760–90.

Figure 3.3). This space proximity is not surprising in a tight-knit community with little contact with distant and external parties. In fact, only a handful of lenders or borrowers came from the outside (represented in green on the graph) meaning there was almost no flow of outside capital in this market. Similarly, between 10% and 30% of the transactions bound kin in a biosocial web. The likelihood that parties knew each other before contracting with the notary is thus very high.

Why Did People Choose to Certify Their Loans with the Notary?

The notarial credit market of Delle and Florimont was smaller than the non-intermediated market. It is clear that parties preferred to contract privately rather than certify their agreements at the notary's office. By doing so, they saved the notary's fee and other associated costs such as transportation and time. One question thus persists: why did people choose to contract at the notary's office against a fee rather than contracting privately? Who turned to the notary? This part explores several possible answers. It first debunks a few common assumptions before turning to other hypotheses.

Common Assumptions Debunked

Because notaries drafted various kind of contracts related to the wealth of individuals, families, and households, scholars have emphasized their exceptional access to a vast array of information.[112] With such information, especially regarding creditworthiness, notaries could presumably overcome asymmetric information, lower transaction costs, and match lenders and borrowers effectively, precluding the role of commercial banks in the nineteenth century. Recent historiography highlights, thus, their role as intermediaries between investors and borrowers.

Yet, peer-to-peer lending brokered by a notary did not necessarily mean that lenders and borrowers did not know each other. In most instances, they did. In an anonymous city like Paris, where locating large capital was made more difficult due to anonymity, lack of strong bonds and therefore trust, notaries certainly did help putting individuals in touch and contributed to reducing asymmetric information. To what extent, is a question that remains open to debate.

In tight-knit rural communities, where most individuals knew each other, were related to each other, and conducted business on a daily basis with each other, notarial brokerage remained limited. In the south of Alsace, the majority of creditors and debtors contracting with the notary displayed not only homophily but also geographical propinquity. More than a third of the loans were made between people living in the same village, tied by strong norms of cooperation, emotional bonds, and kinship. Only a handful of individuals came from villages located more than 25 kilometres from the main town. And even then, in most cases, parties presented a connection of some sort. In 1742, for example, Catherine Carillon and her husband owed 80 livres to a creditor from Paris. Jean Germain Carillon, her uncle, had emigrated there and sold

---

[112] Hoffman, Postel-Vinay, and Rosenthal, *Priceless Markets*; Hoffman, Postel-Vinay, and Rosenthal, "What Do Notaries Do?"; Levy, *The Making of a Market*; Julie Hardwick, *The Practice of Patriarchy: Gender and the Politics of Household Authority in Early Modern France* (University Park, PA: Pennsylvania State University Press, 1998); Hoffman, Postel-Vinay, and Rosenthal, *Dark Matter Credit*.

her, on credit, several plots of land he had inherited. In 1752, the rural doctor, George Lacour, borrowed 650 livres from his sister, who was living and working in Colmar, more than 100 kilometres away. Long distance loans did not necessarily imply that borrowers and lenders did not know each other. Contrary to the old idea of the 'immobile village', individuals, including those living in rural areas were quite mobile.[113]

Evidence of the parties' prior knowledge of each other is also evident in the notarial loan contracts. A significant proportion of transactions could not have been realized simply by notarial brokerage. This is the case, for example, of deferred payments, especially for livestock, which suggest prior negotiations between parties, outside of the notary's office. In April 1760, Francois Deur bought a couple of oxen from Ignace Bluem at the Delle fair. Satisfied with their deal, they went straight away to the notary to sign an obligation. They even brought the animals in front of the notary.[114]

Some authors have argued that the illiteracy rate prevented rural dwellers from drafting written contracts themselves.[115] Supposedly, they preferred turning to the notary to write down the contract. But, as we have seen in the previous chapter, parties that did not know how to read and write could turn to a third person, often acting as a witness on a promissory note. Illiteracy did not hinder contracting and was certainly not a sufficient reason to encourage people to pay a fee to the notary in exchange for his services.

Another reason why this argument is not tenable lies in the actual literacy rate in the eighteenth century. If one considers the signature of both creditors and borrowers at the bottom of contracts, most of the parties knew how to sign their names. This argument for literacy can be problematic as knowing how to write one's name does not necessarily equate to literacy. In addition, knowing how to write did not mean that one knew how to read. In any case, at least one of the parties knew how to sign and possibly knew how to write. The rate of literacy based on signatures increased throughout the eighteenth century. We can possibly discard illiteracy as one of the main reasons to turn to a notary.[116] The notary's intermediation might have served another purpose, other than just the simple act of writing contracts.

---

[113] Jeremy Hayhoe, "Rural Domestic Servants in Eighteenth-Century Burgundy: Demography, Economy, and Mobility," *Journal of Social History* 46, no. 2 (2012): 549–71. Jeremy Hayhoe, *Strangers and Neighbours: Rural Migration in Eighteenth-Century Northern Burgundy* (Toronto: University of Toronto Press, 2016).

[114] ADTB 2E4/222.

[115] Hoffman, Postel-Vinay, and Rosenthal, *Dark Matter Credit*, p 57.

[116] See Elise Dermineur, "Trust, Norms of Cooperation, and the Rural Credit Market."

Several Hypotheses

If people did *not* turn to the notary because they were illiterate or because they lacked information on the other party, why then did they use the notary? Because credit transactions were embedded in the social fabric of communities, multiple reasons prevailed.

A deficit of trust needed to be compensated for by the official seal of the notary. On 25 April 1735, a livestock fair took place in Delle. The fair attracted both farmers and clients from nearby villages. On this occasion, André Glare from Traubach-le-Bas bought a pair of oxen from the Jewish breeder Hannelot Levy from Zilisheim. They agreed on a price, 177 livres. As Glare could not pay outright, they went to the notary of Delle to sign an obligation. The oxen were to be paid for within one year. Glare and Levy probably did not know each other well, they lived more than 20 kilometres apart, and it is unlikely that either of them knew the notary personally. The obligation contract represented a security net for the seller and a proof of good faith for the buyer.[117]

Oftentimes, lenders decided to make their private agreement official via a notarial loan after a few missed payments had occurred or after the initial trust between the parties had been damaged. As difficulties began to appear, certification of the loan reassured creditors that they would be compensated in case of default. But I also think that the certification step was used as a warning to the borrowers, indicating that the lender's forbearance was wearing down. The certification was thus the occasion for the parties to renegotiate the terms of their agreement and add extra compensation(s) for the lender, either included in the price or on the side. In 1774, the miller Richard Kirchner recognized he owed a couple of farmers from Suarce 300 livres. The initial loan had been signed privately via a promissory note six years earlier. The capital was still outstanding. Perhaps because Kircher had missed a few payments, the farmers' forbearance had worn down.[118] Jean Baptiste Grissey and his wife Elisabeth Vauthier had also contracted a loan privately with their neighbour Jean Carnat in 1765 and 1766. They had missed a few payments. Now, the obligation stipulated both the outstanding capital and they had failed to pay; interests would have to be paid on all of this.[119]

Notarial contracts thus filled a deficit gap between the parties. Evidently, this lack of trust might have occurred *ex ante* or *ex post*. Reasons proper to lenders – and to a lesser extent to borrowers – explained the notarization of contracts: deficiency of trust including

---

[117] ADTB 2E4/155.   [118] ADTB 2E4/444.   [119] ADTB 2E4/444.

defiance; doubt over the debtor's creditworthiness and reputation; uncertainty over the borrower's repayment capacity; and absence of repeated exchanges certainly ranked high. But other personal circumstances might have played a role, too.

Parties sought the notary's services to secure a transaction because of the value of the notary's official imprimatur. Certification was necessary if judicial proceedings were required to retrieve the sum loaned. Lenders who presented written evidence at court were almost always assured of a judicial decision in their favour. We have seen that promissory notes were also enforceable at court. The signatures sealed the promise between the parties and made both a promissory note and an obligation contract peremptory. But in case of a repayment issue, the judicial process was different, depending on the nature of the contract itself. For a promissory note, a lender needed to have a court ruling against his debtor first. A notarized obligation, on the other hand, allowed a lender to directly move towards the seizure of the borrower's assets might he wish to do so.[120].

Thus, one of the reasons why a notary's deed might be more attractive than a promissory note lay in the mortgage clause. Securities in the form of land or real estate were legally binding if the notary drew up the contract. If there was a repayment problem, the lender could turn to the securities and have them sold to get reimbursed. We will see in the next chapter that asset seizure remained rare. Again, I believe that certification was a strategy to coerce the debtor to repay, a sort of ultimatum.

The average size of notarial loans was significantly higher than the average of non-intermediated agreements. With higher sums of money at stake, creditors sought to add an extra layer of protection to their loan, even if they had prior knowledge of the borrower. The possibility of turning to the mortgaged assets was an interesting safety net, worth paying a premium via the notarial fee. And the lender could easily compensate for this fee by adding extra provisions. How many notarial loans enter into this category is difficult to say. Those interested in the insurance aspect (i.e., the mortgage clause) might have been the lenders with no other social leverage option to enforce repayment, such as unmarried women or widows for example. It might also have been those with more power in their hands such as the better-off and the new category of non-manual workers. For these creditors, lending might have been purely an investment strategy, depleted of other norms. They counted on the investment of their savings in the credit market to receive a regular *rente*.

[120] Rodolphe Dareste de la Chavanne, "Note sur l'origine de l'exécution parée," *Bibliothèque de l'école des Chartes* 11, no. 1 (1850): 452–58, p 457.

Other reasons led parties to the notary for the certification of their loans. Jacques Patingre was an industrious livestock farmer. He raised and sold cows, oxen, and horses to his neighbours. He was active between at least 1766 and 1789. Over the course of three decades, he appeared on the notary's loan registers 139 times as creditor. He allowed the deferred payment of the livestock he sold. But because he had access to cash, he engaged in redistribution and loaned some of his gains. Overall, his outstanding claim in the notarial register was over 32,000 livres, a fortune. Jacques Patingre always contracted first privately with his clients. He seems to have only certified the debts due with an obligation in case of late payment. Pierre Antoine Laibe and Barbe Charpiot his wife had bought a horse from him; after 4 years, they had still not reimbursed Patingre. The livestock breeder made them contract at the notary.

Family arrangements such as inheritance preference payment was another reason to turn to the notary. Joseph Frossard and his wife Marie Barbe Caillet ran into financial difficulties in the second half of the eighteenth century. They borrowed 300 livres tournois from their daughter Catherine Frossard, a domestic worker in Belfort. The repayment would be effective at the parent's death. The daughter would be given preference and therefore seniority in the division of the estate regardless of her share for the 300 livres tournois owed.[121] She was both an heir and a creditor. In another example, François Charmois promised his wife would be reimbursed 1,000 livres at his death because of land they had sold that belonged to her.[122]

Similarly, a guardian had an incentive to use a notarial contract on behalf of his ward. In early modern France, a guardian's responsibility for children's welfare was a serious commitment.[123] One of the tasks that fell to a tutor was the management of his ward's assets. In case of waste, fraud, or neglect, the guardian was liable for the loss incurred and his own property was at stake. Because a tutor had to report and justify his actions to the family council, he often chose to make official any kind of contract he initiated.[124]

---

[121] ADTB 2E4/410.   [122] ADTB 2E4/157.

[123] Hardwick, *The Practice of Patriarchy*, p 122. Sylvie Perrier, *Des enfances protégées: la tutelle des mineurs en France (XVIIe-XVIIIe siècles): enquête à Paris et à Châlons-sur-Marne* (Saint-Denis: Presses universitaires de Vincennes, 1998).

[124] Charles P. Sherman, "Debt of the Modern Law of Guardianship to Roman Law," *Michigan Law Review* 12, no. 2 (1913): 124–31. See also Christopher Corley, "Preindustrial 'Single-Parent' Families: The Tutelle in Early Modern Dijon," *Journal of Family History* 29, no. 4 (2004): 351–65.

Pauline Vaicle was born in July 1761 in the village of Suarce. Her parents were better-off farmers who owned valuable assets. At some point, her father, Jean Francois Vaicle, even managed to purchase the charge of *sergent seigneurial*, a low police office. Her mother, Marie Françoise Monnier, died in 1765 when Pauline Vaicle was four years old. Her father remarried briefly before dying in 1769. At the age of eight, Pauline Vaicle found herself an orphan without any living siblings. Her maternal uncle Pierre Monnier became her tutor. As such, he took the responsibility to lend part of her capital; some of these loans were in cash, while some were credit sales for grain sold, possibly from her land. In total, Monnier extended over 5,700 livres via 20 notarial obligations on behalf of his ward.

Besides guardians of minors, other individuals needed the official imprimatur of the notary to avoid trouble. This was the case of community officers, borrowing for a purpose related to the village. Parish vestry officials, for example, had to report a summary of accounts at the end of their term, and often found themselves owing money. An obligation acknowledged the outstanding balance and offered greater protection to the institution and the next officers to serve.

Concluding Remarks

In the south of Alsace, the notarial credit contracts show a high degree of flexibility for the parties on at least three levels. First, parties could negotiate the terms of their agreement beforehand and could skirt around the standardized or legally-imposed interest rate limit. Second, parties had the possibility to soften contractual repayment terms through tacit 'rolling over', whereby each side was satisfied with the on-going agreement. Finally, a degree of elasticity existed regarding the guarantees backing loans and the function of such guarantees. Apart from providing an alternative return, also to avoid forfeiture of their lands, borrowers could offer the payment of interest in kind.

But this flexible framework was also available to households with private agreements such as promissory notes, as we saw in the last chapter. Why did households choose to contract for their loans at the notary's office against a fee? In a small traditional community, households sought his official imprimatur. A notarial obligation granted more security to parties in a situation of trust deficit because the lien backing the loan was easily seizable. A notarial obligation also offered a legal protection to lenders whose position required it. Tutors and representatives of communal institutions had to secure the transaction the best they could because the capital exchanged did not belong to them and they were accountable to others.

Finally, some lenders chose to contract with the notary because they used the certification as a leverage tool to seek repayment. Those lenders might have found themselves with little social bargaining capital to coerce debtors into repayment, unmarried women and widows, for example, among them.

4   Women and Credit

Introduction

In contemporary developing economies, women wield significant influence within the peer-to-peer credit landscape. Notably, microfinance institutions exhibit a clear preference for female borrowers, with approximately 95% of the Grameen Bank's clientele comprised of women. Moreover, informal credit networks, such as African stokvels, susus, tontines, and diaspora credit circles across the globe, predominantly feature women as the primary participants.[1] Women often assume the pivotal responsibilities of overseeing daily consumption, healthcare, education, housing, and other essential expenditures. While they actively engage in financial transactions, their role is frequently relegated to a secondary position in societal perceptions.[2]

Some scholars contend that in pre-industrial Europe, women's involvement in credit activities presented the same features. Women remained constrained to 'the small loan market, but a particular and not very prized slice of it, namely, the very smallest loans, (…) the domestic part of the market'.[3] In a context of severe constraints put on women's opportunities and resources by patriarchal institutions and

---

[1] Aspha Bijnaar, "Akuba & Kasmoni. Surinamese Women in a Traditional Banking System in Amsterdam." In Fenneke Reysoo and Christine Verschuur, eds. *Femmes en mouvement: genre, migrations et nouvelle division internationale du travail*, (Genève: Graduate Institute Publications, 2016), 197–202; Svetiev, Dermineur, and Kolanisi, "Financialization and Sustainable Credit"; Caroline Shenaz Hossein and P. J. Christabell, eds., *Community Economies in the Global South: Case Studies of Rotating Savings and Credit Associations and Economic Cooperation* (Oxford, NY: Oxford University Press, 2022).

[2] Célia Drouault, "Aller chez le notaire: un moyen d'expression pour les femmes ? L'exemple de Tours au XVIIIᵉ siècle," *Genre & Histoire* 6 | Printemps 2010, mis en ligne le 24 juillet 2010, consulté le 18 octobre 2023. URL : http://journals.openedition.org/genrehistoire/961.

[3] William Chester Jordan, *Women and Credit in Pre-Industrial and Developing Societies* (Philadelphia, PA: University of Pennsylvania Press, 2016), p 23. See also Fontaine, Laurence. "Women in the micro finance economy of early modern Europe." *Quaderni storici* 46, no. 137(2) (2011): 513–32.

147

practises, women's access to property and capital was often restricted, as was their legal capacity.[4] As such, women's role in the credit market is often deemed ancillary.

Yet, 'there is something distinctive and significant about women's role in credit'.[5] Despite much recent interest, we still know little about women's role as creditors and debtors and the impact of their credit activities for their community.[6] This chapter uncovers the specificities and significance of female credit activities in the south of Alsace. How and why did women participate in credit transactions? What was the extent of female credit capacity and women's abilities in terms of lending and borrowing? What did it mean for rural women to be active agents in credit markets? Previous chapters have emphasized the significance of cooperative norms in traditional communities. Did this pattern also apply to women?

To answer these questions, this chapter considers mainly the notarial loan registers of the seigneuries of Delle and Florimont from 1730 to 1790. It leaves partly aside other source materials such as probate inventories. While probate inventories draw a picture of non-intermediated transactions, they often left women out and are not the most adequate for a gender analysis of credit transactions. Writing the name of the male head of the household rather than a woman, who could be at the origin of a loan, was often the norm. Additionally, marital status was often missing in probate lists of claims and liabilities making it difficult to properly identify debtors and lenders.

Women as Debtors in the Rural Credit Market

'If influential women could readily lend', note Philip Hoffman and his co-authors, 'it is true that they still had difficulty borrowing'.[7] Early modern society and its institutions were fundamentally patriarchal; access to wealth and capital was often more arduous for women, attributable to limitations placed on opportunities and their legal rights. In the

---

[4] Fontaine, Laurence. "Women's Economic Spheres and Credit in Pre-Industrial Europe." In Beverly Lemire, Ruth Pearson and Gail Campbell, eds. *Women and Credit. Researching the Past, Refiguring the Future*, (Oxford: Berg, 2001).

[5] Jordan, *Women and Credit*.

[6] See for example the recent Sara T. Damiano, *To Her Credit: Women, Finance, and the Law in Eighteenth-Century New England Cities* (Baltimore, MD: Johns Hopkins University Press, 2021); Dermineur ed., *Women and Credit in Pre-Industrial Europe*, 2018; Cathryn Spence, *Women, Credit, and Debt in Early Modern Scotland*, (Manchester: Manchester University Press, 2016); Cathryn Spence, *Women, Gender and Credit in Early Modern Western European Towns* (Routledge Handbooks Online, 2017).

[7] Hoffman, Postel-Vinay, and Rosenthal. "Information and Economic History," p 91.

Table 4.1 *Borrowers according to their marital status in the seigneuries of Delle and Florimont, 1733–89*

	N	N %	Volume	Volume %	Mean	Median	Std Dev
Man	994	47.5	370,521.4	49.2	372.75	178.4	835.24
Unmarried woman	26	1.24	4,389	0.6	168.81	133	113.24
Married couple	862	41.26	296,219.09	39.3	343.64	200	678.41
Widow	119	5.70	43,818.20	5.8	368.22	200	641.21
Group	91	4.31	38,184.95	5.1	419.6	279	411.5

Source: dataset: notarial records

absence of capital and landed wealth to secure loans, women's access to credit markets was thus restricted.[8]

Yet, in the south of Alsace, women regardless of marital status represented about half the number of debtors, borrowing 46% of the total capital exchanged (Table 4.1). Considering these figures more closely, marital status played a key role in the allocation of funds. Unmarried women and widows represented the minority of the borrowers. The proportion of married couples, on the other hand, increased throughout the century (Figure 4.1).[9]

Depending on their marital status, female borrowers had different needs, legal rights, and different opportunities to access resources. To grasp the significance of female borrowing activities in the notarial credit market, it is essential to make a distinction between female debtors based on their marital status.

Unmarried Women as Borrowers: Necessities and Emergencies

The category 'unmarried woman' alludes to a heterogeneous group of women who have reached reproductive age, who were able to sell their manpower, who remained single for some time, or who never been married at all. All these women had in common that they lived without

---

[8] Elena Reboul, *Gender and Debt, Past and Present: Financing Social Reproduction*, Doctoral thesis, 2020. See Christian Hagen, Margareth Lanzinger, and Janine Maegraith, *Competing Interests in Death-Related Stipulations in South Tirol c. 1350–1600* (Leiden: Brill, 2018).

[9] It is rather difficult to establish meaningful comparisons with non-intermediated transactions. Probate inventories were household-based documents. There was very little distinction between the spouses' assets. Appraisers often recorded the name of the male head of the household regardless of who precisely had incurred the debt. And marital status was often missing.

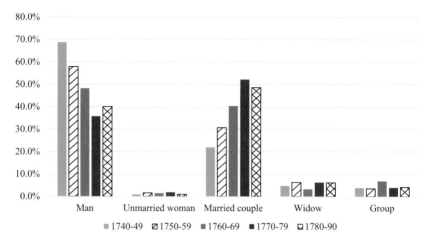

Figure 4.1 Borrowers according to their marital status and according to the percentage of money borrowed per period throughout the period, seigneuries of Delle and Florimont, 1740–80.
(*Source*: notarial records dataset)

the authority and social protection of a husband. Some of them lived with their employers or with their families. A handful lived alone. Some were still minors, living on the familial farm under the authority of their fathers. Some were over the age of majority and could legally carry their interests forward on their own. The authorities, in fact, did not always legally enforce this minority/majority boundary. In the south of Alsace, unmarried women could represent their interests on their own whatever their adult age; they often appeared alone, without a male guardian, in the notary's office.

It is difficult to get a precise picture of how many unmarried women lived in the south of Alsace. Marital status was usually perceived as a transition status. Traditional societies discouraged young people, regardless of sex, from remaining unwed. Marriage was a religious, moral, economic, and natural norm. In rural areas, only a few remained unwed all their lives, either by necessity or by lack of opportunity. It has been suggested that out of the people born between 1575 and 1700 in England, between 13% and 27% remained unwed.[10] In the town of Southampton in 1696, 34.2% of adult women were not married.[11]

---

[10] Amy M. Froide, *Never Married: Singlewomen in Early Modern England* (Oxford: Oxford University Press, 2007), p 2.
[11] Ibid.

Closer to us, in Württemberg, between 10% and 15% of women never married.[12]

Yet, in the south of Alsace, only a few unmarried women acted as debtors in the credit market, accounting for less than 1% of the borrowers in the notarial credit market. The amount unmarried women sought was usually low compared to what other borrowers asked for. Who were the women who sought credit and what were their reasons for doing so?

The most common profile was usually a woman with only a few relatives alive, whose parents were dead, and who was not married (either because of her young age or because of lack of resources). She either had a few social connections left that enabled her to seek credit or she was forced to renew old agreements.[13]

Marie Anne Blanchard is a good example. In April 1743, she borrowed 146 livres in cash from her aunt Anne Eve Betry, her mother's sister. Blanchard's mother passed away in 1732 and it seems that her father was dead too at the time of the loan. Blanchard promised to reimburse her aunt within two years and assured her that the loan was safely guaranteed by her brother's property. Betry allowed her aunt to use her brother's lands as interest payments; there had been no news from him, then in the army, for a while. Like Blanchard, most of the unmarried women who sought credit found it primarily through a familial network but had nonetheless to offer a guarantee of repayment and pay interest fees.[14]

Most unmarried women's loans were motivated by a real need for cash or by an emergency. In April 1751, Catherine Jeanmaire borrowed 190 livres from her sister for her 'needs and necessities'. Her sister Marie lent her the money without asking for interest but nonetheless secured the transaction with land as collateral. We do not know whether Jeanmaire had the opportunity to repay her sister. But this latter would certainly have received the pieces of land mortgaged in the loan at Jeanmarie's death in 1758, not as legal heir but as primary creditor.[15]

In 1777, Marie Liron inherited some property from her deceased parents and with it some debts. Unable to repay the creditors right away, she asked her sister Catherine to advance the money to her for her share, 50 livres. Marie Liron promised to reimburse her sister '*à première requisition*' (upon request) with 5% interest. She also pledged her portion of the parental house to secure the transaction.[16] In another example, Madelaine Michelat from Florimont promised to repay 255 livres to a

---

[12] Ogilvie, Sheilagh. *A Bitter Living: Women, Markets, and Social Capital in Early Modern Germany*. (Oxford: Oxford University Press, 2003), p 296.
[13] Amy Froide reminds us that single women were not alone. Froide, *Never Married*.
[14] ADTB 2E4/157.   [15] ADTB 2E4/409.   [16] ADTB 2E4/444.

couple of bakers living in Delle. The debt was in fact incurred by her brother, by then deceased.[17] Inheriting debts often meant renewing the loan agreement with the creditor before the notary.

Like Marie Liron or Catherine Jeanmaire, unmarried women borrowed cash or deferred payments in the case of necessity or emergency. None of these single women borrowed capital for a productive investment. The amount of money sought was usually low (see Table 4.1). Most of the unmarried women's deeds stipulated either collateral or guarantees (or both) to secure the deal. It is in fact the landed securities that most often enabled the drafting of a notarial contract and conditioned the access these women had to the credit market.

Alternatively, unmarried women who needed to borrow money usually could find access to cash via informal means. Yet, it is difficult to assess exactly how many did relying on probate inventories; these inventories rarely mention marital status in the list of claims and liabilities. And even so, the proportion of women in the claims or liabilities list remained very low. I suspect unmarried women could benefit from the solidarity and empathy of others in case of difficulties. Often young, these women could sell their labour force to another.

Widows as Borrowers: Necessities and Investments

In traditional assumptions and historiography, widows were easily subjected to poverty.[18] Contemporaries ranked widows among the groups characterized by poverty, 'on the same level as orphans, the infirm and the elderly'.[19] Between a quarter and a third of widows were on the verge of indigence in the eighteenth century.[20] Yet, some widows, despite having lost their spouse, could continue living comfortably: they might have inherited a portion of the community property and lineage property; some continued to manage their farms; rural widows could often count on their children for board and lodging. In late-seventeenth century Languedoc, for example, only a handful of widows lived alone.[21] Who were the women who borrowed money and to what end?

---

[17] ADTB 2E4/281.

[18] There were several levels of poverty, ranging from temporary financial difficulty to extreme poverty leading to beggary. On this topic see especially Jütte, Robert. *Poverty and Deviance in Early Modern Europe.* (Cambridge: Cambridge University Press, 1994).

[19] Fontaine, Laurence. "Women's Economic Spheres," p 20.

[20] Beauvalet-Boutouyrie, Scarlett. *Etre veuve sous l'Ancien Régime.* (Paris: Belin, 2001), p 269.

[21] Dousset, Christine. "Familles paysannes et veuvage féminin en Languedoc à la fin du xviie siècle." *Dix-septième siècle* 249, no. 4 (2010): 583–96, p 586.

Table 4.2 *Widows as borrowers in the seigneuries of Delle and Florimont, 1730–89*

	N %	V %	Mean	Min	Max
1730–39[22]	6.9	5.7	149.2	62	300
1740–49	4.7	2.7	153	66	283
1750–59	6.3	6.2	95	42	2,500
1760–69	3.2	4.7	148	48	2,400
1770–79	6.3	9.4	256	18	5,000
1780–89	6.2	4.4	240	56	2,000

Throughout the period, widows represented between 3% and 6% of the borrowers (Table 4.2). They were part of a heterogeneous category of debtors. One of the most common profiles of widow borrowers were women held responsible for their share of the household debt after their husbands' death (18% of the cases by number). These women were often liable for half of the debt.[23] Marie Anne Fahy, the widow of Jean Pierre Bouat, for example, had to repay her share after her husband's death. The couple had contracted a debt to an Anabaptist family; with her spouse now gone, she signed a new loan with the heirs of her creditor.[24]

Many widows found themselves in a similar situation. Upon their spouse's death, it is possible they had inherited assets but also debts; these women needed to keep the land and livestock received to continue making a living. Some widows might have been forced to sell a few plots to repay pressing debts. Yet, many of these women chose to renegotiate the debt with their creditors. Anne Herbelin, for example, had to renegotiate with the priest of Courtelevant for her share of the household debt, 164 livres. She signed a new notarial obligation with him stipulating the new conditions. They agreed on a repayment deadline of 6 years. Her house was offered as collateral.[25]

In matters like this, creditors displayed understanding and flexibility. Many were willing to renegotiate the debt with a widow, continuing the relationship with the family and its new head. Creditors could certainly take advantage of their position by asking for new compensation. Yet,

---

[22] Data available only for the seigneurie of Delle.

[23] In the seigneuries of Delle and Florimont, the customary law stipulated that a widow inherited a third of the community property. Therefore, she also inherited a third of the debt. However, if she had signed loans along with her husband or if they decided to divide the community property in half in their marriage contract, she was held responsible for half of the debt.

[24] ADTB 2E4/280.   [25] ADTB 2E4/409.

debt renegotiation was also a means to avoid losing money; creditors were better-off renegotiating the initial agreement, continuing to receive regular payments. Forcing a debtor to sell off her land to repay a loan would reflect badly on the creditor within the community. Creditors' and widows' interests certainly met half-way.

Another group of widows were those in a delicate financial situation, who sought credit primarily from their relatives, their first circle of interaction. Marie Michelat, the widow of Henri Monnier from Croix acknowledged that she owed sixty-six livres to her daughter. Vuillemette Monnier delivered cash to her mother on several occasions in order to help her cope with her recurrent difficulties.[26] They chose a written notarial deed that authenticated the debt in the case of the mother's death. Monnier was not an heir but a creditor, the repayment would not impinge on her share of the inheritance. Using the notary for a debt contracted with a family member was a means of last resort. Many small debts between kin remained incurred without certification.

Widows experiencing difficulties could also turn to their neighbours. Marie Anne Erard borrowed some cash from Joseph Paschaly to buy grain. The loan amounted to forty-two livres and had to be repaid within a year. Not only was the widow obliged to sign a notarial obligation, she also had to mortgage a specific plot of land and bring a guarantor.[27] Widows who borrowed out of necessity might have attracted suspicion. Creditors were eager to ask for greater guarantees as an insurance against non-repayment.

Another group consisted of widows who borrowed to make a productive investment (18% of the cases by number). Catherine Bandelier bought a piece of meadow from Pierre Vuillaumier for the amount of eighty-one livres and twelve sols.[28] Vuillaumier deferred the payment and the widow had three years to repay him. Jean François Montandon, the miller of Grosne, sold two bullocks to the widow Anne Marguerite Monnier. The miller agreed to defer part of the payment. The widow had to reimburse sixty-six livres within two years. The very next year, the miller had received his payment in full.[29] We find, therefore, some widows who were borrowing money in order to make investments to ensure the continuity of their business. As the heads of their farms, widows were now fully in charge.

Overall, even if some widows sought credit for their investments, many of them lacked the necessary resources to secure their transactions. The credit market was open to widows who were morally and financially

[26] ADTB 2E4/158.   [27] ADTB 2E4/257.   [28] ADTB 2E4/222.
[29] ADTB 2E4/156.

creditworthy, with landed guarantees and pledges ready to stand for them, undoubtedly a difficult combination for some of them. In the seigneurie of Delle, a third of the widows who borrowed had to bring a third-party underwriter with them. Despite the legal capacity conferred by the state of widowhood, the material aspect remained an issue for some of these women. They had to use a guarantor as a proxy of wealth.

Married Women as Borrowers: Economic Partnership and Patriarchy

Marriage in early modern Europe, and above all in traditional communities, was considered as a multi-utilitarian partnership between two individuals. It was the legal basis and unit for biological reproduction and inheritance that sustained community survival. But more importantly, it was a survival alliance between two individuals. Each spouse fully collaborated with the other.[30] They actively participated in all the activities of the household, from chores to remunerated tasks, often but not always according to gendered division. Individualism had no rightful place. In this respect, women have always been considered as the partner who needed this partnership the most to avoid destitution. Yet, couples borrowing together present another picture.

Married women in early modern France could not legally borrow money without their husband's permission. But many of them turned out to be key in the allocation of capital.[31] In the south of Alsace, the proportion of married women as borrowers increased dramatically throughout the eighteenth century. Why was there such an increase in married couples signing deeds at the notary? Married couples not only sought more funds but were also gradually more numerous in doing so. This phenomenon could be observed in both seigneuries and the shift occurred at the same time (Figure 4.2).

Contextual conditions and factors such as inflation, high demographic pressure, fragmentation of lands, undoubtedly pushed more and more people to locate available funds in the credit market. But how and why did married couples become the main debtors in the second half of the eighteenth century? Why did this particular group of debtors come to

---

[30] Maria Ågren and Amy Louise Erickson (eds.), *The Marital Economy in Scandinavia and Britain, 1400–1900* (Burlington, VT: Ashgate, 2005).

[31] On married women see particularly Marjorie McIntosh, "Women, Credit, and Family Relationships in England, 1300–1620," *Journal of Family History* 30, no. 2 (2005): 143–63; Gordon DesBrisay Thomson and Karen Sander Thomson, "Crediting Wives: Married Women and Debt Litigation in the Seventeenth Century," in Elizabeth Ewan and Janay Nugent, eds. *Finding the Family in Medieval and Early Modern Scotland* (Aldershot: Ashgate, 2008), 101–14.

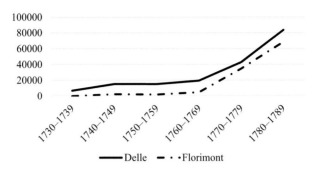

Figure 4.2 Volume of money borrowed by married couples in the seigneuries of Delle and Florimont, 1733–89.

monopolize almost half of the capital available in the credit market? Peasants had increasingly mortgaged a good deal of their land to secure their transactions in the seventeenth and beginning of the eighteenth century. Some pieces of land had been mortgaged for long periods of time, and some may very well have been over-collateralized. In the absence of central registers, creditors had little information about this phenomenon. In the meantime, the numbers of default proceedings at court increased after the 1760s (see the next chapter). In this context of lack of information and trust deficit, creditors were eager to secure their investments through new guarantees.

In the 1730s and 1740s, most of the notarial obligations contained specific mortgage guarantees, usually land. At the end of the period, however, the notary laconically inscribed on most contracts that the debtor(s) would mortgage '*tout ses biens tant meubles qu'immeubles*' (all his property, both movable and immovable). Third party underwriters were also gradually associated with the deed. And women's lineage property became even more interesting to creditors, especially because of their dowries. There was a dramatic increase in the number of married women who were involved in loan deeds after the 1760s. Husbands and wives borrowed together, offering greater insurance to their lenders. Mortgaged lands no longer represented enough of a guarantee. And married women's property (mostly un-mortgaged plots of land and cash either inherited or through dowries) now represented an additional and perhaps better guarantee in the eyes of creditors. Finally, and perhaps more importantly, lenders could seek repayment by turning to the widow for her share of the debt in the case of her husband's death. If a husband borrowed money on his own, the repayment fell to his heirs. Following the partible inheritance system, his wife, then, was responsible for only a third of the debt but could in theory refuse the inheritance and let down the creditors. His children were liable for the other two thirds. But if a husband and his wife signed a loan together, she became responsible for half of it. As such, she became a joint-partner.[32]

Between 1786 and 1788, Pierre Bandelier and Catherine Vuillaumier from Lebetain borrowed cash on three occasions for a total of 360 livres. All their assets were pledged to secure the transactions and two out of the three loans featured guarantors.[33] Bandelier, the husband, never appeared alone. To make the deal with borrowers, married couples added increasingly more guarantees.

Similarly, in May 1781, Henri Fahy borrowed 336 livres from a wholesale merchant in Delle. He had two years to repay the capital plus the interest.[34] Yet, in December 1784, the debtor reappeared again in the notary register for a new loan with the same creditor. This time the amount was 348 livres. Perhaps Fahy failed to deliver the repayment and this was a loan renewal rather than a new transaction. But the most interesting difference was that now Fahy added his wife to the deal. Jeanne Marie Bourquin became liable for half of the loan.[35] It indicates that the lender was looking for insurance of repayment in the future.

One may legitimately wonder if married women were forced to sign loans along with their husbands. Considering the traditional and patriarchal nature of rural societies, this is a legitimate question. A few examples help us to understand the contract mechanisms. In April 1770, André Duprez and his wife borrowed 200 livres from the local judge in order to buy two new steers for their farm. In January 1778, Pierre Joseph Rouge consented to extend credit to a couple of peasants, Ignace le Jeune and his wife, Marie Catherine Surlet, who wanted to build a new house. In August 1780, Jean Baptiste Girardin and his wife Sophie Erard bought several items for their inn from a merchant. These three examples illustrate the partnership existing between husband and wife. Both benefitted from the loan. Credit was definitively an integral part of the household's daily lives both as a leveller and as a survival strategy.

Women had always contributed to their households' revenues in one way or another. Signing an official deed at the notary perhaps made them more responsible as they were held liable for half of the debt. A few scholars have underlined the fact that their property was at stake and therefore this represented a sign of submission. I rather think that women became critical 'business' partners at this point. The fact that women's

[32] Elise Dermineur, "Widows' Political Strategies in Traditional Communities."
[33] ADTB 2E4/281.   [34] ADTB 2E4/279.   [35] ADTB 2E4/280.

lineage property and assets were at stake did not necessarily represent a reinforcement of patriarchy, but rather a breach of it. Women retained the right not to sign the deed if they did not want to; I did find evidence of aborted deeds because of the wife's refusal. But, more importantly, women were able to withdraw their assets by requesting a legal separation of property before the judge if they considered that the financial situation of their household was endangered by their husband's decisions.[36] To a larger extent, the fate of these indebted households forced to pledge all their assets and properties subjugated them not to patriarchy but to an economic system in which they began to lose control over their own agency and fate.[37]

Finally, this part closes by asking if female debtors did repay their debts. Answering this question is difficult. We know that debt repayment in the early modern past was an issue for many households. Yet, there is no direct way to appreciate female repayment. If we compare judicial and notarial records, one can highlight some general trends. Widows seem to have had a hard time repaying their debts, which explains the prudence of creditors in the examples mentioned above. The proportion of unmarried women as debtors in notarial records is almost equivalent to their proportion in judicial records. Married couples, on the other hand, did seem to prioritize notarial debt repayment. Their proportion as defendants at court was lower than their proportion as debtors. It is not impossible that repayment issues for married couples were recorded by scribes writing only the name of the male head of the household in debt litigations (Figure 4.3).

If women had access to the credit market as borrowers, they also played a key role in the extension of credit as lenders. Marital status, once again, remains a key tool of analysis.

Women as Creditors in the Rural Credit Market

In fourteenth-century Ghent, women accounted for 16% of its money-lenders. In Writtle, an English village, female lenders represented 14% of creditors.[38] In fourteenth-century Nottingham, this proportion oscillated between 8% and 14%.[39] In Paris, 23% of female lenders provided 20%

---

[36] On this topic see especially Hardwick, Julie. "Seeking Separations."

[37] Dermineur, "Women in Rural Society"; Elise Dermineur, "Les femmes et le crédit dans les communautés rurales au 18e siècle," *Traverse Revue d'Histoire - Zeitschrift Für Geschichte* 2 (2014): 53–64.

[38] Jordan, William Chester. *Women and Credit*, p 20.

[39] Teresa Phipps, "Creditworthy Women and Town Courts in Late Medieval England." In Elise Dermineur, ed. *Women and Credit in Pre-Industrial Europe*, (Turnhout: Brepols Publishers, 2018), 73–94, p 79.

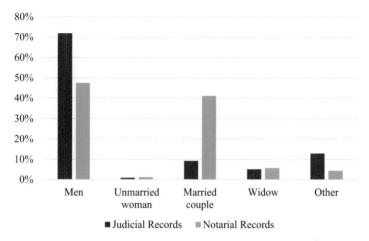

Figure 4.3 Proportion of debtors in notarial records and defendants in judicial records according to marital status, 1680–1790.

of the credit volume in the eighteenth century.[40] And in Milan, women were 15% of creditors in the 1770s.[41] How many female lenders were in the South of Alsace? The same range can roughly be found in Delle and Florimont. Overall, women signed 19% of the notarial obligations extending 21.5% of the capital (Table 4.3). Once again, marital status played a key role in the distribution of loans.

Were women useful to the development of the economic life of their community and why did peasants need female capital? Considering the entire period, the involvement of female moneylenders increased progressively both in term of numbers and in terms of volume, indicating that their assets were indeed sought after (Figure 4.4).

Unmarried Women: Credit and Empowerment?

Scholars have underlined the dynamism of unmarried women in credit allocation.[42] In seventeenth- and eighteenth-century Southampton, 45%

[40] Philip T. Hoffman, Gilles Postel-Vinay, and Jean-Laurent Rosenthal. "Private Credit Markets in Paris, 1690–1840." *The Journal of Economic History* 52, no. 2 (1992): 293–306, p 300.
[41] Marcella Lorenzini, "The Other Side of Banking: Private Lending and the Role of Women in Early Modern Italy." In *Change and Transformation of Premodern Credit Markets: The Importance of Small-Scale Credits* (Heidelberg: heiBOOKS, 2019), p 185.
[42] Elise M. Dermineur, ed. "Women and Credit in Pre-Industrial Europe: An Overview," in *Women and Credit in Pre-Industrial Europe* (Turnhout: Brepols Publishers, 2018), 1–18.

Table 4.3 *Marital status and the allocation of capital in the credit market of the seigneuries of Delle and Florimont, 1733–89*

	Count	N %	Sum	Sum %	Mean	Standard Deviation
Man	1,637	78.3	577,607.25	76.7	352.84	724.09
Unmarried woman	211	10.1	64,004.20	8.5	303.34	568.62
Married couple	74	3.5	40,663.10	5.4	549.50	1383.99
Widow	121	5.8	57,583.10	7.6	475.89	809.01
Group	15	0.7	6,172.85	0.8	411.52	476.75
Institution	34	1.6	7,102.14	0.9	208.89	226.02

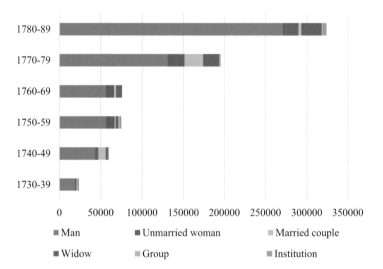

Figure 4.4 Creditors in the seigneuries of Delle and Florimont according to their marital status by volume lent 1730–89.

of single female testators mentioned loans due to them.[43] A similar percentage can be found in British cities such as Bristol, Oxford, and York.[44] In seventeenth-century England, 'single women had on average 73% of their personal assets tied up in lending'.[45] Few estimates are currently available for rural areas. In the south of Alsace, unmarried women and widows represented the majority of women who extended

---

[43] Amy M. Froide, *Never Married*, p 130.   [44] Ibid.
[45] Judith M. Spicksley, "'Fly with a Duck in Thy Mouth': Single Women as Sources of Credit in Seventeenth-Century England" *Social History* 32, no. 2 (2007): 187–207, p 202.

Table 4.4 *Single women as creditors in the seigneuries of Delle and Florimont, 1730–89*

	Number	N%	Mean	Volume	V%	Min	Max
1730–39	11	8.4	153.64	1,690	7.2	60	300
1740–49	22	9.4	168.95	3,717	6.2	60	700
1750–59	30	11.8	342.50	10,275.1	13.7	48	3,998
1760–69	33	11.9	292.76	9,661	12.8	39	2,701
1770–79	59	12.3	341.36	20,140.1	10.3	50,7	6,000
1780–89	56	7.8	330.73	18,521	5.7	50	1,880
	211			64,004.20			

Source: notarial dataset

credit. And unmarried women ranked before widows.[46] They signed 211 notarial obligations (10.1%) lending 8.5% of the total capital.

In theory, minors of either sex (under twenty-five years old) could not sign contracts without the express authorization of their fathers. Once they reached their majority, men and women could contract and manage their property under their own name. Unmarried women above twenty-five years old could, for instance, borrow and lend money on the credit market without being accompanied by a male relative.[47]

Looking closely at the data, the number of unmarried women lending money increased throughout the eighteenth century. In the second half of the eighteenth century, they also lent more on average per contract (Table 4.4).

Being able to lend money supposed sufficient financial means. Yet, young and single people had limited access to capital. Marriage remained the main determining factor in transferring parental assets to wedded couples. The origins of the money invested is thus of interest. Where did unmarried women find the necessary resources to have surplus to lend? While most of the unmarried female creditors had a limited lending capacity as the mean per contract indicates, several profiles of single women creditors can be drawn out.[48]

---

[46] Amy Froide also remarks that in Southampton single women loaned out more money than widows. Froide, Amy M. *Never Married*, p 133.

[47] Most of the single women encountered in the notarial records, however, extended credit in their own name without the assistance of a male relative, suggesting that either they were all over the age of twenty-five, or that both the notary and the debtors were not particularly attentive to their gender and legal rules.

[48] William Jordan argues that women were providers of small or 'domestic' loans. But their importance, despite their limited lending capacity, should not be overlooked as these

First, many of these women invested their wages in the local credit market. In the seigneuries of Delle and Florimont, young men and women often worked as domestics in wealthy farms or in small shops before establishing their own households.[49] Young women in particular were numerous in turning to this option, as their domestic wages contributed to their dowries.[50] Elisabeth Bettevy, daughter of better-off peasants, for instance, signed an apprentice contract with a *maîtresse tailleuse d'habits* (female master tailor) who lived in Porrentruy, a neighbouring town located in a Swiss canton.[51] Even if some of these young domestics had to emigrate to enter service, they remained strongly connected to their native villages. Marie Anne Vilbois, a cook in Delle, agreed to lend 200 livres to one of her relatives in Lachapelle-Sous-Rougemont, the village she was from.[52] Marguerite Duprez, a domestic in Delle, extended credit to people from her native village on several occasions, maintaining thus a strong bond.[53] Those who migrated were able to inject their savings into the local credit market of their native village.

Olwen Hufton estimates that 'in Brittany a farm *servante* could expect about twenty livres annually, in the Sologne she could expect anything from 60 to 90 livres [...] A servant spinner or the type who was an industrial employee housed by a master carder could expect about 100 livres as she could in Bordeaux'. Hufton also states that 'normally a girl expected to work for fourteen to sixteen years before marriage'.[54] In Alsace, Jean-Michel Boehler found that the monthly wage of a female servant varied between 13 and 18 livres, between 156 and 216 livres annually.[55] In Florimont, Barbe Bettevy, employed in the service of the seigneur, earned 100 livres per year. The annual wage was often received in cash. Female domestics could accumulate a substantial capital over the years.[56] The savings amassed could not be kept safely at home and it was undoubtedly more secure invested in the credit market. As Laurence

---

loans did serve a purpose as well. William Chester Jordan, *Women and Credit*, p 23. See also Spence, *Women, Credit, and Debt*, chapter 5.

[49] Labour service was a common feature for early modern rural young women. Allyson M. Poska, *Women and Authority in Early Modern Spain: The Peasants of Galicia* (Oxford: Oxford University Press, 2006), p 60.

[50] Rural domestics usually received room, board, and clothing, in addition to a small salary every year. The literature on domesticity is vast. See especially Bridget Hill, *Servants: English Domestics in the Eighteenth Century* (Oxford: Clarendon Press Oxford, 1996). R. C. Richardson, *Household Servants in Early Modern England* (Manchester: Manchester University Press, 2010).

[51] ADTB 2E4/389.   [52] ADTB 2E4/257.   [53] ADTB 2E4/279 and ADTB 2E4/280.

[54] Olwen Hufton, "Women and the Family Economy in Eighteenth-Century France," *French Historical Studies* 9, no. 1 (1975): 1–22, p 6–7.

[55] Jean-Michel Boehler, *Une société rurale en milieu rhénan*, p 1045.

[56] To the annual wage paid in cash, should be added room and board, and some clothing.

Fontaine puts it, female creditors were at the heart of a system of capital redistribution.[57] Overall, single women invested their income in the credit market to keep it safe, and also to make a small profit thanks to the payment of annual interest in the prospect of a future marriage.

Marie Margueritte Beuné is a good example. She lent 512 livres in May 1745 to three different creditors, thus diversifying her investment. In November 1747, she married Antoine Betevy and could count on her returns from the credit market to increase her dowry and her new household's capital.[58] Her assets returned a small profit into the bargain.

Marguerite Duprez, the domestic working in Delle in the earlier example, also opted for this strategy. She was born in the village of Saint Dizier L'Evêque in 1739.[59] The eldest of at least six siblings, she was sent to the town of Delle to enter service. As such, she accumulated some savings and was able to extend credit at least twice. In November 1777, she lent 120 livres to Joseph Tallon from her native village. She secured her investment by asking for a guarantor. Tallon promised to repay her within a year.[60] Six years later, she lent 220 livres in cash to a couple of innkeepers from Lebetain. The pair promised to repay her in a year. The transaction was also secured with a guarantor.[61] In January 1786 Marguerite Duprez married Joseph Berger, a baker and a widower from Delle.[62] She had probably worked in service for over ten years, amassing savings for her dowry. Her marriage contract specified that the bride contributed 600 livres. This money remained her own property.[63] Rosenthal observes that 'quantitative analysis of credit activity suggests that individuals used these markets to invest their savings and withdrew their funds when they needed to provide for their children'; in the case of single women, it is likely they withdrew their money in order to get married, demonstrating a certain independence from their families, opportunities in the labour market, and an appreciation for investment and the protection of their assets.[64] Thanks to the greater monetization of the local economy, and its greater penetration in rural areas throughout the eighteenth century, domestics were truly at the heart of the redistribution system.

Some of these unmarried women – a minority though – investing their capital in the credit market were seeking regular *rentes* in lieu of labour to assure independent living. This phenomenon is rather well-documented among women of the urban bourgeoisie and women of the

---

[57] Laurence Fontaine, *L'économie morale*, p 156.   [58] ADTB 2E4/157.
[59] ADTB Registre paroissial Saint Dizier l'Evêque 090 E-dépôt GG1–8.
[60] ADTB 2E4/279.   [61] ADTB 2E4/280.
[62] ADTB Registre paroissial 033-E-dépôt GG1–5.   [63] ADTB 2E4/525.
[64] Rosenthal, "Rural Credit Markets and Aggregate Shocks," p 305.

nobility.[65] Marie Elisabeth Taiclet was the daughter of the bailiff of the seigneurie of Delle, Pierre Francois Taiclet. Born in 1725, we find evidence of her involvement in the credit market after the death of her parents. From 1762 to her death in 1779, Marie Elisabeth Taiclet extended credit 22 times for a total amount of 4,568 livres, making her one of the largest portfolios in the seigneurie. She extended credit to artisans and peasants living in different villages around Delle. Most of her contracts had fixed-term repayment provisions and stipulated interest fees and collateral ensuring both profit and security. It is possible the notary, a close acquaintance of hers, managed to find safe clients for her investments. Marie Elisabeth Taiclet remained unmarried throughout her life.[66] She could potentially count on her investments in the credit market to generate an annual income, which in turn contributed to her independence. Women such as Taiclet belonged to the upper strata of the rural community and had capital to make use of. Their families had been active in lending before them and they followed a path already set.

Property and money inherited constituted a source of available capital for some unmarried women. In seventeenth-century England, inheritance was the main motivation for single women to engage in lending activities.[67] It is rather difficult to know precisely the provenance of the capital lent on the credit market. We find traces of legal guardians lending the inherited capital of their young wards, tasked with making it fructify on behalf of the minors. Yet, they had to make sure not to put the assets at risk. Pauline Vaicle was four when her mother died. She was eight years old and the only child of the rural seigneurial sergeant Jean François Vaicle, when her father died. He left his daughter both money and property.[68] Pierre Monnier, her guardian, invested part or most of this inheritance in the credit market. On her behalf, capital was extended to several individuals, diversifying her investments. When in 1783 she married Jean Claude Simon Dadez, the son of a rich *laboureur*, she was able to bring a significant dowry to her new household as her initial capital had grown over the years.[69]

The amount of money lent by unmarried women was usually small when compared to men or widows. Unmarried women had not yet accumulated

---

[65] Ann M Carlos, Larry Neal, "Women Investors in Early Capital Markets, 1720–1725," *Financial History Review* 11, no. 2 (2004): 197–224. Lorenzini, "The Other Side of Banking." In Anne Laurence, Josephine Maltby, and Janette Rutterford, eds., *Women and Their Money, 1700–1950: Essays on Women and Finance* (London: Routledge, 2008).

[66] ADTB 0033 E-dépôt GG1-5. She died in 1779 at fifty-five years old, unmarried.

[67] Judith M. Spicksley, "Fly with a Duck in thy Mouth," p 198.

[68] ADTB Registre paroissial de Suarce, 095 E dépôt GG 1-5. Her mother had previously died, her father remarried Anne Marie Grimont in 1767 (ADTB 2E4/391).

[69] ADTB Registre paroissial de Suarce, 095 E dépôt GG 1-5.

enough capital to make bigger loans. Most of the active single women creditors were rather young and participated in the credit market before getting married. Many young women (and young men) waited until their parents died before getting married, as lineage property often determined matches. Unmarried women creditors invested their domestic wages in the credit market for at least two reasons. First, it was unsafe to keep cash at home, even if in well-hidden places, as it could be stolen or even used by family members and never reimbursed. Second, unmarried women placing their wages in the credit market could hope to make a profit through fructifying their capital, indicating their good management of their own assets. On the other hand, spinsters who grew older without marrying, and thus had no children, might decide to invest their small assets in the credit market, perhaps to provide security for their old age, a strategy that widows also employed.[70] Finally, single women's attractiveness as creditors came from cash generating labour and accumulating capacities, especially since domestics did not have to pay for board and lodging. Finally, I should also add that these women who extended money in the credit market could bring this experience with them when they entered matrimony.

We might therefore wonder whether single women with regular incomes, such as domestics and rural workers, and/or with inherited assets, were constrained to extending credit to their relatives.[71] Bernard Derouet suggests, for instance, that in regions where partible inheritance was applied, women had to give up their pretentions to their parents' land in favour of their brothers.[72] Were single women constrained to extending credit to their relatives as a result of their lack of spousal support and their so-called vulnerability because of their sex? Were they in a position to resist such demands? Points of comparison are currently lacking to answer this complex question.[73] In the seigneurie of Delle,

[70] Rosenhaft, Eve. "Did Women Invent Life Insurance?: Widows and the Demand for Financial Services in Eighteenth Century Germany." In David R. Green and A. Owens, eds. *Family Welfare: Gender, Property and Inheritance since the Seventeenth Century.* (Westport CT: Praeger Publishers, 2004): 163–94.

[71] See for example Wherry, Seefeldt, and Alvarez, "To Lend or Not to Lend to Friends and Kin."

[72] Bernard Derouet, "Le partage des frères: héritage masculin et reproduction sociale en Franche-Comté aux XVIIIe et XIXe siècles," *Annales. Histoire, Sciences Sociales* 48, no. 2 (1993): 453–474.

[73] In England, Holderness found that 40% of lenders and borrowers were blood related, while Wrightson and Levine counted 17% of loans contracted by family members in a British village. B. A. Holderness, "Widows in Pre-Industrial Society: An Essay Upon Their Economic Functions," in Richard M. Smith, ed., *Land, Kinship and Life-Cycle*, 423–42 (Cambridge: Cambridge University Press, 1984), p 441. Keith Wrightson, and David Levine, *Poverty and Piety in an English Village: Terling, 1525–1700.* (Oxford: Oxford University Press, 1995), p 100.

Table 4.5 *Distribution of same family obligation contracts in the seigneuries of Delle and Florimont, 1730–90, based on the marital status of the creditor*

	N %	Sum %	Mean
Man	6.5	6.7	364.50
Unmarried woman	14.7	14.3	294.81
Married couple	21.6	17.3	439.00
Widow	6.6	35.7	275.63
Group	20	19.8	469.33

Source: notarial dataset

10.6% of single women extended credit to their relatives, while 23.7% did so in Florimont; but in this latter, households were also less numerous, which in turn biases the significance of this percentage. As a point of comparison, Spicksley found that a third of single women lenders provided credit for family and kin.[74] While these figures were slightly higher than average, nothing indicates that family members took advantage of the incomes of single women (Table 4.5).

Compared to male creditors, single women did extend credit more often to their relatives (Table 4.5). They lent money to people in their immediate circle of interaction. Yet, the fact that unmarried women took the precaution to register their transactions before the notary reinforced the argument that even a loan to a family member had to be repaid.

The following example illustrates well the complexities of family ties and credit. Catherine Frossard was the daughter of a couple of innkeepers living in the village of Florimont. Like many other girls, Frossard was sent off to work as a domestic in a household away from home. In Belfort, she managed to find a good position, perhaps because her parents belonged to a rather better-off strata in their village, with good connections. She saved at least 300 livres for her *établissement*, in other words, her marriage.[75] In 1765, however, her parents had to repay a debt to the mayor of the village. They turned to their daughter and borrowed 300 livres without interest, which she would get back at their deaths.[76] By helping her indebted parents, she undoubtedly delayed her own future marriage. It is interesting to note that her parents also borrowed 200 livres on the same day from their son François Frossard. In 1765, Catherine Frossard was already 32 years old and still in service. In 1771,

---

[74] Judith M. Spicksley, "Fly with a Duck in thy Mouth," p 198.
[75] 'Somme provenant de son pécule et de ses épargnes pour son établissement.'
[76] ADTB 2E4/410.

Table 4.6 *Behaviour of single women creditors in the seigneuries of Delle and Florimont, 1730–89*

Single women lent to	N	N %	V	V %	Mean	Standard deviation
Man	98	46.4	37,280.6	58.2	380.4	795.26
Unmarried woman	5	2.4	987	1.5	197.4	88.03
Married couple	81	38.4	20,625.1	32.2	254.6	246
Widow	21	10	4,132.50	6.5	196.8	152.35
Group	6	2.8	979	1.5	163.1	74.97

Source: notarial dataset

a few years later, she can be found working in the town of Masevaux, probably still as a domestic. She extended credit to her father, Joseph Frossard,[77] lending him 150 livres, refundable within three years.[78] Her parents died within a few years of signing the deeds and Catherine Frossard married Jean Antoine Clerc, a widower, in 1776, at the age of 43.[79] Catherine Frossard certainly had to work for longer in service and marry when it was almost impossible for her to have children. It is nonetheless interesting to note that parents and children made their transactions official before the notary. In this case, we can assume that they did so to protect Catherine and François Frossard's loans from other potential heirs and/or other creditors on the deaths of their parents.

Examining closely the network of single women's debtors, these women chose to extend capital principally to men and married couples (Table 4.6). In the case of married couple debtors, both spouses guaranteed the loan. If one of the borrowers died, the other was still accountable for that share of the debt along with the heirs, increasing somehow the safety of the capital investment. Men were also sought after borrowers as they could easily bring collateral and mortgages to secure the transactions. Amy Froide has highlighted the same lending strategy on the part of single women in Bristol. There, women also overwhelmingly extended capital to men.[80] Single women also lent money to people in their immediate circle, preferably living in the same community (Table 4.7). Single women were thus careful investors.

[77] Marie Barbe Caille, her mother, had died in 1767. ADTB registre paroissial de Florimont 0046 E-Dépôt GG1–4.
[78] ADTB 2E4/411.   [79] Archives Municipales de Belfort GG 09-36.
[80] Amy M. Froide, *Never Married*, p 135.

Table 4.7 *Single women lending to debtors living in the same village and lending to their relatives*

Single women lent to	N same village	V same village	N Kin	V Kin
Man	39 (39.8%)	18,734 (50.25%)	17 (17.3%)	6,647 (17.8%)
Unmarried woman	4 (80%)	841 (85%)	2 (40%)	336 (34%)
Married couple	40 (49.4%)	8,440 (40.9%)	8 (9.9%)	1,488 (7.2%)
Widow	7 (33.3%)	1,329.75 (32.2%)	4 (19%)	668 (16%)
Group	2 (33.3%)	379 (38.7%)	0 (0%)	0 (0%)

Source: notarial dataset

One might legitimately ask whether single women's allocation of credit to men was a premarital strategy to secure a potential alliance with a possible suitor. In cross-checking the names of single women creditors with parish registers, no evidence can be found that any marriage between a female creditor and a debtor took place. The credit market was not a place in which to strengthen a promise of marriage. For unmarried women creditors, credit was a means to save and to make money grow, possibly by redistributing money in their own community.

Unmarried women creditors did play a dynamic role in the local economy, increasingly extending more capital throughout the eighteenth century. Their participation in the local credit market may correspond to an increasing demand for liquidity and funds. Yet, these women did benefit from their lending activities. They received dividends for their capital. But they also enjoyed a strengthening of their social status and position.[81]

These women, who invested their savings and domestic wages in the credit market, might have been able to relieve their parents of part, or perhaps all, of their endowment at marriage. Several marriage contracts in the area mentioned cash in the dowry provision.[82] In regions where partible inheritance applied, historians have asserted that, in practise, daughters were often excluded from their parent's inheritance after they had been endowed at marriage. Their brothers, on the other hand, would be endowed *and* receive their share of the family property at the death of their parents, creating an inheritance practise that was highly discriminatory and based solely on gender.[83] In the case that some women were

---

[81] See Chris Briggs "Empowered or Marginalized? Rural Women and Credit in Later Thirteenth- and Fourteenth-Century England," *Continuity and Change* 19, no. 1 (2004): 13–43, p 31.
[82] Dermineur. "Women in Rural Society," chapter 3.
[83] See especially Bernard Derouet, "Le partage des frères."

Table 4.8 *Married couples as creditors in the*
seigneuries of Delle and Florimont, 1733–89

	Married couple as creditors
Number of contracts	74
Amount exchanged	40,663.1
Mean	549.5
Standard deviation	1,383.9
Min	22
Max	10,764

Source: notarial dataset

able to provide their dowry themselves, there was no obstacle to them accessing their parent's property and inheriting the same share as their brothers. While this is an interesting hypothesis, more data and research could help to verify it. Along the same lines of reasoning, these unmarried women might have had more freedom to choose their life partner thanks to their ability to negotiate loan contracts, their access to resources, and their possible dowry provision. This issue would need more data and research but could prove to be significant.

Married Couples as Creditors

Married women represented only a marginal proportion of creditors (Table 4.8).[84] Why did so few married couples extend money? Who invested and what type of profiles emerge? In theory, husbands could not engage their wives' property and assets without their consent. A married couple could decide to place those assets in the credit market to make them profitable.

There were three main profiles of married female creditors. First, a married woman may appear on the deed because she and her husband sold some items and/or property that belonged to her as part of her lineage property via a deferred payment. For instance, it was likely that Anne Arnoux and her husband Christophe Belet sold a house to Jean Claude Girardin that belonged to the wife in the first place.[85]

---

[84] Married women credit activities were widespread in urban environments. Alexandra Shepard, "Minding Their Own Business: Married Women and Credit in Early Eighteenth-Century London," *Transactions of the Royal Historical Society* 25 (2015): 53–74.

[85] ADTB 2E4/157.

Second, a married female creditor could have been added to the deed because she may have signed in place of her absent husband. Pierre Vauthier and Catherine Fridez borrowed some money from Joseph Rouge and his wife to reimburse a debt. Rouge was absent when the deal was signed at the notary's office, only his wife, Marie Francoise Cravanche, was present. She may have delivered the money and even negotiated the contract with the tacit agreement of her husband.[86] Catherine Payot was also the only one present to extend fifty-two livres to one of her neighbours. Her husband's name was written on the deal, but the notary specified he was absent.[87]

Finally, a married woman could also be on the deed as a creditor along with her husband because she extended money to her relatives. Anne Grevillot was married to Thiebaud Duringer. In March 1778 she lent eighty livres to her brother Barthelemy Grevillot, possibly using her own funds. In any case, Grevillot and her husband secured the transaction with an official deed, but the loan negotiation and agreement may have involved only Anne Grevillot and her brother.

As the examples of married women creditors show, creditors' motivations and profiles could differ. Yet, husbands often presented themselves under their name only to lend money. The capital extended, in theory, might have belonged to both spouses as community property; upon the husband's death, the debt was still owed to his heirs, including his wife. Without her name correctly written alongside her husband's, she might have been entitled to only a third of the repayment upon his death because of local customs, unless the spouses had made another arrangement.[88]

Widows as Creditors

Anne Marie Monnier was married to the *laboureur* Nicolas Jeantine. Perhaps because her husband was busy, or perhaps because she was extending credit on her own money, she alone was present before the notary on November 1771 and on June 1777. On the first occasion, she extended credit to Pierre Jacquet and Marie Anne Liron, a married couple living in her village of Suarce, for a total of 500 livres.[89] A few years later, in 1777, she agreed to renew an old obligation and to extend a new loan to Catherine Frin, the widow of Henri Werther, in order for Catherine to rebuild her house destroyed by a fire. Anne Marie Monnier

[86] ADTB 2E4/155.   [87] ADTB 2E4/285.
[88] Elise Dermineur, "Widows' Political Strategies in Traditional Communities."
[89] ADTB 2E4/443.

lent Catherine Frin 880 livres.[90] She delivered her debtors the money and her husband countersigned the deeds later, but he had left her to go to the notary on her own each time.

Monnier's husband passed away in 1779 at fifty years old. The now widow did not remarry. She managed her property in her own name as head of the household.[91] She continued to extend credit to her neighbours and friends. But in 1783, perhaps feeling she was not getting any younger and perhaps because she could not work anymore, she invested a lot of money in the credit market, thus securing a regular income for her retirement. Like her, widows were eager to invest in the credit market in order to secure a fixed annual income, especially if they had no offspring.[92] She extended a total of 3,173 livres to ten different borrowers, all living in her village, spreading the risk.[93] Most of the capital repayment deadlines were on demand, indicating her willingness to receive a fixed amount of money from the interest every year (possibly 158 livres a year).[94] The transactions were all risk-limited as all the borrowers lived in her village. Most of them were married (if one spouse died, the other was still responsible for his or her share of the debt). The repayment date was on demand, meaning the widow could withdraw her capital at any time (with notice) if needed. Most of the widows extending credit sought an annual return; especially ageing widows who attempted to diversify their income.

In a common assumption and in traditional historiography, widows were usually active creditors in credit markets (despite the fact – and paradoxically – that widowhood also equalled poverty).[95] Throughout early modern Europe, historians have noted that widows lent money extensively.[96] In England, the 'most prominent economic function of the widow in rural society between 1500 and 1900 was moneylending'.[97] In early modern France, Laurence Fontaine evaluates that widowed

---

[90] ADTB 2E4/444.   [91] ADTB Registre paroissial 095 E dépôt GG 1-5.

[92] In Württemberg, widows invested in state mortgages. See Sabean, David Warren, *Property, Production, and Family in Neckarhausen, 1700–1870.* (Cambridge: Cambridge University Press, 1991), p 47. Laurence Fontaine has noted the same thing for early modern French widows. Fontaine, Laurence. *L'économie morale*, p 157.

[93] ADTB 2E4/445.

[94] Barbe Bettevy, the housekeeper in chief of the local seigneur made 100 livres a year.

[95] Dousset, "Familles paysannes et veuvage féminin en Languedoc," p 584.

[96] Holderness, "Widows in Pre-Industrial Society"; Dermineur, Elise M. "Female Peasants, Patriarchy, and the Credit Market in Eighteenth-Century France," *Proceedings of the Western Society for French History* 37 (2009): 61–84. Hoffman, Philip T., Gilles Postel-Vinay, et Jean-Laurent Rosenthal. "Private Credit Markets in Paris." Sabean, David. *Property, Production, and Family in Neckarhausen*, p 47.

[97] Holderness, B. A., "Widows in Pre-Industrial Society" p 435.

Table 4.9 *Widows as creditors in the seigneuries of Delle and Florimont, 1733–89*

	Widows as creditors
Number of contracts	121
Amount exchanged	57,583.1
Mean	475.9
Standard deviation	809
Min	24
Max	6,000

Source: notarial dataset

creditors had at least a third of their assets tied up in credit.[98] Who were these women and what were their motivations and goals in extending money?

In the south of Alsace, 5.8% of widows extended money, allocating 7.6% of the capital available (Table 4.9). Some of these women extended credit several times throughout the period. During the eighteenth century, their participation in the credit markets was quite irregular, with the exception of the seigneurie of Florimont where they gradually came to participate more in terms of number and volume. It is worth noting that their loans were, on average, no smaller than the ones of men.

Marie Catherine Monnier, the widow of Jean Jacques Dadey, was one of these widow moneylenders. In 1772, her husband died, only a few years after their wedding.[99] Monnier, the legal guardian of her two young sons, became the head of a quite wealthy household. As the guardian of her children, she was in charge of managing their inherited estates until they reached their majority, as well as her own property. The widow inherited a third of the community property while her sons inherited two thirds of it. The probate of Jean Jacques Dadey, her late husband, mentions a large patrimony; a house covered with tiles with adjacent barn and stable, surrounded by a garden and an orchard, various pieces of land (arable land, meadows, and flax fields), 1,273 livres worth of livestock including many horses, and ploughing materials in good condition. The probate also mentions many pieces of clothing belonging to the deceased, which had been auctioned to different individuals for a total of 94 livres. The clerk reported that 200 livres in cash had been found in the house. And the widow declared that various individuals owed 600 livres to the household. She added that she and her husband had not yet

---

[98] Fontaine, Laurence. *L'économie morale*, p 159.   [99] They married in January 1765.

Table 4.10 *Widows network of creditors in the seigneuries of Delle and Florimont, 1733–89*

Widows lent to	N	N %	V	V %	Mean	Standard deviation
Man	63	52.1	28,538.5	49.6	452.9	866.3
Unmarried woman	1	0.8	50	0.1	50	
Married couple	43	35.5	15,111.6	26.2	351.4	264.75
Widow	7	5.8	10,571	18.4	1,510.1	1,819.9
Group	7	5.8	3,312	5.8	473.1	369.3

Source: notarial dataset

finished paying for the purchase of a piece of land and that 200 livres remained to be paid. No loom was reported in the probate, but the significant amount of fabric and yarn indicated artisanal textile work on the side.[100]

Marie Catherine Monnier's household, therefore, was one of the better-off of her community with important and diversified means of resources and production (land, textile homemade production, livestock). It is rather unclear how she successfully managed the farm after the death of her husband, whether she decided to rent out the lands in her possession and/or whether she hired workers. But she appeared active as a money-lender on several occasions. She extended a total of 4,294 livres within 13 years to 9 different creditors. Some loans were bigger than others. She agreed to lend 1,100 livres to Jean Jacques Thomas in June 1783 (repaid in full in 1787), and Richard Kircher, the miller of Chavanatte, and his wife Claudine Chatelot received 500 livres from Monnier to purchase pieces of land. Towards the end of her life, she lent larger amounts of money repayable on demand, indicating her willingness to receive an annual profit. Monnier not only never remarried – which could have threatened the management of her and her children's patrimony – but also managed her financial assets well. She asked for guarantees and extended credit almost exclusively to married couples from her village, therefore maximizing the security of her investment.

Her example was not unique. Many widows who became heads of wealthy households also invested their capital in the credit market, especially when they were ageing. Securing their invested capital was an important preoccupation. Widows uppermost lent to men and to married couples (Table 4.10). Widows, like unmarried women, took

[100] ADTB 2E4/435.

Table 4.11 *Widows lending to debtors living in the same village and lending to their relatives*

Widows lent to	N same village	V same village	N Kin	V Kin
Man	35 (53.8%)	13,646 (42%)	4 (50%)	1,415 (64.2%)
Unmarried woman	1 (1.5%)	50 (0.2%)	1 (12.5%)	50 (2.3%)
Married couple	23 (35.4%)	9,301.6 (28.6%)	3 (37.5%)	740 (33.6%)
Widow	4 (6.2%)	8,837 (27.2%)	0	
Group	2 (3.1%)	650 (2%)	0	

Source: notarial dataset

minimal risks and looked for safe investments with trustworthy debtors. Their capital for their old age was at stake.

Laurence Fontaine suggests that widows were very active in proximity lending.[101] This pattern is similar to the one we have observed for unmarried women and married couples. Capital extended to their neighbours was high but not higher than any other category (Table 4.11).

Typology of Female Loans

Notarial contracts rarely mentioned the precise purpose of loans. As Thomas Brennan notes 'it is rarely clear how borrowers used their loans'.[102] Therefore, it is difficult to know why women allocated their money in particular ways. Did they extend credit to support investment? Were they more inclined to charity? Were female creditors extending credit in cash or were they granting deferred payments? Were their loans different from those of men? Many transactions elude us. Consequently, all the figures and proportions given in this part must be seen as a means of evaluation only.

Considering notarial records, female creditors, regardless of their marital status, avoided deferred payments (which might not have prevented them to do so via non-intermediated loans). Evidence suggests that they rather extended loans in cash and more frequently than men (Table 4.12). Unmarried women rarely granted deferred payments for livestock, grain, or other items. More than 62% of their loan allocations went to loans supposedly in cash, possibly for productive investments. This high proportion can be explained by unmarried women's wages invested in the credit market. Widows also prioritized cash when

---

[101] Fontaine, Laurence. *L'économie morale*, p 159.
[102] Thomas Brennan, "Peasants and Debt in Eighteenth-Century Champagne," p 177.

Table 4.12 *Creditor loan types distribution in the seigneuries of Delle and Florimont, 1730–89*

Type of loan	Man	Unmarried woman	Married couple	Widow	Group	Institution
Loan without specification	48.7%	62.6%	45.9%	57.0%	33.3%	11.8%
Livestock	14.4%	0.9%	2.7%	8.3%	6.7%	0%
Grains	0.8%	0%	0%	0.0%	6.7%	0%
House and building	5.3%	5.7%	6.8%	2.5%	0%	0%
Land	4.9%	4.7%	8.1%	1.7%	0%	26.5%
Foodstuff	1.0%	0%	1.4%	0%	13.3%	0%
Mix	6.0%	6.6%	1.4%	6.6%	0%	35.3%
Merchandise	2.2%	1.4%	5.4%	2.5%	0%	0%
Wage	0.4%	0%	1.4%	0%	0%	0%
Justice fees	2.9%	0.9%	1.4%	0.8%	0%	0%
Rent	0.9%	0.5%	1.4%	0%	0%	0%
Old debt	11.0%	13.7%	24.3%	17.4%	40%	17.6%
Tax	0.9%	1.4%	0%	0.8%	0%	5.9%
Community related	0.3%	0%	0%	0.8%	0%	2.9%
Other	0.4%	1.4%	0%	1.7%	0%	0%

Source: notarial dataset

allocating money (57%); they granted slightly more deferred payments than unmarried women but less than men.

Did women lend the same amount as men? Were they able to match the loans made by male creditors? William Chester Jordan argues that women's specialty in the Middle Ages 'was small loans and, indeed, the smallest of the small, usually only one half to one-third the size of loans made by male moneylenders'.[103] Female wealth accumulation was limited owing to legal restrictions and prospects of a reduced income. Yet, some women were able to extend large amounts of money. Focusing on single loans – rather than on the general picture – women did lend significant amounts, and not just the smallest of the small. When one looks at the mean figures, widows for instance were able to lend large amounts of money at once (Table 4.13).

Scholars have argued that, traditionally, women tended to extend credit to other women in large proportion, underlining, therefore, the pattern of solidarity and mutual help existing between them. While this

[103] Jordan, William Chester. *Women and Credit*, p 23.

Table 4.13 *Mean per type of loans according to marital status of the creditors in the seigneuries of Delle and Florimont, 1730–90*

Type of loan	Man Mean	Unmarried woman Mean	Married couple Mean	Widow Mean
Loan without specification	319.81	197.66	470.29	403.85
Livestock	169.29	69.50	141	137.30
Grains	126.92			
House and building	566.53	257.67	429.20	410
Land	544.69	398.60	444.83	593
Foodstuff	323.88		150	
Mix	339.95	778.46	313	380.25
Merchandise	409.34	384.72	630.75	1,058.53
Wage	188.26		136	
Justice fees	214.41	228.50	35.10	115
Rent	624.10	2250	227	
Old debt	558.38	510.47	899.56	849.90
Tax	303.60	107		300
Community related	1,594.80			1,200
Other	262.58	270.67		124

Source: notarial dataset

pattern has been found in cities, there appears to have been no such solidarity among women in the south of Alsace, at least not in the notarial market.[104] In fact, female solidarity was very low; female creditors preferred to extend credit to credit-worthy clients and were, therefore, more likely to turn to married couples or men, who had landed assets and often better guarantees to offer (see Table 4.6 and Table 4.10). I rather think that female-to-female loans might have occurred frequently via uncertified loans.

In a world where debt repayment was often delayed and where patriarchal structures prevailed, we might wonder whether female lenders were being repaid. Using the local court registers, we see a greater proportion of female plaintiffs in debt repayment cases throughout the eighteenth century. While female moneylenders represented about 19% of all creditors, they represented between 8% and 13% of plaintiffs.[105]

[104] Jordan, *Women and Credit*.
[105] Hereafter the judicial dataset: ADTB 8B18, 19, 20, 21, 22, 31, 32, 33, 81, 83, 84, 85, 86, 87, 88, 89, 90, 91, 92, 93, 94, 95, 96, 97, 98, 156, 157, 158, 159, 160 (seigneurie of Delle). ADTB 12B14, 15, 16, 17, 42, 43, 44, 45, 46, 47, 48, 72, 73, 78, 79, 80, 81, 82 (seigneurie of Florimont). See Elise Dermineur, "Women in rural society."

Table 4.14 *Proportion of plaintiffs in judicial registers for debt collection according to sex, seigneuries of Delle and Florimont, 1680–1785*

	1680–85	1700–05	1740–45	1780–85
Man	90%	84%	83%	86%
Women	5%	12%	13%	10%
Other	5%	4%	4%	4%

Source: judicial dataset

These figures suggest that women might have experienced a certain degree of difficulty in retrieving their capital and the interest. Yet, these proportions are slightly inferior with what has been observed in other regions. In seventeenth-century Aberdeen, 19% of debt pursuers were female. In Exeter, 16% of plaintiffs were unmarried women and widows. They were 19% in Bristol.[106] In larger urban areas where it is possible ties between people were looser, retrieving one's money might have been more difficult. People might have turned to institutions to this end. In traditional communities featuring a high degree of social intimacy between debtors and creditors, negotiations and arrangements outside the courtroom might have been made easier.

The results featured in Table 4.14 corroborate the observation made previously. Unmarried women and widows tended to ask for more securities and guarantees when they lent money because the risk of non-repayment was greater for them. Single women, for example, might have encountered difficulties retrieving their capital because of their sex and marital status. Yet, they were very few among the plaintiffs in debt repayment cases, compared to other groups.[107] In the seigneurie of Delle, about 70% of single women secured their transactions with specific material goods and/or with guarantors, while only 30% secured them in their deeds, with the normative sentence 'all movables and immovable goods'. Single female lenders, therefore, seemed to make safer investments, which in turn could partly explain their absence from court records as plaintiffs.

Finally, it is likely that the proportion of married women was higher in debt suits. They might have been represented only by their husbands and left out of the records.[108]

---

[106] Thomson, "Crediting Wives," p 93.
[107] A feature also observed by Judith M. Bennett, *Ale, Beer and Brewsters in England: Women's Work in a Changing World, 1300–1600* (Oxford: Oxford University Press, 1999), p 203, and Chris Briggs. 'Empowered or Marginalized?' pp 17–18.
[108] Thomson, "Crediting Wives."

Concluding Remarks

In the last century of the Old Regime, in a context of intense economic upheavals, the local credit market experienced significant shifts in the system of capital allocation and redistribution, especially in reference to the increasingly greater participation of women, whether as creditors or debtors. Women's marital status played a determining factor in their capacity to either extend capital or to locate available funds.

As debtors, in a background of growing indebtedness, married women helped secure transactions thanks to their personal assets, dowries, and lineage property. They became incontrovertible partners in their households and with their spouses. Their presence on the deed reinforced lenders' confidence that repayment would be met.

As creditors, women actively participated in their community's life. Single women, in particular, increasingly invested their wages and savings in the local credit market throughout the eighteenth century, thereby injecting liquidity into the community and making cash circulate. Their actions were aligned with the norms of cooperation and solidarity applicable to traditional communities. Unmarried women participated fully in the economic dynamism of their communities. More importantly, unmarried women who extended money may have been able to supply their own dowries and thus may have been more independent when it came to a choice of marriage partners. In any case, their participation in the credit market certainly had repercussions on their social capital and image. A lot of work remains to be done on this form of empowerment.

Overall, women's participation in this market gradually became more and more significant in terms of capital injected and participation, engendering a modification to the social fabric of the community. The traditional pattern of patriarchy in which women had very limited access to financial exchange and business because of their lack of opportunity, capital and rights is no longer valid. Women were essential to the circulation of credit. The indirect result was a dramatic change in the gender equilibrium of the community, in which women appeared undisputed and capable business and household partners.

5 Insolvency and Default

Introduction

Despite the norms of solidarity, cooperation, and fairness that character-ized pre-industrial society, breach of agreement did occur. When lenders and debtors had exhausted all the possibilities available to settle their disagreement, taking the matter to court was often the last resort. The aim was to recover the capital invested. But often, the emotional and social implications of a lawsuit went beyond the straightforward eco-nomic dimension. Throughout the period, the burden of debt increased rapidly, as did the number of discontented creditors. This phenomenon was assuredly not circumscribed to France; debt collection lawsuits also filled the docks of courtrooms here and there across the Western world.[1]

The apparent dichotomy is intriguing. Financial arrangements were often non-intermediated, flexible, and renegotiable. Yet, contract enforcement at court was sought after.[2] As most of the pre-industrial transactions were contracted privately and without certification, we can assume that enforcement mechanisms would remain confined to an informal enforcement mechanism and not find their way to the courts. Why did creditors resort to an external arbiter in their conflict with their debtors? What kind of debts were being recalled? By whom? In the meantime, in close-knit societies, complex chains of credit were entan-gled in different social and economic networks. As financial disputes grew in volume in the courts, this chapter is concerned with the impact of the growing importance of market relations on the social fabric of the community. Cornelia Hughes Dayton refers to this process as 'the

---

[1] Craig Muldrew, "Credit and the Courts"; Muldrew, *The Economy of Obligation*; Chris Briggs, "'Can't Pay' and 'Won't Pay' in the Medieval Village," *Common Knowledge* 17, no. 2 (2011): 363–70; Briggs, *Credit and Village*; B. Zorina Khan, "'Justice of the Marketplace': Legal Disputes and Economic Activity on America's Northeastern Frontier, 1700–1860," *The Journal of Interdisciplinary History* 39, no. 1 (2008): 1–35.

[2] On this see Benoît Garnot, "Justice, infrajustice, parajustice et extra justice dans la France d'Ancien Régime." *Crime, Histoire & Sociétés/Crime, History & Societies* 4, no. 1 (2000): 103–20.

litigated economy', while Zorina Khan talks about the 'justice of the marketplace'.[3] Did the growing litigation – and institutionalization – of debt have an impact on social relations?

To answer these questions, the present chapter focuses on the enforcement of financial transactions and the failure to repay a debt with particular emphasis not only on the legal process of debt collection, but especially on its practises. Judicial records from civil courts in Delle and in Florimont constitute the basis for this study. Through the analysis of a sample of 3,700 lawsuits, among them 1,799 for debt collection, from 1680 to 1785, I study closely the economic and social origins as well as the outcomes of default.[4] Local courts dealt with a great number of insolvency cases. These lawsuits are rich sources of information for the historian. They highlight the shortcomings and failures of debtors, and the (im)patience of creditors. But above all, they display the complex and multiple layers of the dynamics of social and economic relationships.

The Judicial Process: An Overview

Civil lawsuits contained most of the disputes related to debt. There are two main types of civil record: the trial records (often registered in *registre d'audiences* or *registres des causes*) are by far the most exhaustive documentation available, and all the related documents produced by the court to inform and complement the investigation (*procès-verbaux*, expert witnesses, testimonies, and other documents useful for the judge's decision). The *registres d'audiences* are perhaps the most useful source of information. These bound registers contain the name(s) of the plaintiff(s) and defendant(s), the place of residence, and their occupation. These also state the *moyens* – the arguments of both parties – set before the judge, who also listened to the prosecutor's arguments. The magistrate could subsequently give a final decision on the matter, render a sentence, and assess court costs, or he could decide he needed to gather more evidence (expert witnesses, receipts, paperwork, or testimonies for instance) and another hearing would take place. Finally, he could also

---

[3] Cornelia Hughes Dayton, *Women Before the Bar: Gender, Law, and Society in Connecticut, 1639–1789.* Chapel Hill, NC: University of North Carolina Press, 2012; Craig Muldrew, *The Economy of Obligation*; Chris Briggs, "'Can't Pay' and 'Won't Pay'"; Khan, "Justice of the Marketplace."

[4] Hereafter the judicial dataset: ADTB 8B18, 19, 20, 21, 22, 31, 32, 33, 81, 83, 84, 85, 86, 87, 88, 89, 90, 91, 92, 93, 94, 95, 96, 97, 98, 156, 157, 158, 159, 160 (seigneurie of Delle). ADTB 12B14, 15, 16, 17, 42, 43, 44, 45, 46, 47, 48, 72, 73, 78, 79, 80, 81, 82 (seigneurie of Florimont).

indicate that his court was not competent on the matter and order a *pourvoi* (an appeal).

Most of the hearings took place, in theory, with all parties present.[5] Each party, sometimes but not always represented by a lawyer, brought their arguments forward. The *greffier* (clerk) wrote the summary of the hearing after it took place, based on his notes. The summary contained a few sentences for each parties' arguments and the judge's decision.[6] The historian has, therefore, a truncated version of the debates at their disposal.

The access to civil justice was, in principle, free to all litigants. But the loser usually had to pay the judicial fees, part of it serving to cover the magistrates' fees. Litigants could use the services of lawyers for a fee; a few did.

The hearing registers contain, in theory, all the civil lawsuits of a local jurisdiction.[7] These cases reflect the daily pulse of the community, where we find lawsuits involving just about anything. Categorization often does not do justice to the complexity of the cases. These lawsuits covered many things, such as violence, inheritance disputes, property issues, and financial matters. They often amounted to layers of quarrels and antagonistic relationships. Family feuds, neighbourhood enmity, the struggle for local power, among other types, filled the dockets of the courts. A case might require several hearings. Note that I have counted the number of lawsuits, not the number of hearings.[8]

Increasingly, throughout the period, unrepaid debt lawsuits came to represent the main category of suits (see Table 5.1). The registers of these hearings are therefore of enormous help in quantifying the volume of problematic and unpaid debt. Unfortunately, the scribe often left out

---

[5] The Civil Ordonnance of 1667 enacted this.

[6] Claire Dolan, *Entre justice et justiciables: les auxiliaires de la justice du Moyen Âge au XXe siècle* (Quebec: Presses Université Laval, 2005); Fabrice Mauclair, "Des gens de justice à la campagne," *Annales de Bretagne et des Pays de l'Ouest. Anjou. Maine. Poitou-Charente. Touraine*, no. 116–2 (2009): 81–103, p 108.

[7] On seigneurial justice see especially François Brizay, Antoine Follain, and Véronique Sarrazin, eds. *Les justices de village: administration et justice locales de la fin du Moyen Âge à la Révolution*. Histoire. (Rennes: Presses universitaires de Rennes, 2015). Hayhoe, Jeremy. *Enlightened Feudalism: Seigneurial Justice and Village Society in Eighteenth-Century Northern Burgundy*. (Rochester, NY: University of Rochester Press, 2008). Fabrice Mauclair, *La justice au village: justice seigneuriale et société rurale dans le Duché-Pairie de La Vallière*. (Rennes: Presses Universitaires de Rennes, 2008). Isabelle Mathieu, *Justices Seigneuriales En Anjou et Dans Le Maine*. (Rennes: Presses Universitaires de Rennes, 2011). Frédéric Chauvaud, *Justice et sociétés rurales: du XVIe siècle à nos jours, approches pluridisciplinaires*. (Rennes: Presses Universitaires de Rennes, 2011).

[8] Hervé Piant, "Des procès innombrables," *Histoire & mesure*, Déviance, justice et statistiques, XXII, no. 2 (2007): 13–38.

Table 5.1 *Proportion of debt lawsuits per cases in hearing registers in the seigneuries of Delle and Florimont, 1680–1785*[a]

	1680–85		1700–05		1740–45		1780–85	
	N	%	N	%	N	%	N	%
Debt lawsuits in hearing registers	82/377	21.7	156/425	36.7	535/1,090	49	1,026/1,808	56.7

[a] Only the year 1700 is available for the seigneurie of Delle.

information the historian would find valuable. Judicial transcripts of lawsuits for the seventeenth century tended to be short, vague, and oftentimes confusing. Only a few sentences summarised the arguments of both parties and the judge's decision. In debt cases, the nature of the debt and its amount often went missing, as well as the date of the initial contract. The complexity of the disputes did not always materialize in neat details. Distraint, for instance, did appear but the actual procedure was recorded on loose sheets. All of these other documents, like loose reports contributing to the lawsuit, are usually housed elsewhere in the archives, and constitute a chaotic, uncatalogued, and enormous mass of documents.[9]

Debt collection suits reflect a truncated reality. Their number is only the tip of the iceberg as we are ignorant of the real number of debt conflicts. How many debtors failed their creditors? How many of these disputes were settled out of court? It is impossible to answer these questions with precise figures. Negotiations, renegotiations, and private settlements with private mediators occurred frequently.[10] It is certain that not all disputes were brought to court. Benoît Garnot and Avner Greif, among others, argue that most disputes were settled out of court, corroborating the argument of community self-regulation.[11]

As a whole, there was a general democratization of the use of courts throughout the kingdom. The intendant of Alsace, Jacques de la Grange, remarked on the worrying tendency in 1697:

[9] Recently, Sylvain Soleil has denounced the chaos in the archiving of judicial sources in French archives. Sylvain Soleil, "Nouveau scénario pour séries b: les fonds des tribunaux d'ancien régime." *Les Cahiers du Centre de Recherches Historiques*, Officiers "moyens" (1), no. 23 (1999). See also Piant "Des procès innombrables."

[10] Bonzon, *La paix au village.*

[11] Benoît Garnot, *Histoire de la justice: France, XVIe-XXIe siècle.* (Paris: Gallimard, 2009); Benoît Garnot, "Justice, infrajustice, parajustice et extra justice." Avner Greif, "Contract Enforceability and Economic Institutions in Early Trade: The Maghribi Traders' Coalition." *The American Economic Review*, no. 3 (1993): 525–48, p 525.

In the past, the people of Alsace went to court only rarely. Justice was rendered informally, and cases ended with low costs. Since the number of courts has multiplied (...) they have started to use them. Once they did not even know what a summons was, and now their number increases daily. The use of a summons is so common that one is presented every day, whether they are right or not, and this even for the smallest thing.[12]

The general increase in the volume of lawsuits could be imputed partly to the development of formal institutions enforcing market transactions. These institutions became better staffed and more reliable towards the end of the Old Regime. The growing affirmation of private property rights paralleled with a weakening of the feudal grip played a role in the growing use of local courts. Regarding insolvency specifically, the development of a market economy in the Late Middle Ages onwards brought new reasons for lawsuits.[13] In the seventeenth and eighteenth century, the growth of economic and commercial activities and opportunities, as well as the refinement of credit instruments led to an increase in default suits. In the late-seventeenth century, in the south of Alsace, 21% of cases concerned repayment of a debt, while a century later this proportion reached 57%. The proportion of cases concerning debt corresponds to what other historians have observed elsewhere. Hervé Piant found that in the late-seventeenth century 39% of the *causes d'audience* concerned the repayment of loans and debt, while this reached 76% in the eighteenth century.[14] As Muldrew states, 'it appears reasonable to assume that with an increase in transactions there would have been more credit, more defaults, and more litigation'.[15]

Not only did the number of judicial proceedings for non-repayment increase tremendously during the period, but non-economic lawsuits declined, including those relating to the regulation of society. Cases relating to violence and improper social behaviour, for instance, greatly decreased in the eighteenth century. Obviously, this does not mean that violence per se subsided.[16] But litigants resorted more to local courts to settle their financial issues, pushing aside other matters, perhaps

[12] De la Grange, *Extrait d'un mémoire sur la province d'Alsace*, Strasbourg, 1697, reprinted in 1858, Bibliothèque Nationale et Universitaire de Strasbourg, M116.430. pp 1–4. On this topic see also Loyseau, Charles. *Discours de l'abus des justices de villages*, 1603.

[13] See Smail, *The Consumption of Justice*, pp 158–59; Richard L. Kagan *Lawsuits and Litigants in Castile: 1500–1700*. (Chapel Hill, NC: University of North Carolina Press, 1981), p XIX; Muldrew, *The Economy of Obligation*, p 3.

[14] Piant, Hervé. *Une justice ordinaire: justice civile et criminelle dans la prevôté royale de Vaucouleurs sous l'Ancien Régime*, (Rennes: Presses Universitaires de Rennes, 2006), p 143. Piant mentions that J.-A. Dickinson found between 30% and 40% of debt litigations in the bailiwick of Falaise and that D. Martin found over 50% of these cases in Basse en Auvergne.

[15] Muldrew. "Credit and the Courts," p 25.

[16] These cases were not handled by another court.

resorting to auto-regulation when it came to violent conflict. Finding the same results for colonial Maine, Zorina Khan contends that 'this pattern should not be surprising; it accords well with the notion that market expansion is accompanied by a rationalization of social and economic practices'.[17] Just like in Maine, legal institutions in early modern France had abandoned their persuasive supervisions of social interactions and behaviours in the course of the eighteenth century.

Debt Collection Mechanism: Taking an Insolvent Debtor to Court

In the south of Alsace, a debt lawsuit always began with a libel, that is, when a creditor formally lodged a complaint to the judge to ask for redress of an insolvent debtor. A lawyer or a clerk often wrote the request on the behalf of a creditor. A messenger then dispatched the summons to the debtor's house. Neighbours witnessed the delivery of the summons to court, and that knowledge of the upcoming lawsuit spread within the community; 'publicity is crucial to the practice of justice'.[18]

Most of the lawsuits for debt were usually short and involved only one hearing. A creditor presented himself, asking that the debtor acknowledge his debt and pay his dues. In the seventeenth century, creditors seldom provided written evidence to the judge, supposedly because the literacy rate was still low. Instead, witnesses appeared at court to testify on behalf of both parties.[19] Under oath, witnesses contributed to the community's self-enforcing mechanism. In the eighteenth century, however, a creditor often presented written evidence, such as a contract between the two parties or an account book signed by the debtor as proof. The debtor or the judge officially recognized the debtor's signature and the debt incurred. In many cases, the debtor did not show up to court despite the summons. In 99% of the cases, the judge condemned the debtor to reimburse the creditor and assessed the court fees. The loser, in that case the debtor, always had to pay the fees.

What happened next? Most of the debt collection lawsuits stopped there. There was no second appearance before the judge.[20] Did the

---

[17] Khan, "Justice of the Marketplace," p 15.

[18] Smail, Daniel Lord, *The Consumption of Justice*, pp 22, 34.

[19] This practise involving witnesses was suppressed in 1667 with the promulgation of the civil *ordonnance*. In practise, however, witnesses continued to testify on behalf of litigants in debt collection cases. See Isambert, *Recueil général des anciennes lois françaises, depuis l'an 420 jusqu'à la révolution de 1789*, XVIII, p 137, title XX.

[20] In Burgundy, in the period 1750–1759, 43% of the suits do not have a final ruling while 33% did not have one in 1780–89. Jeremy Hayhoe, *Enlightened Feudalism*. In Château-la-Vallière, one case out of five did not have a final sentence in the eighteenth century. Fabrice Mauclair, *La justice au village* .

debtor repay his debt right away? Probably not. If he could not meet his obligation before the hearing, it is unlikely that his financial situation improved in such a short time. But an injunction to attend court might have been enough to restore communication between a creditor and his debtor. In June 1683, the children of Jacques Garriat found themselves unable to repay their creditor. They 'were in a state of extreme indigency and had no money to pay'. At the hearing, they attempted to renegotiate the terms of their agreement and proposed to pay half of what was due on Christmas Day and the other half on Easter Day. The judge showed little empathy and ordered them to pay half of twenty-four livres bâloises in fifteen days and the other half on St Martin's day in November.[21] There are no document to tell us whether they tried to renegotiate with their creditors after appearing in court.

The disputants might have found a negotiated solution after the hearing, outside the courtroom, and through informal enforcement mechanisms.[22] Livestock or some household items might have been exchanged. A new promissory note might be signed between the parties with new provisions. Or litigants might have decided on a new schedule for repayment. We cannot exclude that they agreed on an informal increase of the initial interest rate. Unfortunately, there is no written evidence left to support this idea and we can only speculate. But, as the creditor appeared in a position of power after the hearing, he might have been able to force the debtor to compensate for the renegotiation. Surely, the appearance at court hurt the creditworthiness of the debtor, but was this shaming process enough to satisfy the creditor? I think we can imagine that to restore communication and trust, creditor and debtor might have added new terms to their initial contract, possibly to the advantage of the creditor.

While a debtor's reputation might be hurt via a summons to court, it is equally true that a creditor's prestige might have been reinforced. In the same vein, a fair and charitable creditor would not push the suit forward by seizing a defaulting household's assets. Punishing a defaulting debtor with the court fees appeared enough. Overall, litigants oscillated between the official channel of justice through the court process and the informal means of regulation embodied by negotiation outside the courtroom, mediated or not. The ultimate goal was perhaps not entirely the enforcement of the terms of the contract but rather a pressure to restore dialogue and negotiation.

---

[21] ADTB 8B19.

[22] Hervé Piant, "Vaut-Il mieux s'arranger que plaider? Un essai de sociologie judiciaire dans la France d'Ancien Régime." In *Les justices locales dans les villes et villages du XVe au XIXe siècle* (Rennes: Presses Universitaires de Rennes, 2006), 97–124. See also Thomas Kuehn, *Law, Family & Women* (Chicago: University of Chicago Press, 1994), p 22.

Debtors were better-off cooperating rather than persisting in their default. Credit was embedded so much in the social fabric of the community that refusing a payment had disastrous consequences for future transactions. The debtor's reputation and creditworthiness would be hurt. The sentence, therefore, acted as a warning. The next step would be foreclosure. Both parties had the incentive to find a solution.

In cases where the litigants quarrelled over the terms of their agreement and disagreed over figures and calculations, the judge often invited them to settle their dispute via his court clerk. They all sat down and reviewed the evidence. Claude Francois Paillard had allowed the deferred payment of some goods to the mayor Joseph Tallon. The agreement between the two featured no written contract, it was only oral. But the sum of thirty-seven livres was contested. The judge invited the parties to settle the matter with the court clerk.[23] These cases were closed via this arbitration and no further appearance at court was necessary.

A few lawsuits, however, continued after the first hearing. A defendant could appeal the judge's decision and contest the debt. Appeals, however, remained very rare. Written agreements were strong evidence difficult to challenge. Some debtors nonetheless chose to appeal the magistrate's ruling. This strategy was perhaps meant to gain time, but it was a costly move as it added to the fees to be paid by the loser. Moreover, only a few debtors resorted to this weapon, presumably because it would have further hurt their creditworthiness. The final decision remained inevitably the same: the judge ruled that a debt had to be repaid.

Not all lawsuits were straightforward. Some insolvents claimed they owed nothing and denied the debt. The magistrate always based his final judgement on written evidence. Unless a debtor could prove the repayment of his dues via a receipt, the primary agreement prevailed. Notarized contracts, but also private agreements and account books, were irrefutable evidence. Some dishonest insolvents produced false receipts, claiming repayments whose true nature was subsequently questioned at court. The growing spread of false private claims also worried the authorities. In the mid-eighteenth century, the *Conseil Souverain d'Alsace* (Sovereign Council of Alsace) decreed a set of rules for the writing of private agreements. These contracts, from then on, needed to be written by the hand of the parties and the sum needed to be stipulated in full in letters, not in numbers.[24] In the south of Alsace, these counterfeited deeds remained, nonetheless, rare.

Male fide debtors sometimes attacked their creditors' integrity to contest the debt. In 1773, Jean Monnier contested the amount of money he

---

[23] ADTB 8B96.   [24] De Boug, *Recueil des édits*. vol 2, p 51.

presumably owed to a shoemaker, claiming that his creditor 'has a pettifogger character'.[25] Jewish lenders were often the target of a debtor's contempt. In 1770, Marie Herbelin, a widow living in Courtelevant, pretended that she and her husband had repaid their debt to their creditor, Cerf Levy, a Jew from a neighbouring village. She declared Levy denied it because 'Jews are used to cheating people'.[26]

Once a creditor had called in a debt, other creditors often imitated this judicial move and also asked for their capital back. This snowball effect can be explained by the desire to be assigned a place of seniority, to be the first in line to recoup a loan. Many feared seeing their capital vanish. Once a summons was dispatched to a debtor's house, information regarding the bad state of a debtor's affairs travelled throughout the community. As hearings took place with more or less frequency, different creditors could call in their loans at the same hearing for the same debtor. In Florimont, for instance, in the 1740s, lawsuits were examined once a month. On 16 July 1783, Maurice Dietrich from the village of Puis had to face four creditors on the same day. It is unclear which of the creditors had made the first move. Jean Carnal, a successful livestock farmer, called in three different outstanding debts from 1779, for a total of 308 livres tournois. The surgeon-doctor Lacour asked that his fees be paid for the sum of 40 livres 15 deniers and 4 sous, indicating that someone in Dietrich's household might be unwell and thus unable to work. Jean Pierre Patingre, a neighbour from the same village, asked for the 66 remaining livres for the sale of a piece of land in June 1781. And finally, Joseph Sprinsele, also a neighbour, called in 100 livres lent in January 1781, plus 21 livres for another loan.[27]

In a majority of debt collection lawsuits, the defendant did not present himself at the hearing. When Nicolas Rot's house vanished in flames, Catherine Guiot, one of his neighbours, lent him thirty-six livres to help rebuild it. She also lent him grain on six different occasions over the following months, perhaps to help his household overcome difficulties in the aftermath of the fire. We do not know what happened between them. But Guiot came forward and asked for the repayment of her loan and reclaimed the grain. Rot failed to attend the hearing.[28] Was this because of shame and guilt? Was it a way to deny the claim? Was it a way to gain time and avoid the necessary renegotiation of the debt with the creditor?

---

[25] ADTB 12B73.

[26] ADTB 12B72. Throughout the period, a growing number of Jewish lenders asked for redress. Jewish moneylenders experienced a high rate of default and forgery in the eighteenth century. They were eager, therefore, to take both untrustworthy and defaulting debtors to court. They also lacked other informal channels of enforcement.

[27] ADTB 12B81.   [28] ADTB 12B44.

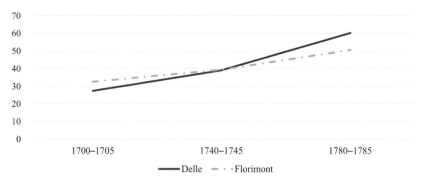

Figure 5.1 Percentage of failures to appear at court in the seigneuries of Delle and Florimont in the eighteenth century.
(*Source*: judicial dataset)

In an increasing number of debt lawsuits throughout the eighteenth century, debtors deliberately chose not to attend the hearing. In the south of Alsace, this absence was particularly noticeable in debt collection cases. In both seigneuries, the level of non-presentation at court rose increasingly throughout the eighteenth century. It reached 60.3% in Delle and 50.2% in Florimont in the 1780s (see Figure 5.1). Elsewhere, historians have observed the same phenomenon. Along the Loire river, in Château-La-Vallière between 1761 and 1765, more than half of the defendants did not attend their hearing. In the same region, in Saint Christophe, between 1770 and 1774, the proportion of absent defendants reached 55.7%.[29]

Why did an increasing number of debtors choose not to appear at court? Insolvent debtors might have thought they could spare themselves the embarrassment of appearing at court for debt collection, especially because the issue would have been ultimately the same whether they attended the hearing or not. They also might have preferred to avoid an embarrassing and shameful encounter with their creditor. It might have been a strategy to gain time. Not attending the hearing led inexorably to the loss of the lawsuits for defaulting debtors.

Those attending their hearing came usually to contest the debt. In 1781, Henri Labouebe from Chavannes-les-Grands asked Pierre Sabourin from the village of Grosne for the repayment of eighty-seven livres. Sabourin claimed he had repaid the money. The judge ruled that

---

[29] Fabrice Mauclair, La justice au village, p 274.

he had to prove he made the payment.[30] No further hearing could be found. The parties had likely found an agreement.

Foreclosure was the last possible legal action against an insolvent debtor. Evidently, foreclosure often meant financial distress and possibly indigence for many low-income debtors. Jean Pierre Chavanne, a farmer from Réchésy, struggled financially. In 1737, he had signed a couple of obligations to the profit of Charles Fleur. Charles Fleur was, in comparison, a wealthy man with cash readily available. He managed the foundry in Grandvillars, a respectable and profitable position. In 1740, he took Chavanne to court to collect 438 livres, the remaining sum of the obligations. The judge ruled in the plaintiff's favour. Despite the verdict, Chavanne was unable to meet his obligations and could not repay. In November 1741, Fleur asked for the foreclosure of Chavanne's assets.[31]

Some other debtors experienced foreclosure as merely a bump in the road, a result of poor financial management and with limited economic consequences. Maurice Dietrich was one of them. A better-off labourer living in the village of Puis, together with his first wife, they owned about 4,200 livres worth of land, a substantial amount. The couple also produced fabric on the side, likely destined for the marketplace and therefore generating a complementary income. Their house was one of the nicest in the village, with a tiled rather than straw roof. Their furniture and other household items could not be labelled as extravagant but were, by comparison, decent. They were one of the few households, for instance, to own items such as a book, a clock, and a rifle.[32] The couple had nonetheless incurred many debts. When Dietrich's wife, Madelaine Guyot, died in 1776, they owed 2,173 livres and 10 deniers to various creditors, a fortune. Better-off households were usually the most indebted ones; this particular one was no exception. Sales on credit for land and livestock, as well as loans, were among the outstanding debts. After the death of his spouse, Dietrich encountered some difficulty. Most of the couple's creditors tried to retrieve their dues at court. Dietrich appeared at court as the defendant in nine debt collection cases (see Table 5.2).

In 1783, Maurice Dietrich appeared to be unable to meet some of his debts.[33] One of his creditors, George Dermineur, asked for the foreclosure of Dietrich's assets. Dermineur could certainly have asked for the simple repayment of his dues but he preferred the assets of his debtor to be seized and sold. There is no previous lawsuit between the two parties recorded. As Dermineur asked for foreclosure, a clerk listed the debtor's land as well as items in the debtor's house to be auctioned.

[30] ADTB 8B156.   [31] ADTB 2E4/43-44.   [32] ADTB 2E4/439, Madelaine Guyot.
[33] ADTB 12B81.

Table 5.2 *Debt collection suits against Maurice Dietrich, seigneurie de Florimont, 1780–85*

Date	Plaintiff	Reason	Date of the initial agreement	Amount
6 February 1781	Moïse Bluem	Private written agreement unpaid	September 1779	216
15 May 1781	Jacques Patingre	Livestock, sales on credit	Unknown	96
16 April 1782	Antoine Schwartz	Land, sales on credit	1768	477.25
8 May 1783	Jacques Dadey	Remains of a debt	Unknown	39
16 July 1783	Jean Carnal	Various written agreements unpaid	1779	318
16 July 1783	George Lacour	Medical fees	Unknown	40.75
16 July 1783	Jean Pierre Patingre	Land, sales on credit	1781	66
19 August 1783	George Dermineur	Foreclosure	Unknown	
16 March 1784	Jacob Gilot	Private written agreement unpaid	1782	37,5
				1,290.5

Source: ADTB 12B79, 12B80, 12B81, 12B82

The local judge often appointed a private individual to watch over the seized movables before the public auction to avoid any possible removal of assets. After the list of assets was ready, the judge decided whether the defendant's items would suffice to repay his debts. At the foreclosure hearing, both parties could also present their views. This was the last opportunity for the defendant to avoid foreclosure. Dietrich declared that he hoped that not more land than necessary would be sold at the auction, for about the '600 or 700 livres' due to Dermineur. The judge declared the foreclosure valid. The auction took place. The suit mentions other potential creditors, but none are listed. It is unclear what happened next; in any case, it does not seem to have had a strong impact on Dietrich. He still had some possessions afterwards; he married twice after this. In 1788, he donated all his remaining assets and land to his children.[34] He built for himself and his wife a small house and lived off the pension

[34] ADTB 2E4/389.

his son was paying him. The foreclosure certainly deprived him of some land but enough remained. We do not know how his social credit was affected.

In theory, when a debtor had defaulted and found himself unable to repay, the judge ordered his assets to be seized and auctioned, as in the example above. Household items were listed first, depending on the amount owed. Land came thereafter. The assets of the guarantor could also be at stake. In the eighteenth century, *fidejussion* (guarantee) became both increasingly in demand but also a greater risk. Guarantors, after having paid the debtor's dues, could in turn sue him. In the case that a debtor had mortgaged a specific piece of land, the said piece was auctioned. The judge also assigned seniority among the potential various creditors on a pro-rata basis. Foreclosure often involved several creditors. In 1679, Pierre Bidelle experienced financial difficulty; to repay his numerous creditors, his house was seized. The winning bidder offered 295 livres bâloises. This amount did not seem to be below market price but matched perfectly the overall amount due. It was often the case that auctioned assets were sold not for the highest price possible but rather to match the amount of debt to be repaid. The money was then distributed among Bidelle's creditors on a pro-rata basis. The hôpital took the largest share, 140 livres bâloises, while the other twelve creditors shared the rest according to what was owed to them.[35]

Auctions were public events. People learnt about the event at church where auctions were often advertised on the door.[36] Two types of auctions were usually performed. The first was a regular sale by auction to the highest bidder (called *encan* in French, from Latin *in quantum*). The second used a candlestick – or several depending on local practises – and was called *à la chandelle*. The last bidder when the candlelight went out won the prize. This type of auction seems to have been less and less common throughout the period.

It is a common assumption that the seizure of assets related to indebtedness is perceived as a creditor's weapon. Marxist historiography has claimed that indebted peasants were forced to cede their land to their rapacious creditors. Recently, historians have shown that this picture did not correspond to reality for at least two reasons.[37] First, creditors preferred to roll over an overdue debt rather than enforce the repayment

---

[35] ADTB 2E4/53.   [36] ADTB 12B45.

[37] B. A. Holderness, "Credit in a Rural Community, 1660–1800: Some Neglected Aspects of Probate Inventories." *Midland History* 3, no. 2 (1975): 94–116. Postel-Vinay, Gilles, *La terre et l'argent l'agriculture et le crédit en France du XVIIIe au début du XXe siècle.* (Paris: Albin Michel, 1997), p 33. Brennan, "Peasants and Debt in Eighteenth-Century Champagne." Fontaine, "Antonio and Shylock," p 44. P. R. Schofield, "Alternatives

of their capital. Creditors preferred to continue receiving the payment of the interest rather than suing their debtors in court, as we saw in previous chapters. Several reasons may explain this. Creditors may not have wanted to damage the long-standing relationship with their debtor and his family. Bringing the debtor before a court was not a guarantee to retrieve one's capital in its entirety; a long list of creditors could also present themselves. In addition, the plot of land mortgaged could have been over-mortgaged to several creditors. Second, village solidarity played a role at auctions. Historians have noted that, here and there in Europe, family members, friends, and neighbours often bought the auctioned property before handing it over to the original owner. They often offered low prices on auctioned land in order for the debtor to retrieve his assets.[38] Joseph Frossard and his wife faced financial difficulties to the point where their assets were seized. At the auction, only one bidder made an offer, but it was too low to cover the debt. The judge had no choice but to decide the adjournment of the auction. Not bidding at all seemed to have been a strategy in some instances to make the auction impossible. In February 1786, Marie Bandelier, an unmarried rural domestic, successfully placed a bid at an auction to retrieve her mother and father's seized land. She had to borrow 100 livres tournois but the land could remain in the family.[39]

If private individuals showed leniency towards insolvent debtors and rarely used foreclosure, institutions' strategies differed. The *hôpital des pauvres* in Delle extended credit from its creation at the beginning of the seventeenth century. It did not tolerate late payments very easily and often sent the bailiff to seize goods to be auctioned in place of interest payments. In 1709, it seized a couple of pigs from Jacques Gainon who owed 5.4 livres bâloises for the interest. In Moris Boige's house, grain was seized for a value of 3 livres tournois. And in

---

to Expropriation: Rent, Credit and Peasant Landholding in Medieval Europe and Modern Palestine." *Continuity and Change*, 36, 2, 2021: 36 (2) 141–148. Antoni Furió, 'Rents Instead of Land. Credit and Peasant Indebtedness in Late Medieval Mediterranean Iberia: The Kingdom of Valencia'. *Continuity and Change* 36, no. 2 (2021): 177–209. Laurence Fontaine and Paul Servais, "Relations de crédit et surendettement en France: XVIIème–XVIIIème siècles." In *Des personnes aux institution: Réseaux et culture du crédit du XVIe au XXe siècle en Europe*, edited by Laurence Fontaine, Gilles Postel-Vinay, and Jean-Laurent Rosenthal. (Louvain-la-Neuve, Belgium: Bruylant-Academia, 1997).

[38] Antoni Furió, "Crédit, endettement et justice: Prêteurs et débiteurs devant le juge dans le royaume de Valence (XIIIe–XVe siècle)." In Julie Claustre, ed. *La dette et le juge: juridiction gracieuse et juridiction contentieuse du XIIIe au XVe siècle (France, Italie, Espagne, Angleterre, Empire)*. (Paris: Publications de la Sorbonne, 2006), 19–54, p 50.

[39] ADTB 2E4/281.

Francois Girardot's house, the bailiff took some pieces of clothing worth 3 livres bâloises.[40]

In fact, most people preferred to renegotiate the term of their agreement or find alternative solutions. In 1765, Elisabeth Gainon loaned fifty livres to a couple living in her village for their '*affaires et besoins*' (business and needs). Jacques Bonjean and Suzanne Vuilaumier, however, could not repay Gainon after the three-year deadline. They preferred to write a land sale and cede one of their pieces of land to her at a negotiated price.[41] Their case did not appear at court, meaning they preferred to negotiate the matter privately. Private arrangements and negotiation often prevailed. Those arrangements are obviously difficult to track.

The proportion of foreclosures remained low for most of the period, indicating that creditors did not favour this strategy.[42] In the last period observed, however, more cases were noted. In the seigneurie of Delle, there were sixty-seven foreclosures while only seventeen took place in the seigneurie of Florimont. In Delle, for instance, thirty-nine of the plaintiffs asking for foreclosure, out of sixty-seven, belonged to the upper strata of the population. Twenty-three belonged to the nobility and the civil servants/services group and nine belonged to the middling sort.[43] The remaining seven were institutions. The same pattern can be observed in Florimont. Why did these individuals in particular ask for foreclosure? First, as their saving capacity was usually higher, the middling and upper sort might have lent more money than any other group. They had, therefore, potentially a greater incentive to retrieve their capital. Second, and I think this is key, these individuals might not have shared the same values and norms of cooperation and fairness as the peasantry. Christophe Lotz sat on the city council of Porrentruy; as such, there is little doubt he was a wealthy man. Councillors in Porrentruy often counted among them the merchant bourgeoisie and the non-manual professionals, almost never among the peasantry. So when in April 1741, he summoned the labourer Pierre Antoine Hantz for the payment of an obligation amounting to one hundred livres bâloises, he had no incentive to be patient with his defaulting debtor.

---

[40] Cited by Jules Joachim, "La fondation des pauvres ou vieil hôpital de Delle 1600–1820," *Bulletin de la Société Belfortaine d'Emulation*, no. 50, 1936: 151–207, p 169. On this topic see also Smail, *Legal Plunder*.

[41] ADTB 2E4/257.

[42] Foreclosure remained therefore an exception, as did land evictions. In Suecia, a town in the south of Valencia in Spain, between 1485 and 1515, foreclosure took place in 20% of the judicial cases and auction of the assets occurred in only 4% of these cases. See Antoni Furió, "Crédit, endettement et justice." p 50.

[43] See Hunt, *The Middling Sort*.

With no sign of repayment in sight, Lotz asked for foreclosure on Hantz's assets in October 1741.[44] Concerning the middling sort, artisans, retailers and service-oriented labourers had a stronger incentive to retrieve their dues to keep afloat and assure the sustainability of their business.

Despite the resort to court, debt collection did imply a strong degree of cooperation between creditors and debtors to recover the unpaid debt. To a certain extent, the coercive power of judicial courts remained limited. Foreclosure and auctions did happen but their process implied that the debtor let the assessors enter his house to list and seize his assets.

An important question needs to be asked at this point. Why would someone take a debtor to court to collect debt via a third party? The most obvious answer is to retrieve one's capital. The creditor might have needed the money that had been lent. But even by summoning a debtor to court, there was absolutely no guarantee that the capital lent would be recovered in full. A second reason might be that court fees were always paid by the party who lost the case. In 99% of debt lawsuits, the debtor lost the case and was condemned to repay his debt. It was, therefore, a safe gambit for a creditor to take a debtor to court knowing it involved no transaction cost. Debt collection suits served another purpose; seniority ranking of a debt could be established, which was rather important in the case of a debtor's insolvency and the subsequent foreclosure. As we have seen, actors in the credit market had very little knowledge regarding their debtor's financial standing. There was no register showing whether land has already been mortgaged. If a debtor became insolvent, several creditors could claim part of his assets. The judge's ruling helped in identifying existing creditors and assessing seniority ranking. In the seigneuries of Delle and Florimont, access to court was made fairly easy; the geographical distance to the courthouse was no greater than fifteen kilometres for the farthest village.

But as most loans were highly personalized, summoning a defaulting debtor before the judge signalled that all other informal enforcement mechanisms to recover the debt had failed. Nicolas Laloz, the smith of Faverois declared that he 'had repeated his demand for payments on several occasions' to his debtor Simon Barré, without success.[45] Beyond economic considerations, a court action certainly spelt the end of a good friendship and possibly the rupture of the communication channel between the debtor and the creditor.

I believe that debt collection suits featured a broken promise that needed to be addressed in the public eye. Jean Pierre Fleury had known

[44] ADTB 12B44.   [45] ADTB 8B19.

his neighbour Jacques Herbelin for several years. They lived in the same village where Herbelin often frequented Fleury's inn. In 1771, the innkeeper lent 100 livres to his neighbour, using a private written contract. As it is often the case, we do not know what the money was for. Six years later, in 1777, Fleury agreed to yet another loan of 100 livres. But this time, the pair signed an obligation at the notary's office, indicating perhaps a certain distrust on the part of the innkeeper or, more likely, the renewal of the original loan. Between 1777 and 1780, Fleury let Herbelin run a tab for food and drink. He agreed to additional small cash loans here and there, which he registered in his account book. After all, innkeepers extended credit in the form of running tabs and cash, often contributing to the redistribution of specie. At some point, the innkeeper attempted to retrieve his capital, either because he needed the money himself or because he had lost patience and trust in Herbelin. None of the debt had been satisfied after all. It is likely that Fleury tried to talk and negotiate with Herbelin. In July 1780, presumably tired of his fruitless attempts, he took the matter to court. At the hearing, he showed the judge the two contracts and his account book. Herbelin failed to appear to contest the charge. The costs were awarded to Fleury.[46] There were no further hearings between the two litigants, indicating that the matter had been resolved. Either Fleury had repaid his debts straight away or the innkeeper had renegotiated the terms of their agreement. We do not know if friendship was restored.

Litigants had the *choice* to bring a case before the judge or not. Most inhabitants had the capacity to do so. In theory, every subject had the right and the freedom to seek justice. The reason why a creditor took this step might not be the result of pure economic reasoning and logic. As credit was highly personalized, a court action often fell within mechanisms of trust and friendship. Economic exchanges, after all, took place between individuals and as such were 'nearly always embedded within a social context'.[47] It is thus interesting to pause for a moment on the emotional dimension of judicial debt collection. Emotion was an inherent component of the action of lending money. In the strong ties within communities, friendship and a sense of obligation often engendered and cemented credit transactions. It is not surprising to witness the rise of strong emotions in the case of disputes.

---

[46] ADTB 12B79.

[47] Marcel Fafchamps. "Formal and Informal Market Institutions: Embeddedness Revisited." In Jean-Marie Baland, François Bourguignon, Jean-Philippe Platteau, and Thierry Verdier, eds. *The Handbook of Economic Development and Institutions* (Princeton, NJ: Princeton University Press, 2020), pp. 375–413, p 375.

Marie Eve Chavanne was a rural domestic working at Jean-Baptiste Galliat's farm. In July 1781, she came before the judge to claim the payment of her salary. Less than a month later, Melchior Galliat, brother of her former master, accused her of being a 'slut and a slob' and physically attacked her, perhaps because she had claimed her dues at court, defaming her former employer and his family in the public eye.[48] We cannot possibly know for sure. The exact same thing happened to Anne Marie Huguelin from the village of Seppois-le-Haut. She had been working at Georges Surgaud's farm as a domestic. Her master owed her six livres and a muslin handkerchief, the remainder of her salary. In March 1762, she took the case before the judge who ruled in her favour. Two months later, when she ran into her former master, who still had not paid her, in the street, a fight between the two occurred. She claimed that Surgaud pulled her hair, knocked her down three times, and held her down while his new servant, Madelaine Burget, beat her head with a stick.[49] Strong emotions and financial matters were often entangled even if correlation does not equate causation. Financial disputes could lead to or fuel existing hatred and violence.

Some lawsuits highlight how friendship could turn into hatred when the norms of cooperation were infringed. In December 1741, a widowed baker, Marguerite Durand, came before the judge of Florimont to ask for the payment of nine livres tournois for some bread she had sold on credit to Henri Monnier, the mayor of Florimont. As we have seen, cooperation was such that it was usual to keep a tab at the local store for this kind of transaction. The amount of money was rather small. The fact that the baker had to request payment before the local judge indicates that she had not been successful in getting it earlier by more direct means and that she was now in open conflict with Monnier. The story is a little bit complicated as the bread ordered by the mayor was consumed by a carpenter working for the community of Florimont and therefore commissioned by the mayor. The judge asked to hear all the parties involved and the mayor claimed that he had paid for the bread, which the baker continued to deny, as her books made no mention of it. The parties appeared in the courtroom on two further occasions and witnesses were summoned to testify as to whether or not the bread had been paid for. In March 1742, three months after the initial complaint of the widow, whose case was still open and under investigation, she reappeared before the judge as a plaintiff. This time, she came to request 100 livres of 'dommages et intérêts' (compensation) as the wife of the mayor, Marie

---

[48] ADTB 8B156.   [49] ADTB 8B132.

Bettevy, had physically attacked her. She claimed that the mayor's wife 'beat her up, knocked her down to the ground several times and punched and kicked her, and that she lost so much blood that she had to stay in bed at home for several days.' We cannot fail to note the use of a dramatic narrative here. Marie Bettevy, the mayor's wife, on the other hand, simply declared that the baker insulted her saying she was a 'silly woman and a thief' ('*une sotte et une voleuse*'). Several court hearings took place afterwards regarding the two cases. On 11 October 1742, the mayor's wife was charged to pay 10 livres of *dommages et intérêts* to the baker, to pay for medicines and expenses, and she was also fined 4 livres and 16 sols for disturbing the public peace. The very next day, her husband, the mayor, was charged to pay the baker 19 livres for the bread and late interest fees; he also had to pay all the legal fees of about 30 livres.

This short example highlights several important features about the local courts, money, and sentiments. Financial issues could trigger strong sentiments such as enmity, revenge, hatred, and humiliation. For the payment of nine livres and in defence of their honour, the mayor's wife severely injured the baker, which tends to show that the matter and its development was extremely important to her and her husband. It also reveals the flip side of trust as a complaint was lodged against the mayor. When the norms of cooperation were infringed, in this case the default of payment for the bread and the breach of trust, both material reparations and moral reparations were looked for in the courts. Legal sanctions often implied moral sanctions because the bond between the parties had been broken. It is also interesting to note that lawsuits for defamation often featured insults related to honesty. The term 'thief' is by far the most common insult featured in judicial registers.

Emotions could arise as a consequence of legal sanctions (shame/pride, anger, hatred/joy, feelings of justice/injustice, indignation, desire for vengeance, etc). Enmity was exposed to the public eye and news was spread and conveyed within a tight-knit community. In this community, emotions could be manipulated in order, for instance, to emphasize a prejudice and seek compassion, understanding, and sympathy from others, to diminish an opponent through giving them a bad reputation, to seek pity or admiration from others. The description of Durand's injury in this respect might have been manipulated and overdramatized. The public nature of this small case was quite important as witnesses had to give information on the payment or otherwise for the bread and, consequently, had to take sides. And finally, emotions such as those in this example have meaning and send information to the participants. Marie Bettevy's attack on the baker refers to her husband's conflict with Margueritte Durand and expands the network of emotionality in the community. The mayor's wife was the one attacking the baker and not the mayor himself.

Similarly, a creditor might sue an insolvent debtor in order to protect his own reputation and his own affairs. By suing a debtor, a creditor flexed his muscles before other existing or potential borrowers. But by stopping short of a lawsuit, he also showed his charitable and fair character. Overall, debt collection lawsuits triggered strong emotions because of the embeddedness of debt in social relations.

Characteristics of Default: Nature of Debt

In general, in court rolls, most of the plaintiffs asked for monetary redress in one way or another. Even in suits for battery and defamation, litigants assessed the reparations they estimated they deserved in monetary value. The characterization of debt is therefore challenging as one needs to disentangle which cases come under debt collection. In Tables 5.3 and 5.4, debt collection lawsuits are divided according to the type of initial agreement they were based on.

Non-intermediated contracts, that is non-notarized agreements, such as promissory notes and sales on credit, accounted for most of the lawsuits throughout the period. The same results have been found along the Loire Valley in Château-la-Vallière and Saint Christophe. There too, private agreements outnumbered notarial obligations.[50] This is hardly surprising considering this type of agreement accounted for most of the existing transactions as noted in Chapter 2.

This type of transaction concerned modest amounts of money. Most of these debts did not represent the entire amount lent but most likely the *remainder* of it. In any case, it seems that creditors were eager to sue a debtor at court even for a small amount. When a burgher of Porrentruy asked for the repayment of seven livres tournois for an obligation of the labourer Jacques Brahier in 1683, it was likely the remainder of a greater sum.[51] Jean Jacques Schmitt, the butcher of Florimont did not hesitate to summon his neighbour for a debt of four livres and eight deniers owed to him for meat sold.[52] Overall, the mean value for deferred sales and private agreements remained below eighty-two livres. It is important to note that account books presented by plaintiffs had to be signed by the debtor to be recognized as legitimate. The initial debt was likely made verbally and was later recorded in the account book.

---

[50] Hervé Piant, *Une justice ordinaire.*   [51] ADTB 8B22.   [52] ADTB 12B81.

Table 5.3 *Overview of the debt lawsuits in the seigneuries of Delle and Florimont, 1680–1789*

	Count	Sum	Mean	Min	Max	Standard deviation
Notarized loan	179	31,337.22	182.19	3	2,400	289.81
Non-notarized loan	617	49,885.94	82.18	0. 25	780.05	110.58
Unpaid credit sales	404	58,239.08	147.81	0.10	12,150	873.94
Services	121	5,077.68	47.45	0.1	554	77.83
Inherited debt	50	6,406.76	133.47	3	576	134.29
Tax related	121	7,747.11	74.49	0.10	1,158	156.83
Parish vestry	43	3,806.57	90.63	5.14	1,126.60	226.94
Rent	69	7,762.85	127.26	1	2,954	403.36
Foreclosure	147	429.80	143.27	27	352.80	181.83
Other	48	8,440.87	175.85	5.25	2,000	323.44

Source: judicial dataset

These short-term small debts overloaded the dockets of the judicial courts (Tables 5.2 and 5.3). Shopkeepers and artisans selling craft products and other items had to make sure they did not run into bankruptcy themselves to assure the continuity of their business. Innkeepers were particularly exposed as most of their sales were made on credit. In addition, we cannot discard the idea that the middling sort used the justice system to recover their dues to emphasize their own creditworthiness as good business managers.

Some of the sales in credit disputes took place because creditors did not keep their account books in proper order. In towns and cities, artisans, retailers, and better-off households often had account books to help them keep track of their affairs.[53] But the two accounting columns were often not filled properly.[54] In traditional communities where the literacy rate was supposedly low, people carefully archived their transactions in bundles in wooden boxes. Not only did better-off peasants have account books, but increasingly others did too. In the late-eighteenth century, most households kept track of their expenses, financial assets, and income in writing, either in account books or in the form of bundled papers. Plaintiffs and defendants frequently quarrelled over calculations and the exact standing of accounts. For example, a defendant would claim he had already repaid part of the money due while the plaintiff would claim the contrary or advance another figure. Often, the judge had to invite them to tell their history together with the help of any written

---

[53] See Daniel L. Smail, *Legal Plunder*, p 93.
[54] As shown by Julie Hardwick, "Banqueroute," pp 90–91.

Table 5.4 *Categories of debt featured in lawsuits in the seigneuries of Delle and Florimont, 1680–1785*

	1680–85[a]		1700–05[b]		1740–45		1780–85		Total	
	N	%	N	%	N	%	N	%	N	
Notarized loan	21	25.6	25	16.0	56	10.5	77	7.5	179	
Non-notarized loan	16	19.5	32	20.5	152	28.4	417	40.7	617	
Unpaid credit sales	15	18.3	37	23.7	108	20.2	244	23.8	404	
Services	11	13.4	14	9.0	43	8.0	53	5.1	121	
Inherited debt	3	3.7	7	4.5	11	2.1	29	2.8	50	
Tax related	8	9.8	19	12.2	52	9.7	42	4.1	121	
Parish vestry	3	3.7	2	1.3	18	3.4	20	2.0	43	
Rent	3	3.7	12	7.7	17	3.2	37	3.6	69	
Foreclosure	0	0.0	6	3.8	57	10.7	84	8.2	147	
Other	2	2.4	2	1.3	21	3.9	23	2.2	48	
Total	82	100	156	100	535	100	1,026	100	1,799	

[a] Only data available for Delle.
[b] Only the year 1700 available for Delle.
Source: judicial dataset

evidence they could provide. In 1773, Joseph Piquerez, the innkeeper of Réchésy, claimed before the judge that Pierre Antoine Quinkre owed him four livres and four sols for wine he had drunk with others in his house over a year earlier. He brought his account book to support his claim. The defendant responded that he had paid the amount and had left the money on the table. The court case does not transcribe the entirety of the verbal exchange. But both parties seem to have reached some sort of agreement. And the judge dropped the case.[55]

The falling proportion of notarial obligations featured in the judicial records is perhaps surprising, especially since the number of notarial loans increased throughout the period (see Figure 5.2). This can be explained because obligations, as notarized documents, gradually included more pledges and securities throughout the period. People might have had a greater incentive to reimburse those loans first. In the same vein, a very few lawsuits dealt with loans enacted by the *hôpital des pauvres*, a charitable institution. Debtors also had a greater incentive to pay the interest as a priority since their lands were mortgaged and a guarantor was on the deed. Note that annuities did not appear in lawsuits. In theory, these credit instruments did not have a deadline for repayment. Their length was unlimited as long as the interest remained paid in cash or in kind. In theory, therefore, a creditor could not claim the payment of the capital in court.

Apart from notarized loans, private agreements, and unpaid sales credit, we find other lawsuits regarding debt collection. I have already mentioned foreclosure cases. Payments for services and wage arrears also filled the courts' dockets. Marie Eve Chavanne, a domestic at Jean Baptiste Galliat's mill sued her master as part of her salary remained unpaid, ninety-nine livres and twelve sols.[56] Alix, the daughter of Antoine Dion also had a difficult time getting paid. Her master, Jacques Franquin, had not paid her salary. The same goes for Georges Verne, a farm worker on Jean Terrier's farm. His master had just died, and the widow Jeanne Riche had not yet paid him the twenty livres bâloises of his salary.[57] He might have feared that while the widow was settling the estate, the payment of the debt would eat up his wages. Asking for justice was a strategy to appear as a creditor of the household in the absence of a working contract. With a sentence, he had an official dated document in his hand acknowledging the debt.

There were many reasons why people defaulted on their debt. Harvests might have been insufficient. Cash was often scarce. Borrowing beyond

[55] ADTB 12B73.   [56] ADTB 8B156.   [57] ADTB 12B15 and 16.

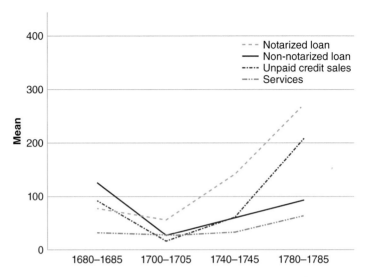

Figure 5.2 Mean amount of money at stake in debt lawsuits in the seigneuries of Delle and Florimont, 1680–1785.
(*Source*: judicial dataset)

their means, households might have had a hard time to service their debt. Death, illness, and other physical incapacities might have reduced the productive abilities of a family. Feuds, personal conflicts, and sundered friendship ties might have made the reclaiming of loans difficult. People tended to delay the repayment of their debts as long as their creditors tolerated it. Yet, justice records very rarely delve into these reasons.

Who Defaulted and on Whom?

Debt is a relationship of power between two parties; 'handing over wealth is the expression of the superiority of the giver to the recipient'.[58] This aspect is magnified further if there was a discrepancy between the socio-professional status of the parties.

Disputants are divided into groups based on their socio-professional categories with particular attention given to their social status: farmers, middling sorts (innkeepers, doctors, artisans, millers, etc.), and upper strata or better sorts (local representatives, civil servants, lawyers,

---

[58] Bronislaw Malinowski, *Argonauts of the Western Pacific: An Account of Native Enterprise and Adventure in the Archipelagoes of Melanesian New Guinea [1922/1994]* (London: Routledge, 2013), p 177.

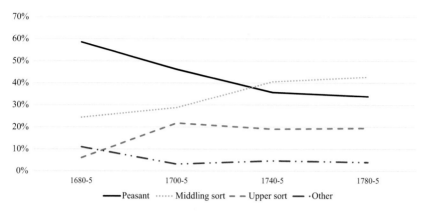

Figure 5.3 Plaintiffs in the seigneuries of Delle and Florimont by socio-professional categories, 1680–1785.

nobility, clergy).[59] The social status of each category mattered, especially in cases where the plaintiff was better-off than the debtor. A non-manual worker might have a greater incentive to sue a defaulting farmer to retrieve his capital but also, and perhaps above all, to protect his prestige capital.

In 1680–85, 58.5% of the plaintiffs were peasants, and only 33.8% a century later. In the meantime, the number of plaintiffs from the middling sort rose. The proportion of plaintiffs from the upper sort remained stable. In the last decade of the Ancien Regime, 42.7% of the plaintiffs belonged to the middling sort and 19.5% to the upper sort (see Figure 5.3). By contrast, the number of peasants as defendants remained about the same throughout the period. There was a slight increase of the middling sort proportion as defendants throughout the eighteenth century. The upper sort percentage of defendants was negligible (see Figure 5.4). Considering these trends, more plaintiffs belonged to the middling and upper sort while defendants remained peasants, which created an imbalance of power, including bargaining power. Those with a superior social status within the community pursued the enforcement of debt against those of a lower status.

The growing commercialization of the exchanges, the rise of non-manual workers under the impulse of the venality of charges, technological improvements, and amelioration in agricultural productivity contributed to the rise of new socio-professional categories. It is also a trend we observed in the notarial credit market where more middling sort and

---

[59] Hunt, *The Middling Sort*; Dolan, *Entre justice et justiciables*.

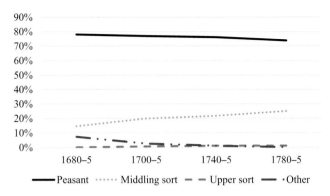

Figure 5.4 Defendants in the seigneuries of Delle and Florimont by socio-professional categories, 1680–1785.

upper sort households extended credit. These households proceeded with debt enforcement at court to assure the sustainability of their business. In the meantime, they also sought the preservation of their newly acquired social status and reputation. These categories displayed perhaps less forbearance with their peasant debtors with whom they shared presumably less similar conditions and social norms.

Debt was not only highly personalized, it was also well embedded in the social structure of a community. The network in Figure 5.5 is based on the debt collection lawsuits in the seigneurie of Florimont in 1780–85. Each node represents a litigant while the direction of the arrow is from a plaintiff to a defendant. A node's size is weighted according to its out degree, in other words, the number of complaints appearing as a plaintiff. The network features a collection of dyadic nodes. But most strikingly perhaps, it shows one massive component in the middle. It highlights particularly well how debt was a community matter with connections linking many agents with each other. And some households were at turn plaintiff and defendant.

Litigants were often neighbours (see Table 5.5). A third of the parties lived in the same village. This proportion remained more or less constant throughout the eighteenth century.[60] This geographical propinquity is perhaps not surprising given that debt was highly personalized and often formed between people who had previous knowledge of each other and frequent interaction. Personal conflicts could also be stirred up by proximity and frequent encounters.

---

[60] Data for 1700–05 shows a higher proportion but it is certainly due to the fact that data for the seigneurie of Delle is incomplete.

Table 5.5 *Relationships between litigants in the seigneuries of Delle and Florimont, 1680–1785*

	1680–85	1700–05	1740–45	1780–85
% Same village	32.9	46.9	33.3	30.9
% Same family	1.2	1.2	4.1	3.3

Source: judicial dataset

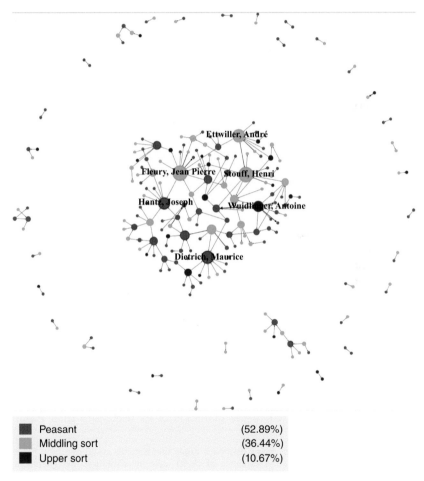

■ Peasant	(52.89%)
▨ Middling sort	(36.44%)
■ Upper sort	(10.67%)

Figure 5.5 Network of litigants in the seigneurie of Florimont, 1780–85.
(*Source*: judicial dataset)

It is perhaps not surprising either that litigations for debt rarely took place between family members. While 14% of promissory notes, 8% of deferred payments, and 13.5% of notarial loans took place among relatives, only a few lawsuits featured such relations. Less than 4% of the debt litigations featured conflicts between relatives. Families preferred to resolve their disagreements privately, perhaps with the help of intermediaries such as the priest or other family members.[61]

Finally, one should note that the number of female plaintiffs for debt was low. It was 4.4% for widows and 2.5% for single women. Single women often claimed their dues as domestics. And widows asked for the repayment of a debt after their husbands' death, a critical period when they often had to assert their authority and rights to bad faith debtors.

Turning to the proportion of female defendants, the case of married couples is of interest. In 1680–85, they were 1.2% to be brought before the judge. In 1780–85, their proportion increased to 12.6%. We have seen that the proportion of married couples as borrowers rose in the notarial credit market throughout the eighteenth century. There is a correlation here between these two tendencies. Yet, we could have expected a higher percentage of defaulting married couples due to the high proportion of married debtors found in notarial obligations.

The proportion of widows (under 6%) and single women (about 1%) remained marginal. Widows were often brought to court to settle debts they incurred with their deceased husband. In December 1741, Anne Oeuvrard from Suarce was condemned to pay twenty-two livres to Jacques Belet for a promissory note made with her late husband.[62]

Concluding Remarks: The Social and Economic Implications of Default and the Migration of Trust

The judicial system played a critical role in contract enforcement mechanisms. The increasing volume of lawsuits for debt collection throughout the eighteenth century proved that litigants found its services adequate. The judicial institution itself acquired expertise in debt settlement and benefited from greater public confidence in return. Embedded in society, the local court responded to the demands of its users and their input

---

[61] Bonzon, *La paix au village.* Some historians argue that notaries could also have filled these functions. I have found evidence of clerks' role in arbitration. See Stéphane Trayaud, "Notariat et infrajustice: le rôle de médiation du notaire sous l'Ancien Régime à travers la pratique de Pierre Thoumas de Bosmie, notaire royal à Limoges (1735–1740)," *Revue d'histoire de l'enfance "irrégulière." Le Temps de l'histoire,* no. Hors-série (2001): 207–20.

[62] ADTB 12B44.

shaped the form of the institution, contributing to its development into a more specialized court, efficient in debt conflict resolution and strong enough to sustain the major change that would constitute capitalism later on. Scholars such as Zorina Khan argue that third party collection through the courts in colonial Maine was in fact meant to economize on transaction costs. I rather think that the greater use of this institution was the result of a social strategy intended to re-establish sundered ties of friendship and resume communication via an intermediary.[63]

As most of the debt collection lawsuits did not go beyond the first hearing and as the number of foreclosures remained low, the court acted mainly as a pressure leveller on debtors, sending them a warning. Ultimately, the social implications were perhaps even greater than the economic. A summons to court sent a signal to other members of the community regarding the state of one's affairs. A debtor's reputation was at stake in an age when information remained scarce and when a credit score did not yet exist. For a debtor, a summons to court, in the public eye, equates to a stain on her reputation. Some debtors ran the risk of seeing other debts being suddenly recalled. Yet, taking an insolvent debtor to court mattered also to the creditor's reputation. Notables and middling sorts both protected their business affairs and asserted the prestige pertaining to their status through the use of courts, again in the public eye. Meanwhile, moral norms of cooperation and fairness were somehow preserved. Foreclosures remained an exception. Both parties preferred to renegotiate outside the courtroom after a first hearing. In the last decades of the Old Regime, however, creditors from the upper sort and the middling sort, both recalled more debts than farmers and asked for foreclosure in greater numbers than peasants. This group of plaintiffs moved their confidence into the arms of official authorities such as the local court, an institution capable of providing public recognition and a form of coercion. It is perhaps a critical moment when trust began to migrate from personalized ties towards institutions.

Economic changes partly shaped the institution of justice as locals resorted more often to the judge for enforcing debt collection. The grip of the upper and middling sort on resources and capital defined their position in society and constituted the major vector of change. This group of plaintiffs, a selected few, furthered objectives and were a force of change, increasing perhaps inequality at the institutional level, especially with reference to the treatment of their cases to the detriment of others. As a result, legal institutions abandoned their persuasive supervision of social interaction and behaviour over the course of the eighteenth century.

[63] Khan, "Justice of the Marketplace," p 23.

6   The Growing Institutionalization of Credit

It is now an accepted fact that a shift occurred from the prevalence of personal transactions to the emergence of impersonal exchanges.[1] At some point in time, transactions embedded in social exchanges governed by reciprocity and repetition ceased to be personal. With the increasing complexity of societies, formal structures emerged. These formal structures, acting *de facto* as intermediaries or brokers, imposed their rules and mechanisms, weakening and shoving aside previous communal norms and practises governing traditional exchanges. This growing institutionalization was facilitated by modernity. Modern times brought technological changes and developments such as better communication tools or novel contractual instruments favouring conformity. But this movement forward was not linear and not self-evident. Scholars have trouble defining its contours and identifying its origins. Douglass North, referring to this shift between personal and impersonal exchanges, remains vague as to the conditions of its exact emergence.[2] David Graeber, by contrast, points to the responsibility of capitalism.[3] While this depersonalization of exchange now has the consensus of scholars, the forces and mechanisms behind the switch still remain to be determined.[4]

This process of institutionalization also finds an echo in the history of credit.[5] There, too, traditional financial exchanges based on communal norms made way for more formal and intermediated types of transactions.[6] Gradually, peer-to-peer lending ceased to be personalized and

---

[1] North, *Institutions, Institutional Change and Economic Performance*; Tonnies, *Community and Society*; Graeber, *Debt*.

[2] North, *Institutions, Institutional Change and Economic Performance*.

[3] Graeber, *Debt*, 2011.

[4] Lemercier and Zalc, "Pour une nouvelle approche de la relation de crédit en histoire contemporaine," p 983.

[5] Berthe, ed., *Endettement paysan et crédit rural*, p 18.

[6] See Pierre-Cyrille Hautcoeur, "Les transformations du crédit en France au XIXe siècle," *Romantisme*, vol 151 no. 1 (2011): 23–38.

became intermediated, either for the conclusion of the contract and/or its enforcement. In eighteenth-century Alsace, there was a growing use of the notary's services for the drafting of loan contracts and increasing resort to the local court of justice for the execution and enforcement of debt contracts. What exactly did cause this growing institutionalization of credit? Why did households begin to turn to institutions to handle their financial matters? What were the forces behind this phenomenon?

Parallel and concomitant to this growing institutionalization of credit is the challenge of mutual arrangements and subsequently moral norms. Pre-industrial credit exchanges took place within the framework of a moral economy. Transactions were, for the most part, fair, flexible, and renegotiable. Non-intermediated credit implied reciprocal trust and the adherence to communal social norms for both the conclusion of the contracts and their enforcement. Even notarial credit, an intermediated form of credit featuring, in theory, more rigid legal norms, displayed norms of the moral economy. Notarial loans were negotiable and renegotiable and offered both input and elasticity to the parties.

Yet, in the last decades of the Ancien Regime, one observes a split in this model. The moral economy framework began to crack. Rigidity and distrust made an appearance. Idiosyncratic exchanges featuring high inputs were progressively replaced by more standardized contracts. Rules and routines developed and became more codified. This chapter explores two elements that pointed in this direction. First, we observe a growing resort to institutions such as the notary and the local court of justice for cases related to debt. Various forces pushed for this growing institutionalization of credit, including the emergence of a new category of lenders. Royal and seigneurial officials as well as legal professionals with saving capacities began to invest massively in the local credit market. As a result, exchanges became unbalanced and lost their flexibility, introducing a lack of stability. Second, this growing institutionalization of credit was partly the result of a growing distrust. Notarial contracts progressively exhibited greater demands for securities. Specific pieces of land offered to back loans had suddenly lost their attractiveness. Borrowers now had to systematically add their wife – and their assets – to the deal. A pledge was also more and more frequently requested. These changes, pertaining to the substance of contracts, suggest a growing distrust between the parties. This growing distrust can be explained by fundamental changes in both the population structure and the emergence of new market realities.

This chapter thus examines in detail the forces and mechanisms behind the growing institutionalization of credit. To understand what happened and why households chose to turn to institutions, one needs to examine credit, households, and institutions, and the migration of trust in a holistic fashion.

Credit, Households, and the Rise of Institutions

In the early modern period, institutions such as the notary or the local court of justice were familiar, they had both existed since at least the Middle Ages. People knew about their existence, functions, and the opportunities they offered. But in the early modern period, people began to use them in a more systematic way. Households turned more and more frequently to institutions either to facilitate their transactions (notaries) and/or to enforce them (local court of justice). The increase was especially visible after the 1760s. An external party – an institution – acting as an arbiter and intermediary came thus to play a central role.

Growing Use of Formal Institutions: The Local Court of Justice

In the middle of the eighteenth century, one observes an increased demand for intermediation at the local court. Throughout the eighteenth century, the number of local civil lawsuits kept increasing. In 1680–85, a total of 377 conflicts were settled in both seigneuries. In 1780–85, a century later, the judges of Delle and Florimont pronounced judgement on 2,686 cases, about 537 trials a year. Considering that there were probably about 1,500 households living in this area in the last decades of the Ancien Regime, the local courts became very popular with the population.[7] Among the legal proceedings, a significant proportion pertained to debt repayment issues.

In Delle, in the late-seventeenth century, 21.7% of all lawsuits were related to debt. A century later, this proportion had jumped to 61.7%. In Florimont, in the period 1700–05, a third of the lawsuits pertained to debt matters (see Figure 6.1). In the last decade of the Ancien Regime, the proportion increased to 42%. Therefore, almost half of the cases handled by the local judge now concerned debt repayment issues. Not only was the local court increasingly used, it was also sought after significantly more for debt matters.

Evidently, as credit activity increased throughout the period, as we have seen in the previous chapters, one might expect to find more debt-related conflicts. Craig Muldrew observes an increase in credit supply

---

[7] A phenomenon commonly noted by historians. Julie Hardwick, *Family Business: Litigation and the Political Economies of Daily Life in Early Modern France* (Oxford: Oxford University Press, 2009), p 129. See especially Muldrew, "Interpreting the Market," p 172.

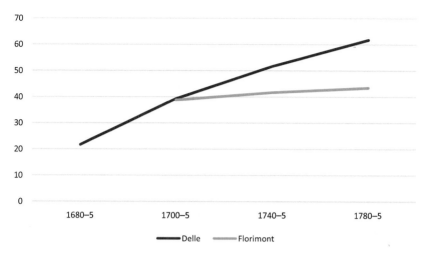

Figure 6.1 Proportion of debt lawsuits in % in registers of court hearings in the seigneuries of Delle and Florimont, 1680–1785. (*Source*: judicial register)

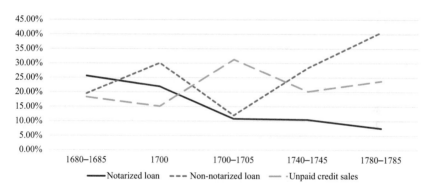

Figure 6.2 Proportion of debt lawsuits per type of contractual engagement in the seigneuries of Delle and Florimont, 1680–1785. (*Source*: judicial dataset)

and demand associated with more defaults in court in sixteenth-century England; a logical correlation between intensification of credit activities and failure to repay one's obligation.[8]

Interestingly, there was a diminution of lawsuits pertaining to notarized loans over time (Figure 6.2). In the seigneurie of Delle, notarized

---

[8] Muldrew, *The Economy of Obligation*, p 124.

loan proceedings accounted for about a quarter of all the debt lawsuits in the period 1680–85. A century later, this proportion had dropped to 8%. But in the meantime, the proportion of non-notarized loan lawsuits jumped from 19.5% to 40.8% for the same period. The trend was similar in Florimont, albeit less marked. These results highlight two tendencies: households seem to have prioritized the repayment of notarial obligations over other commitments; and this rise in debt lawsuits also points to a dynamic non-intermediated credit market. Private credit grew throughout the period. But as it grew, parties did encounter difficulties in the execution of their agreements. Households tended to default on their private deeds more easily. In terms of number, there was an explosion of such cases over the years 1780–85. This did not necessarily mean that households were more encumbered with debts and could not meet their obligations any longer (even though the volume of liabilities did rise as probate inventories show for the last period). It might also entail that households began to prefer the services of a mediator to settle their conflicts.

If one looks at the median amount in debt collection lawsuits, we see a net increase between the 1740s and the 1780s for all sort of loans, both non-intermediated and notarized. In 1780–85, households defaulted on bigger debts than before. The mean for deferred payments was multiplied by more than 3 between 1740–45 and 1780–85. The mean for notarial loans was almost multiplied by two, while the mean for non-intermediated loan was multiplied by 1.5 between the two periods. One might suppose a positive correlation between the weight of the debt and its default; the heavier the burden the more likelihood of default.[9]

If the use of the local court could be explained thanks to increasing credit activities, other factors also favoured its rise and should not be overlooked. Some actors were increasingly required to use the local court to pursue their dues and settle contractual obligations. Guardians, for example, used the courts to settle conflicts on behalf of their trustees. Other plaintiffs represented an institution and were obliged to use the court, even though they appeared under their own name before the judge. Tax collectors, for example, often pursued the repayment of outstanding taxes; although it is unclear if they pursued the tax payment itself or the loans they made thanks to the collection of taxes.[10] These

---

[9] The price for both wheat and land did increase throughout the eighteenth century. Therefore, it is not too surprising to observe bigger loans towards the end of the eighteenth century.

[10] Daphne L. Bonar, "Debt and Taxes: Village Relations and Economic Obligations in Seventeenth-Century Auvergne," *French Historical Studies* 35, no. 4 (2012): 661–89.

litigants were increasingly bound to use official means of conflict resolution like the court to shield themselves from backlash. And the central
authorities, through their officials, also requested that entities such as
communities use the official channels of conflict resolution.[11]

Examining closely the socio-professional categories of the litigants,
there is a fall in the number of peasants among the plaintiffs.
In 1680–85, 58.5% of the plaintiffs were peasants against 33.8% a
century later. In the meantime, the number of plaintiffs from the
middling and upper sort rose. In the last decade of the Ancien Regime,
42.7% of the plaintiffs belonged to the middling sort and 19.5% to the
upper sort. By contrast, the number of peasants as defendants remained
about the same throughout the period. Therefore, more plaintiffs
belonged to the middling and upper sort while defendants remained
peasants, creating an imbalance of power.

Turning to the local court was the result of a social strategy intended to
re-establish sundered ties of friendship and resume communication via
an intermediary. It was also a shaming strategy via which lenders exposed
defaulting borrowers in the public eye. The middling and upper sorts
were increasingly more numerous in their use of the local courts. These
elites preferred to resort to an intermediary to settle their conflicts with
the peasants. They might also have wanted to use the services of the
judicial institutions in order to distinguish themselves from the peasants,
assert their identities and control, and shame those who had wronged
them by not respecting their promises. To the same extent, these elites
did not abide by the traditional community self-regulation process.

Growing Use of Formal Institutions: The Notary

Parallel with the growing resort to the local judge, there was a growing
use of the notary's services. In the south of Alsace, peasants had turned to
the notary to draft their contracts, including loans, for a long time.
However, it is not easy to draw an exact chronology of this use.
We know that notaries drafted loan contracts in the seventeenth century;
in the absence of remaining notarial ledgers, the few probate inventories
that have survived attest their existence. But we do not know how often
households turned to them to contract compared to the use of private
agreements.[12]

---

[11] Livet, *L'intendance d'Alsace sous Louis XIV*. The *intendance* in Strasbourg increasingly
gained in power and closely supervised communities.
[12] As we saw in Chapter 2, for the eighteenth century, only a few deceased had notarial
loans specified in their probates. The proportion of notarial obligations even decreased

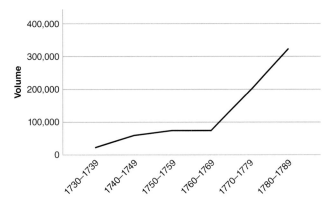

Figure 6.3 Volume exchanged per period in the notarial credit market
in the seigneuries of Delle and Florimont, 1730–89.
(*Source*: notary dataset)

The examination of notarial ledgers for the period 1730–90 shows that
households increasingly used the services of the notary. The volume of
notarial obligations in the south of Alsace grew throughout the period with
a net surge in the last two decades of the Ancien Regime. Both the volume
of transactions and the number of loans increased (see Figure 6.3). The
mean per contract more than doubled on average between the 1730s and
the 1780s. Most of the notarial credit activity observed was albeit concentrated between 1770 and 1790, featuring 62% of the total volume in Delle
and 77% in Florimont. Yet more loans in terms of number were drafted
during this period than any others. Credit activities were therefore
dynamic, both in terms of volume and number.[13]

This dynamic trend was not limited to the south of Alsace and can also
be observed elsewhere. In Paris, even though the number of notarial
loans declined during the eighteenth century, the volume of exchange
increased between 1740 and 1780.[14] From 1750 to the French

---

over time. We should not read too much into probate inventories as they often present a
truncated picture of reality. It is possible that deceased preferred to repay obligations as a
priority over any other debts. And it is also possible that ageing households did not
contract obligations towards the end of their lives because of the productive character
and higher mean of these contracts over any others, in other words, notarial obligations
took longer to reimburse.

[13] Even though loans grew larger, this does not mean that small ones vanished. As we saw
in Chapter 2, the number of small private loans either in the form of deferred payments
or private deeds did progress in this period (see Figure 2.4). It seems by contrast that
small loans did not find their way to the notary's ledgers any longer.

[14] Hoffman, Postel-Vinay, and Rosenthal, *Priceless Markets*.

Revolution, the notarial credit market in Paris grew by +3.75% annually in terms of volume. In the countryside around Albi, it grew by +1.86% annually. In the town of Maubeuge, for the period 1710–1780, the volume of loans increased by +2.41% annually.[15] For the kingdom of France as a whole, the size of notarial credit contracts doubled on average between 1740 and 1780.[16] How can we explain this dynamism?

First, I'd like to remind the reader that there was no legal requirement to use the service of a notary to draft a loan contract. Legal provisions encouraging the use of notaries were in fact of little incentive. From 1666 onwards, loans of more than 100 livres had to be registered before the notary against a fee *or* had to be written down between the parties.[17] The central authorities sought to rule out verbal agreements and control the flux of exchanges. This legal provision, however, did not seem to have influenced the drafting of more notarial contracts in the south of Alsace. Peasants seem to have continued contracting privately, mostly because a notarial contract represented an additional cost.[18]

Second, if one considers the reasons households borrowed, there was no radical change over time for the period 1730–90. All loan categories remained more or less stable in terms of proportion. There was no sudden shift towards a particular type of investment. What did change, though, was the mean per contract. In terms of volume, households tended to borrow more (see Table 6.1). Loans for the purchase of land and real estate objects, for example, show a significant increase in the mean per contract in the last two decades of the Ancien Regime, which is correlated by the increase in price for plots of land.

As households borrowed, on average, more money, it is likely that lenders progressively turned more to notaries to draft their contracts as they might have doubted the capacity and capability of borrowers to meet their obligations. Distrustful, they might have wanted to strengthen the security of their loans.

Third, the absence of major shocks such as armed conflicts, severe epidemics, or famines in the second half of the eighteenth century favoured the development and boom of investments in general and credit markets in particular. As a result, there was a climate of general prosperity. Prices increased by 0.3% annually in eighteenth-century France,

[15] Postel-Vinay, Gilles. *La terre et l'argent: l'agriculture et le crédit en France*, p 134.
[16] Hoffman, Postel-Vinay, and Rosenthal, *Dark Matter Credit*, p 55.
[17] François Isambert, *Recueil général des anciennes lois françaises* (Paris: Belin-Le-Prieur, Verdiere, 1829), p 137.
[18] As we have seen, illiteracy did not seem to have given rise to more notarial contracts either.

Table 6.1 *Mean per contract in the seigneuries of Delle and Florimont, notarial ledgers, 1730–90*

	1730–39	1740–49	1750–59	1760–69	1770–79	1780–89
Loan without specification	178.25	217.01	245.47	258.61	380.05	360.87
Livestock	123.27	170.45	130.89	169.71	178.21	187.21
House and building	381.6	312.25	1,180.57	385.11	374.75	697.71
Land	281.5	412	209.78	270	537.79	843.69
Old debt	149.6	329.54	234.38	181.3	878.84	938.5

Source: notarial register

contributing to stimulating the offer and demand for credit.[19] In the seigneurie of Delle, land prices grew by 1.57% annually between the beginning of the eighteenth century and the 1780s.[20] And wheat prices almost doubled between 1750 and 1790.[21] This increase in prices, however, cannot justify entirely the demand and the dynamism of credit markets in the eighteenth century.[22] By contrast, rising incomes might have enabled some households with saving capacities to sustain this climate of investment and innovation.

In the south of Alsace, the emergence of a new category of creditors played a critical role in the dynamism of the local notarized credit market. While the notarial credit market expanded in the last decades of the Ancien Regime, the source of the capital lent began to change. From the 1730s to the 1760s, peasants represented roughly a bit less than half of the total creditors, while in the last decade of the Old Regime they represented only 26.6% of all creditors investing 23.1% of the capital exchanged.[23] Throughout the period, their importance as creditors in the local credit market thus decreased.

Alongside the peasants, the middling sort's investments via notarial loans remained more or less stable throughout the period. The middling

---

[19] Postel-Vinay, *La terre et l'argent: l'agriculture et le crédit en France*, p 134.

[20] In the period 1700–05, the mean for one journal of land equalled 46 livres. In the period 1780–85, it increased to 160. For both periods, the mean of one journal might have been drastically undervalued, as we saw in Chapter 1.

[21] Yvette Baradel, *Belfort: de l'Ancien Régime au siège de 1870–1871*.

[22] Hoffman, Postel-Vinay, and Rosenthal, *Des marchés sans prix*, pp 127–28.

[23] Loans registered by the notary rarely specified the occupations of debtors, largely because most of them were peasants. The rate of professions known for creditors was much higher, around 60%. See also Rosenthal, "Rural Credit Markets and Aggregate Shocks," p 291.

sort, composed of town artisans, lower administrators, shopkeepers, innkeepers, millers, grocers, medical professionals, military, schoolmasters, and religious minorities, continued to lend about a third of the total volume throughout the period. In the last decade of the Ancien Regime, they lent 33.5% of the total volume. This group could be assimilated to what French historians called the 'coqs de village', the non-aristocratic better-off strata of traditional communities. Some of them had retained an agricultural activity on the side but had assumed another occupation enabling them to generate a surplus they could reinvest in the credit market. A large proportion of this group filled positions in the local police and administration, giving them exposure, information, and prestige, as mayors for example.

In the last decades of the Ancien Regime, the upper sort came to play a more prominent role in the local credit market. This category of lenders was mainly composed of the local nobility, clerical elite, and local upper bourgeoisie. Among these latter, a new category of lenders appeared. The new 'investors' came from an emerging bourgeoisie, from the liberal professions and the increasingly growing category of seigneurial agents (upper sorts such as judges, clerks, administrators, and civil servants).[24] These new creditors had less of a connection to land and agriculture; some did own land but did not exploit it themselves. They formed a new type of rural elite of non-manual workers, educated, and aspiring to climb the social ladder to the top.

In the 1730s, the upper sort together lent nearly 20.5% of the volume exchanged (34.6% by the peasants), while in the last decade of the Old Regime, they lent together 41.2% of the total volume (23.1% by the peasants). They mostly lent to peasants. In terms of number and volume, peasant creditors declined while the middling and upper sorts progressed over time, see Table 6.2.[25]

Within the upper sort group, those engaged in non-manual service and administrative work, such as the local judges, notaries, clerks, and other civil servants became active lenders in the last decades of the Ancien Regime. This new group of investors, coming from a different socio-professional category than the peasants, had different goals, financial strategies, and expectations, which did not necessarily match the traditional pattern of stability, mutual cooperation, and norms of reciprocity of the peasants. They did not have strong ties to their debtors; they had

[24] Among such creditors, only a handful had good information on potential borrowers, such as the seigneurial judges or agents.

[25] It is interesting to note that the local nobility lost ground and no longer engaged in private lending in the late-eighteenth century.

Table 6.2 Creditors according to their socio-professional categories over time in the seigneuries of Delle and Florimont, 1733–89

	1733–39[a]		1740–49		1750–59		1760–69		1770–79		1780–89	
	N%	V%	N%	V%	N%	V%	N%	V%	N%	V%	N%	V%
Peasants	47	34.6	44.6	42.5	45	29	28.4	21.2	28.1	26.4	26.6	23.1
Middling sort	32.8	36.3	27.5	21.1	18.4	15.6	46.7	35.8	47	30.5	44.2	33.5
Upper sort	14.5	20.5	21	33	27	41.4	18.3	28.7	20	40.1	22.9	41.2

[a] Only data available for the seigneurie of Delle
Source: notarial dataset

commercial interests. They did not necessarily belong to the same family, nor to the same socio-professional category, and in some cases did not even live in the same village. In other words, they were social and economic outsiders with little concern for other-regarding norms.

Interestingly, the same pattern was noted elsewhere. In Paris, in the 1660s, 46% of creditors and borrowers shared strong ties. Almost half of the loans Parisian notaries recorded involved borrowers and creditors from the same family, neighbourhood, or professions.[26] But in the 1780s, by contrast, only 31% of the Parisian loans featured such strong ties.[27] In the heart of the Jura mountains, in the village of Arinthod, the notary recorded 254 obligations from 1779 to 1785. While 83% of the borrowers were small peasants, 58% of the lenders were 'bourgeois'. Only 8% of the creditors were peasants.[28] In the seigneuries of Delle and Florimont the percentage of strong connections between lenders and borrowers also decreased throughout the eighteenth century, corroborating this idea of loosening ties.

The Taiclet family is a good example of this new category rapidly ascending the social ladder. At the beginning of the eighteenth century, the Taiclet family settled in Delle. Originally from a distant village, Jean Pierre Taiclet purchased the position of tax farmer before buying a position as a seigneurial judge. After him, his son, grandson, and the husbands of his great-granddaughter and great great-granddaughter succeeded him. They all kept the position of judge in Delle and purchased additional positions as judges of nearby administrative entities, expanding their networks. Rapidly, the Taiclet family grew richer and more connected as the number of their loan transactions indicate (see Table 6.3). Just like the Lacombe family of Gaillac in the south of France, the Taiclets were not only trusted in positions of power within their communities but also became relatively important lenders. Apart from their offices, their favourite investments did not lie in land but in loans.

The Taiclet family lent over 77,000 livres in the course of the eighteenth century. As some of the family's most prominent members were local judges and even notaries, they possibly had access to better

---

[26] Gilles Postel-Vinay, "Change and Transformation of Premodern Credit Markets." In Stephan Nicolussi-Köhler, ed. *Change and Transformation of Premodern Credit Markets: The Importance of Small-Scale Credits* (Heidelberg: heiBOOKS, 2021), 23–38, p 24.
[27] Hoffman, Postel-Vinay, and Rosenthal, "Information and Economic History," p 83.
[28] Colette Merlin, *Ceux des villages: la société rurale dans la "Petite Montagne" jurassienne à la veille de la Révolution* (Besançon: Presses Universitaires de Franche-Comté, 1994), p 225.

Table 6.3 *The Taiclet and Lacombe families' investments throughout the eighteenth century*

	Lacombe family in Gaillac[a]			Taiclet family in Delle		
	Number of loans	Mean	Volume	Number of loans	Mean	Volume
1740–49	2	88	175	3	77.9	233.9
1750–59	14	480	6,245	13	271.8	3,533
1760–69	25	264	6,611	20	170.5	3,410
1770–79	68	280	19,024	28	442.9	12,400.85
1780–89	47	450	21,166	73	788.4	57,555.5
Total	156	341	53,221	137	563	77,133.3

[a] Postel-Vinay, *La terre et l'argent*, p 61.

information than most people. It is difficult to assess whether or not they exploited this pool of information well. The Taiclet family extended money to various kinds of people, all living in the seigneuries. A third of the borrowers lived in the same town. The Taiclet seem to have been familiar with some of their borrowers; some of them were clerks and lower administrators working closely with or for them. Interestingly, the Taiclet family members rarely lent money to the same individuals: each member of the family seems to have had their own distinctive network. This category of investors did secure their transactions well; the Taiclet family secured their notarized contracts by requiring a pledge on 57% of their deeds and 52% of the borrowers were married couples, highlighting their desire for insurance.

Like the Taiclet family, the new group of investors had an increasingly greater savings and lending capacity, but also fewer ties to land. Their primary aim was to generate a regular annual return of their investment; they belonged to the rentiers category, not the one generating revenue from land ownership but the one getting an income from their capital. This new category of lenders turned to the notary to draft their deals.

In theory, a notary could exert a certain influence on the substance of the contract. He supposedly had both the required legal expertise and social authority to advise and persuade the parties. He could emphasize the mutual benefits but also disadvantages the parties committed to. He could give his opinion on the price. As a broker, parties might have resorted to him to ensure the deal would go through. Philip Hoffman and his colleagues argue that notaries increasingly came to play a key role in intermediation, providing both essential information and security to investors, which thus explains not only the dynamism of notarial credit markets but also the attraction they had for the middling and better sorts with saving capacities and interest for investments.[29] Brokerage assured by notaries meant that not only did deals go through but there was low risk. For the elite, it is possible that the notary offered them both brokerage and security. This role as intermediaries might have been especially important for the better sort of creditors who had looser ties to the peasants to whom they extended money.

Marie Elisabeth Taiclet was the daughter of the bailiff of the seigneurie of Delle, Pierre Francois Taiclet. Born in 1725, we find evidence of her involvement in the credit market after the death of her parents. From 1762 to her death in 1779, Marie Elisabeth Taiclet extended credit 22 times for a total amount of 4,568 livres, meaning she held one of the largest portfolios in the seigneurie. She extended credit to artisans and peasants living in different villages around Delle. Most of her investments had a fixed term repayment and stipulated interest fees and collateral, ensuring her profit and security. The notary, a close acquaintance of hers, managed to find her safe clients for her investments. Jacques Vieillard from the village of Meroux, 15 kilometres away from Delle, was looking for funds in order to finish building his house. Marie Elisabeth Taiclet agreed to extend credit to him, securing the transaction with the house pledged and collateral.[30] It is likely that the notary of Delle introduced a debtor in need of cash and a potential creditor interested in a fruitful investment, such as Taiclet. Using the notary to seal a loan would reassure both parties who presented notable differences in their bargaining and political power.

It is also possible that the middling and upper strata developed a growing consciousness of status based on wealth and authority.[31] Using the notary could have been a way for people of these categories to distinguish themselves from the peasants. By using an intermediary, they signified their willingness to mark a social distance.

In the seigneuries of Delle and Florimont, the new bourgeoisie seem to have turned their back on the traditional investment in land for a more 'urban', modern investment. There, the increasing appetite of new lenders for the credit market could also be explained by the uncertainties pertaining to the land market. Demographic pressure, coupled with fragmentation of land due to partible inheritance, increased the competition for land and pulled prices up. It is possible that new investors did not wish to compete with wealthy farmers for plots of land. In Delle, for example, the Taiclet family did not seem especially eager to take part in the land market. In other regions, credit and investment in the land

---

[29] Hoffman, Postel-Vinay, and Rosenthal, *Dark Matter Credit*, pp 56–57.
[30] ADTB 2E4/245.   [31] It is also the contention of Le Gendre, *Confiance*, p 102.

market often went hand in hand as a strategy to spread risk.[32] Second, bad weather and poor harvests could make the land market highly unpredictable and affect the returns negatively.[33] The costs associated with collecting rents and dealing with payment in kind could also have been discouraging to these investors. In the same vein, the transaction costs associated with the financial investment could have been less important than in the case of land, provided the chosen borrower did not default. But more importantly, the non-aristocratic elite was subjected to taxes on their landed property (contrary to the nobility and the clergy).

A Migration of Trust?

Households turned to institutions more and more often for the facilitation and enforcement of their contracts and gradually abandoned the traditional pattern of community self-regulation. What happened? What caused such a shift? Part of the answer could lie in an examination of the notarial loan provisions. The substance of the contract did change. Lenders requested progressively more and better guarantees to secure the exchanges. This desire to insure oneself further against uncertainty and risk points to a context of distrust. Several elements pertaining to demographic changes and new market realities explain the emergence of distrust. In such a context, institutions appeared as an answer adapted to providing a secure mitigation of risk.

A Growing Distrust: Changes in the Substance of Notarial Credit Contracts, from Idiosyncrasy to Standardization

Notarial contracts were not indispensable tools to obtain credit in early modern France. There was no legal requirement for credit to be notarized. Parties could contract privately. Without intermediation, strong shared social norms made both lenders and borrowers comply with the ex-ante provisions as well as facilitating enforcement. A notarial deed was often superfluous between households intimate with each other, and did not therefore add much value to the transaction itself. Yet, notarial credit contracts increasingly gained in popularity in the eighteenth century.

---

[32] In Gaillac, the Lacombe family invested in both the credit market and the land market. See Postel-Vinay, *La terre et l'argent,* p 61.

[33] There was a total of sixteen significant famines in the eighteenth century in France. This number excludes the multitude of local famines here and there throughout the kingdom.

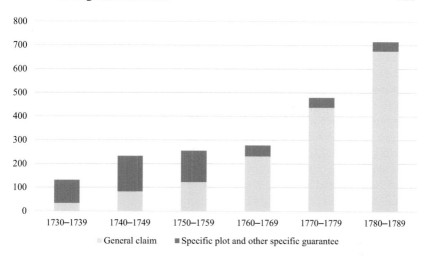

Figure 6.4 Securities backing notarial loans in the seigneuries of Delle and Florimont, 1730–90.
(*Source*: notarial dataset)

The substance of notarial loan contracts progressively changed. Provisions went from being idiosyncratic to being more standardized and codified. Namely, three major provisions pertaining to guarantees and collateral were modified: specific pieces of land lost their attractiveness as sureties and were replaced by a general claim on the borrower's assets; a pledge (or several) were more frequently requested; and wives' property was increasingly added to the deed.

Land was often offered as a guarantee to back loans in rural areas. At the beginning of the eighteenth century and up to the 1760s, parties agreed on a specific plot of land to secure the transaction (see Figure 6.4). Well-defined and negotiated plots were added to the deed by the parties. The notary often took great care in describing these specific pieces. In November 1735, for example, George Lorrest pledged a plot of '*trois journeaux situés au finage de Croix au lieud au bas de la mairie entre le créditeur de bise la terre et grands mont de vent*' ('three journaux of land located on the territory of Croix, in the hamlet called "bas de la mairie" between on the north east side of the creditor and on the opposite side the land called "grands monts"') to secure a 100 livres loan.[34] It is likely that parties decided and negotiated beforehand which plots would secure the transaction. At the beginning of the period, about 65% of the

[34] ADTB 2E4/155.

contracts mentioned a specific type of security, most often a specific piece of land. Only 35% of the deeds mentioned solely a general claim on the borrower's goods and assets.

These specific plots of land were put on the deed as collateral for various reasons. Parties often secured a deferred payment with the very item they just bought. If the deal was not executed to its completion, this mortgaged object would return to the seller. Perhaps more importantly, specific plots of land guaranteed loans because the lender could *use* them. If cash became scarce or unavailable, land represented a resource to be exploited to get compensation. In particular, the payment of interest could be executed in kind, presumably by harvesting the lien.[35] In the previous example, the pledged land was next to the creditor's own land making it easier to exploit if necessary.

There are traces of this practise especially at the beginning of the eighteenth century. Several deeds mention that land serving as a security would be used 'à titre précaire', a temporary usufruct of the land. This practise, inherited from Roman law, consisted in letting the lender use the land until the contract was fully executed.[36] In April 1739, Jean Fredey *le vieux* borrowed 116 livres from the local judge Pierre Francois Taiclet to reimburse an old debt. He secured the transaction with not only a general claim on his assets but also by pledging three different plots of land. One of them was mortgaged 'à titre précaire'.[37] This practise allowed the lender to claim the fruits of a specific plot and it allowed the borrower to pay interest either with a mix of cash and kind, or in kind only.[38] Presumably, with this practise, the payment of the annual interest was flexible and open to negotiation. One may add that this practise might also entail a higher interest rate. The yield on the lien could be far superior to the 5% and/or could be added to the payment in cash. Notarial contracts were purposely vague about the execution of this payment, presumably to circumvent usury laws. Parties might have had some latitude of action. Let us consider the following example. In 1736, Joseph Girard bought a piece of meadow from the innkeeper Léger Terrier. As he could not pay outright, it was agreed that 115 livres would be repaid within 5 years. The meadow backed the loan. The parties stipulated that the money would have to be reimbursed at the same rate as in 1736. And they added: 'Within the five years mentioned, the lender would of course be obliged to accept all of what the borrower would give

---

[35] Even though it was illegal to stipulate a repayment in kind in a notarial contract.
[36] Fedou, *Lexique historique du Moyen Age.*   [37] ADTB 2E4/156.
[38] One cannot exclude that the borrower had to sow and harvest himself the plot of land to the benefit of the lender.

him to reimburse the capital either in kind, labour, or cash and the interest would be diminished accordingly'.[39] The deal seemed to be mutually advantageous and elastic. The use of the adverb 'of course' seems to underline the commonality of this practise.

Yet, fast forward to the last decade of the Ancien Regime, almost 95% of the transactions mentioned a general claim only. The practise of temporary usufruct had now totally disappeared. Specific plots of land were no longer used as liens. Borrowers offered all their goods and assets instead. Two reasons might explain this shift. First, the payment of interest in kind might not have been as attractive as before. Yields might have fallen behind, the weather might have had an impact on the expected return, and storage costs might have risen. In other words, a large number of transaction costs were associated with this practise. As Figure 6.4 shows, the change began to take place in the 1760s. This matches, more or less, with an increase in wheat prices in the area. As grains became more expensive, the practise of temporary usufruct might have represented a loss for the borrowers, who might have found themselves paying more for their loans. Second, the practise of using a specific plot of land to back a loan might have disappeared because of land encumbrance. No official control and no public ledger of mortgaged land existed then in Alsace. Lenders ignored whether or not a specific plot had already been mortgaged. A general claim, by contrast, offered presumably more guarantees in the case of insolvency.

While the practise of offering a specific plot of land increasingly receded, a new practise emerged almost simultaneously; more and more often parties agreed on adding a pledge to the deed (see Chapter 3). The number of underwriters per contract grew throughout the eighteenth century. From the beginning of the period until the 1760s, fewer than 10% of the contracts featured guarantors (see Figure 6.5). But then, the number rose progressively to reach almost half of the contracts in the last decade of the Ancien Regime (46%). After the 1760s, a pledge was often added when a borrower offered a general claim on his assets to back a loan.

Admittedly, the mean amount per loan did increase throughout the period. It more than doubled between 1730 and 1790. The same trend can be observed in Paris and also in other parts of Alsace.[40] But it does not necessarily mean that borrowers would not be able to meet their obligations or that their assets would not suffice to cover an eventual default. Adding a pledge might be an incentive for borrowers to pay their

---

[39] ADTB 2E4/155.   [40] Boehler, *Une société rurale en milieu rhénan*, p 1198.

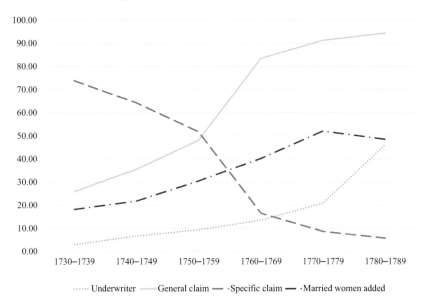

Figure 6.5 Changes in guarantees offered in notarial loans in the seigneuries of Delle and Florimont (in % of contracts), 1730–89. (*Source*: notarial dataset)

interest on time and repay the capital without too much delay. To some extent, resorting to a pledge activated mutual solidarity for the borrowers while it gave greater insurance of repayment to the lenders.

Finally, almost around the same time, another change in the contract provisions occurred. Parties began to add married women's assets to the deed (see Chapter 4). The number of married couples who borrowed money together increased throughout the period from 22% in 1730–39 to almost 50% in 1780–89, meaning that men progressively attached their wives' names to deeds and fewer men borrowed alone in the credit market. Married women's holdings in the form of dowry, cash, or inherited property became a source of additional guarantee eyed by creditors. The property a wife inherited from her family was now subject to foreclosure in the event of a breach in the contract's terms and provisions, especially insolvency. Repayment could be sought by turning to the widow for her share of the debt, in the case of her husband's death, as she was legally liable for half of the loan, a much more efficient process and security than turning to several heirs in the case of the debtor's death. Interestingly, in the period 1780–89, a third of married couples borrowing money also presented a pledge.

To some extent, notarial contracts while available for a fee, certainly eased the exchanges. Parties consented to pay a price to reduce uncertainties pertaining to the transaction. Contracts can be perceived as necessary costs to prevent opportunistic behaviours.[41] Yet, at the turn of the mid-eighteenth century, a need emerged to strengthen the guarantees that a loan would be repaid. The combination of a change in the guarantees offered, the growing insertion of a pledge, and the increasing use of women's property in contracts points to several aspects of the credit relationship. The strengthening of the guarantees was appealing to households, which turned henceforth to the notary in greater number. These changes in the substance of the contract also suggest a growing deficit of trust. Lenders wanted to make sure their investment would not be completely lost if there were difficulties. Greater guarantees gave them greater insurance. And last, all the new changes pertaining to the substance of the contract introduced rigidity and standardization. Until then, notarial loan contracts, even though they were intermediated, remained elastic because of parties' inputs. Offering a specific plot of land as security to eventually repay the interest in kind, for example, gave debtors choices and options. With the new provisions introduced, parties seem to have had less room to design their own contract and deal. Idiosyncrasy vanished.

How to Explain the Growing Distrust?

The changes observed pertaining to the growing use of institutions for credit matters and the greater emphasis on guarantees point towards both a growing distrust and the subsequent migration of trust towards institutions. But what caused this distrust in the first place?

Distrust can be defined as 'an absence of assurance and reliance, with the special quality of a certainty of the absence of trustworthiness in the other person'.[42] A loan is in fact a promise that repayment would be executed in the future. A lender never knew if a debt would be repaid at some point; ignorance surrounded whether a borrower could possibly create future wealth through labour, the production of goods and services for sale to pay both the interest and the capital. Lenders could only rely on the information at their disposal and their trust in the borrower. In the mid-eighteenth century, the belief that a loan would be repaid began to be challenged. Lenders began to doubt.

---

[41] Cook, *Cooperation Without Trust?* p 52.

[42] S. Isaacs, M. Alexander, and A. Haggard, "Faith, Trust and Gullibility," *International Journal of Psycho-Analysis* 44 (1963): 461–69, p 463.

At least two elements can help us to understand this growing distrust. Jean-Philippe Platteau, argues that 'mutual insurance arrangements and practises are subject to gradual erosion under the influence of new forces, particularly population growth and market penetration'.[43] In the south of Alsace, demographic pressure increased throughout the eighteenth century. From 1667 to 1751, the population in Delle increased by 195%, 1.29% per year. From 1751 to 1806, it increased by a total of 52%, 0.81% every year. More people lived in the seigneuries of Delle and Florimont, and they lived longer. The logical conclusion is that these demographic changes meant more numerous households to borrow and to lend. As these village communities grew, the number of social relationships an individual was able to maintain did not budge. New social relations were more distant in all senses of the word, and ties between individuals became looser. As a result, these new social relations were stretching and weakening the social bonds between people, bonds that were previously tightly enmeshed. The smallness of scale gives scope to interpersonal effects because it fosters mutual trust. But when the scale of relations becomes larger and social networks expand, interpersonal relations are affected and become *de facto* stretched out.[44] Cooperation became more difficult to navigate with a 'larger number of players'.[45] Mutual insurance arrangements like personalized lending were subject to erosion precisely because of this population growth.[46]

Demographic pressure only partly explains the weakening of social bonds, changes in the socio-professional structure is another important factor. In both the notarial credit market and the local court of justice, one witnesses a weakening of ties in social relations with the emergence of a new type of actor. A new elite began to take part in the exchanges as creditors (and subsequently as plaintiffs); their presence in the credit market, as outsiders, *de facto* altered the fabric of the community because their different socio-professional status meant they adhered to different values and norms than the peasants. This elite might have concerned themselves little with other-regarding norms, so central to traditional communities; their expectations were more market oriented. And because of this, they drove part of this growing distrust. They asked for better guarantees to mitigate uncertainties and reduce risks. To some

---

[43] Platteau, "Solidarity Norms and Institutions in Village Societies," p 822.
[44] Mary Douglas, *How Institutions Think* (London: Routledge & Kegan Paul, 1987), p 21.
[45] Douglass C. North, "Institutions," *Journal of Economic Perspectives* 5, no. 1 (1991): 97–112, p 97.
[46] Platteau, "Solidarity Norms and Institutions in Village Societies," p 822.

extent, the strengthening of securities resembled to an insurance, a way to insure one's capital against default.

Evidently, these new creditors had more wealth, greater bargaining power, and a connection to institutions in terms of social networks that could possibly serve them better (remember the Taiclet was a dynasty of local judges). As a result, I believe this discrepancy in power between the parties introduced de facto another layer of distrust. It weakened cooperation and prevented reciprocity. Trust emerges in 'ongoing relationships when both parties have an incentive to fulfil the trust'.[47] When this is not the case, institutions can fill the gap and provide the incentive structure to push through the exchange.

New market realities could also be held accountable for this erosion of mutual insurance arrangements and the rise of institutions. Selling on the market for profit tended to break down village communities based on local custom and co-operation. It led to what Christopher Hill called the 'spirit of individualism'.[48] A growing demand for credit was correlated with an increase in the price of grain. In the second half of the eighteenth century, there was a sharp surge in the price of wheat in the kingdom of France in general and in Alsace in particular (see Figure 6.6). Between 1764 and 1770, an abrupt increase took place. After that, the price continued to increase steadily to reach an all-time record just before the French Revolution.[49] In fact, all necessities were subject to sharp inflation in the second half of the eighteenth century. The pressure on prices could explain both why people needed to borrow more, and justify the erosion of confidence in the future. As prices grew, lenders might worry more about the capacity of borrowers to create wealth to repay their debt.

Distrust and uncertainty went hand in hand. Uncertainties about both the future and borrowers' capacity to repay, and distrust in new stretched out social relations, called for a new form of trust. And this is precisely when institutions came into the picture. Institutions put uncertainty under control.[50] They created order. As Mary Douglas recalls, 'the more fully the institutions encode expectations, the more they put uncertainty under control with the further effect that behaviour tends to conform to the institutional matrix: if this degree of coordination is achieved, disorder and confusion disappear'.[51] Institutions such as the notary and the

---

[47] Cook, *Cooperation without Trust?* p 42.
[48] Cited in Muldrew, *The Economy of Obligation*, p 167.
[49] Labrousse, *Esquisse du mouvement des prix et des revenus en France au XVIIIe siècle.* 122. The new liberalization of the grain markets in 1764 might explain the pressure on prices, although this argument is refuted by Labrousse.
[50] Douglas, *How Institutions Think*, p 48.   [51] Douglas, p 48.

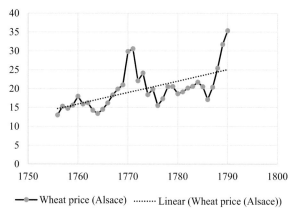

Figure 6.6 Wheat price in Alsace in livre tournois (sétier de Paris) according to Labrousse.

local court of justice were *de facto* elevated to the rank of defenders of property rights.[52]

How Institutions Responded to Uncertainty and Distrust

Local institutions such as the notary and the local court of justice were within geographical reach for most of the population. In the South of Alsace, most people did not have to travel far to use their services. But it is also true that these institutions' existence often did clash with traditional customs and moral norms. Some legal ordinances, old and new alike, might have been perceived as unfamiliar, nay foreign.[53] These institutions and their rules were the product of the political elite to ensure control and public order. And if one adds that access to these institutions was conditional on the payment of a fee or a price, one understands the resistance, even the reluctance, they could engender on the part of traditional communities to turn to them. In other words, the use of these institutions was not self-evident.

In the eighteenth century both the growing use of the notary for the conclusion of loan contracts and the resort to the local judge for contract enforcement force us to rethink the place of institutions in the society and their meaning for people.

---

[52] See Claire Priest, *Credit Nation: Property Laws and Institutions in Early America* (Princeton: Princeton University Press, 2021).
[53] Graeber, *Debt*, 2011, p 332–33.

It seems clear that local institutions such as the notary and the local court of justice grew more legitimate in the eighteenth century. In this respect, legitimacy corresponds to 'a generalized perception or assumption that the actions of an entity are desirable, proper, or appropriate within some socially constructed systems of norms, values, beliefs and definitions'.[54] Both the notary and the local court seem to have been entities or conventions providing a valuable and needed service to the population upon new market realities, population growth, and disentanglement of social bonds. Then, all parties had a common interest in there being a rule to insure coordination.[55]

In the seventeenth century, the local court was often an instrument of social control for the seigneur. His prosecutor frequently initiated lawsuits against the peasants for infringements of the seigneur's rights or the disruption of public order. By contrast, increasingly in the eighteenth century, the local justice served the interests and the demands of the local population more and almost ceased being an instrument of public control alone. It became progressively an instrument of intermediation and arbitrage defending property rights.[56]

In this sense, the progressive institutionalization of the local court of justice, i.e. its growth into a modern institution, gaining more and more in legitimacy, replaced traditional conflict mediators. The priest or the village elders, traditional figures of arbitration, drifted away to the benefit of the institution of justice.[57] Their loss of influence might be explained by a growing distrust placed in their persons and/or their status. But, perhaps more importantly, the court of justice offered an arena for public shaming. Plaintiffs, increasingly coming from the middling sort and the better sort, asserted their class identity by differentiating themselves from the peasants. Humiliation of debtors in difficulty at court might have been a more efficient tool of conflict resolution but also one that offered these elites a tool to express their social superiority. *De facto*, the confidence entrusted in the priest or the elders for the resolution of conflicts was displaced to the local court of justice where plaintiffs became themselves empowered.

---

[54] Mark C. Suchman, "Managing Legitimacy: Strategic and Institutional Approaches," *The Academy of Management Review* 20, no. 3 (1995): 571–610.

[55] David Lewis, *Convention: A Philosophical Study* (Hoboken, NJ: John Wiley & Sons, 2008).

[56] B. Zorina Khan, "'Justice of the Marketplace': Legal Disputes and Economic Activity on America's Northeastern Frontier, 1700-1860," *The Journal of Interdisciplinary History* 39, no. 1 (2008): 1–35.

[57] Anne Bonzon, *La paix au village – clergé paroissial et règlement des conflits dans la France d'Ancien Régime* (Paris: Éditions Champ Vallon, 2022).

The same parallel can be drawn for the growing use of the notary in the eighteenth century. A new elite, distrustful of the peasants and concerned to differentiate themselves from them, used the notary to draw a social line between the groups.

In a complacent assumption, institutions could, in theory, enforce anyone's rights and privileges on a legal and fair basis, thus erasing the social inequalities that existed within the society.[58] 'Nothing else but institutions can define sameness', Mary Douglas argues.[59] In practise, however, those who seemed to have been more prompt to turn to institutions were in fact those who were estranged from the self-regulation process, the outsiders of the community. The elites showed preference for an intermediary above the community and outside the traditional pool of mediators. By relying on a mediator from their own group – the judge – they generally found a positive echo to their claims. And by choosing the notary for the conclusion of their contracts, they potentially introduced both standardization of contracts – cutting short any idiosyncratic demands on the part of the peasants – and a degree of responsibility by requesting more and better guarantees. They did control the conclusion and enforcement of contracts mechanisms, imposing their authority on the peasants who had very little other choice than to comply.

Yet, I am not excluding the possibility that institutions conferred sameness to the peasants as a group as well. As population growth sundered the previously enmeshed ties of the community, peasants might have attempted to recreate a network of reciprocal exchanges via a structure in which they could find both sameness and a renewed communal contract for common norms. But by turning to institutions for this, they lost in independence and became subject to third party rules.

This loss of input was visible as the evolution of the purposes of the lawsuits shows for example. Users increasingly brought their debt conflicts before the court to the detriment of other cases. Albeit it did not mean that battery and violence stopped altogether. But the court of justice was now heralded as a mediator and a guarantor of private property and capital. And as such, the institution developed a specialism. The judge, at the centre of the edifice, turned into an expert, or rather was perceived as an expert.[60] He could possibly resolve debt repayment conflicts while the community could continue to engage in

---

[58] Muldrew, *The Economy of Obligation*, p 179.
[59] Douglas, *How Institutions Think*, p 55.
[60] It seems unlikely that the local judge gained in knowledge or sharp expertise in the seigneuries of Delle and Florimont, but was increasingly considered an expert who could disentangle conflicts.

self-regulation for its more intimate conflicts such as violence, defamation, and battery.

In the same vein, not all the debt conflicts found their way to the dock of the local judge. Some householders certainly continued to privilege self-regulation outside the courtroom with or without traditional intermediaries. And many loans were still contracted outside the notary's office. A quasi-complete migration of trust would not occur until much later.

And there was no complete and clear rupture either. Trust in institutions did not occur all of a sudden. Some households chose to trust institutions for the conclusion of their contracts and/or their enforcement. But the same households often continued to practise deferred payments for daily items and services.

Side Effects of the Growing Institutionalization of Credit

Many scholars would argue that institutions are generally a good thing. They provide 'the incentive structure for the economy' and may sustain economic growth.[61] They are a natural response to the problem of agency, information asymmetry and uncertainties. By enforcing debt contracts, the legal system safeguards creditors' rights and capital.

Yet, the shift between community self-regulation and institutionalized enforcement, between personalized exchanges and impersonal ones was not without its downsides. One of the side effects of the institutionalization of credit was the introduction of rigidity in the exchanges. Parties were able to contribute significantly to their transactions up until the mid-eighteenth century. But when mistrust appeared, under the impulse of demographic changes with notably the participation of a new elite in the credit market, flexibility disappeared. Evidently, this emergence of rigidity is difficult to measure. Before the 1760s, many contracts, either notarized or non-intermediated, featured parties' contribution and tended to accommodate them in a mutually beneficial agreement. The progressive institutionalization of credit standardized contracts.

Before the 1760s, both contract provisions and the post ante enforcement mechanisms were elastic. Parties negotiated and renegotiated their agreements. They let the contract roll on without enforcing the provisions as long as the interest was paid. Repayment deadlines were often ignored. But in the last decades of the Ancien Regime, parties turned more and more to the judge to seek arbitration. The possibility of renegotiation between the parties remained but had to be monitored and intermediated

---

[61] North, "Institutions," p 97.

by a third party. The debt and its default were exposed to the public eye. To some extent, the judge codified the default applying labels, rules, and sanctions different from the traditional communal norms.

In the same vein, another side effect of institutionalization lay in the loss of independence. Ronald Coase argues that 'the legal system will have a profound effect on the working of the economic system and may in certain respects be said to control it'.[62] As contracts became standardized, parties' contribution was cast aside. There was less room for idiosyncrasy. Evidently, these changes in the local credit markets had a tremendous impact on the social fabric of the community, challenging old societal patterns. Both the growing distrust and the subsequent institutionalization of credit, for example, led to the erosion of patriarchy.[63] The male head of the household saw his authority eroded by the association of his wife as a joint partner, the co-signer with a say in his personal finances, while institutions gained in legitimacy. Additionally, because women were made joint partners and were now held responsible for their household finances on the same footing as their husbands, new legal norms in marriage contracts emerged, giving them greater property rights.[64]

Concluding Remarks

'The story of the origins of capitalism', writes the late anthropologist David Graeber, 'is not the story of the gradual destruction of traditional communities by the impersonal power of the market. It is, rather, the story of how an economy of credit was converted into an economy of interest; of the gradual transformation of moral networks by the intrusion of the impersonal – and often vindictive – power of the state'.[65] Perhaps we should not be surprised that Graeber, an anarchist anthropologist, attributes to the State the responsibility for the emergence of impersonal exchanges. For him, the State strengthened institutions to monitor and criminalize debt with devastating effects on communal solidarity.[66]

[62] R. H. Coase, "The Institutional Structure of Production," *The American Economic Review* 82, no. 4 (1992): 713–19, p 713. See also Katharina Pistor, "The Standardization of Law and Its Effect on Developing Economies," *The American Journal of Comparative Law* 50, no. 1 (2002): 97–130.

[63] Dermineur, "Women in Rural Society: Peasants, Patriarchy and the Local Economy in Northeast France, 1650–1789," 2011; Dermineur, *Women and Credit in Pre-Industrial Europe*, 2018.

[64] Dermineur, "Widows' Political Strategies in Traditional Communities."

[65] Graeber, *Debt*, 2011, p 32.

[66] An argument also developed in David Graeber and David Wengrow, *The Dawn of Everything: A New History of Humanity*, First ed. (New York: Farrar, Straus and Giroux, 2021).

While I share Graeber's diagnosis regarding the erosion of traditional moral norms and the implication of the market in this process, I rather think the causes are lodged elsewhere. The authorities did provide some infrastructure for the facilitation and conclusion of agreements. But they did not pay too much attention to the substance of the contracts, apart from their price. Households' contribution and input still mattered a great deal. I rather believe that structural changes pertaining to communities *themselves* eroded traditional communities' practises and moral norms.

In this chapter, we have seen that institutions like the notary and the local court of justice gained in legitimacy in the last decades of the Ancien Regime. The notary gradually drafted more contract obligations and the local judge adjudicated more debt-related lawsuits. There was therefore a movement towards institutions, a shift from community self-regulation to third party arbitration.

This development was the result of two main factors. First, the structure of local communities changed significantly. Population growth partly provoked the erosion of traditional communal norms. As social networks expanded, the ties binding personal relations became looser.[67] And because those ties were paramount to ensure the smoothness of cooperation, their alteration had a negative impact on coagency. Trust was no longer a given. Additionally, the social homogeinity of those traditional communities was challenged after the 1760s. The emergence of a new group of lenders from a nascent non-manual cast altered and damaged the social fabric of the community. The practises and expectations of these new lenders were fundamentally different from those of the peasants. Not only did these new players contribute to expanding the social bounds between people further but they also imposed new rules for their exchanges. As their goals and expectations were anchored in the logic of investment and returns, they contributed to displacing trust to the institutions. Additionally, by turning to the institutions, parties not only displaced the trust they had in one another but also in other traditional mediators whose intermediation and therefore power and influence were greatly challenged. Second, new market realities also contributed to this process of institutionalization of credit. An upsurge in prices, especially in the second half of the eighteenth century, created a climate of uncertainty. Lenders increasingly doubted the capacity of borrowers to honour their obligations. Institutions not only helped them to bring uncertainty under control and minimize risk but gave them the opportunity to proceed further with their investments.

---

[67] Mark S. Granovetter, "The Strength of Weak Ties," *American Journal of Sociology* 78, no. 6 (1973): 1360–80.

Overall, the growing use of contract law and third parties (notaries and courts of justice) points towards the creation of a credible commitment.[68] It sent a positive signal not only to investors but also to future partners. In theory, cooperation was made smoother and easier. The willingness to cooperate might even have increased because the incentive structure changed in a favourable way.[69] But, by contrast, this migration of trust also entailed the erosion of moral norms. I believe that institutions did embrace households' expectations and practises at first, as we have seen with contract provisions for example. But with time institutions grew and responded to the imperatives of the market rather than on a case-by-case basis.

As Graeber and others have noted there was de facto a migration of trust from peer-to-peer exchanges to institutionalized transactions, a shift between community self-regulation to institutionalized supervision and monitoring. However, a complete institutionalization of credit would not be complete until much later. The notarial credit market was growing and was attracting more households, but the number of loans drafted compared to the number of inhabitants remained modest. Households continued to practise peer-to-peer exchanges and continued to pursue self-regulation. In the last decades of the Ancien Regime, the traditional model of the moral economy came under attack and started to recede, albeit it did not yet disappear.

---

[68] Cook, *Cooperation without Trust?* p 37.   [69] Ibid.

Epilogue: The Community of Advantage

The book opened with a reference to the financial crisis of 2008. The financial meltdown occurred for a wide range of reasons. One of them was what David Graeber called the 'impersonal arithmetic' of the exchanges. Throughout the twentieth century and onwards, the financial sector has grown disembedded and disconnected from the real economy through both formalization – at the expense of embedded relationships – and the growing use of novel and more complex financial instruments. As a result, there is simply little flexibility and input left.

In contrast, pre-industrial financial markets were highly personalized and embedded in the social tissue of communities. As a result, mutual agreements were often struck to the satisfaction of both parties. Flexibility, input, and even fairness characterized those exchanges *ex* and *post ante*. This did not mean that all transactions were harmonious and consensual. But there was space for negotiation, consensus, and a degree of input from both parties.

In this conclusion, I would like to insist on the social dimension of preindustrial financial markets and reflect on the lessons that can be drawn from the making of credit and debt in preindustrial France. We need first to recall how the embeddedness of credit in the social tissue of communities worked in a world where credit was an inherent part of communal life. Then, both endogenous and exogenous changes pertaining to credit markets led to the etiolation of previously enmeshed ties. As a result, the institutionalization of credit exchanges was set to rise.[1] Yet, the migration of credit, from peer-to-peer exchanges towards formalization, was neither simple nor linear. The persistence of peer-to-peer lending in

---

[1] See also D'Maris Coffman, "Towards the Institutionalisation of Credit," in *Financing in Europe: Evolution, Coexistence and Complementarity of Lending Practices from the Middle Ages to Modern Times*, ed. Marcella Lorenzini, Cinzia Lorandini, and D'Maris Coffman, 347–53, (Cham: Springer, 2018); and Masahiko Aoki and Yujiro Hayami, *Communities and Markets in Economic Development* (Oxford: Oxford University Press 2001).

today's world sheds light on the significance of personal ties and offers some food for thought.

Credit and the Communal Organization of Life

In pre-industrial Europe, the making of credit and debt involved various actors and circuits of exchange. Private, non-intermediated exchanges and notarized transactions between households, and credit supplied by professional lenders and non-personalized lenders represented a vast constellation of actors and opportunities. Parties could choose from among various credit instruments to tailor their needs and preferences. Contracts aimed to mitigate risks and offered a certain degree of insurance.

Among these various credit circuits, credit without certification played an important role for households. Non-intermediated transactions were very common for all sorts of deferred payments or cash transfers. Households did not hesitate to turn to non-intermediated credit for the payment of labour, services, livestock, seeds, foodstuffs, craft items, and even land. In other words, for everything that was for sale. The recurring lack of cash because of a shortage of specie, but above all because of irregular cash flows, made peer-to-peer lending necessary.

But the success of these non-intermediated transactions pertained, in fact, to the nature of small traditional communities.[2] In these close-knit communities, strong social norms were pervasive and were reflected in mutual arrangements such as credit. The wealth gap and discrepancies in bargaining power remained limited. There were strong predispositions toward altruistic or norm-following behaviour.[3] Such communities also provided fertile ground for trust because access to information was made easier.[4] Competences, assets, and motivations were often aspects easy to assess. Cooperation was thus straightforward. As a result, formal certification was often deemed unnecessary. Agreements were often subjected to parties' input and bargaining, as well as renegotiation *ex ante*, precisely because of households' social propinquity.

This flexibility of arrangements entailed a constant search for fairness, especially when the conditions to fulfil the deal had changed over time. And those conditions often did change in a world full of risks and uncertainties.[5] Borrowers frequently encountered difficulties in the

---

[2] On cooperation see especially Joseph Heath, "The Benefits of Cooperation."
[3] Platteau, "Solidarity Norms and Institutions in Village Societies."
[4] Cook, *Cooperation Without Trust?* p 91.
[5] Jean-Yves Grenier, *L'Economie d'Ancien Régime: Un monde de l'échange et de l'incertitude* (Paris: Albin Michel, 1996).

repayment of their obligations. Renegotiation of contract provisions often occurred *ex ante*. And yet, lenders were typically accommodating to the borrower's ability to pay in ways that avoided harsh adjustments. They did so because of the intimate nature of these societies, the embeddedness of credit relations in the social tissue of communities, and the necessary repetition of exchanges. It was this continual readjustment to fairness that stabilized relations and made togetherness bearable, creating a certain social equilibrium within the community.

This equilibrium was not necessarily perfect. Fairness did not mean that credit relations were egalitarian; they were not for the most part. Borrowers were often indebted economically but also morally to their lenders. There were, without doubt, constraints, obligations of all sorts, and use and abuse of power. Judicial litigations, as highlighted in Chapter 5, shed light on the complexities of both social relations and embeddedness.

The prevalence and significance of non-intermediated transactions therefore forces us to rethink the significance and the role of more formal transactions such as notarial transactions.[6] In a context where non-intermediated credit thrived, one might question the ultimate utility of notarial contracts. Notarial contracts displayed similar norms of cooperation and fairness to non-intermediated agreements. Parties had the possibility to negotiate contract provisions *ex* and *post ante* regarding guarantees, the interest rate, and length of repayment. As Chapter 3 highlights, there was a degree of elasticity even for these intermediated notarial contracts. And there, too, there was a constant readjustment towards fairness. The 'rolling over' of contracts is perhaps the most telling example. Few notarial loans were repaid on time. The initial length specified in the contract mattered very little. Borrowers took longer to repay than what had initially been agreed upon. But as long as the interest continued to be paid on time, both parties remained satisfied with this tacit arrangement. Such practises suggest that if the agreed upon exchange term became harsh for one party, parties jointly adjusted terms by continuing their agreement past the deadline, avoiding an open conflict leading to judicial enforcement. We can imagine that other forms of compensation might have been required in the meantime.

In fact, notarial deeds were sought after because of the notary's official imprimatur. Despite the norms of cooperation highlighted above, uncertainty sometimes prevailed. Parties were reassured by a notarial contract, which granted them better access to the borrower's assets, especially

---

[6] A question also tackled by Fontaine, "L'activité notariale (Note Critique)."

landed assets. This insurance on repayment mattered in the cases where there was uncertainty over the borrower's competences and motivations. A notarial contract was also, and perhaps above all, used as a leverage tool to seek repayment when forbearance began to wear down. It might have been used as a tool when negotiations came to no avail. Finally, creditors with little social capital or little social bargaining power, such as widows or unmarried women, showed strong preferences for notarial contracts. For these creditors, arrangements without certification could often lead to repayment difficulties precisely because these arrangements entailed constant bargaining and a power discrepancy due to patriarchal structures.

Overall, both non-intermediated and notarial credit enabled people to reach fair deals. Credit agreements were flexible because of the cooperative nature of traditional societies. Communities faced constant risks, hurdles, and uncertainties. People had to constantly revise their terms of agreements to insure the sustainability of their communities. This reciprocal system was made of short-run altruistic acts, which made *de facto* both parties better-off.[7]

I have mentioned that notarial contracts were often sought after because of the greater security they granted. This implies that repayment was not always a given. Conflicts and repayment issues were, in fact, common. All kinds of credit arrangements were concerned, notarial as well as non-intermediated. And yet, default is not contradictory to the norms of cooperation I have stated above. In fact, conflicts did occur precisely because of the intimate character of these communities.

Despite the pervasive social norms in agrarian communities, mutual arrangements sometimes broke down. Repayment issues were common. And activation of commitments had to be reiterated forcefully on several occasions. When lenders' forbearance broke down, matters had to be mediated and arbitrated. How many repayment conflicts did in fact occur it is impossible to say. Yet, we know that mediation outside the courtroom occurred. It is likely that the use of the local judge as an arbitrator was reserved for infringements and conflicts that could not be solved by other means. By taking the matter before justice, lenders exposed their debtors' failure to the public eye. This public humiliation was an effective mechanism to discipline individuals to act in other-regarding ways. The efficiency of this mechanism resided in the fact that members of the community shared the same system of beliefs and norms.[8] The use of the judicial institution was not only a form of punishment but also a social strategy intended to re-establish sundered

---

[7] Taylor, *Community, Anarchy and Liberty*, p 29.
[8] Platteau, "Solidarity Norms and Institutions in Village Societies," p 825.

ties of friendship and resume communication via an intermediary. In fact, as most of the debt collection lawsuits did not go beyond the first hearing and as the number of foreclosures remained low, the court acted mainly as a pressure leveller on debtors, sending them a warning.

Overall, pre-industrial credit markets were characterized by their strong pro-social nature. In small communities, credit was understood as a flexible and renegotiable commitment. A credit arrangement had to fit into the social norms and the other-regarding norms of the community. Yet, such norms and cooperative behaviour did not preclude conflicts. They were part of the constant readjustment to fairness. I would like to insist that the making of credit and debt was never unproblematic. Embeddedness did not mean harmonious and consensual exchanges.[9] But as long as some equilibrium was respected, this model applied. In the south of Alsace, this pattern was valid roughly until the 1760s. In the last decades of the eighteenth century, however, cracks started to appear.

The Gradual Erosion of Personal Ties and the Rise of Institutions

In the last decades of the eighteenth century, a series of important changes took place. There was a gradual transformation of credit markets through both endogenous and exogenous factors. As a consequence, credit transactions turned more and more impersonal.

The main vectors of these transformations were the acceleration of the economy and demographic change. These two factors contributed to the erosion of the social norms that governed traditional communities.

First, credit markets became increasingly dynamic. Notarial credit rose. Judicial litigations for debt also increased. Women's capital was increasingly more invested in credit markets, suggesting a rise in demand. And the emerging rural bourgeoisie, the non-manual workers engaged in services and administrative work, was also gradually more numerous in placing their savings in the local credit market. Overall, everything pointed to the intensification of such exchanges, in other words, a growing demand and supply of credit. Local credit markets thrived.

Second, changes pertaining to demographic and socio-professional composition had tremendous consequences for the social equilibrium of communities. By demographic and socio-professional changes I mean two things. To begin with, there were more people living in the area. Consequently, the number of both agents and personal ties increased,

---

[9] On the same idea see Lemercier and Zalc, "Pour une nouvelle approche de la relation de crédit en histoire contemporaine."

resulting in the lengthening of these ties. Sustaining and navigating these expanding personal networks became increasingly more difficult. Information access became more challenging. Cooperation was not a given anymore and distrust crept in, as we saw in the previous chapter. With less social proximity, norm compliance was eroded.[10] And next, a new category of actors appeared. An emerging bourgeoisie with greater wealth accumulation and saving capacity invested increasingly in the credit market. This non-manual cast altered and damaged the social fabric of the community because of their superior/different social status, their greater wealth and their disregard for traditional social norms. Population homogeinity was no longer the rule, and cooperation was made more difficult.

As a result, there was a movement towards institutions for both the conclusion of loan contracts and their enforcement. Craig Muldrew refers to this phenomenon as the emergence of a 'contractual society'.[11] Parties relied increasingly on the local notary and the judge. Personal ties, voluntaristic constraints, and social ostracism 'were no longer effective as more complex and impersonal forms of exchange emerge'.[12]

Finally, as I mentioned earlier, the acceleration of the economy meant that new sources of capital had to be found. Female capital was more and more sought after. In parallel, the proportion of female borrowers, in particular married borrowers, increased significantly. Personal ties in credit markets under demographic pressure were stretched, the emergence of new actors, and new economic conditions made uncertainty a weighty factor in the making of credit. As a result, women became joint-partners liable for half of the debt. Their lineage property and dowries were progressively at stake in any repayment issue. Because of this new role, women gained both in responsibility and social capital. Male heads of household were no longer fully in charge of their finances. Lenders had imposed on them new constraints in terms of guarantees. The forced association with their wives was a survival strategy. But it eroded patriarchy as a societal model.

Yet, if there were signs of erosion of the peer-to-peer lending model for greater formalization, one can question the extent. There was no abrupt transition towards institutionalization. People did turn to institutions for the conclusion and enforcement of their contracts, but they also remained attached to non-intermediated credit and continued to come

---

[10] Bicchieri, Cristina, Eugen Dimant, Simon Gächter, and Daniele Nosenzo. "Social proximity and the erosion of norm compliance." Games and Economic Behavior 132 (2022): 59–72.

[11] Muldrew, *The Economy of Obligation.* Conclusion.

[12] North, *Institutions, Institutional Change and Economic Performance*, p 99.

to agreements privately. This cohabitation of formal and non-intermediated credit was meant to last.

The Persistence of Peer-to-Peer Lending and the Renewal of Communal Norms

Despite the increasing degree of depersonalization of the exchanges, peer-to-peer lending did in fact persist, and it did so long after the scope of this book. Commercial banking did not replace peer-to-peer lending easily.[13] In fact, it is difficult to point to the exact moment when peer-to-peer lending faded away. The evolution of credit institutionalization has never been linear.[14] In modern France, commercial banks began to emerge in the 1820s. And yet, in 1926, peer-to-peer lending still represented between 35% and 40% of industrial companies' indebtedness.[15] One must wait until the 1970s for French households to become 'banked' at 87%; in 1966, only 18% owned a bank account.[16] Well into the 1990s, small shopkeepers continued to run tabs for their customers.

And this is not only proper to France. The same trend can be found elsewhere in the Western world. In Sweden, for example, peer-to-peer lending resisted competition from commercial banks up until at least World War I.[17] And, in small rural communities, deferred payments were still practised widely in the 1960s. In the United States, well into the twentieth century, personal ties remained an important factor in lending. Morris Plan Banks, for example, made small loans in the inter-war period relying exclusively on co-signers to ensure repayment.[18] Personal character rather than collateral assets were preferred for assessing borrowers' repayment capacity.

Today, in developing countries, peer-to-peer lending resists well, despite being promised a quick death upon the increasing formalization and technologization of the exchanges. Samuel Popkin claimed that the

---

[13] See especially this brilliant overview Lemercier and Zalc, "Pour une nouvelle approche de la relation de crédit en histoire contemporaine."

[14] Oscar Gelderblom et al., "Exploring Modern Bank Penetration: Evidence from Early Twentieth-Century Netherlands," *The Economic History Review* 2023, 76, pp 892–916.

[15] Michel Lescure and Alain Plessis, "Le financement des entreprises françaises de la fin du XIXe à la Seconde Guerre Mondiale," *Études et Documents* 10 (1998): 277–91, p 286.

[16] Jeanne Lazarus, "Faire crédit: de la noble tâche à la corvée," *Revue Française de Socio-Economie* 9, no. 1 (2012): 43–61, p 43.

[17] Håkan Lindgren, "The Modernization of Swedish Credit Markets, 1840–1905"; Elise Dermineur, "Peer to Peer Credit Networks in Sweden, 1810–1910," in *Beyond Banks: A Comparative Framework for Understanding Credit Markets and Intermediation* (Basingstoke: Palgrave). Forthcoming.

[18] Gunnar Trumbull, *Consumer Lending in France and America: Credit and Welfare* (Cambridge: Cambridge University Press, 2014), p 8.

survival of mutualist schemes was theoretically unlikely because they were non-inclusive and insufficient for survival.[19] In South Africa, for example, despite an increasing proportion of households being 'banked', informal lending via stokvels, a type of rotating savings and credit association, is currently thriving.[20] It represents an economy of millions of US dollars. The same trends are observed elsewhere in the Global South.[21]

How can we explain the resistance and persistence of peer-to-peer lending? In a common assumption, such as in Popkin's, informal exchanges are archaic and inefficient. They should be replaced by formal instruments offering better security, information, and efficiency. The results of this book can help us shed light on this conundrum; I would like to put forward especially the significance of the relational aspect.

There is a rich literature presenting informal loans as a necessity for poor households in the developing world.[22] Informal lenders provide cash to poor people, usually to smooth consumption. These borrowers would not have access to formal loans because the amount they sought is typically too low to be profitable for banks and/or because they lack valuable collateral to pledge. Informal lending steps in when formal banking does not. But it is not the whole picture. Economic necessity is one approach. Peer-to-peer lending also persists because of its social dimension.

Peer-to-peer lending usually flourishes best in close-knit communities. In such communities, strong social norms prevail. Cooperation is thus made easier. People share the same set of beliefs and expectations. The size of such communities also matters for closeness makes mutual observation possible. And as a result, the collection of information is made easy. No intermediary is therefore needed to obtain information about a potential debtor's competences and motivations. This is why today successful ROSCAs (rotating savings and credit associations) throughout the world are usually made up of a handful of people sharing the same set of beliefs. Stokvel associations in South Africa, for example, have, on average, thirty-one persons, and enrolment happens upon recommendation or co-optation. Members often belong to the same community, live

---

[19] Samuel Popkin, "The Rational Peasant: The Political Economy of Peasant Society," *Theory and Society* 9, no. 3 (1980): 411–71.

[20] In 2018, 65% of South Africans had a bank account. Svetiev, Dermineur, and Kolanisi, "Financialization and Sustainable Credit."

[21] Hossein and Christabell, *Community Economies in the Global South.*

[22] Abhijit Banerjee and Esther Duflo, *Poor Economics: A Radical Rethinking of the Way to Fight Global Poverty* (New York: Public Affairs, 2011). Nicolas Lainez, "Informal Credit in Vietnam: A Necessity Rather Than an Evil," *Journal of Southeast Asian Economies* 31, no. 1 (2014): 147–54.

in the same street, frequent the same church, or are involved in the same trade, allowing mutual observation and control.[23]

In a common assumption, informal loans are more expensive than formal ones.[24] Commercial banks often offer better deals. (Yet, they rarely extend small amounts to smooth consumption expenditure. ROSCAs do.) But beyond this credit rationing problem, many black South Africans choose to stay within a stokvel mainly because of its relational value, with awareness of the frequent cost of a higher interest rate.

The relational value of informal credit is tremendously important for those who live in communities where the welfare state is not, or not very, present. Facing similar hurdles, these communities need to assist each other as past societies did to insure their survival.[25]

In fact, this relational dimension of credit exchange is well understood by microcredit institutes. To ensure repayment, they frequently extend money to groups, not individuals. They often used co-signers. As such, they seek to incorporate the discipline of social monitoring, mimicking, therefore, the relational nexus between debtors and creditors in non-intermediated credit markets.[26] But, *in fine*, these organizations are intermediaries, outsiders who can exercise their power upon borrowers. The relationship between lenders and creditors is unequal, not prone to flexibility, reciprocity, or fairness. After being praised, microloans today do not fulfil their promise.[27] Their failure may well reside in the use of intermediaries who stretch further relational ties and their lack of flexibility, ignoring people's circumstances.

Beyond the persistence of non-intermediated credit, we even observe a renewal of peer-to-peer credit. Throughout the world, new forms of peer-to-peer lending have emerged. Their aim is to short-circuit

---

[23] Svetiev, Dermineur, and Kolanisi, "Financialization and Sustainable Credit."

[24] Although recent research has shed light on zero interest loans. Platteau mentions interest free loan systems here, for example: Jean-Philippe Platteau and Anita Abraham, "An Inquiry into Quasi-credit Contracts: The Role of Reciprocal Credit and Interlinked Deals in Small-scale Fishing Communities," *The Journal of Development Studies* 23, no. 4 (1987): 461–90. See also Jonathan P. Thomas and Timothy Worrall, "Gift-Giving, Quasi-Credit and Reciprocity," *Rationality and Society* 14, no. 3 (2002): 308–52.

[25] Elise M. Dermineur and Unathi Kolanisi, "Mutual Aid and Informal Finance: The Persistence of Stokvels," *The Thinker* 95, no. 2 (2023): 35–43.

[26] Becky Hsu, "The 'Impossible' Default: Qualitative Data on Borrower Responses to Two Types of Social-Collateral Microfinance Structures in Rural China," *The Journal of Development Studies* 52, no. 1 (2016): 147–59.

[27] Abhijit Banerjee, Esther Duflo, Rachel Glennerster, and Cynthia Kinnan. "The miracle of microfinance? Evidence from a randomized evaluation," *American Economic Journal: Applied Economics* 7, no. 1 (2015): 22–53. Isabelle Guérin, Santhosh Kumar, and Isabelle Agier, "Women's Empowerment: Power to Act or Power over Other Women? Lessons from Indian Microfinance," *Oxford Development Studies* 41, no. sup1 (2013): 76–94.

traditional banking. In southern Italy, in the 1990s, for example, a non-intermediated system of credit facilitated exchanges between farmers, millers, and bakers using 'flour bonds'. They could all trade in wheat, flour, and bread to operate without the apparent mediation of money. Far from being an inherited system from the past, it was implemented in the early 1960s and developed further in the 1990s.[28] And what to make of the Irish bank strikes between 1966 and 1976? A series of bank strikes closed down all bank counters in Ireland. People could no longer access their bank accounts. They could neither withdraw nor make deposits. Very surprisingly, this turn of events had very little impact on the Irish economy. And more importantly, it did not affect Irish households much. How was it possible? With limited possibilities to use cash, individuals began instead to use cheques, which they traded among themselves. Cheques circulated like a species, albeit in small social networks.[29] Again, in these examples the relational aspect is key. Examples of face-to-face credit like these can be multiplied.[30]

This attachment to mutual arrangements, despite the evident flaws, contradicts the *Homo economicus* model put forward by neo-classical economists. The work of Daniel Kahneman, Amos Tversky, and Richard Thaler among others makes clear that people are 'not nearly as farsighted, calculating, and consistent in their decision making'.[31] People are simply not rational and self-interested actors. They prefer mutually beneficial cooperation.

Mutual arrangements like the ones of southern Alsace in the early modern period, despite their flaws, point to several benefits. The flexibility, reciprocity, and fairness of the exchanges allowed parties to reach consensus. As a result, these features engendered sustainable credit, in the sense that it was not destabilizing. Yet, many today are of the opinion that returning to such a system is neither likely nor desirable. Non-intermediated credit formats, though persistent, continue to evolve, change, and manifest in new ways. Consequently, they hold valuable

---

[28] Valeria Siniscalchi, "La monnaie de farine," *Terrain. Anthropologie & sciences humaines*, no. 52 (March 5, 2009): 152–63.

[29] Anne L. Murphy, *The Origins of English Financial Markets: Investment and Speculation before the South Sea Bubble* (Cambridge: Cambridge University Press, 2009).

[30] Miller, Michelle, "Mutual Aid as Spiritual Sustenance," *Daedalus, Journal of the American Academy of Arts & Sciences* 152, no. 11 (2023): 125–31. Caroline Shenaz Hossein, "Money Pools in the Americas: The African Diaspora's Legacy in the Social Economy," *Forum for Social Economics* 45, no. 4 (2016): 309–28; Hossein and Christabell, *Community Economies in the Global South*. Frederick F. Wherry et al., *Credit Where It's Due: Rethinking Financial Citizenship*, (New York: Russell Sage Foundation, 2019).

[31] Bowles, *The Moral Economy*, p 7.

insights for regulators, policymakers, and financial institutions. Rather than regarding these mutual arrangements solely as alternatives or temporary transitions to formal finance, it is imperative to foster a better dialogue between financial institutions and non-intermediated credit. This approach would address the limitations of both models, while empowering consumers to have a more influential role in shaping the future of finance.

Bibliography

Primary sources

Registers and archival documents kept at the Archives Départementales du Territoire de Belfort (ADTB hereafter).

Archives départementales du Territoire de Belfort (ADTB)

1.   Série B: Justice (Judicial Dataset)

1.1.   Seigneurie de Delle (8 B)
     18: 20 juillet 1678–13 juillet 1680
     19: 20 juillet 1680–2 mai 1682
     20: 9 mai 1682–29 janvier 1684
     21: 29 janvier 1684–15 juin 1685
     22: 30 juin 1685-29 novembre 1686
     31: 9 janvier 1699–22 avril 1700
     32: 6 mai–22 décembre 1700
     33: 27 janvier–16 décembre 1705
     81: 13 juin-9 septembre 1739
     83: 23 décembre 1739–7 mai 1740
     84: 11 mai–20 juillet 1740
     85: 27 juillet–23 novembre 1740
     86: 23 novembre 1740–8 mars 1741
     87: 13 mars–14 juin 1741
     88: 14 juin–29 juillet 1741
     89: 31 juillet–25 octobre 1741
     90: 7 novembre 1741–26 février 1742
     91: 6 mars–13 juin 1742
     92: 20 juin–31 octobre 1742
     93: 6 novembre 1742–18 mars 1743
     94: 27 mars-26 juin 1743
     95: 26 juin 1743–29 janvier 1744
     96: 12 février–15 juillet 1744
     97: 15 juillet–14 novembre 1744
     98: 18 novembre 1744–14 avril 1745
     156: 30 septembre 1779–10 octobre 1781

157: 10 octobre 1781–5 février 1783
158: 19 février–13 août 1783
159: 3 septembre 1783–10 novembre 1784
160: 18 novembre 1784–19 juillet 1786

Not part of the dataset:
132: 12 décembre 1761–7 juillet 1762

1.2   *Seigneurie de Florimont (12 B)*
14: 26 mars 1699–3 mars 1701
15: 28 juillet 1701–19 novembre 1703
16: 15 janvier 1704–19 juin 1704
17: 21 juillet 1705–5 novembre 1705
42: 22 septembre1739–26 février 1740
43: 26 mars 1740–16 mai 1741
44: 17 mai 1741–19 décembre 1741
45: 20 mars 1742–11 juillet 1742
46: 6 septembre1742–18 mars 1743
47: 20 avril 1743–25 janvier 1745
48: 27 janvier 1745–17 novembre 1745
72: 23 février 1770–21 novembre 1771
73: juin 1772–25 octobre 1773
78: 15 juin 1779–18 juillet 1780
79: 18 juillet 1780–15 mai 1781
80: 10 juillet 1781–18 avril 1782
81: 4 février–30 décembre 1783
82: 16 mars 1784-1er février 1785
12B183: Livre de comptes de J Lajanne, notaire et tabellion. 1696–1697

2.   *Série 2 E 4: Notariat*

2.1   *Protocoles, Seigneurie de Delle*
24: 10 juin 1681–4 mars 1683
25: 1er février 1684–7 juillet 1685
38: 15 juin 1699–5 mars 1700
39: 9 mars–31 décembre 1700
40: 25 janvier 1701–27 juin 1702
41: 1er janvier 1701–10 août 1703
42: 5 janvier 1704–31 décembre 1704
101: 5 janvier 1739–10 août 1740
102: 21 août 1740–7 janvier 1742
103: 3 février 1742–5 mars 1743
104: 6 mars 1743–28 février 1745
268: 26 novembre 1779–15 mars 1783
269: 20 mai 1782–19 juillet 1784
270: 21 juillet 1784–25 février 1788

2.2   *Protocoles, Seigneurie de Florimont*

323: 1700
324: 1701
325: 1704
352: 1696–1731
366: 24 juin 1739–21 janvier 1740
367: 30 janvier–28 octobre 1740
368: 6 novembre 1740–2 juin 1741
369: 9 juin 1741–7 avril 1742
370: 9 avril–31 octobre 1742
371: 11 novembre 1742–11 novembre 1743
372: 30 novembre 1743–7 juillet 1745
389: 19 mars 1745–15 avril 1788
428: 4 février 1780–21 novembre 1781
429: 22 novembre 1781–1 septembre 1783
430: 25 août 1783–21 juin 1785

2.3   *Contrats de Mariage, seigneurie de Delle*

25:1684
39: 1700
40: 1701
42: 1704
74: 1720
102: 1740
103: 1743
111: 1733–1739
276: 1776–1780

2.4   *Contrats de Mariage, Seigneurie de Florimont*

342: 1699–1703
344:1704–1707
345: 1711–1719
347: 1725–1731
390: Courtelevant. 1er novembre 1749–10 février 1791
391: Chavanatte, Suarce. 26 avril 1744–22 avril 1776
392: Faverois, Réchésy, Courcelle, Fêche-l'Eglise, Normanvillars et forains. 20 septembre 1750–5 février 1791.
393: Florimont. 17 février 1760–25 octobre 1784.
525: 1769–1791

2.5   *Obligations, Seigneurie de Delle (Notarial Dataset)*

155: 3 juin 1733–27 février 1736
156: 8 janvier 1737–28 janvier 1741
157: 3 mars 1741–30 novembre 1746
158: 21 décembre 1746–26 juillet 1750
159: 7 septembre 1750–29 avril 1754

194: 19 mai 1754–22 mai 1758
222: 28 octobre 1758–5 mars 1764
223: 3 avril–15 décembre 1764
257: 28 novembre 1769–5 juin 1772
258: 22 juin 1772–3 mars 1777
279: 8 mars 1777–23 juillet 1781
280: 23 juillet 1781–10 novembre 1785
281: 24 octobre 1785–4 février 1791
285: 1774–1791

2.6   *Obligations, Seigneurie de Florimont (Notarial Dataset)*
408: 21 mars 1740–22 juin 1745
409: 11 juillet 1745–6 août 1753
410: 16 octobre 1753–26 juin 1769
443: 17 février 1768–7 janvier 1773
444: 20 janvier 1773–28 juin 1781
445: 27 mars 1781–19 juin 1784
446: 30 juillet 1784–18 février 1791

3.   *Inventaire après décès (Probate Dataset)*

Seigneurie de Delle
10: 1607–1660
53: 1660–1708
54: 1648–1709
55: 1672–1709
56: 1672–1708
85: 1711–1728
86: 1711–1728
87: 1711–1728
114: 1728–1750
203: 1759–1764
210: 1759–1764
228: 1765–1769
252: 1769–1773
260: 1769–1779
261: 1769–1779
262: 1769–1779
287: 1774–1791
288: 1774–1791
296: 1774–1791
299: 1774–1791

Seigneurie de Florimont
309: 1676–1683
315: 1684–1688
317: 1689–1691

348: 1696–1731
349: 1698–1729
350: 1696–1731
351: 1696–1731
397: 1751–1777
399: 1747–1759
401: 1733–1760
402: 1748–1760
403: 1733–1756
404: 1747–1758
405: 1733–1759
407: 1748–1760
411: 1706–1790
435: 1764–1785
436: 1761–1787
437: 1762–1790
438: 1762–1787
439: 1763–1788
440: 1761–1771
441: 1772–1781
442: 1782–1790
12B165

4.   *Archives des Fabriques*

2G29 Florimont
2G13 Courtelevant
12B182 Florimont
GG15-1-37 fabrique de Delle
GG16-1-36 fabrique de Delle

5.   *Etat civil d'Ancien Régime*

033 E-dépôt AA, BB, DD, FF, GG, JJ
055 E-dépôt GG
028 E-dépôt GG
046 E-dépôt GG
095 E-dépôt GG1-5

6.   *Miscellaneous*

6.1   *Archives de l'intendance d'Alsace*

ADTB 1C22
ADTB 1C31
ADTB 1C34

ADTB 1C92
ADTB1C111
ADTB 1C165

6.2   Other

ADTB 4B/249
ADTB 1Fi323
ADTB 1Fi326
21 J 1 Etat et remembrement de la subdélégation de Belfort en 1751.
  (Fonds Noblat)
3 E Fonds Mazarin

7.   Other archives

Archives Municipales de Belfort (AMB) GG09-36
Archives départementales du Bas-Rhin (ADBR) 338
Archives départementales du Haut-Rhin (ADHR) C1284

Printed Sources

Bois de Chêne, Hugues. *Recueil mémorable de Hugues Bois-de-Chesne, chronique inédite du XVIIe siècle*. Montbéliard: Charles Deckherr, 1856.
Bonvalot, Édouard. *Les coutumes du val de Rosemont*. Paris: Durand, 1866.
Les coutumes de l'Assise et les terriers de 1573 et de 1742. Paris: Durand, 1866.
Coutumes de Haute Alsace dites de Ferrette publiées pour la première fois avec introduction. Colmar: Barth, 1870.
Colney, Michel. *Complete Works of Aristotle, Volume 2*, 1984. https://press.princeton
  .edu/books/hardcover/9780691016511/complete-works-of-aristotle-volume-2.
De Boug, François-Henri. *Recueil des edits, déclarations, lettres patentes, arrêts du Conseil d'État et du Conseil Souverain d'Alsace. Ordonnances et règlemens concernant cette province avec des observations* (Colmar: Jean-Henri Decker) 1775. vol 1, p 80.
De la Grange. *Extrait d'un mémoire sur la province d'Alsace*, Strasbourg, 1697, reprinted in 1858, Bibliothèque Nationale et Universitaire de Strasbourg, M116.430.
Ferrière, Claude de. *La science parfaite des notaires*. Paris: Charles Osmont, 1682.
Dictionnaire de droit et de pratique, contenant l'explication es termes de droit, d'ordonnance, de coutume et de pratique, avec les jurisdictions de France, Paris: Chez Babuty Fils, 1758.
Furetière, Antoine. (1619–1688) *Dictionnaire universel*. Paris: Arnout et Reinier Leers, 1690.
Dictionnaire Universel contenant généralement tous les mots françois tant vieux que modernes & les termes des sciences et des arts. La Haye: A. & R: Leers, 1701, entry: rente constituée, pp 483–84.

Isambert, François André. *Recueil général des anciennes lois françaises, depuis l'an 420 jusqua'à la révolution de 1789; contenant la notice des principaux monumens des Mérovingiens, des Carlovingiens et des Capétiens, et le texte des ordonnances, édits, déclarations, lettres-patentes, réglemens, arrêts du Conseil, etc., de la troisième race, qui ne sont pas abrogés, ou qui peuvent servir, soit à l'interprétation, soit à l'histoire du droit public et privé, avec notes de concordance, table chronologique et table général analytique et alphabétique des matières.* Paris: Belin-Le-Prieur, 1821.

L'Hermine, Jacques de. *Guerre et paix en Alsace au XVIIe siècle: les mémoires de voyage du sieur J. de L'Hermine.* Mulhouse: Editions Veuve Bader, 1880.

Lagrange, Jacques de. *L'Alsace en 1700. Mémoire de l'intendant Lagrange publié par Raymond Oberlé.* Colmar: Alsatia, 1975. Taverne de Longchamps, "Mémoire", in Bulletin de la Société belfortaine d'émulation, no 8, 1886.

Loyseau, Charles. *Discours de l'abus des justices de villages.* Paris: A. l'Angelier, 1603.

Pothier, Robert-Joseph. *Traité du contrat de constitution de rente.* Paris: Béchet aîné, 1763.

Taverne, de Longchamps, "Mémoires" in Bulletin de la Société belfortaine d'émulation, 1886, no 8, p 79.

Young, Arthur. *Voyages en France, 1787–1788–1789.* Paris: Armand Colin, 1976.

Secondary Sources

Ågren, Maria. "Land and Debt: On the Process of Social Differentiation in Rural Sweden, circa 1750–1850." *Rural History* 5, no. 01 (1994): 23–40.

Ågren, Maria, and Amy Louise Erickson, eds. *The Marital Economy in Scandinavia and Britain, 1400–1900.* Burlington, VT: Ashgate, 2005.

Ahlquist, John S., and Levi, Margaret. *In the Interest of Others: Organizations and Social Activism.* Princeton, NJ: Princeton University Press, 2013.

Albert, Anaïs. "Le crédit à la consommation des classes populaires à la Belle Époque: invention, innovation ou reconfiguration?" *Annales. Histoire, Sciences Sociales* 67, no. 4 (2012): 1049–82.

Angleraud, Bernadette. "Les boulangers lyonnais aux XIXe-XXe siècles (1836–1914): Une étude sur la petite bourgeoisie boutiquière." Thèse de doctorat, Université Lyon 2, 1993.

Aoki, Masahiko, and Yujiro Hayami. *Communities and Markets in Economic Development.* Oxford: Oxford University Press, 2001.

Arnoux, Mathieu, and Olivier Guyotjeannin. *Tabellions et tabellionages de la France médiévale et moderne.* Mémoires et documents de l'École des chartes. Paris: École des Chartes, 2011.

Audisio, Gabriel. *L'historien et l'activité notariale: Provence, Vénétie, Egypte, XVe–XVIIIe siècles.* Toulouse: Presses Universitaires du Midi, 2005.

Baland, Jean-Marie, Catherine Guirkinger, and Charlotte Mali. "Pretending to Be Poor: Borrowing to Escape Forced Solidarity in Cameroon." *Economic Development and Cultural Change* 60, no. 1 (2011): 1–16.

Balestracci, Duccio, Betsy Merideth, and Paolo Squatriti. *The Renaissance in the Fields: Family Memoirs of a Fifteenth-Century Tuscan Peasant.* University Park, PA: Pennsylvania State University Press, 1999.

Banerjee, Abhijit, and Esther Duflo. *Poor Economics: A Radical Rethinking of the Way to Fight Global Poverty*. New York: Public Affairs, 2011.
Good Economics for Hard Times: Better Answers to Our Biggest Problems. London: Penguin, 2020.

Banerjee, Abhijit, Esther Duflo, Rachel Glennerster, and Cynthia Kinnan. "The Miracle of Microfinance? Evidence from a Randomized Evaluation." *American Economic Journal: Applied Economics* 7, no. 1 (2015): 22–53.

Baradel, Yvette. *Belfort: De l'Ancien Régime au siège de 1870–1871: fonction régionale, impact national, 1780–1870*. Belfort: Société belfortaine d'émulation, 1993.

Bardy, Henri. "Les Suédois dans le Sundgau (1632–1648)," *Revue d'Alsace*, 7:241–56. Fédération des sociétés d'histoire et d'archéologie d'Alsace, 1856.

Barral, Pierre. "note historique sur l'emploi du terme 'paysan.'" *Études Rurales*, no. 21 (1966): 72–80.

Baulant, Micheline. "Niveaux de vie paysans autour de Meaux en 1700 et 1750." *Annales. Histoire, Sciences Sociales* 30, no. 2–3 (1975): 505–18.

Béaur, Gérard. "Foncier et crédit dans les sociétés préindustrielles: des liens solides ou des chaînes fragiles?" *Annales. Histoire, Sciences Sociales* 49, no. 6 (1994): 1411–28.
"Les catégories sociales à la campagne: repenser un instrument d'analyse." *Annales de Bretagne et des pays de l'Ouest* 106, no. 1 (1999): 159–76.
"Credit and Land in Eighteenth-Century France." In Thijs Lambrecht and Phillipp R. Schofield, eds. *Credit and the Rural Economy in North-Western Europe, c. 1200–c. 1850*, Turnhout: Brepols Publishers, 2009, 153–67.

Beauvalet-Boutouyrie, Scarlett. *Etre veuve sous l'Ancien Régime*. Paris: Belin, 2001.

Béguin, Katia. "La circulation des rentes constituées dans la France du XVIIe siècle: une approche de l'incertitude économique." *Annales. Histoire, Sciences Sociales* 60, no. 6 (2005): 1229–44.

Bennett, Judith M. *Ale, Beer and Brewsters in England: Women's Work in a Changing World, 1300–1600*. Oxford, New York: Oxford University Press, 1999.

Berthe, Maurice, ed. *Endettement paysan et crédit rural: dans l'Europe médiévale et moderne*. Toulouse: Presses Universitaires du Midi, 2020.

Bicchieri, Cristina. *The Grammar of Society: The Nature and Dynamics of Social Norms*. Cambridge: Cambridge University Press, 2006.

Bicchieri, Cristina, Eugen Dimant, Simon Gächter, and Daniele Nosenzo. "Social proximity and the erosion of norm compliance." Games and Economic Behavior 132 (2022): 59–72.

Bicchieri, Cristina, Ryan Muldoon, and Alessandro Sontuoso. "Social Norms." In Edward N. Zalta, ed. *The Stanford Encyclopedia of Philosophy*, Winter 2018. Stanford, CA: Metaphysics Research Lab, Stanford University, 2018. https://plato.stanford.edu/archives/win2018/entries/social-norms/

Bijnaar, Aspha. "Akuba & Kasmoni. Surinamese Women in a Traditional Banking System in Amsterdam." In Fenneke Reysoo and Christine Verschuur, eds. *Femmes en mouvement: genre, migrations et nouvelle division internationale du travail*, eds. Genève: Graduate Institute Publications, 2016, 197–202.

Birgy, Odile. "Une occupation originale de l'espace rural. La communauté Anabaptiste de Normanvillars dans le Sundgau au XVIIIe siècle." *Histoire & Sociétés Rurales* 41, no. 1 (2014): 17–54.

Bischoff, Georges. *Gouvernés et gouvernants en Haute Alsace à l'époque Autrichienne.* Strasbourg: Librairie Istra, 1982.

"Les blancs de la Carpe. Pisciculture et pouvoir: l'exemple de l'Alsace autrichienne (14e–17e siècle)." In Jean-François Chauvard et Isabelle Laboulais, eds. *Les fruits de la récolte, études offertes à Jean-Michel Boehler*, Strasbourg: Presses Universitaires de Strasbourg, 2007, 179–95.

Bochove, Christiaan van, and Heleen Kole. "Uncovering Private Credit Markets: Amsterdam, 1660–1809." *Tijdschrift Voor Sociale En Economische Geschiedenis* 11, no. 3 (2014): 39–72.

Boehler, Jean-Michel. "Communauté villageoise et contrastes sociaux: laboureurs et manouvriers dans la campagne strasbourgeoise de la fin du XVIIe au début du XIXe siècle." *Études rurales* 63, no. 1 (1976): 93–116.

Une société rurale en milieu rhénan: la paysannerie de la plaine d'Alsace (1648–1789). Strasbourg: Presses Universitaires de Strasbourg, 1995.

La terre, le ciel et les hommes à l'époque moderne: des réalités de la plaine d'Alsace aux horizons européens: 35 années de recherches d'histoire rurale, 1968–2003. Strasbourg: Société savante d'Alsace, 2004.

"L'art d'être propriétaire sans l'être tout en l'étant." *Revue d'Alsace*, no. 140 (2014): 79–96.

"Quelle reconstruction dans la campagne alsacienne au lendemain des guerres du XVIIe siècle?" *Revue d'Alsace*, 142 (2016): 11–25.

"Étrangers et étranges: terre et paysans d'Alsace vus par les ressortissants d'outre-Rhin et d'outre-Vosges aux XVIIe et XVIIIe siècles." In Dominique Dinet and Jean-Noël Grandhomme, eds. *Les formes du voyage: approches interdisciplinaires*, Sciences de l'histoire. Strasbourg: Presses Universitaires de Strasbourg, 2019, 11–23.

Bonar, Daphne L. "Debt and Taxes: Village Relations and Economic Obligations in Seventeenth-Century Auvergne." *French Historical Studies* 35, no. 4 (2012): 661–89.

Bonzon, Anne. *La paix au village – clergé paroissial et règlement des conflits dans la France d'Ancien Régime.* Paris: Éditions Champ Vallon, 2022.

Bossy, John. *Christianity in the West 1400–1700.* New York: Oxford University Press, 1985.

Bourdieu, Pierre. "Les stratégies matrimoniales dans le système de reproduction". *Annales. Économies, Sociétés, Civilisations* 27, 4 (1972).

Outline of a Theory of Practice. Translated by Richard Nice. of Cambridge Studies in Social and Cultural Anthropology. Cambridge: Cambridge University Press, 1977.

Practical Reason: On the Theory of Action. Translated by Randall Johnson. 1st ed. Stanford, CA: Stanford University Press, 1998.

Pascalian Meditations. Cambridge, UK: Polity Press, 2000.

Bowles, Samuel. *The Moral Economy: Why Good Incentives Are No Substitute for Good Citizens.* New Haven, London: Yale University Press, 2016.

Braudel, Fernand. *Civilisation matérielle, économie et capitalisme, XVe–XVIIIe siècle. 1 - Les Structures du quotidien.* Paris: Le Livre de Poche, 1993.

Brennan, Thomas. "Peasants and Debt in Eighteenth-Century Champagne." *The Journal of Interdisciplinary History* 37, no. 2 (2011): 175–200.

Briggs, Chris. "Empowered or Marginalized? Rural Women and Credit in Later Thirteenth- and Fourteenth-Century England." *Continuity and Change* 19, no. 01 (2004).

Credit and Village: Society in Fourteenth-Century England. New York: Oxford University Press, 2009.

"'Can't Pay' and 'Won't Pay' in the Medieval Village." *Common Knowledge* 17, no. 2 (2011): 363–70.

Briggs, Chris, and Jaco Zuijderduijn. *Land and Credit: Mortgages in the Medieval and Early Modern European Countryside.* Cham, Switzerland: Palgrave Macmillan, 2018.

Brizay, François, Antoine Follain, and Véronique Sarrazin, eds. *Les justices de village: administration et justice locales de la fin du Moyen Âge à la Révolution.* Rennes: Presses Universitaires de Rennes, 2015.

Bruch, Charles A. "Taking the Pay Out of Payday Loans: Putting an End to the Unsurious and Unconscionable Interest Rates Charged by Payday Lenders Comment." *University of Cincinnati Law Review* 69, no. 4 (2001 2000): 1257–88.

Brunet, Serge. "Fondations de messes, crédit rural et marché de la terre dans les Pyrénées centrales (XVe–XVIIIe siècle): les communautés de prêtres du Val d'Aran." In Maurice Berthe, ed. *Endettement paysan et crédit rural: Dans l'Europe médiévale et moderne.* Toulouse: Presses Universitaires du Midi, 1998, 217–37.

Burns, Kathryn. "Notaries, Truth, and Consequences." *The American Historical Review* 110, no. 2 (2005): 350–79.

Calder, Lendol. *Financing the American Dream: A Cultural History of Consumer Credit.* Princeton, NJ: Princeton University Press, 2009.

Carlos, Ann M., and Larry Neal. "Women Investors in Early Capital Markets, 1720–1725." *Financial History Review* 11, no. 2 (2004): 197–224.

Carruthers, Bruce G. *The Economy of Promises: Trust, Power, and Credit in America.* Princeton, NJ: Princeton University Press, 2022.

Casari, Marco, and Claudio Tagliapietra. "Group Size in Social-Ecological Systems." *Proceedings of the National Academy of Sciences* 115, no. 11 (2018): 2728–33.

Chauvaud, Frédéric. *Justice et sociétés rurales: du XVIe siècle à nos jours, approches pluridisciplinaires.* Rennes: Presses Universitaires de Rennes, 2011.

Christophers, Brett. *Rentier Capitalism: Who Owns the Economy, and Who Pays for It?* London: Verso Books, 2020.

Claustre, Julie. "De l'obligation des corps à la prison pour dette: l'endettement privé au Châtelet de Paris au Xve siècle." In Julie Claustre ed. *La dette et le juge. Juridiction gracieuse et juridiction contentieuse du XIIIe au XVe siècle (France, Italie, Espagne, Angleterre, Empire). Actes de la Table ronde, 15–16 mai 2003 au Collège de France.* Paris: Publications de la Sorbonne, 2005, 121–34.

Dans les geôles du roi. L'emprisonnement pour dette à Paris à la fin du Moyen Âge. Paris: Publications de la Sorbonne, 2007.

"Vivre à crédit dans une ville sans banque (Paris, XIVe–XVe siècle)." *Le Moyen Age* CXIX, no. 3 (2013): 567–96.

Coase, R. H. "The Institutional Structure of Production." *The American Economic Review* 82, no. 4 (1992): 713–19.

Coffman, D'Maris. "Towards the Institutionalisation of Credit." In Marcella Lorenzini, Cinzia Lorandini, and D'Maris Coffman, eds. *Financing in Europe: Evolution, Coexistence and Complementarity of Lending Practices from the Middle Ages to Modern Times*, Cham: Springer, 2018, 347–53.

Collectif, Olivier Guyotjeannin, Jean-Louis Gaulin, Giampaolo Cagnin, Claude Denjean, Kathryn Reyerson, Noël Coulet, Gaëlle Le Dantec, François Menant, and Odile Redon. *Notaires et crédit dans l'Occident méditerranéen médiéval*. Rome: Ecole Française de Rome, 2004.

Colney, Michel. *Delle au XVIIIe siècle*. Colmar: Coprur, 1989.

Cook, Karen Schweers. "Networks, Norms, and Trust: The Social Psychology of Social Capital-2004 Cooley Mead Award Address." *Social Psychology Quarterly* 68, no. 1 (2005).

Cook, Karen S., Russell Hardin, and Margaret Levi. *Cooperation Without Trust?* New York: Russell Sage Foundation, 2007.

Coquery, Natacha. "Vente, troc, crédit: les livres de comptabilité d'un joailler-bijoutier parisien à la fin du XVIIIe siècle," in *Actes des Sixièmes Journées d'histoire de la comptabilité et du management, faculté Jean Monnet, 23–24 mars 2000*, 133–44.

   Tenir boutique à Paris au XVIIIe siècle: luxe et demi-luxe. Paris: Éd. du comité des travaux historiques et scientifiques, 2011.

Corbin, Alain. *Archaïsme et modernité en Limousin au XIXe siècle, 1845–1880: La rigidité des structures économiques, sociales et mentales*. Limoges: Presses Universitaires de Limoges, 1999.

Corley, Christopher. "Preindustrial 'Single-Parent' Families: The Tutelle in Early Modern Dijon." *Journal of Family History* 29, no. 4 (2004): 351–65.

Craddock, Fred B. *L'Hostie et le denier: les finances ecclésiastiques du haut Moyen Age à l'époque moderne: actes du Colloque de la Commission internationale d'histoire ecclésiastique comparée, Genève, août 1989*. Genève: Labor et Fides, 1991.

Crowston, Clare Haru. "Credit and the Metanarrative of Modernity." *French Historical Studies* 34, no. 1 (2011): 7–19.

Damiano, Sara T. *To Her Credit: Women, Finance, and the Law in Eighteenth-Century New England Cities*. Baltimore, MD: John Hopkins University Press, 2021.

Dareste de la Chavanne, Rodolphe. "Note sur l'origine de l'exécution parée." *Bibliothèque de l'école des Chartes* 11, no. 1 (1850): 452–58.

Dattler, Philippe. *La métallurgie dans le Comté de Belfort: 1659–1790*. Belfort: Société Belfortaine d'Emulation, 1980.

Dayton, Cornelia Hughes. *Women Before the Bar: Gender, Law, and Society in Connecticut, 1639–1789*. Chapel Hill, NC: University of North Carolina Press, 2012.

Debard, Jean-Mard. *Les monnaies de la principauté de Montbéliard du XVIe au XVIIIe siècle* (Besançon: Presses Universitaires de Franche-Comté: 1980)

de Vries, Jan. *The Industrious Revolution: Consumer Behavior and the Household Economy, 1650 to the Present*. Cambridge, NY: Cambridge University Press, 2008.

"Peasant Demand Patterns and Economic Development: Frieland 1550–1750." In William N. Parker and Erik L. Jones eds. *European Peasants and Their Markets. Essays in Agrarian Economic History*. Princeton, NJ: Princeton University Press, 1976.

Dermineur, Elise M. "Female Peasants, Patriarchy, and the Credit Market in Eighteenth-Century France." *Proceedings of the Western Society for French History* 37 (2009).

"The Civil Judicial System in Early Modern France." *Frühneuzeit-Info* 22 (2011): 44–53.

Women in Rural Society: Peasants, Patriarchy and the Local Economy in Northeast France, 1650–1789. Doctoral thesis West Lafayette, IN: Purdue University, 2011.

"Les femmes et le crédit dans les communautés rurales au 18e siècle." *Traverse Revue d'Histoire - Zeitschrift Für Geschichte* 2 (2014): 53–64.

"Trust, Norms of Cooperation, and the Rural Credit Market in Eighteenth-Century France." *Journal of Interdisciplinary History* 45, no. 4 (2015): 485–506.

"Widows' Political Strategies in Traditional Communities: Negotiating Marital Status and Authority in 18th c France." In James Daybell and Svante Norrhem eds. *Gender and Political Culture, 1500–1800*, 123–39. Farnham: Routledge, 2016.

"Rural Credit Markets in 18th-Century France: Contracts, Guarantees and Land." In Chris Briggs and Jaco Zuijderduijn (eds.), *Land and Credit: Mortgages and Annuities in the Medieval and Early Modern European Countryside*. London: Palgrave Macmillan, 2017, 205–31.

ed. *Women and Credit in Pre-Industrial Europe*. Turnhout: Brepols Publishers, 2018, 205–231.

"Credit, Strategies, and Female Empowerment in Early Modern France." *Women and Credit in Pre-Industrial Europe*, 12:253–80. Early European Research 12. Turnhout: Brepols Publishers, 2018.

Pre-Industrial Europe, 12:1–18. Early European Research 12. Turnhout: Brepols Publishers, 2018.

"Peer-to-Peer Lending in Pre-Industrial France." *Financial History Review* 26, no. 3 (2019): 359–88.

"Women in Early Financial Markets." In Vulkan, *Past, Present and Future: Economic History in Eli F. Heckscher's Footsteps*. Stockholm: Erik Lakomaa, 2020, 75–105.

"The Evolution of Credit Networks in Pre-Industrial Finland." *Scandinavian Economic History Review* 70, no. 1 (2022): 57–86.

"Peer to Peer Credit Networks in Sweden, 1810–1910." In Christiaan Van Bochove and Juliette Levy, eds. *Beyond Banks: A Comparative Framework for Understanding Credit Markets and Intermediation*. Basingstoke: Palgrave. Forthcoming.

Dermineur, Elise M., and Unathi Kolanisi. "Mutual Aid and Informal Finance: The Persistence of Stokvels." *The Thinker* 95, no. 2 (2023): 35–43.

Dermineur, Elise M., and Yane Svetiev. "The Fairness of Contractual Exchange in a Private Law Society: A Case Study of Early Modern Credit Markets." *The European Review of Contract Law* 11, no. 3 (2015): 229–51.

Derouet, Bernard. "Le partage des frères: héritage masculin et reproduction sociale en Franche-Comté aux XVIIIe et XIXe siècles." *Annales. Histoire, Sciences Sociales* 48, no. 2 (1993).

Dolan, Claire. *Le notaire, la famille et la ville: Aix-en-Provence à la fin du XVIe siècle.* Toulouse: Presses Universitaires du Midi, 1998.

Entre justice et justiciables: les auxiliaires de la justice du Moyen Âge au XXe siècle. Quebec: Presses Université Laval, 2005.

Dormard, Serge. "Le marché du crédit à Douai aux XVIIe et XVIIIe siècles." *Revue du Nord* 362, no. 4 (2005): 803–33.

Douglas, Mary. *How Institutions Think.* London: Routledge & Kegan Paul, 1987.

Dousset, Christine. "*Familles paysannes et veuvage féminin en Languedoc à la fin du xviie siècle.*" *Dix-septième siècle* 249, no. 4 (2010).

Drouault, Célia. "Aller chez le notaire: un moyen d'expression pour les femmes ? L'exemple de Tours au XVIIIe siècle." *Genre & Histoire*, no. 6 (2010).

Elster, Jon. *Explaining Social Behavior: More Nuts and Bolts for the Social Sciences.* 1st ed. Cambridge: Cambridge University Press, 2007.

Fafchamps, Marcel. "Solidarity Networks in Preindustrial Societies: Rational Peasants with a Moral Economy." *Economic Development and Cultural Change* 41, no. 1 (1992): 147–74.

"Formal and Informal Market Institutions: Embeddedness Revisited." In Jean-Marie Baland, François Bourguignon, Jean-Philippe Platteau, and Thierry Verdier, eds. *The Handbook of Economic Development and Institutions*, Princeton, NJ: Princeton University Press, 2020, 375–413.

Fairchilds, Cissie. *Domestic Enemies: Servants and Their Masters in Old Regime France.* Baltimore, MD: Johns Hopkins University Press, 2019.

Faraizi, Aminul, Taskinur Rahman, and Jim McAllister. *Microcredit and Women's Empowerment: A Case Study of Bangladesh.* London: Routledge, 2013.

Fedou, René. *Lexique historique du Moyen Age.* Paris: Armand Colin, 1980.

Fernández Cuadrench, Jordi. "Crédit juif et solidarité villageoise dans les campagnes barcelonaises au XIIIe siècle." In Maurice Berthe, ed. *Endettement paysan et crédit rural dans l'Europe médiévale et moderne*, Toulouse: Presses Universitaires du Midi, 1998.

Finlay, Steven. "The History of Credit." In Steven Finlay, ed. *Consumer Credit Fundamentals.* London: Palgrave Macmillan, 2009, 33–53.

Finn, Margot C. *The Character of Credit.* Cambridge: Cambridge University Press, 2003.

Firth, Raymond. *Elements of Social Organisation.* London: Routledge, 2013.

Follain, Antoine. "L'administration des villages par les paysans au XVIIe siècle." *Dix-septième siècle* 234, no. 1 (2007): 135–56.

Le village sous l'Ancien Régime. Paris: Fayard, 2008.

"L'exercice du pouvoir à travers les fonctions communautaires dans les campagnes françaises modernes." In Jean-Pierre Jessenne and François Menant, eds. *Les élites rurales: dans l'Europe médiévale et moderne.* Toulouse: Presses Universitaires du Midi, 2020, 149–62.

Fontaine, Laurence. "L'activité notariale (Note critique)." *Annales. Histoire, Sciences Sociales* 48, no. 2 (1993): 475–83.

"Espaces, usages et dynamiques de la dette: dans les Hautes Vallées Dauphinoises (XVIIe–XVIIIe siècles)." *Annales. Histoire, Sciences Sociales* 49, no. 6 (1994): 1375–91.

"Antonio and Shylock: Credit and Trust in France, c. 1680–c. 1780." *The Economic History Review*, 54, no. 1 (2001): 39–57.

"Women's Economic Spheres and Credit in Pre-Industrial Europe." In Beverly Lemire, Ruth Pearson, and Gail Campbell, eds. *Women and Credit. Researching the Past, Refiguring the Future*, Oxford: Berg, 2001.

L'économie morale: pauvreté, crédit et confiance dans l'Europe préindustrielle. Paris: Editions Gallimard, 2008.

"Women in the micro finance economy of early modern Europe." *Quaderni storici* 46, no. 137(2) (2011): 513–32.

"Pouvoir, relations sociales et crédit sous l'Ancien Régime." *Revue Française de Socio-Économie*, 9, no. 1 (2012): 101–16.

Le marché: histoire et usages d'une conquête sociale. Paris: Gallimard, 2014.

"Introduction." In Maurice Berthe, ed., *Endettement paysan et crédit rural: dans l'Europe médiévale et moderne*, Toulouse: Presses Universitaires du Midi, 1998

Vivre pauvre. Quelques enseignements tirés de l'Europe des Lumières. Paris: Editions Gallimard, 2022.

"Le genre du capital et la difficile conciliation des logiques." *Genèses* 126, no. 1 (2022): 140–46.

Fontaine, Laurence, and Jürgen Schlumbohm. *Household Strategies for Survival, 1600–2000: Fission, Faction and Cooperation*. Cambridge: Cambridge University Press, 2000.

Fontaine, Laurence, and Paul Servais. "Relations de crédit et surendettement en France: XVIIème–XVIIIème siècles." In Laurence Fontaine, Gilles Postel-Vinay, and Jean-Laurent Rosenthal and Paul Servais, eds. *Des personnes aux institution: Réseaux et culture du crédit du XVIe au XXe siècle en Europe*. Louvain-la-Neuve: Bruylant-Academia, 1997.

Fontaine, Laurence, Gilles Postel-Vinay, Jean-Laurent Rosenthal, and Paul Servais. *Des personnes aux institutions. Réseaux et culture du crédit du XVIe au XXe siècle en Europe. Actes du colloque international «Centenaire des FUCAM» (Mons, 14–16 Novembre 1996)*. Louvain-la-Neuve: Bruylant-Academia, 1997.

Froide, Amy M. *Never Married: Singlewomen in Early Modern England*. Oxford: Oxford University Press, 2007.

Furió, Antoni. "Crédit, endettement et justice: Prêteurs et débiteurs devant le juge dans le royaume de Valence (XIIIe–XVe siècle)." In Julie Claustre, ed. *La dette et le juge: juridiction gracieuse et juridiction contentieuse du XIIIe au XVe siècle (France, Italie, Espagne, Angleterre, Empire)*. Paris: Publications de la Sorbonne, 2006, 19–54.

"Rents Instead of Land. Credit and Peasant Indebtedness in Late Medieval Mediterranean Iberia: The Kingdom of Valencia." *Continuity and Change* 36, no: 2 (2021): 177–209.

Garnot, Benoît. "Justice, infrajustice, parajustice et extra justice dans la France d'Ancien Régime." *Crime, Histoire & Sociétés/Crime, History & Societies* 4, no. 1 (2000): 103–20.

Histoire de la justice: France, XVIe-XXIe siècle. Paris: Gallimard, 2009.

Gehler, L. "Les Juifs de Marmoutier." *Bulletin de La Société d'histoire et d'archéologie de Saverne*, no. 3–4 (1954).

Gelderblom, Oscar. *Cities of Commerce: The Institutional Foundations of International Trade in the Low Countries, 1250-1650.* Princeton, NJ: Princeton University Press, 2015.

Gelderblom, Oscar, Mark Hup, and Joost Jonker. "Public Functions, Private Markets: Credit Registration by Aldermen and Notaries in the Low Countries, 1500–1800." In Marcella Lorenzini, Cinzia Lorandini, and D'Maris Coffman, eds. *Financing in Europe: Evolution, Coexistence and Complementarity of Lending Practices from the Middle Ages to Modern Times.* Cham: Springer, 2018, 163–94.

Gelderblom, Oscar, Joost Jonker, Ruben Peeters, and Amaury de Vicq. "Exploring Modern Bank Penetration: Evidence from Early Twentieth-Century Netherlands." *The Economic History Review*, 76 (2023): 892–916.

Gelfand, Michele J., Jana L. Raver, Lisa Nishii, Lisa M. Leslie, Janetta Lun, Beng Chong Lim, Lili Duan, et al. "Differences Between Tight and Loose Cultures: A 33-Nation Study." *Science* 332, no. 6033 (2011): 1100–104.

Gervais, Pierre. "Early Modern Merchant Strategies and the Historicization of Market Practices." *Economic Sociology*, Cologne: Max Planck Institute for the Study of Societies MPIfG 15, 3, (2014), 19–29.

"Why Profit and Loss Didn't Matter: The Historicized Rationality of Early Modern Commerce." In Pierre Gervais, Yannick Lemarchand et Dominique Margairaz, eds. *Merchants and Profit in the Age of Commerce, 1680-1830.* London: Pickering & Chatto, 2014.

Gilomen, Hans-Jörg. "La prise de décision en matière d'emprunts dans les villes suisses au 15e siècle." In Marc Bookne, Karel Davids, and Paul Janssens eds. *Urban Public Debts, Urban Government and the Market for Annuities in Western Europe (14th–18th Centuries)*, Turnhout: Brepols Publishers, 2003: 127–48.

Goubert, Pierre. *Beauvais et le Beauvaisis de 1600 à 1730: contribution à l'histoire sociale de la France du XVIIe siècle.* Paris: Publications de la Sorbonne, 2013.

Goujard, Philippe. "L'abolition de la féodalité dans le Pays de Bray (1789–1793)." *Annales Historiques de La Révolution Française* 224, no. 1 (1976): 287–94.

Graeber, David. *Debt: The First 5,000 Years.* Brooklyn, NY: Melville House, 2011.

The Democracy Project: A History, a Crisis, a Movement. 1st ed. New York: Spiegel & Grau, 2013.

Graeber, David, and David Wengrow. *The Dawn of Everything: A New History of Humanity.* 1st ed. New York: Farrar, Straus and Giroux, 2021.

Granovetter, Mark. "The Strength of Weak Ties." *American Journal of Sociology* 78, no. 6 (1973): 1360–80.

"Economic Action and Social Structure: The Problem of Embeddedness." *American Journal of Sociology* 91, no. 3 (1985): 481–510.

Greif, Avner. "Contract Enforceability and Economic Institutions in Early Trade: The Maghribi Traders' Coalition." *The American Economic Review*, vol 83, no. 3 (1993): 525–48.

Grenier, Jean-Yves. *L'Economie d'Ancien Régime: Un monde de l'échange et de l'incertitude.* Paris: Albin Michel, 1996.

Grevet, René. "Les intendants des généralités septentrionales et le commerce des grains à la fin du règne de Louis XV," *Revue du Nord* 400–1, no. 2–3 (2013): 335–49.

Guérin, Isabelle, Santhosh Kumar, and Isabelle Agier. "Women's Empowerment: Power to Act or Power over Other Women? Lessons from Indian Microfinance." *Oxford Development Studies* 41, no. sup1 (2013): 76–94.

Guinnane, Timothy W. "Trust: A Concept Too Many." Working Paper. Economic Growth Center, Yale University, 2005.

Hagen, Christian, Margareth Lanzinger, and Janine Maegraith. *Competing Interests in Death-Related Stipulations in South Tirol c. 1350–1600.* (Leiden: Brill, 2018).

Hardin, Russell. *Collective Action.* Baltimore, MD: John Hopkins University Press, 1982.

Hardwick, Julie. "Widowhood and Patriarchy in Seventeenth Century France." *Journal of Social History* 26, no. 1 (1992): 133–48.

The Practice of Patriarchy: Gender and the Politics of Household Authority in Early Modern France. University Park, PA: Pennsylvania State University Press, 1998.

"Seeking Separations: Gender, Marriages, and Household Economies in Early Modern France." *French Historical Studies* 21, no. 1 (1998): 157–80.

Family Business: Litigation and the Political Economies of Daily Life in Early Modern France. Oxford: Oxford University Press, 2009.

"Banqueroute: la faillite, le crime et la transition vers le capitalisme dans la France moderne." *Histoire, Economie Societé,* 30e année, no. 2 (2011): 79–93.

Hart, Keith. "Informal Income Opportunities and Urban Employment in Ghana," *The Journal of Modern African Studies* 11, no. 1 (1973): 61–89.

Hautcoeur, Pierre-Cyrille. "Les transformations du crédit en France au XIXe siècle." *Romantisme,* vol 151, no. 1 (2011): 23–38.

Hayhoe, Jeremy. *Enlightened Feudalism: Seigneurial Justice and Village Society in Eighteenth-Century Northern Burgundy.* Rochester, NY: University of Rochester Press, 2008.

"Rural Domestic Servants in Eighteenth-Century Burgundy: Demography, Economy, and Mobility." *Journal of Social History* 46, no. 2 (2012): 549–71.

Strangers and Neighbours: Rural Migration in Eighteenth-Century Northern Burgundy. Toronto: University of Toronto Press, 2016.

Heath, Joseph. "The Benefits of Cooperation." *Philosophy & Public Affairs* 34, no. 4 (2006): 313–51.

Hildesheimer, Françoise. "Insinuation, contrôle des actes et absolutisme." *Bibliothèque de l'École des chartes* 143, no. 1 (1985): 160–70.

Hill, Bridget. *Servants: English Domestics in the Eighteenth Century.* Oxford: Oxford University Press, 1996.

Himly, François Jacques. *Les conséquences de la Guerre de Trente Ans dans les campagnes alsaciennes.* Strasbourg: F. X. Leroux, 1948.

Hoffman, Charles. *L'Alsace au XVIIIe siècle au point de vue historique, juridique, administratif, économique, intellectuel.* Colmar: A.M.P. Ingold, 1899.

Hoffman, Philip T. *Growth in a Traditional Society: The French Countryside, 1450–1815.* New ed. Princeton, NJ: Princeton University Press, 2000.

Hoffman, Philip T., Gilles Postel-Vinay, and Jean-Laurent Rosenthal. "Private Credit Markets in Paris, 1690–1840." *The Journal of Economic History* 52, no. 2 (1992): 293–306.

"What Do Notaries Do? Overcoming Asymmetric Information in Financial Markets: The Case of Paris, 1751." UCLA Economics Working Paper. UCLA Department of Economics, 1994.

"Information and Economic History: How the Credit Market in Old Regime Paris Forces Us to Rethink the Transition to Capitalism." *American Historical Review* 104, no. 1 (1999): 69–94.

Des marchés sans prix: une économie politique du crédit à Paris, 1660–1870. Paris: Editions de l'Ecole des Hautes Etudes en Sciences Sociales, 2001.

Priceless Markets: The Political Economy of Credit in Paris, 1660–1870. Chicago, Il: University of Chicago Press, 2001.

"The Role of Trust in the Long-Run Development of French Financial Markets." In Karen Cook, Russell Hardin, and Margaret Levi, *Whom Can We Trust? How Groups, Networks, and Institutions Make Trust Possible.* Russell Sage Foundation, New York: 2009, 249–85.

"Entry, Information, and Financial Development: A Century of Competition between French Banks and Notaries." *Explorations in Economic History* 55 (2012): 39–57.

Dark Matter Credit: The Development of Peer-to-Peer Lending and Banking in France. Princeton, NJ: Princeton University Press, 2019.

Holderness, B. A. "Credit in a Rural Community, 1660–1800: Some Neglected Aspects of Probate Inventories." *Midland History* 3, no. 2 (1975): 94–116.

"Widows in Pre-Industrial Society: An Essay Upon Their Economic Functions." In Richard M. Smith ed., *Land, Kinship and Life-Cycle.* Cambridge: Cambridge University Press, 1984.

Holmes, Oliver Wendell. *The Common Law.* Revised ed. New York: Dover Publications, 1991.

Homer, Sidney. *A History of Interest Rates.* New Brunswick: Rutgers University Press, 1963.

Hossein, Caroline Shenaz. "Money Pools in the Americas: The African Diaspora's Legacy in the Social Economy." *Forum for Social Economics* 45, no. 4 (2016): 309–28.

Hossein, Caroline Shenaz, and Christabell P. J., eds. *Community Economies in the Global South: Case Studies of Rotating Savings and Credit Associations and Economic Cooperation.* Oxford, NY: Oxford University Press, 2022.

Hsu, Becky. "The 'Impossible' Default: Qualitative Data on Borrower Responses to Two Types of Social-Collateral Microfinance Structures in Rural China." *The Journal of Development Studies* 52, no. 1 (2016): 147–59.

Hudson, Michael. *…. And Forgive Them Their Debts: Lending, Foreclosure and Redemption from Bronze Age Finance to the Jubilee Year.* Dresden: ISLET-Verlag, 2018.

Hufton, Olwen H. *The Poor of Eighteenth-Century France 1750–1789.* Oxford: Clarendon Press, 1974.

"Women and the Family Economy in Eighteenth-Century France." *French Historical Studies* 9, no. 1 (1975).

Hunt, Margaret R. *The Middling Sort: Commerce, Gender, and the Family in England, 1680–1780.* Berkeley: University of California Press, 1996.

Isaacs, S., M. Alexander, and A. Haggard. "Faith, Trust and Gullibility." *International Journal of Psycho-Analysis* 44 (1963): 461–69.

Jackson, Matthew. *Social and Economic Networks.* Princeton, NJ: Princeton University Press, 2010.

"Networks in the Understanding of Economic Behaviors." *Journal of Economic Perspectives* 28, no. 4 (2014): 3–22.

Jacquart, Jean. "L'endettement paysan et le crédit dans les campagnes de la France moderne." In Maurice Berthe, ed. *Endettement paysan et crédit rural: dans l'Europe médiévale et moderne.* Toulouse: Presses Universitaires du Midi, 2020, 283–97.

Jacquemet, Gérard. "Belleville ouvrier à la Belle Epoque." *Le Mouvement Social,* no. 118 (1982): 61–77.

Joachim, Jules. *La fondation des pauvres ou vieil hôpital de Delle 1600–1820.* Belfort: Bulletin de la Société Belfortaine d'Emulation, 1936, no. 50, 151–207.

Johnson, Creola. "Payday Loans: Shrewd Business or Predatory Lending." *Minnesota Law Review* 87, no. 1 (2003 2002): 1–152.

Johnson, Paul. "Small Debts and Economic Distress in England and Wales, 1857–1913." *Economic History Review* 46, no. 1 (1993): 65–87.

Jordan, William Chester. *Women and Credit in Pre-Industrial and Developing Societies.* Philadelphia, PA: University of Pennsylvania Press, 2016.

Jütte, Robert. *Poverty and Deviance in Early Modern Europe.* Cambridge: Cambridge University Press, 1994.

Kadens, Emily. "The Last Bankrupt Hanged: Balancing Incentives in the Development of Bankruptcy Law," *Duke Law Journal* 59, no 7 (2010): 1229–1319.

Kagan, Richard L. *Lawsuits and Litigants in Castile: 1500–1700.* Chapel Hill, NC: University of North Carolina Press, 1981.

Kaplan, Debra. "Transactions financières entre Juifs et chrétiens dans l'Alsace du XVIe siècle." *Archives Juives* 47, no. 2 (2014): 29–46.

Kaplan, Steven Laurence. *The Bakers of Paris and the Bread Question, 1700–1775.* 1st ed. Durham, NC: Duke University Press Books, 1996.

Keibek, Sebastian A. J. "Correcting the Probate Inventory Record for Wealth Bias." Working Paper No. 28, Cambridge Group for the History of Population and Social Structure & Queens' College, March 2017.

Khan, B. Zorina. "'Justice of the Marketplace': Legal Disputes and Economic Activity on America's Northeastern Frontier, 1700–1860." *The Journal of Interdisciplinary History* 39, no. 1 (2008): 1–35.

Kuehn, Thomas. *Law, Family & Women.* Chicago: University of Chicago Press, 1994.

Kuuse, Jan. "The Probate Inventory as a Source for Economic and Social History." *Scandinavian Economic History Review* 22, no. 1 (1974): 22–31.

Labrousse, Ernest. *Esquisse du mouvement des prix et des revenus en France au XVIIIe siecle*. Paris: Editions des archives contemporaines, 1984.

Ladurie, Emmanuel Le Roy. *Montaillou, village occitan de 1294 à 1324*. Édition revue et corrigée. Paris: Folio, 2008.

Laferté, Gilles. "Théoriser le crédit de face-à-face: un système d'information dans une économie de l'obligation." *Entreprises et histoire*, 2 no. 59 (2010): 57–67.

Laferté Gilles et al. "Le crédit direct des commerçants aux consommateurs: persistance et dépassement dans le textile à Lens (1920–1970)." *Genèses* 79, no. 2 (2010): 26–47.

Laffont, Jean L. *Le notaire, le paysan, et la terre dans la France méridionale à l'époque moderne*. Toulouse: Presses Universitaires du Midi, 1999.

Lagadec, Yann. "Elites villageoises et pouvoir local." *Enquêtes rurales*, no. 11 (2007): 45–61.

Lagrange, Jacques de. *L'Alsace en 1700: Mémoire sur la Province d'Alsace de l'Intendant Jacques de La Grange*. Colmar: Ed. Alsatia, 1975.

Lainez, Nicolas. "Informal Credit in Vietnam: A Necessity Rather Than an Evil." *Journal of Southeast Asian Economies* 31, no. 1 (2014): 147–54.

Lambrecht, Thijs. "Rural Credit and the Market for Annuities in Eighteenth-Century Flanders." In Thijs Lambrecht, Phillipp R. Schofield, eds., *Credit and the Rural Economy in North-Western Europe, c. 1200-c. 1850*, Turnhout: Brepols Publishers, 2009: 75–97.

Lambrecht, Thijs, and Phillipp R Schofield, eds. *Credit and the Rural Economy in North-Western Europe, c. 1200-c. 1850*. Turnhout: Brepols Publishers, 2009.

Lange, Tyler. *Excommunication for Debt in Late Medieval France: The Business of Salvation*. Cambridge: Cambridge University Press, 2016.

Lanzinger, Margareth. "Movable Goods and Immovable Property: Interrelated Perspectives." In Annette Cremer, ed., *Gender, Law and Material Culture*, London: Routledge, 2020.

Lauer, Josh. *Creditworthy: A History of Consumer Surveillance and Financial Identity in America*. New York: Columbia University Press, 2017.

Laurence, Anne, Josephine Maltby, and Janette Rutterford, eds. *Women and Their Money, 1700–1950: Essays on Women and Finance*. London: Routledge, 2008.

Lazarus, Jeanne. "Faire crédit: de la noble tâche à la corvée." *Revue Française de Socio-Economie* 9, no. 1 (2012): 43–61.

Lazzarato, Maurizio. *The Making of the Indebted Man: An Essay on the Neoliberal Condition*. Los Angeles, CA: Semiotext(e), 2012.

Le Cerf, René. "Le général d'une paroisse Bretonne." *Revue de Bretagne et de Vendée. Etudes d'Histoire Local*, Juillet 1888, 54–65.

Le Gendre, Romain. *Confiance, épargne et notaires: le marché du crédit à Saint-Maixent et dans sa région au XVIe siècle*. Paris: Ecole des Chartes, 2020.

Lemercier, Claire, and Claire Zalc. "Pour une nouvelle approche de la relation de crédit en histoire contemporaine." *Annales. Histoire, Sciences Sociales* 67e année, no. 4 (2012): 979–1009.

Lemercier, Claire, and Francesca Trivellato. "1751 and Thereabout: A Quantitative and Comparative Approach to Notarial Records." *Social Science History* 46, no. 3 (2022): 555–83.

Lemire, Beverly. "Petty Pawns and Informal Lending: Gender and the Transformation of Small-Scale Credit in England, circa 1600 – 1800." In Kristine Bruland and Patrick O'Brien, eds., *From Family Firms to Corporate Capitalism: Essays in Business and Industrial History in Honour of Peter Mathias*. Oxford: Clarendon Press, 1998, 112–38.

Lerch-Boyer, Anne. *Esquisse d'une seigneurie de Haute Alsace au XVIIIe s.: La seigneurie de Florimont*, Mémoire de maîtrise, Strasbourg: Université de Strasbourg, 1973.

Lescure, Michel, and Alain Plessis. "Le financement des entreprises françaises de la fin du XIXe à la Seconde Guerre Mondiale." *Études et Documents* 10 (1998): 277–91.

Le Velly, Ronan. "La notion d'encastrement: une sociologie des échanges marchands," *Sociologie du travail* 44, no. 1 (2002): 37–53.

"Le problème du désencastrement," *Revue du MAUSS* 29, no. 1 (2007): 241–56.

Levy, Juliette. *The Making of a Market: Credit, Henequen, and Notaries in Yucatan, 1850–1900*. University Park, PA: Penn State University Press, 2012.

Lewis, David. *Convention: A Philosophical Study*. Hoboken, NJ: John Wiley & Sons, 2008.

Lindgren, Håkan. "The Modernization of Swedish Credit Markets, 1840–1905: Evidence from Probate Records." *The Journal of Economic History* 62, no. 3 (2002): 810–32.

"Parish Banking in Informal Credit Markets: The Business of Private Lending in Early Nineteenth-Century Sweden." *Financial History Review* 24, no. 1 (2017): 83–102.

Lis, Catharina, and Hugo Soly. *Poverty and Capitalism in Pre-Industrial Europe*. Atlantic Highlands, NJ: Humanities Press, 1979.

Livet, Georges. *L'intendance d'Alsace sous Louis XIV, 1648–1715*. Paris: Société d'Edition Les Belles Lettres, 1956.

Lorenzini, Marcella. "The Credit Market and Notaries in Verona in the Second Half of the Seventeenth Century" *The Journal of European Economic History*, 44, no. 1 (2015): 123–48.

"Borrowing and Lending Money in Alpine Areas During the Eighteenth Century: Trento and Rovereto Compared." In Marcella Lorenzini, Cinzia Lorandini, and D'Maris Coffman, eds. *Financing in Europe: Evolution, Coexistence and Complementarity of Lending Practices from the Middle Ages to Modern Times*. Cham: Springer, 2018: 107–34.

"The Other Side of Banking: Private Lending and the Role of Women in Early Modern Italy." In Stephan Nicolussi-Köhler, ed., *Change and Transformation of Premodern Credit Markets: The Importance of Small-Scale Credits*. Heidelberg: heiBOOKS, 2019.

Lorenzini, Marcella, Cinzia Lorandini, and D'Maris Coffman. *Financing in Europe: Evolution, Coexistence and Complementarity of Lending Practices from the Middle Ages to Modern Times*. Cham: Springer, 2018.

Maegraith, Janine. "Financing Transfers: Buying, Exchanging and Inheriting Properties in Early Modern Southern Tyrol." *The History of the Family* 27, no. 1 (2021): 11–36.

Malinowski, Bronislaw. *Argonauts of the Western Pacific: An Account of Native Enterprise and Adventure in the Archipelagoes of Melanesian New Guinea [1922/1994]*. London: Routledge, 2013.

Mann, Bruce H. *Republic of Debtors: Bankruptcy in the Age of American Independence*. Cambridge, MA: Harvard University Press, 2009.

Mathieu, Isabelle. *Justices seigneuriales en Anjou et dans le Maine*. Rennes: Presses Universitaires de Rennes, 2011.

Mauclair, Fabrice. "Des gens de justice à la campagne." *Annales de Bretagne et des Pays de l'Ouest. Anjou. Maine. Poitou-Charente. Touraine*, no. 116–2 (2009): 81–103.

La justice au village: justice seigneuriale et société rurale dans le Duché-Pairie de La Vallière. Rennes: Presses Universitaires de Rennes, 2008.

Mauss, Marcel. *The Gift: Forms and Functions of Exchange in Archaic Societies*. Translated by Ian Cunnison. Jefferson, NC: Martino Fine Books, 2011.

Mazzucato, Mariana. *The Value of Everything: Making and Taking in the Global Economy*. Illustrated ed. New York: Public Affairs, 2018.

McIntosh, Marjorie. "Women, Credit, and Family Relationships in England, 1300–1620." *Journal of Family History* 30, no. 2 (2005): 143–63.

Menant, François and Odile Redon, (eds). *Notaires et crédit dans l'Occident méditerranéen médiéval*. Rome: Ecole Française de Rome, 2004.

Merlin, Colette. *Ceux des villages: la société rurale dans la "Petite Montagne" jurassienne à la veille de la Révolution*. Besançon: Universitaires de Franche-Comté, 1994.

Meyer, John W., and Brian Rowan. "Institutionalized Organizations: Formal Structure as Myth and Ceremony." *American Journal of Sociology* 83, no. 2 (1977): 340–63.

Miller, Michelle. "Mutual Aid as Spiritual Sustenance." *Daedalus, Journal of the American Academy of Arts & Sciences* 152, no. 11 (2023): 125–31.

Mirowski, Philip. *Never Let a Serious Crisis Go to Waste: How Neoliberalism Survived the Financial Meltdown*. London: Verso, 2013.

Muldrew, Craig. "Credit and the Courts: Debt Litigation in a Seventeenth-Century Urban Community." *The Economic History Review*, 46, no. 1 (1993): 23–38.

"Interpreting the Market: The Ethics of Credit and Community Relations in Early Modern England." *Social History* 18, no. 2 (1993): 163–83.

The Economy of Obligation: The Culture of Credit and Social Relations in Early Modern England. Basingstoke: Palgrave Macmillan, 1998.

"'Hard Food for Midas': Cash and Its Social Value in Early Modern England." *Past & Present*, vol 170, no. 1 (2001): 78–120.

Murphy, Anne L. *The Origins of English Financial Markets: Investment and Speculation before the South Sea Bubble*. Cambridge, New York: Cambridge University Press, 2009.

Murray, James M. *Bruges, Cradle of Capitalism, 1280-1390*. Cambridge: Cambridge University Press, 2005.

Nakaya, So. "Credit Networks between City and Countryside in Late Medieval Lucca." In Stephan Nicolussi-Köhler ed. *Change and Transformation of Premodern Credit Markets: The Importance of Small-Scale Credits*. Heidelberg: heiBooks, 2021, 133–56.

Nicolussi-Köhler, Stephan, et al. *Change and Transformation of Premodern Credit Markets: The Importance of Small-Scale Credits*. Heidelberg: heiBOOKS, 2021.

Noonan, John Thomas. *The Scholastic Analysis of Usury*. Cambridge, MA: Harvard University Press, 1957.

Nootens, Thierry, and Nathalie Ricard. "Petites gens, petites dettes: monétarisation de la vie sociale et rapports de domination dans le district judiciaire d'Arthabaska (Québec), 1880–1930." *Histoire Sociale/Social History*, vol 53, no 109 (2020): 491–518.

North, Douglass C. *Institutions, Institutional Change and Economic Performance*. Cambridge: Cambridge University Press, 1990.

"Institutions." *Journal of Economic Perspectives* vol 5, no. 1 (1991): 97–112.

O'Brien, Rourke L. "Depleting Capital? Race, Wealth and Informal Financial Assistance." *Social Forces* 91, no. 2 (2012): 375–96.

Ogilvie, Sheilagh. *A Bitter Living: Women, Markets, and Social Capital in Early Modern Germany*. Oxford: Oxford University Press, 2003.

Ogilvie, Sheilagh, Markus Küpker, and Janine Maegraith. "Household Debt in Early Modern Germany: Evidence from Personal Inventories." *The Journal of Economic History* 72, no. 1 (2012): 134–67.

O'Neil, Cathy. *Weapons of Math Destruction: How Big Data Increases Inequality and Threatens Democracy*. New York: Crown, 2016.

Ostrom, Elinor. "Collective Action and the Evolution of Social Norms." *Journal of Economic Perspectives* 14, no. 3 (2000): 137–58.

Pacaut, Marcel et al. *L'Hostie et le denier: les finances ecclésiastiques du haut Moyen Age à l'époque moderne: actes du colloque de la commission internationale d'histoire ecclésiastique comparée, Genève, août 1989*. Genève: Labor et Fides, 1991.

Parr, Thomas, Giovanni Pezzulo, and Karl J. Friston. *Active Inference: The Free Energy Principle in Mind, Brain, and Behavior*. Cambridge, MA: The MIT Press, 2022.

Patalano, Robert, and Caroline Roulet. "Structural Developments in Global Financial Intermediation: The Rise of Debt and Non-Bank Credit Intermediation," *OECD Working Papers on Finance, Insurance and Private Pensions*. No. 44, Paris: OECD Publishing, 2020.

Peebles, Gustav. "The Anthropology of Credit and Debt." *Annual Review of Anthropology* 39, no. 1 (2010): 225–40.

"Washing Away the Sins of Debt: The Nineteenth-Century Eradication of the Debtors' Prison," *Comparative Studies in Society and History* 55, no. 3 (2013): 701–24.

Perlinge, Anders. "Sockenbankirerna: kreditrelationer och tidig bankverksamhet: Vånga socken i Skåne 1840–1900." Stockholm, Nordiska museets förlag, 2005.

Perrier, Sylvie. *Des enfances protégées: la tutelle des mineurs en France (XVIIe–XVIIIe siècles): enquête à Paris et à Châlons-sur-Marne*. Saint-Denis: Presses Universitaires de Vincennes, 1998.

Pfister, Ulrich. "Le petit crédit rural en Suisse aux XVIe–XVIIIe siécles." *Annales. Histoire, Sciences Sociales* 49, no. 6 (1994): 1339–57.

"Rural Land and Credit Markets, the Permanent Income Hypothesis and Proto-Industry: Evidence from Early Modern Zurich." *Continuity and Change* 22, no. 03 (2007): 489–518.

Phipps, Teresa. "Creditworthy Women and Town Courts in Late Medieval England." In Elise M. Dermineur, ed., *Women and Credit in Pre-Industrial Europe*. Turnhout: Brepols Publishers, 2018: 73–94.

Piant, Hervé. *Une justice ordinaire: justice civile et criminelle dans la prévôté royale de Vaucouleurs sous l'Ancien Régime*. Rennes: Presses Universitaires de Rennes, 2006.

"Vaut-Il mieux s'arranger que plaider? Un essai de sociologie judiciaire dans la France d'Ancien Régime." In Antoine Follain, ed., *Les justices locales dans les villes et villages du Xve au Xixe siècle*. Rennes: Presses Universitaires de Rennes, 2006: 97–124.

"Des procès innombrables." *Histoire & mesure*, Déviance, justice et statistiques, XXII, no. 2 (2007): 13–38.

Pistor, Katharina. "The Standardization of Law and Its Effect on Developing Economies." *The American Journal of Comparative Law* 50, no. 1 (2002): 97–130.

Platteau, Jean-Philippe. *Institutions, Social Norms, and Economic Development*. London: Routledge, 2000.

"Solidarity Norms and Institutions in Village Societies: Static and Dynamic Considerations." In Serge-Christophe Kolm and Jean Mercier Ythier, eds. *Handbook of the Economics of Giving, Altruism and Reciprocity*. Foundations. Amsterdam: Elsevier, 2006: 819–86.

Platteau, Jean-Philippe, and Anita Abraham. "An Inquiry into Quasi-credit Contracts: The Role of Reciprocal Credit and Interlinked Deals in Small-scale Fishing Communities." *The Journal of Development Studies* 23, no. 4 (1987): 461–90.

Polanyi, Karl. *The Great Transformation: The Political and Economic Origins of Our Time*. 2nd Beacon Paperback ed. Boston, MA: Beacon Press, 2001.

Pompermaier, Matteo. *"Le vin et l'argent": osterie, bastioni et marché du crédit à Venise au XVIIIe siècle*, Rome: Publications de l'École Française de Rome, 2019.

Poncet, Olivier. "Nommer et décrire les actes des notaires de l'époque moderne, entre théorie, pratique et histoire." *Bibliothèque de l'école des Chartes* 172, no. 1/2 (2014): 449–53.

Popkin, Samuel. "The Rational Peasant: The Political Economy of Peasant Society." *Theory and Society* 9, no. 3 (1980): 411–71.

Poska, Allyson M. *Women and Authority in Early Modern Spain: The Peasants of Galicia*. Oxford: Oxford University Press, 2006.

Postel-Vinay, Gilles. *La terre et l'argent, l'agriculture et le crédit en France du XVIIIe au début du XXe siècle*. Paris: Albin Michel, 1997.

"Change and Transformation of Premodern Credit Markets." In Stephan Nicolussi-Köhler, ed. *Change and Transformation of Premodern Credit Markets: The Importance of Small-Scale Credits*. Heidelberg: heiBOOKS, 2021, 23–38.

Priest, Claire. *Credit Nation: Property Laws and Institutions in Early America*. Princeton: Princeton University Press, 2021.

Raphaël, Freddy. "Les Juifs de la campagne alsacienne: les marchands de bestiaux," *Revue des sciences sociales de la France de l'Est*, 9, (1980): 220–45.

Reboul, Elena. *Gender and Debt, Past and Present: Financing Social Reproduction.* doctoral thesis, Université Paris-7 Diderot unpublished, 2020.

Reuss, Rodolphe. *L'Alsace au dix-septième siècle au point de vue géographique, historique, administratif, économiqe, social, intellectuel et religieux.* Paris: É. Bouillon, 1897.

Richardson, R. C. *Household Servants in Early Modern England.* Manchester: Manchester University Press, 2010.

Roos, Jerome E. *Why Not Default?: The Political Economy of Sovereign Debt.* Princeton: Princeton University Press, 2019.

Rosenhaft, Eve. "Did Women Invent Life Insurance? Widows and the Demand for Financial Services in Eighteenth-Century Germany." In D. R. Green, and A. Owens, eds. *Family Welfare: Gender Property and Inheritance Since the Seventeenth-Century.* Westport, CT: Praeger Publishers, 2004: 163–194.

Rosenthal, Jean–Laurent. "Credit Markets and Economic Change in Southeastern France 1630–1788." *Explorations in Economic History* 30, no. 2 (1993): 129–57.

"Rural Credit Markets and Aggregate Shocks: The Experience of Nuits St. Georges, 1756–1776." *The Journal of Economic History* 54, no. 02 (1994): 288–306.

Sabean, David Warren. *Property, Production, and Family in Neckarhausen, 1700–1870.* Cambridge: Cambridge University Press, 1991.

Sahlins, Marshall. *Stone Age Economics.* New York: Routledge, 2020.

Sarazin, Jean-Yves. "L'historien et le notaire: acquis et perspectives de l'étude des actes privés de la France moderne." *Bibliothèque de l'école des Chartes* 160, no. 1 (2002): 229–70.

Schmitt, Jean-Marie, and David Jenkins. "The Origins of the Textile Industry in Alsace: The Beginnings of the Manufacture of Printed Cloth at Wesserling (1762–1802)." *Textile History* 13, no. 1 (1982): 99–109.

Schnapper, Bernard. *Les rentes au 16e Siècle. Histoire d'un instrument de crédit.* Paris: Editions de l'Ecole des Hautes Etudes en Sciences Sociales, 1995.

Schneider, Zoë A. *The King's Bench: Bailiwick Magistrates and Local Governance in Normandy, 1670–1740.* Rochester, NY: University of Rochester Press, 2008.

Schofield, P. R. "Alternatives to Expropriation: Rent, Credit and Peasant Landholding in Medieval Europe and Modern Palestine." *Continuity and Change* 36, no. 2 (2021): 141–48.

Scott, James C. *The Moral Economy of the Peasant: Rebellion and Subsistence in Southeast Asia.* New Haven: Yale University Press, 1977.

Seeing Like a State: How Certain Schemes to Improve the Human Condition Have Failed. New Haven, CT: Yale University Press, 1998.

Semin, Jeanne. "L'argent, la famille, les amies: Ethnographie contemporaine des tontines africaines en contexte migratoire." *Civilisations. Revue internationale d'anthropologie et de sciences humaines,* vol 56 (2007): 183–99.

Servais, Paul. "De la rente au crédit hypothécaire en période de transition industrielle: stratégies familiales en région Liégeoise au XVIIIe siècle." *Annales. Histoire, Sciences Sociales* 49, no. 6 (1994): 1393–1409.

Shammas, Carole. "Constructing a Wealth Distribution from Probate Records." *The Journal of Interdisciplinary History* 9, no. 2 (1978): 297–307.

The Pre-Industrial Consumer in England and America. Oxford: Clarendon Press, 1990.

Shaw, James E. "Market Ethics and Credit Practices in Sixteenth-Century Tuscany." *Renaissance Studies* 27, no. 2 (2013): 236–52.

"The Informal Economy of Credit in Early Modern Venice." *The Historical Journal*, 61, no. 3, (2018): 623–642.

Shepard, Alexandra. "Minding Their Own Business: Married Women and Credit in Early Eighteenth-Century London." *Transactions of the Royal Historical Society* 25 (2015): 53–74.

Sherman, Charles P. "Debt of the Modern Law of Guardianship to Roman Law." *Michigan Law Review* 12, no. 2 (1914 1913): 124–31.

Siniscalchi, Valeria. "La monnaie de farine." *Terrain. Anthropologie & sciences humaines*, no. 52 (2009): 152–63.

Smail, Daniel Lord. *The Consumption of Justice: Emotions, Publicity, and Legal Culture in Marseille, 1264–1423*. Ithaca: Cornell University Press, 2003.

Legal Plunder: Households and Debt Collection in Late Medieval Europe. Cambridge, MA: Harvard University Press, 2016.

Smith, Adam, and Alan B. Krueger. *The Wealth of Nations*, Annotated ed. New York, NY: Bantam Classics, 2003.

Soleil, Sylvain. "Nouveau scénario pour séries b: les fonds des tribunaux d'ancien régime." *Les Cahiers du Centre de Recherches Historiques*, Officiers "moyens" (1), no. 23 (1999).

Spang, Rebecca L. *Stuff and Money in the Time of the French Revolution*. Cambridge, MA: Harvard University Press, 2015.

Spence, Cathryn. *Women, Credit, and Debt in Early Modern Scotland*. Manchester: Manchester University Press, 2016.

Women, Gender and Credit in Early Modern Western European Towns. Routledge Handbooks Online, 2017 in Deborah Simonton, ed., The Routledge History Handbook of Gender and the Urban Experience, p. 21–32.

Spicksley, Judith M. "'Fly with a Duck in Thy Mouth': Single Women as Sources of Credit in Seventeenth-Century England" *Social History* 32, no. 2 (2007): 187–207.

Spufford, Peter. "Long-term Rural Credit in Sixteenth- and Seventeenth-Century England: The Evidence of Probate Accounts." In Christopher Marsg, Tom Arkell, Nesta Evans, and Nigel Goose, eds, *When Death Do Us Part: Understanding and Interpreting the Probate Records of Early Modern England*. Oxford: Leopard's Head Press, 2000, 213–28.

Spufford, Peter, and Dominique Taffin. "Les liens du crédit au village: dans l'Angleterre du XVIIe siècle." *Annales. Histoire, Sciences Sociales* 49, no. 6 (1994): 1359–73.

Stiglitz, Joseph. "Rational Peasants, Efficient Institutions, and the Theory of Rural Organization: Methodological Remarks for Development Economics." Working Paper. Princeton, NJ: Woodrow Wilson School, 1988.

Storti, Marie-Lyse. "Coutume de Ferrette et/ou coutume du comté de Belfort." *Revue d'Alsace*, no. 132 (2006): 205–44.

Stout, Noelle. *Dispossessed: How Predatory Bureaucracy Foreclosed on the American Middle Class*. Oakland, CA: University of California Press, 2019.

Strange, Susan. *Casino Capitalism*. New ed. Manchester: Manchester University Press, 1997.

Suchman, Mark C. "Managing Legitimacy: Strategic and Institutional Approaches." *The Academy of Management Review* 20, no. 3 (1995): 571–610.

Sugden, Robert. *The Community of Advantage: A Behavioural Economist's Defence of the Market*. Oxford, NY: Oxford University Press, 2018.

Svetiev, Y., E. Dermineur, and U. Kolanisi. "Financialization and Sustainable Credit: Lessons from Non-Intermediated Transactions?" *Journal of Consumer Policy* 45, no. 4 (2022): 673–98.

Taylor, George V. "Noncapitalist Wealth and the Origins of the French Revolution." *The American Historical Review* 72, no. 2 (1967): 469–96.

Taylor, Michael. *Community, Anarchy and Liberty*. Cambridge, NY: Cambridge University Press, 1982.

Thomas, Jonathan P., and Timothy Worrall. "Gift-Giving, Quasi-Credit and Reciprocity." *Rationality and Society* 14, no. 3 (2002): 308–52.

Thompson, Edward Palmer. "Time, Work-Discipline, and Industrial Capitalism." *Past & Present*, no. 38 (1967): 56–97.

"The Moral Economy of the English Crowd in the Eighteenth Century." *Past & Present*, 50, no. 1 (1971): 76–136.

Thomson, Gordon DesBrisay, and Karen Sander Thomson. "Crediting Wives: Married Women and Debt Litigation in the Seventeenth Century." In Elizabeth Ewan, and Janay Nugent, eds. *Finding the Family in Medieval and Early Modern Scotland*. Aldershot: Ashgate, 2008.

Tönnies, Ferdinand. *Community and Society: Gemeinschaft und Gesellschaft*. Mineola, NY: Dover Publications, 2003.

Tooze, Adam. *Crashed: How a Decade of Financial Crises Changed the World*. New York: Viking, 2018.

Trayaud, Stéphane. "Notariat et infrajustice: le rôle de médiation du notaire sous l'Ancien Régime à travers la pratique de Pierre Thoumas de Bosmie, notaire royal à Limoges (1735–1740)." *Revue d'histoire de l'enfance « irrégulière ». Le Temps de l'histoire*, no. Hors-série (2001): 207–20.

Trivellato, Francesca. *The Promise and Peril of Credit: What a Forgotten Legend about Jews and Finance Tells Us about the Making of European Commercial Society*. Princeton, NJ: Princeton University Press, 2019.

Trumbull, Gunnar. *Consumer Lending in France and America: Credit and Welfare*. Cambridge: Cambridge University Press, 2014.

Uzzi, Brian. "The Sources and Consequences of Embeddedness for the Economic Performance of Organizations: The Network Effect." *American Sociological Review* 61, no. 4 (1996): 674–98.

Van Bochove, Christiaan. "Seafarers and Shopkeepers: Credit in Eighteenth-Century Amsterdam," *Eighteenth-Century Studies* 48, no. 1 (2014): 67–88.

Varry, Dominique. "Les campagnes de la subdélégation de Belfort au milieu du XVIIIe siècle." In Michel Balard, Jean-Claude Hervé, and Nicole Lemaitre eds. *Paris et ses campagnes sous l'Ancien Régime*, Paris: Éditions de la Sorbonne, 2021: 15–26.

Vickers, Daniel. "Errors Expected: The Culture of Credit in Rural New England, 1750–1800." *Economic History Review* 63, no. 4 (2010): 1032–57.

Vicq, Amaury de, and Christiaan van Bochove. "Historical Diversity in Credit Intermediation: Cosignatory Lending Institutions in Europe and North America, 1700s–1960s." *Social Science History* 47, no. 1 (2023): 95–119.

Vincent, Catherine. "La vitalité de la communauté paroissiale au XVe siècle à travers quelques exemples de fondations rouennaises." *Revue du Nord* 356–357, no. 3–4 (2004): 741–56.

Waddilove, David P. "Mortgages in the Early-Modern Court of Chancery." Chapter 2 "Aspects of Mortgages in Society." Cambridge: Cambridge University, 2014.

Wahid, Abu. "The Grameen Bank and Women in Bangladesh." *Challenge* 42, no. 5 (1999): 94–101.

Wherry, Frederick F., Kristin S. Seefeldt, and Anthony S. Alvarez. *Credit Where It's Due: Rethinking Financial Citizenship*. New York: Russell Sage Foundation, 2019.

"To Lend or Not to Lend to Friends and Kin: Awkwardness, Obfuscation, and Negative Reciprocity." *Social Forces* 98, no. 2 (2019): 753–93.

Wilson, Catharine Anne. *Being Neighbours: Cooperative Work and Rural Culture, 1830–1960*. Montreal: McGill Queen's University Press, 2022.

Woolf, Stuart. *The Poor in Western Europe in the Eighteenth and Nineteenth Centuries*. London: Routledge, 2016.

Wrightson, Keith, and David Levine. *Poverty and Piety in an English Village: Terling, 1525–1700*. Oxford: Oxford University Press, 1995.

Zuijderduijn, Jaco C. "Foreclosures Foregone: Default, Prosecution, and Leniency in a Village in Holland (Sixteenth Century)," Paper for the workshop 'Mortgages in the European countryside, 1200–1700', Cambridge 13 July 2015.

"The Ages of Women and Men: Life Cycles, Family, and Investment in the Fifteenth-Century Low Countries." In Elise M. Dermineur, ed., *Women and Credit in Pre-Industrial Europe*, Early European Research 12. Turnhout: Brepols Publishers, 2018: 95–120.

Index

Printed in the United States
by Baker & Taylor Publisher Services